Geoffrey Cubitt is Lecturer University of York.

THE JESUIT MYTH

THE JESUIT MYTH

*Conspiracy Theory
and Politics in
Nineteenth-Century France*

GEOFFREY CUBITT

CLARENDON PRESS · OXFORD

1993

Oxford University Press, Walton Street, Oxford OX2 6DP

Oxford   New York   Toronto
Delhi Bombay Calcutta Madras Karachi
Kuala Lumpur Singapore Hong Kong Tokyo
Nairobi Dar es Salaam Cape Town
Melbourne Auckland Madrid
and associated companies in
Berlin Ibadan

Oxford is a trade mark of Oxford University Press

Published in the United States
by Oxford University Press Inc., New York

© *Geoffrey Cubitt 1993*

British Library Cataloguing in Publication Data
Data available

Library of Congress Cataloging in Publication Data
Cubitt, Geoffrey.
The Jesuit myth : conspiracy theory and politics in nineteenth-
century France / Geoffrey Cubitt.
p. cm.
Includes bibliographical references and index.
1. Jesuits—France—History—19th century.   2. Jesuits—France—
public opinion.   3. Public opinion—France.   4. France—Church
history—19th century.   5. France—History—19th century.
6. Conspiracies—France—History—19th century.   I. Title.
BX3731.C83 1993   271'.53044'09034—dc20   93—18391
ISBN 0–19–822868–6

1 3 5 7 9 10 8 6 4 2

Typeset by Graphicraft Typesetters Ltd., Hong Kong
Printed in Great Britain
on acid-free paper by
Bookcraft (Bath) Ltd., Midsomer Norton, Avon

Acknowledgements

This book can claim little of the indulgence due to youth: its origins lie in a Ph.D. thesis completed in 1984, and the present version was begun two years later. I am grateful to its editors at Oxford University Press and to a great many others for considerable patience, and in some cases for much else besides. Without a junior research fellowship from Jesus College, Oxford, the book might never really have been started; without the willingness of several other institutions temporarily to assist my swinging from tree to tree in the over-thinned woodlands of academic employment, it might never have been finished. I am indebted to the examiners of the original thesis (Maurice Larkin and the late Patrick Bury) for their comments; to members of the staffs of the Bibliothèque Nationale in Paris, the University Library in Cambridge, and the Bodleian Library in Oxford, for extensive assistance; and to Christine Eckersley for much speedy and efficient typing. I am grateful to Christopher Andrew (who supervised the original thesis) and to Jim McMillan, Ralph Gibson, and John Walsh, both for specific advice and for encouragement over a long period. The list of those without whose companionship, sympathy, or good cheer at various stages the progress towards this book's eventual appearance would have been much harder cannot be recited in full, but it begins with Clive Castaldo and Mat Burrows (in the pleasure of whose company the earliest research towards it was carried out) and must include Nick Atkin, Władek Bartoszewski, Katya Andreyev, Martin Conway, Tom Buchanan, and Gervase Rosser. It also includes those to whom the book is dedicated: my parents, Tom and Rachel Cubitt, my debt to whom began long before the Jesuit myth took a hold; and my wife Katy, whose very practical assistance in breaking that hold, and whose friendship and love meanwhile, have gone well beyond anything I could decently demand.

NOTE

This book was already in the hands of its publishers when Michel Leroy's book, *Le Mythe jésuite, de Béranger à Michelet*, appeared in Paris. M. Leroy and I wrote our books in ignorance of each other's labours, but we have worked on very similar bodies of material, and it is not surprising that our arrangements and interpretations of that material sometimes coincide; the resemblances are most notable in the sections of our books which survey the main themes of the Jesuit myth. In certain respects the two books complement each other: M. Leroy, for example, provides more detailed summaries of the contents of various anti-jesuit tracts, while I have drawn more on newspaper sources in tracing anti-jesuitism's evolving political uses, of which I provide an in some ways more systematic account. I have also covered a significantly longer period, and would question M. Leroy's suggestion that the myth's political and cultural relevance was in definite decline by mid-century. Finally, although M. Leroy's interests and my own have overlapped, our conceptual equipment and analytical concerns have often not been the same: I have explored the structural and dynamic relationships between different elements in the myth in ways which are not paralleled in his study, have reached different kinds of conclusion about its nineteenth-century significance, and have given more attention to establishing its place in a longer and broader history of conspiracy theories. I believe and hope that the reader will find sufficient differences between the two books to justify their coexistence.

Contents

Abbreviations

AN	Archives Nationales
AP	*Archives parlementaires de 1787 à 1860*
ASCD	*Annales du Sénat et de la Chambre des Députés*
ASCL	*Annales du Sénat et du Corps Législatif*
Ass. N.	Assemblée Nationale
BN Est.	Bibliothèque Nationale, département des estampes
BNMS NAF	Bibliothèque Nationale, département des manuscrits: nouvelles acquisitions françaises
CD	Chambre des Députés
Constitutionnel	*Le Constitutionnel*
Courrier	*Le Courrier français*
CP	Chambre des Pairs
Débats	*Le Journal des débats*
Moniteur	*Le Moniteur universel*
Siècle	*Le Siècle*

References to parliamentary debates—e.g. *Moniteur*, CP 12 Apr. 1844—begin with the name of the collection cited (*AP*, *Moniteur*, *ASCL*, or *ASCD*); this is followed by the name of the Chamber (CP, CD, Ass. N., or Sénat), and the date on which the debate took place (not the date of its publication in the *Moniteur*); where appropriate the name of the orator is given at the end in brackets. Note that in the collections *ASCL* and *ASCD* the debates of the two Chambers are paginated separately.

References to the Archives Nationales—e.g. AN F^7 6770 (Moselle), Prefect to *Ministre de l'Intérieur*, 2 Apr. 1827—give the box number, followed by the name or description of the dossier (in brackets), and finally the description of the particular document.

Introduction

THIS book is a study in what has sometimes been called the 'paranoid style' in politics.[1] Another term often used to describe the same sort of thing is 'conspiracy theory'. Each term has its disadvantage: the first hints at too much psychological disorder, and the second at too much theoretical order, in the phenomenon described. Each, however, draws attention to an aspect of that phenomenon which the other unduly neglects: its stylistic or imaginative dimension in the first case, its logical structure in the second. This book deals, then, both with a way of imagining politics and with a form of political analysis, the two being intimately connected.

What each term with its different emphasis refers to is the propensity to think of politics (in the broadest sense) as dominated or controlled by the ill-intentioned and conspiratorial machinations of a group whose aims and values are profoundly opposed to those of the rest of society. There is a major difference between conspiracy theories and the type of analysis whose exponents regard conspiracy as a normal and widespread human activity, and therefore seek to understand politics in terms of conflicting and interacting conspiratorial intrigues. If conspiracies are various and numerous, what happens in politics and society is likely only rarely and irregularly to be what any particular set of conspirators has intended. A conspiracy theory asserts the opposite: that the events or trends with which it is concerned have regularly been the direct and intended products of conspiracy by one particular group. In effect, a behavioural distinction is established between a non-conspiratorial

---

[1] The expression was coined by Richard Hofstadter in the title essay of his *The Paranoid Style in American Politics, and Other Essays* (New York, 1965), and has been used since by American historians like David Brion Davis and Gordon S. Wood. As used by these historians, and by me, it does not imply any necessary connection with definable psychological 'abnormality'. Hofstadter's own clarification (pp. 3–4) may be repeated: 'In using the expression "paranoid style", I am not speaking in a clinical sense, but borrowing a clinical term for other purposes. . . . I use the term much as a historian of art might speak of the baroque or the mannerist style. It is, above all, a way of seeing the world and of expressing oneself.'

majority in society, and a minority who are fundamentally con-spiratorial, whether because they conspire instinctively, or because the ends to which they are devoted could never be realized by other means.

Considered at the most schematic level, then, a conspiracy theory does three things: it attributes the events of history or current affairs to conscious human volition; it sharply distinguishes be-tween the human forces of good and of evil; it implies a hidden reality beneath and at odds with the superficial appearances of the political and social world. It is here, however, that the term 'conspiracy theory' must not be allowed to deceive: in general, the historian encounters such 'theories' less often as fully elaborated interpretations of history or current affairs than as interpretative habits implicit in a stream of assertions or arguments, only some of which have an obviously analytical purpose. It follows that, while reflections on the common structures of conspiracy theory can be illuminating, the temptation to pare the paranoid style down to a central set of immutable theoretical elements needs to be resisted. By their rhetorical emphases, by their choice of imagery and selec-tion of themes, writers and polemicists ensure that the balance between the three basic dimensions of the conspiracy theorist's message is different in different cases and at different times. One of the purposes of this book's Conclusion will be to suggest how one particular conspiracy theory may be related to a broader typology and a longer history.

Materials for a more general history of the paranoid style could easily be assembled. From the Popish Plot alarms of the early modern period (if not from medieval alarms over lepers, Jews, and heretics), via eighteenth-century suspicions of famine plots and ministerial cabals, to the anti-Semitic, anti-communist, and anti-capitalist ideologies of the twentieth century, conspiracy theories have etched their traces deeply and repeatedly into the political culture both of Europe and of North America.[2] During few periods, however, were those traces more pronounced than in the

---

[2] See the case-studies cited in nn. 3 and 4 below and those, listed in the Biblio-graphy, by Bailyn (pp. 144–59), Barber, Billig (esp. pp. 296–343), Birnbaum, Brown, Christie, Clifton, Cohn, Davis, Hibbard, Hofstadter, Kaplan, Kuisel, Lipset and Raab, Nora, Thackray, Thurlow, Wiener, and Wood. L. Poliakov, *La Causalité diabolique*, 2 vols. (Paris, 1980–5), attempts a more general approach. C. F. Grau-mann and S. Moscovici (eds.), *Changing Conceptions of Conspiracy* (New York, 1987), combines psychological and historical perspectives.

century following the French Revolution. This need hardly surprise us. The Revolution was a colossal disruption of social and political relations both in the short and in the long term. Monarchy, Church, aristocracy, the corporate society, were shaken throughout Europe, and in France abruptly swept away, never to return in their old forms. For a brief, traumatic period, the Revolution provided a chaotic laboratory of new political forms and practices, through which France herself passed from long centuries of monarchy and hierarchy into a century of unprecedented political and social turmoil. Though equivalent transformations took place at different rates and with variable violence in other countries, few corners of the European continent could count the nineteenth century as an era of stability. The Revolutionary experience and its ideological elaboration, combined with extensions in suffrage, in education, and in the power and freedom of the press, created a world in which politics was more complicated, of more concern to more people, and less governed by any obvious consensus about political values and institutions than ever before. At the same time, thanks not only to the increased complexity of political processes, but also to the growth and centralization of bureaucracy, to improvements in communications, to the development of financial systems, economic differentiation, and division of labour, nineteenth-century Europeans were probably more likely than their forefathers to have an uncomfortable sense of subjection to remote and mysterious human forces. For many, the nineteenth century was a deeply disconcerting time to be living; no very sophisticated understanding of the psychological dynamics of the paranoid style is needed to see that conspiracy theories might have an appeal in such circumstances.

Nowhere was this propensity to formulate and to accept conspiracy theories more apparent in the nineteenth century than in France itself. This is partly because France, more than any other country, was marked and divided and troubled throughout the century by the memory and legacy of the Revolution, and partly because its parliamentary institutions and relatively extensive political press gave a publicity to conspiracy theories (as to many other forms of political opinion) that was hard to achieve elsewhere. The principal conspiracy theories to which the French resorted in this period were not (at least in general outline) unique to France; nor were they cited only in connection with French events. But a focus on France provides the historian with unusually good opportunities to observe how such theories arose and functioned in the arena of practical politics and as an influence on public opinion, in short to examine their place in a modern and developing political culture. It is with nineteenth-century France, therefore, that this book is concerned.

My purpose is to examine, in the French context, the forms and uses, the connotations and influence, of one of the two leading conspiracy theories of early and mid-nineteenth-century Europe. The other is better known, perhaps because we more instantly divine a psychological basis for its appeal. That men of the Right, whose ideal was an ordered hierarchical society with little mobility, united politically in respect for monarchy and morally in acceptance of an established version of Christian religion, should have been tempted, in their shocked perplexity at the liberalizing, democratizing, secularizing currents of the nineteenth century, to see these currents as the work of antisocial conspirators strikes us as understandable. Their reactions, in France and elsewhere, produced a tradition of counter-revolutionary conspiracy theory, focusing on Freemasonry and revolutionary secret societies, which runs from the classic analyses of the French Revolution by Barruel and Robison in the late 1790s through to the work of the *Revue internationale des sociétés secrètes* and of writers like Léon de Poncins and Nesta Webster in the present century. This tradition (which in its later stages became entangled with anti-Semitism) has been the subject of a number of useful historical studies.[3]

[3] The major work is J. M. Roberts, *The Mythology of the Secret Societies*, 2nd edn. (St Albans, 1974). See also Roberts's *The Paris Commune from the Right* (*English Historical Review* Supplement 6 (London, 1973)); J. Rogalla von Bieberstein, *Die These von der Verschwörung 1776–1945: Philosophen, Freimaurer, Juden, Liberalen und Sozialisten als Verschwörer gegen die Sozialordnung* (Berne, 1976), whose arguments are introduced to English readers in his article 'The Story of the Jewish–Masonic Conspiracy, 1776–1945', *Patterns of Prejudice*, 11/6 (1977), 1–8, 21; K. Epstein, *The Genesis of German Conservatism* (Princeton, NJ, 1966), ch. 10; J. Katz, *Jews and Freemasons in Europe, 1723–1939* (Cambridge, Mass., 1970), chs. 10–12 and 15; G. T. Cubitt, 'Catholics versus Freemasons in Late Nineteenth-Century France', in F. Tallett and N. Atkin (eds.), *Religion, Society and Politics in France since 1789* (London, 1991), 121–36; D. Rossignol, *Vichy et les francs-maçons: La Liquidation des sociétés secrètes 1940–1944* (Paris, 1981). On the 18th-century roots of this tradition, see J. Lemaire, *Les Origines françaises de l'antimaçonnisme (1744–1797)* (Brussels, 1985); A. Hofman, 'Anatomy of Conspiracy: The Origins of the Theory of the *Philosophe* Conspiracy, 1750–1789', Ph.D. thesis (Chicago, 1986), parts of which are summarized in Hofman's article 'The Origins of the Theory of the *Philosophe* Conspiracy', *French History*, 2 (1988), 152–72.

The conspiracy theories of the nineteenth-century Left—of liberals and republicans in particular—have received less attention. The Left's own rhetoric is probably partly responsible for this. Self-proclaimed sons of the Revolution, admirers and defenders of its achievements and of its legacy, 'the modern world', liberals and republicans talked as if progress, liberty, and modernity held no fears for them. Yet words like 'progress', 'liberty', 'Revolution', 'the modern world', had meanings in Revolutionary and post-Revolutionary political discourse very different from those which a historian now might give them. In practice, liberty and democracy have tended to generate diversity and discord in politics, or at least to make them more obvious; what Revolutionary ideology expected, however, was that they would untrammel the General Will, awakening a previously dormant consensus and making it the governing principle in the State. Likewise 'progress', to its devotees from the Enlightenment onwards, meant a leisurely uncoiling of united human reason to encompass its own destiny, not the zigzagging advance of a lurching humanity through an endless forest of factional squabbles and compromises. 'The Revolution' meant a definitive shaking-loose of a 'modern world', embodying fixed and definite new values, from its moribund predecessor. In short, one should not confuse the usually confident and optimistic tone of the Left's theories of historical development with serene acceptance of a rapidly and unpredictably changing and increasingly pluralistic world. Having a principled commitment to change is not the same as enjoying changeability, and a dogmatic belief in the imperious schedules of history is no sure proof against frustration at the survival or resurgence of what ought to have disappeared. The Left was as committed as the Right to the assumption that it was natural for society to rest on consensus and for historical change not to become uncontrollable; like the Right, it felt the need of special explanations when this assumption seemed to fail.

That the appeal of conspiracy theories was not confined to the camp of conservatism or reaction had been clear enough during the Revolution itself, when the counter-revolutionaries' theme of the masonic plot had been more than matched by the repeated denunciations of aristocratic and foreign conspiracy against the sovereign people and its Revolutionary achievement which were the stock in trade of Revolutionary politicians; the 'rhetoric of conspiracy', as one historian has put it, 'permeated revolutionary discourse at every political level'.[4] This version of conspiracy theory played an important part in inspiring and justifying Revolutionary violence, especially during the Terror. Partly for this reason, it had few nineteenth-century continuers. This does not, however, mean that nineteenth-century liberals and republicans eschewed the paranoid style. On the contrary, the Left acquired a tradition of conspiracy theory as highly developed, as tenacious, and as influential as that which conservatives entertained concerning Freemasonry and the secret societies. The enemies denounced in this tradition were the Jesuits.

This book discusses the forms and ingredients of the anti-jesuit conspiracy theory, its impact on French secular politics, and its roots in nineteenth-century political and intellectual culture. In places, it has a broader focus. Belief in a Jesuit conspiracy can no more be explored in isolation from a broader pattern of anti-jesuitism[5] than, for example, belief in a Jewish conspiracy can be isolated from a broader pattern of anti-Semitism. By no means all entrenched hostility to the Jesuit order involved a developed sense of Jesuit conspiracy. I have sought to understand how and why anti-jesuitism became, on several occasions, a potent force in French politics, and how and why the conspiracy theory acquired an influence; these are closely connected but not identical questions.

Another kind of breadth of focus has also been necessary. This book is chiefly concerned with anti-jesuitism as a force in secular politics, and its starting-point is the need for a study of the major conspiracy theory of the nineteenth-century Left. In fact, however, anti-jesuitism was confined neither to the Left nor to the secular

---

[4] L. Hunt, *Politics, Culture, and Class in the French Revolution* (London, 1986), 41. On the significance of counter-conspiratorial rhetoric during the Revolution, see pp. 38–45 of Hunt's book; F. Furet, *Interpreting the French Revolution* (Cambridge, 1981), 53–8; G. T. Cubitt, 'Denouncing Conspiracy in the French Revolution', *Renaissance and Modern Studies*, 33 (1989), 144–58. On popular rumours of conspiracy, see G. Lefebvre, *The Great Fear of 1789: Rural Panic in Revolutionary France* (London, 1973).

[5] The terms *antijésuitisme* and *antijésuite* (both as noun and as adjective) can both be found in use well before the establishment of *anticlérical* in the 1850s. A pro-Jesuit pamphlet of 1762 was entitled *Nouveau Catéchisme sur les affaires présentes des jésuites . . . , ou l'antijésuitisme exposé familièrement, par demandes et réponses*; Villèle in his *Mémoires et correspondance*, 5 vols. (Paris, 1888–90), v. 300, writing in Dec. 1827, applied the adjective *anti-jésuite* to the Chambre des Députés; Michelet in his *Journal*, ed. P. Viallaneix, 4 vols. (Paris, 1959–76), i. 543, recorded a nocturnal visit by 'de prétendus anti-jésuites' in Dec. 1843.

arena. There were anti-jesuits of the Right (at least one of whom —the comte de Montlosier—will figure prominently in my account); equally, there were men of the Left, at every stage in the nineteenth century, who scorned to indulge in suspicions of Jesuit conspiracy, and sections of the Left (Marxian Socialism being the obvious case) for which the Jesuits were not the most probable demons. There were also anti-jesuits whose concerns were religious rather than political, some of whom had little in common with anti-jesuits of a more secular kind, yet whose existence (as I shall argue later) is not irrelevant to an understanding of anti-jesuitism's political role. Finally, there were elements in anti-jesuit mythology which had, on the face of it, more to do with morals or aesthetics than with politics, though anti-jesuits might not have accepted the distinction. Anti-jesuitism was a complex phenomenon whose uses in liberal and republican politics will be ill understood if no other uses and contexts are recognized.

It is nevertheless the major heydays of anti-jesuitism in French secular politics that command attention. To follow them is to see anti-jesuitism at work in a striking variety of political circumstances. Three times in the seventy years that followed the Bourbon Restoration, and each time under a different constitutional regime, the Jesuit question may be said for a time to have dominated French politics. In the mid- and late 1820s it emerged as a damaging thorn in the sides first of the Villèle government, and ultimately of the Bourbon monarchy itself. In the mid-1840s it cast its ominous shadow over the acrimonious debates on secondary education which disturbed the surface of Orleanist politics, and became one of the principal issues used by the opposition in an effort to unsettle the government dominated by Guizot. Finally, at the end of the 1870s it provided the ground for the first great anti-clerical offensive by a Third Republican government. On each of these occasions, one product of the wave of anti-jesuitism was a setback to the Society of Jesus itself: in 1828 a royal *ordonnance* banned Jesuits (along with members of other unauthorized religious orders) from teaching in French schools; in 1845 Guizot's diplomatic overtures to Rome secured a partial dispersal of French Jesuit personnel; in 1880, following the defeat of Article 7 of Jules Ferry's higher-education bill in one of the early Third Republic's most traumatic and keenly fought parliamentary battles, the government decreed the dissolution of the Jesuit order on French soil. On each occasion also, however, anti-jesuitism acquired a broader political significance: the Jesuit question was seen, in certain quarters, not just as an issue of national concern in itself, but as the key to other major issues, and perhaps to national politics in their entirety. The Jesuit interest, and often the Jesuits' directing hand, was detected behind political and religious developments, legislative projects, and shifts in public opinion or morals, many of which seem in retrospect to have had little or nothing to do with the Society of Jesus. Individuals, governments, political groupings, were discredited by being branded as vehicles or fronts for Jesuit ascendancy. Politicians and journalists defined their opponents as Jesuits or Jesuit agents, and themselves and their allies as anti-jesuits.[6]

Historians have studied and narrated the political events that composed these three major episodes of anti-jesuit outcry, but their aim in doing so has seldom been to describe the evolution of anti-jesuitism itself in any detail. To retell the story from this perspective—to pinpoint the moments at which, and the circumstances under which, anti-jesuit rhetoric became available as a political weapon, the types of political use to which it was then put, and the effects of this use both on the practicalities of French politics and on the mythology of anti-jesuitism itself—is the purpose of Chapters 2–4 of this book.

Such a study will be inadequate, however, if it treats each spate of anti-jesuitism in isolation, as if each invented its weaponry afresh. The polemics of the 1820s, the 1840s, and the 1870s tapped a more continuous tradition. The wisdom and folklore of anti-jesuitism, deposited over the centuries by successive waves of Protestant, Jansenist, *philosophe*, and now liberal and republican critics (in a manner which Paul Féval once compared to the steady accretion of guano[7]), lingered in the intervals between the heydays— repeated in the occasional pamphlet, rehearsed perhaps by the few rather than the many, but not lost. Anti-jesuitism cannot, then, be reduced to the proportions of an occasional freakish mass delusion. It was a durable ingredient in the mental make-up of successive generations and varying shades of liberal, republican, and democrat, and in the ideological systems with which they sought

---

[6] Thus Benjamin Raspail claimed that the vote on the Loi Falloux in 1850 would establish a simple division: 'For, Jesuits! *Against*, anti-jesuits!' His own position was clear: 'I have been and will always be one of the latter' (*Moniteur*, Ass. N. 11 Mar. 1850: 837).   [7] P. Féval, *Jésuites!* (Paris, 1877), 22.

to frustrate attempts at legitimist, monarchist, or clerical counter-revolution, and to sustain or establish the political dominance of their own kind. It contributed to a sense of continuity in French political identities, connecting later nineteenth-century republicans in their own minds with earlier nineteenth-century liberals, and both with the Gallican traditions of the past. To understand this dimension of anti-jesuitism's contribution to nineteenth-century politics, we must approach it as a gradually evolving compound of traditional materials—themes and motifs transmitted from generation to generation and adapted, with varying degrees of flexibility, to the analytical needs and historical conditions of successive periods. A study of anti-jesuitism's political uses needs, in other words, to be combined with a study of its repertoire. In Chapters 5–10 of this book, accordingly, I have sought to establish the principal themes and images of nineteenth-century anti-jesuit polemic, and to explore the patterns and structures of argument through which the ingredients of anti-jesuit tradition became the components of contemporary analysis.

A historian of anti-jesuitism in nineteenth-century France has few predecessors either to honour or to abuse. Nineteenth-century conditions, and especially the siege mentality prevalent among both Catholics and anticlericals, hardly encouraged the emergence of a serious historical literature on the subject. Anti-jesuits saw little need for such a literature (except perhaps in the hagiographic vein); for them, it was the history of Jesuitism, to which anti-jesuitism was merely the merited rebuke, that had to be exposed. The Jesuits, for their part, accepted the hostility of their enemies with resignation sometimes tinged with pride. Denying any distinction between their own cause and that of the Church, they and their defenders generally failed to see in anti-jesuitism anything other than a cynical tactical manœuvre. 'They have not dared to attack religion frontally: they have attacked it in its most useful and active servants,' wrote Duparc and Cochin of the Jesuits' persecutors in 1880.[8] Père Burnichon, in the first volume (published in 1914) of his still-standard history of the Society of Jesus in nineteenth-century France, remarked philosophically: 'No doubt it is natural that the enemies of religion detest those who defend it, and they

---

[8] H. Duparc and H. Cochin (eds.), *Expulsions des congrégations religieuses: Récits et témoignages* (Paris, 1881), 5.

could do no greater honour to the Jesuits than by devoting the maximum of their hatred to them.'[9] He was palpably unwilling to push analysis of anti-jesuitism any further, considering it a mystery beyond human explanation. Similar convictions informed the large majority of the numerous works written in the Jesuits' defence during the nineteenth and early twentieth centuries; the refutation of anti-jesuit allegations, not the critical or historical analysis of anti-jesuit ideology, was the object.

Only one Jesuit or pro-Jesuit scholar during this period really stood back from the spiral of proofs and refutations and made anti-jesuitism the object of a serious and systematic historical study. Père Brou remained convinced (understandably in the immediate aftermath of the Separation of Church and State) that anti-jesuitism had been ultimately an attack on the Church and religion, but his energies, in a work which stressed the traditional nature of anti-jesuit beliefs, were devoted to cataloguing its forms and charting the evolution of its salient themes. His analysis identified two polar categories—'l'antijésuitisme populaire' and 'l'antijésuitisme savant'—with a number of others ('l'antijésuitisme de tribune', 'de journal', 'littéraire et critique', 'romanesque et mondain', 'social et pédagogique') fluctuating between. Necessarily impressionistic (since it covered the whole of Europe and the full time-span of Jesuit existence), Brou's survey remains the only extensive historical survey of the anti-jesuit tradition as it existed in nineteenth-century France.[10] Important light has been shed by modern historians on certain aspects or episodes—for example by Bertier de Sauvigny on the Restoration myth of the Congrégation and by Mellon on the political uses of Jesuit history during the same period[11]—but general surveys have been scarce and limited to a few pages.[12] Alec Mellor in his history of French anticlericalism, and Léon Poliakov in a general essay on the paranoid style, have both drawn attention to the French anti-jesuit literature

[9] J. Burnichon, *La Compagnie de Jésus en France: Histoire d'un siècle, 1814–1914*, 4 vols. (Paris, 1914–22), vol. i, p. xlvi.

[10] A. Brou, *Les Jésuites de la légende*, 2 vols. (Paris, 1906–7).

[11] G. de Bertier de Sauvigny, *Le Comte Ferdinand de Bertier, 1782–1864, et l'énigme de la Congrégation* (Paris, 1948), 368–407; S. Mellon, *The Political Uses of History: A Study of Historians in the French Restoration* (Stanford, Calif., 1958), 128–92.

[12] See most recently the discussion of conspiracy themes (anti-Semitic, anti-jesuit, and anti-masonic) in R. Girardet, *Mythes et mythologies politiques* (Paris, 1986), 25–62.

of the nineteenth century, and especially of the Restoration period.
Both, however, favour a quasi-psychiatric vocabulary—'jésuito-
phobie', 'insanités' (Poliakov), 'psychose collective', 'démentielle'
(Mellor)—which neither of them really justifies, and which en-
shrines a certain reluctance to discuss anti-jesuitism as ideology,
tradition, or argument, or as anything except the product of mental
disorder.[13]

The four pages (introducing a useful set of extracts from early
nineteenth-century anti-jesuit texts) which René Rémond devotes
to anti-jesuitism in his study of modern French anticlericalism are
more helpful. Rémond notes the insistence of many anti-jesuits on
a distinction between the Jesuits and the Church, but argues that
their charges against the Jesuits were nevertheless similar to those
made against other clergy. The important difference was one of
intensity: what incurred ridicule when attributed to the secular
clergy was seen as frightening and intolerable when attributed to
the Jesuits. In Rémond's view, it was the sheer elasticity of the anticlerical imagination with regard to the Jesuits, who were deemed
capable of any kind and degree of criminality, which gave anti-
jesuitism its distinctive character. Thanks to it, there developed,
in connection with the Jesuits, 'a veritable myth, comparable in
many respects to those which have formed around witchcraft, the
Templars, Freemasonry or the Jews'.[14]

Like the notion of conspiracy theory (which Rémond does not
employ), this notion of an anti-jesuit 'myth' is central to my own
analysis. My understanding of the term (not necessarily identical to
Rémond's), and the methodological attitudes that inform my use of
it, need to be clarified at the outset. In applying words like 'myth'

[13] Poliakov, *La Causalité diabolique*, i. 61–9; A. Mellor, *Histoire de l'anticléricalisme
français* (Paris, 1978), 244–59. Mellor insists that 'the word [psychosis] should be
understood in its literal sense', because 'psychiatric treatises' have taken note of the
case; regrettably, he neither provides bibliographical details of this literature nor
summarizes its findings. It is difficult anyway to accept the imbalance whereby the
anti-jesuitism of Michelet and Quinet is dismissed as 'delirious hallucination' ('in
the words of G. Lanson', a literary rather than a psychiatric specialist), while the
equally extravagant polemic of clerical writers like Deschamps and Védrine is
treated as a natural though excessive reaction to attacks on Christianity (pp. 257–8).

[14] R. Rémond, *L'Anticléricalisme en France de 1815 à nos jours* (Paris, 1976), 81–4
(quotation 82), with documents 84–104. More recently, Rémond has suggested the
existence within anticlericalism of 'a sort of hierarchical scale, according to the
intensity of the polemic and the passions involved—with the Jesuits at the top'
('Anticlericalism: Some Reflections by Way of Introduction', *European Studies
Review*, 13 (1983), 124).

and 'conspiracy theory' to the anti-jesuit case, one inevitably calls into question the nature and directness of the relationship between anti-jesuit allegations and the facts of Jesuit history. Though I have tried (especially in Chapter 1) to provide such information about the Jesuits as may help to explain the influence of anti-jesuit themes, the question of how much truth there was in anti-jesuit assertions is not a central preoccupation of this book. The idea that a meticulous and systematic sifting of the false from the true (on the basis of a careful scrutiny of real nineteenth-century Jesuit behaviour) is an indispensable preliminary to any useful analysis of anti-jesuitism as a mentality or as a political force has been rejected, as resting on a basic misunderstanding of the frameworks of anti-jesuit thought. My suggestion here is not that no shreds of factual accuracy were woven into the fabric of anti-jesuit conspiracy theory (which would be odd if it were true), but that such elements cannot simply be isolated from the structures and patterns of argument that gave them significance. Whatever the verisimilitude of particular details, the general picture of Jesuit influence that anti-jesuitism in its more developed forms projected was (as later chapters will illustrate) one that was markedly disproportionate not only to the particular capacities of the nineteenth-century Society of Jesus, but also to any conception of the objective possibilities of centralized manipulation in human affairs that would be likely nowadays to win the approval of historians or social scientists, or indeed of ordinary citizens. In accounting for the durability and influence of this picture, something more than a liability to exaggeration or mis-perception in matters of detail has got to be explained. It may be argued that this is to give the conspiracy theory too much concrete-ness—to see it too much as a framework which shaped perceptions, and too little as the *ad hoc* product of perceptions independently shaped. Such a criticism, however, ignores some of the most strik-ing characteristics of anti-jesuit argument. It is here that the notion of myth becomes important.

To suggest that myth, rather than empirical observation of contemporary Jesuit behaviour, was the characteristic mainspring of anti-jesuit analyses is not to dismiss these analyses as mere fantasy. On the contrary, it is to reflect the highly conventional and self-consciously traditional nature of a polemical literature which all too often appears to take its cue from the words with which one of its Third Republican practitioners explained the constant need for further books on the Jesuits: 'There is no longer anything new to say about them, but each day sees the arrival of new generations of readers.'[15] Nineteenth-century anti-jesuits made few genuinely new additions to a polemical arsenal whose principal elements, as Brou showed, had been largely assembled by the end of the seventeenth century.[16] The influence of early modern anti-jesuit texts like the so-called *Monita secreta* and Pascal's *Lettres provinciales* remained profound. Anti-jesuits hoped, by transmitting with urgency the anti-jesuit wisdom of the past, to save the modern world from an enemy which they believed had lost nothing of its ancient spirit of domination. This, most of them seem to have believed, could be done with a minimum of rummaging in modern Jesuit dustbins. Only a handful of nineteenth-century French Jesuits—Pères Ronsin, Loriquet, Gury, Ravignan, and du Lac come to mind—found their way into an anti-jesuit rogues' gallery packed with long-defunct casuists, confessors, and conspirators. Hard information on contemporary Jesuit establishments was equally uncommon in the literature. During the early part of the century, indeed, when French Jesuits were few and shy of publicity, most anti-jesuits were so ignorant about the details of French Jesuit life that proofs of even so basic a fact as the organized presence of the Society of Jesus on French soil were treated as a major revelation. Information of this sort was seized on when it came to light, and placed in a preconceived context which endowed even the most innocent data with sinister significance, but it was not the usual raw material from which allegations of contemporary Jesuit conspiracy arose. Instead (as will be argued more fully in Chapter 5), these allegations were rooted in a certain conception of Jesuit history. They involved the recognition in the fabric of current affairs—and not only in those sections of it where real Jesuits could be directly observed at work—of supposedly traditional, and traditionally Jesuit, patterns of devilry.

No automatic opposition between 'myth' and 'reality', then, is implied in my references to a 'myth' of Jesuit conspiracy. What is asserted is not the prevalence of erroneous beliefs about the Society of Jesus, but the dependence of beliefs about it (whether erroneous or not), and of a broader view of modern history and of current

---

[15] A. Michel, *Les Jésuites* (Paris, 1879), 5.
[16] Brou, *Les Jésuites de la légende*, vol. i, *passim*, esp. p. 76.

affairs, on a fossilized but constantly repeated and extended account of the Jesuit past, in which the theme of conspiracy held a prominent place. Myth, in this sense, is not a superstitious mist that fills the gaps left by rational reflection on contemporary data; it is a way of linking present and past in a common dramatic framework, of reading traditional significance into fresh events and circumstances. People do not make (or accept) a myth by mistaking the facts, whether of history or of current affairs, but by finding a certain version or narrative of the past peculiarly and compellingly pregnant with meaning for their own times. To comprehend this perception of a specific kind of relevance—to grasp what it was about a particular vision of the past that permitted it to condition the analytical imagination that was brought to bear upon the present, and what it was about particular circumstances that provoked the mythical sense of *déjà vu*—must be the major concern of a historian seeking to understand the anti-jesuit mentality and its political influence.

A study of anti-jesuitism is thus, in my view, not obliged to keep one eye constantly on real Jesuits, any more than a study of anti-Semitism needs to keep one eye constantly on real Jews. It by no means follows, however, that no attention of any sort needs to be paid to the Jesuits' place in nineteenth-century European, and especially French, history. It is hard to see how an anti-jesuit myth forged in the conflicts of the sixteenth, seventeenth, and eighteenth centuries could have imposed itself on more than a few fanatics or eccentrics in the quite different circumstances of the nineteenth, if there had been nothing else in those circumstances to direct the thoughts of Frenchmen to the Society of Jesus. It therefore becomes necessary to explore not the bare record of Jesuit action, but the different facets of the nineteenth-century Jesuit reputation, the different ways in which—by a variable combination of its conduct, its doctrine, its legal position, and the more or less well-founded expectations of its friends and foes—the Society of Jesus was implicated in some of the major political, religious, or ideological conflicts of the age. By understanding what was suggestive, equivocal, or provocative about this implication we will not, of course, fully account for the forms and contents of the anti-jesuit myth. We may, nevertheless, gain insights into why particular elements in the mythology were stressed especially strongly in the nineteenth century. At the least, we should begin to see how the contexts in which the Jesuits were talked about helped to produce the sort of shimmering half-light in which the lingering spectres of myth could prey on the imagination. This, rather than a systematic survey of Jesuit activity, is my purpose in Chapter 1.

To loosen the connections between anti-jesuit allegations and empirically observable Jesuit conduct by stressing the role of myth in shaping anti-jesuit perceptions is, however, to raise another methodological problem. How should one deal with the ambiguity and indeterminacy of anti-jesuit language? The Bishop of Chartres was perhaps guilty of a pardonable exaggeration when he complained that the word *jésuite*, as used by his opponents, would soon encompass 'the whole Catholic clergy, the faithful of that communion, the Calvinists, the Lutherans, the Socinians and, a little later, all men who believe in God, more or less'.[17] It cannot be denied, however, that the anti-jesuit vocabulary (*jésuite, jésuitisme, jésuitique, jésuitiquement, jésuitiser,*[18] *jésuitesse, jésuitière,*[19] and so on) was frequently applied to people or things which actually had little or nothing to do with the Society of Jesus. No hard-and-fast rule suggests itself for telling the difference, in such cases, between loose usage (whether deliberate or accidental) and usage informed by a genuinely swollen conception of Jesuit influence or membership. It would certainly be foolish to assume that the word 'Jesuit' was always invested with the same sense.[20] In a passage cherished by the Jesuits' defenders, the Liberal journalist Armand Carrel wrote, in retrospect, about the anti-jesuit language of the Restoration:

[17] AN F[19] 6287 (Surveillance et dispersion): Bishop of Chartres to *Ministre des Cultes*, 18 May 1845.

[18] According to L.-N. Bescherelle, *Nouveau Dictionnaire national; ou Dictionnaire universel de la langue française*, 4 vols. (Paris, 1887), iii. 127, 'jésuitiser' meant 'Faire le jésuite, escobardiser'.

[19] A 'jésuitière' was a 'maison de jésuites', but 'la jésuitière' could mean the whole Jesuit order, according to P. Larousse (ed.), *Grand Dictionnaire universel français*, 17 vols. (Paris, 1865–90), ix. 966.

[20] Thus Balzac draws a protracted (and not readily translated) misogynist witticism out of the tension between two orders of usage: 'Le jésuite, le plus jésuite des jésuites est encore mille fois moins jésuite que la femme la moins jésuite, jugez combien les femmes sont jésuites! Elles sont si jésuites, que le plus fin des jésuites lui-même ne devinerait pas à quel point une femme est jésuite, car il y a mille manières d'être jésuite, et la femme est si habile jésuite qu'elle a le talent d'être jésuite sans avoir l'air jésuite.' H. de Balzac, *Œuvres complètes*, ed. M. Bouteron and M. Longnon, 40 vols. (Paris, 1926–63), xxxiii. 41–2 (*Petites Misères de la vie conjugale*: 'Jésuitisme des femmes').

It was known very well that the Society of Jesus itself posed no great danger. The grudge was against the Jesuit spirit, the *dévot* spirit, the *Tartuffe* spirit; this was the spirit of the ruling dynasty. There was an excellent understanding on the meaning of the word Jesuitism; it was a synonym for devotion to legitimacy. At that time, one said 'Jesuit' for 'royalist'.[21]

Simple ignorance could have a similar effect. In 1827, when pupils of the *collège royal* of Orléans, who had rebelled against a headmaster whom they suspected of 'Jesuitism', were questioned on their understanding of the word 'Jesuit', one replied that a Jesuit was a priest, while the others hesitantly answered 'that they attached to the word Jesuit the idea of falsity'.[22] In this, they concurred with a usage well enough established to figure in the dictionaries: in vulgar language, Bescherelle recorded, 'Jesuit' had become a term of abuse and a synonym for 'a hypocritical, intriguing, artful, disloyal person'.[23]

If, however, there is an obvious danger in taking all linguistic connections at face value, the opposite danger, especially when dealing (as this book does, much of the time) with sources which use anti-jesuit terminology extensively and with apparent seriousness, may be as great. The historian of ideas or mentalities must sometimes connect senses which the lexicographer separates. Against the faltering failure of the schoolboys of Orléans to connect 'Jesuits' with the Society of Jesus must be set the case of François-Vincent Raspail. Few men used the terms of anti-jesuitism with more apparent wildness, and few of his claims were more astonishing than his suggestion that the First International was an agent of 'Jesuitism'. Yet this was meant literally: Raspail stated that he had preferred the word 'Jesuitism' to its effective synonym

---

[21] Quoted in Burnichon, *La Compagnie de Jésus en France*, i. 318, and elsewhere. The reference usually given is to *Le National*, 17 Oct. 1832, but I have failed to locate the passage.

[22] J. Brugerette, *Le Comte de Montlosier et son temps (1755–1838)* (Aurillac, 1931), 217 n.

[23] Bescherelle, *Nouveau Dictionnaire*, iii. 127. Similarly E. Littré, *Dictionnaire de la langue française*, 5 vols. (Paris, 1863–72), ii. 179 ('a hypocrite who is not to be trusted, an expression drawn from the mental reservations of which the moral doctrine of the Jesuits was accused'); Larousse (ed.), *Grand Dictionnaire universel*, ix. 958 ('hypocritical and crafty person'). L. Larchey, *Dictionnaire historique, étymologique et anecdotique de l'argot parisien*, 6th edn. (Paris, 1872), 159, gave the synonym 'cafard'. Though Littré was certainly right to see the attack on Jesuit casuistry as the principal influence behind such 19th-century usages, Brou points out that the use of *jesuita* or *jésuite* as a synonym for 'hypocrite' actually antedates the foundation of the Society of Jesus (*Les Jésuites de la légende*, i. 25–6).

'Ultramontanism', because it went straight to the point, whereas 'Ultramontanism only indicates the *Society of Jesus* after two or three leaps, which the worker of today cannot yet make'.[24] The historian's efforts to gauge the sense of anti-jesuit rhetoric are, however, seldom assisted by such obliging self-clarifications. Any attempt to reduce statements using anti-jesuit terminology to neatly differentiated semantic order is bound in places to founder upon ambiguity, opacity, and apparent inconsistency. The same terms may be used, by a single writer within a few pages, to refer to the Jesuit *Constitutions*, to the spread of Ultramontanism, to the machinations of a political party, and to the prevalence of hypocrisy in public life, without any clear sign either of explicit connection or of conscious discontinuity. 'Jesuits' may be referred to, in ways which leave it unclear (at least to today's reader) to whom, if to anyone in particular, the word was meant to apply, and in how literal a sense it was meant to be understood. Nor need it always have been meant to be understood alike by all; the censor or the general public might be meant to take literally what others would understand in an esoteric sense.

All this may render the interpretation of particular texts or passages problematic, but it has more to teach the historian than patience in adversity. For what it indicates is that the boundaries between different senses attributable to the anti-jesuit vocabulary were neither stably established in practice nor universally agreed in theory. Some writers and orators no doubt cynically exploited this fact, but those who couched their accounts of modern ills in anti-jesuit terms were probably on average no less sincere than other citizens, and no more given to wilful ambiguity of utterance. If they used a single set of terms to refer to things that seem to us to be distinct, this was not necessarily through false economy, but perhaps because those things did not seem so distinct to them. Significant elements in the mythology surrounding the Jesuits encouraged a conflation of the different senses with which anti-jesuit vocabulary might be invested: the sinister figure of the *jésuite de robe courte* (the plain-clothes Jesuit) might be seen in the royalist or clerical politician, and the specific effects of the Jesuit casuists' *morale relâchée* perceived in displays of unscrupulous hypocrisy. Part

---

[24] F.-V. Raspail, *Prévision du temps: Almanach et calendrier météorologique* (for the year 1873), 178–9.

of anti-jesuitism's importance to the historian lies precisely in the connections it established in people's minds between what might otherwise have been considered discrete objects of concern, and in the establishment of these connections loose usage and conspiracy theory interacted, each in some measure preparing the other's ground.

To draw attention to the role of myth and of conspiracy theory in shaping anti-jesuit perceptions is not, then, to suggest that anti-jesuitism can be removed from the realm of ordinary political discourse—a realm whose contours are moulded by rhetoric and imagination as well as by theory, and whose meanings are as often shrouded in ambiguity as fixed in the light of certainty. Anti-jesuitism was not a hallucinatory vision that imposed itself with blinding clarity on the susceptible minds of believers, nor was it an esoteric mystery preserved and perpetuated by crankish intellects. Its exponents included some whom even contemporaries found eccentric or fanatical, but others about whom there was nothing especially outlandish. Many who swam with confidence in the mainstream of nineteenth-century politics subscribed to anti-jesuit ideas, not as a secret vice of the intellect, but as an acceptable, even orthodox, part of their political creed. Anti-jesuitism, and its conspiracy myth, appealed to them because they seemed to make sense within, or as an extension of, familiar patterns of political discourse. To establish the type of sense they made is part of the purpose of this book.

I

Anti-Jesuitism and the Jesuits

THE suspicions and hostilities which attached to the Jesuit name in the nineteenth century had as their focus an order that was simultaneously old and new.[1] Founded by Ignatius of Loyola in 1540, the Society of Jesus had rapidly established itself as the most famous and most controversial of the militant forces of Counter-Reformation, and the activities of its members as teachers, as missionaries, and as confessors had kept it in the forefront of religious and ecclesiastical conflict throughout the seventeenth century. In the first half of the eighteenth century, its prestige and its influence had been at their zenith, both in France and elsewhere: the rulers of Catholic Europe had Jesuit confessors, and the extensive network of Jesuit colleges dominated the educational field. Yet the order's downfall at the hands of the Catholic powers in the third quarter of the century had been as decisive as its strength had seemed assured. Driven successively from Portugal (1759), from France (1764), from Spain, Naples, and Sicily (1767), the Society of Jesus had finally been dissolved, supposedly 'forever', by Pope Clement XIV in 1774. Groups of ex-Jesuits had clung on unofficially in places, and a Jesuit organization had continued in Russia under the protection of Catherine the Great, gaining official papal recognition in 1801, but the Jesuit order as an international force had ceased to exist.[2] The dramatic events of the Revolutionary and Napoleonic years had taken place in its absence. In 1814, however, responding to the general mood of Restoration and to what he chose to regard as the unanimous voice of 'the whole Catholic world', Pope Pius VII re-established the Society of Jesus

---

[1] General histories of the Jesuit order are numerous; see e.g. D. Mitchell, *The Jesuits: A History* (London, 1980).
[2] See O. Chadwick, *The Popes and European Revolution* (Oxford, 1981), ch. 5; D. Van Kley, *The Jansenists and the Expulsion of the Jesuits from France* (New Haven, Conn., 1975); P. Dudon, 'La Résurrection de la Compagnie de Jésus (1773–1814)', *Revue des questions historiques*, 133 (1939), 21–59.

throughout Christendom. Constitutionally and organizationally, the revived order was the replica of its predecessor. In magnifying the Jesuits' influence, early nineteenth-century anti-jesuit opinion made much of this eerie sameness, and largely ignored the practical problems involved in the order's resurrection. In countries like France, however, the Society was scarcely in a position instantly to reproduce its former triumphs.[3] The barest handful of aged French Jesuits survived to bridge the fifty-year gap between the old and new orders; the younger men who joined the order from the crypto-Jesuit association of Pères de la Foi were distinguished more for their zeal than for the solidity of their Jesuit preparation, and the proper training of new recruits often suffered, in the early years, as the Jesuits struggled to meet the escalating demand for their services. Throughout the 1820s, which witnessed the first great wave of nineteenth-century anti-jesuitism, the Jesuits of the French province (novices excluded) numbered well below 500, concentrated in a small number of neighbourhoods, and sorely overstretched in staffing the eight schools for which they were responsible by 1828. Forced to suspend its educational activities inside France between 1828 and 1850, the order was finally able to consolidate. By 1844 its French membership (now divided into two provinces, which would become four by 1863) totalled 770, occupying fifty-five houses. By 1864 the figure (including a significant number serving overseas) had risen to over 2,300, and by 1880 it was close to 3,000. In the latter year, on the eve of a fresh suppression, the number of French Jesuit establishments stood at sixty-nine; the order was responsible for twenty-nine *collèges* within

---

[3] The major work on the Society of Jesus in 19th-century France is Burnichon, *La Compagnie de Jésus en France*; see also J. Crétineau-Joly, *Histoire religieuse, politique et littéraire de la Compagnie de Jésus*, 6 vols. (Paris, 1844–6), vi. 65–276; D. M. Linehan, 'The Society of Jesus in France, 1870–1880', Ph.D. thesis (London, 1984); and entries on particular establishments in P. Delattre (ed.), *Les Établissements des jésuites en France depuis quatre siècles: Répertoire topo-bibliographique*, 5 vols. (Enghien, 1949–57). On Jesuit schools, J. Padberg, *Colleges in Controversy: The Jesuit Schools in France from Revival to Suppression, 1815–1880* (Cambridge, Mass., 1969) is fundamental; see also J. Bush, 'Education and Social Status: The Jesuit *Collège* in the Early Third Republic', *French Historical Studies*, 10 (1975), 125–40; J. Langdon, 'The Jesuits and French Education: A Comparative Study of Two Schools, 1852–1913', *History of Education Quarterly*, 18 (1978), 49–60. The most stimulating study of an individual Jesuit school (lying outside France, but frequented by numerous French pupils and staff) is K. Ashe, *The Jesuit Academy (Pensionnat) of Saint Michel in Fribourg, 1827–1847* (Fribourg, 1971).

France's borders, with almost 11,000 pupils, and for seven diocesan seminaries.[4]

The year 1850 provides a convenient point of division in nineteenth-century French Jesuit history. Before this date, the Jesuits' existence in France, if not quite clandestine, was kept discreetly veiled. Jesuit schools (before 1828) were disguised as diocesan *petits séminaires*, and the Jesuits themselves were cautious about revealing their true identity, preferring to be known as Pères de la Foi (under the Restoration) or to pass outwardly for ordinary clergy. When Père de Ravignan, publishing his *De l'existence et de l'institut des jésuites* in 1844, explicitly declared himself a member of the Society of Jesus, he was deliberately breaking new ground. The more usual reticence, coupled with the relative scarcity of Jesuit establishments and personnel, ensured that, at least until mid-century, the Society of Jesus was notorious rather than well known. Almost inevitably, historical memories, reputations, expectations, and rumour tended to count for more in public debate about the order than did informed assessments of the scale and nature of its current activities. After 1850, when the Loi Falloux once more permitted the establishment of a Jesuit educational network on French soil, a distinctly higher profile was maintained. By then, however, the main lines of nineteenth-century anti-jesuit polemic were largely established; the Jesuits' greater visibility under the Second Empire and Third Republic did little to transform them.

The relationship between past and present antagonisms, between inherited prejudice and contemporary perception, in the genesis of this anti-jesuit polemic must be adjudged a complex one. Contemporary observation could reveal a Society of Jesus which was able, in the two-thirds of a century following its resuscitation, to recapture a measure of its former prestige, and whose members exerted a significant influence in numerous areas of ecclesiastical or religious life. Besides their important but interrupted involvement in Catholic secondary education, French Jesuits were deeply involved in missionary work, in preaching, in the confessional, in the organization of spiritual retreats and of pious confraternities, and in religious publishing; indeed they left their mark, individually or

---

[4] Statistics from Delattre (ed.), *Les Établissements*, ii. 581–2 ('France, assistance de'). Linehan, 'The Society of Jesus', 79, gives a slightly higher figure (3,245) for the number of French Jesuits in 1880.

collectively, on almost every branch of ecclesiastical activity with the significant exceptions of primary education and the parish ministry. There was much in all this to make the Jesuits unpopular in anticlerical quarters, but less, on the face of it, to sustain the sharp distinction which anti-jesuitism drew between the actions and influence of the Jesuits and those of other clergy. Even where nineteenth-century Catholicism appears most noticeably to have been influenced by earlier Jesuit examples—in the fields of spirituality and of moral theology, for example—it is by no means clear that the influence was primarily transmitted through modern Jesuit channels. For contemporary observation to yield the insight that the Jesuits were not merely prominent participants in certain movements of modern Catholicism, but those movements' inspirers, organizers, and principal beneficiaries, it had to interact with some sort of prior alertness to the Jesuit order's significance.

The anti-jesuitism of the nineteenth century was undoubtedly indebted to the accumulated hostilities incurred, over the first two and a half centuries of its existence, by an order that had never been meant to be inoffensive, save in the sight of God. In some cases the debt was bound up with a broader sense of positive tradition. It was scarcely to be expected that a man like the ex-magistrate Louis Silvy, whose life revolved around the cult of Port-Royal, would view with equanimity the revival of the order to whose influence on Louis XIV the persecution and destruction of Port-Royal was generally attributed.[5] Silvy's links with the pre-Revolutionary world were obvious (he was born in 1760), but a later nineteenth-century Protestant like pastor Eugène Bersier could feel the anti-jesuit burden of tradition in a similar way. 'On each page of the history of the reformed Church of France, whose son I am, I see the Jesuits inspiring the implacable persecutions that have smitten my fathers,' he wrote to Jules Ferry in 1879; 'that which I honour the most, they degrade; freedom of conscience has had no fiercer adversaries.' His own liberal principles prevented Bersier from supporting Ferry's intended anti-Jesuit legislation; his hostility to the Jesuits was nevertheless 'one of those reasoned and powerful passions that can cease only with life itself'.[6]

---

[5] On Silvy, see A. Gazier, *Histoire générale du mouvement janséniste depuis ses origines jusqu'à nos jours*, 2 vols. (Paris, 1922), ii. 203–15.

[6] Quoted in L. Andrieux, *Souvenirs d'un préfet de police*, 2 vols. (Paris, 1885), i. 211.

Where such a sense of direct spiritual (or actual) descent from past victims of Jesuit intolerance existed, it was no doubt a major factor in focusing apprehensions on the modern Jesuit order. The importance of such inherited hostilities must not, however, be exaggerated. Most nineteenth-century Frenchmen had only a vicarious connection with the martyrs. Those of them who incorporated traditional images of Jesuit evil into their analyses of the present were seldom being purely atavistic; they were assigning an ancient pedigree to things they found sinister or dangerous in the present. If perceptions of modern Jesuit activity were filtered through the grid of anti-jesuit myth, the myth's own influence depended in part on the broader resonance of the contemporary Jesuit reputation. This reputation was built of associations which were neither the simple echo of past polemics nor the straightforward reflection of modern Jesuit behaviour (though both these things contributed to them), but which defined the Jesuits' relationship to the ideological frameworks which structured nineteenth-century perceptions of politics, religion, and society.

Three strands in the nineteenth-century Jesuit reputation were particularly important in preparing Frenchmen to accept the suggestions of anti-jesuit myth: the order's political image as an élite force of counter-revolution; its involvement in ecclesiastical disputes, especially those between Gallicanism and Ultramontanism; its implication in the legal disputes over the status of unauthorized religious orders.

THE JESUITS AND COUNTER-REVOLUTION

'Take a man in the street, the first who comes along, and ask him: "What are the Jesuits?" He will reply without hesitating: "The Counter-Revolution".'[7] Michelet's purpose, of course, was as much to promote this identification as to record it. He was not wrong, however, to suggest that public notoriety bound the Jesuits firmly to one pole in the dualistic description of politics as a struggle between the Revolution and its enemies, and he might have added that this association was encouraged by the Jesuits' more ardent friends as well as by their opponents. Not that either friends or enemies (with a few exceptions in the latter case[8]) believed that the Jesuits had been actively involved in French politics in the years immediately following 1789; it was well known that the order had been expelled from France a quarter of a century earlier. Precisely this circumstance, however, helped to secure the Jesuits a place of honour in counter-revolutionary thought. Had the Jesuits not been destroyed, men like Joseph de Maistre and abbé (later Bishop) Tharin argued, the proven virtues of their educational system would surely have saved France from the effusion of impious and revolutionary doctrines that had engulfed it; the assault on the order had been the necessary and perhaps the deliberate prelude to the assault on monarchy and on religion. The best strategy for counter-revolution, accordingly, was to call the Jesuits once more to the colours, and confide the education of youth to their care. The forces of Revolution, de Maistre told the Russian Minister of Education in 1810, had 'no enemies more courageous, more intelligent, and more precious for the State' than the members of this order.[9] It was thinking of this kind that Pius VII endorsed when he summoned the 'vigorous and experienced rowers' of the Society of Jesus to help the barque of Peter 'break the waves of a sea which threatens every moment shipwreck and death'.[10] It was no accident that he did so in 1814, the best year for counter-revolution since records began: the restoration of the Jesuits was meant as an integral part of a global strategy of reaction. Liberals and others, who saw the Jesuits as the sinister directors of such a strategy, were to some extent reflecting pro-Jesuit wishful thinking.

The idea that the Jesuits were the natural and necessary champions of counter-revolution tended to rest on two assumptions. The first, increasingly made by both friends and foes of the monarchical and Christian order, was that the war between Revolution and Counter-Revolution would ultimately be won in

---

[8] See below, 35, 90, 151.

[9] J. de Maistre, *Lettres et opuscules inédits*, ed. R. de Maistre, 4th edn., 2 vols. (Paris, 1861), ii. 315–17 ('Cinq lettres sur l'éducation publique en Russie', dated 1810). See also J. de Maistre, *Œuvres inédites (Mélanges)*, ed. C. de Maistre (Paris, 1870), 262–5 ('Étude sur la souveraineté'); [C.-M.-P. Tharin], *Nouvelles Considérations philosophiques et critiques sur la Société des Jésuites, sur les causes et les suites de sa destruction* (Versailles, 1817).

[10] Text of bull *Sollicitudo omnium ecclesiarum* in Burnichon, *La Compagnie de Jésus en France*, i. 532–7.

school. It was the Jesuits' reputation as an order of teachers and educators that first caused reactionary hopes to fix upon them, and it remained throughout the century—despite their wide range of other activities and their actual disqualification from educational functions for lengthy periods—their most distinctive asset. They alone were widely considered capable of building a network of Catholic secondary schools that could rival or even replace the state system, and the academic and social prestige of their establishments was the best-advertised affront to the efforts of liberal or republican educationalists to mould an ideologically homogeneous post-Revolutionary educated élite—a fact reflected in the alarmist visions of a France divided into two educationally determined camps which were a frequent feature of anti-jesuit polemic. Had the ideas of ideological warfare and of educational provision not been so closely connected in nineteenth-century minds, the Jesuits would scarcely have had such ardent friends or enemies.

The second assumption amounted to a conspiracy theory of revolutionary development. The Jesuits were necessary in Russia, de Maistre told the Tsar, 'for you have in this country, as elsewhere, a great sect to fight against; and a sect can only advantageously be fought by a *corps*. Any individual is too weak, and the true enemy of the loathsome *illuminé* is the Jesuit.'[11] Evolving out of the interpretation of the French Revolution formulated by Barruel and others in the 1790s (and finding its fullest development in the researches of the Jesuit Nicolas Deschamps, published posthumously in the 1880s), the idea that the revolutionary movement of modern societies was the work of an organized 'sect', based in Freemasonry and assorted secret societies, whose immediate origins lay in the Bavarian Illuminati of the later eighteenth century (though its roots led back to Protestantism and perhaps to earlier heresies) was a commonplace of nineteenth-century Catholic and conservative thought.[12] By proposing the Society of Jesus as the body best equipped to engage in a sustained struggle with this conspiratorial 'sect', the Jesuits' supporters highlighted just those qualities of the Jesuit order—its discipline, its *esprit de corps*, its capacity for concerted and for long-term action—which might most

[11] J. de Maistre, *Correspondance diplomatique, 1811–1817*, ed. A. Blanc (Paris, 1860), 90–1 (account of conversation with Alexander I in 1812).

[12] See Roberts, *The Mythology of the Secret Societies*; Cubitt, 'Catholics versus Freemasons'.

easily win it a place in the opposing conspiracy theories of the Left.

The Jesuits' reputation as the potential saviours of the counter-revolutionary cause had thus been established by projecting a vision of their former glories on to a picture of present needs. It was never likely that their actions would quite live up to it. Whether the Jesuits were more single-mindedly 'counter-revolutionary' in their attitudes, or more deadly in their effect on the various manifestations of 'Revolution' that confronted them, than were other bodies of Catholic clergy in nineteenth-century France is open to doubt. There was little in their record, however, to undermine the belief that they were dedicated servants of a monarchical and aristocratic as well as a Christian world-view. Energetic involvement in the internal missionary movement of the Restoration marked their acceptance of the prevailing politics of Throne and Altar. After 1830, explicit political commitments were prudently avoided. Social contacts, however, remained. Two French Jesuits went to Prague in 1833, charged with the education of the duc de Bordeaux (the future comte de Chambord). Political pressures forced their removal after a few months. Two more, however, attended Chambord at Frohsdorf in his later years, one of whom, Père Bole, served as his confessor for fourteen years.[13]

More important than these occasional links with the Bourbon court in exile, however, were the Jesuits' close relations, as teachers and confessors, with an aristocratic and all too often legitimist portion of French society. The superior of Saint-Acheul (the most prestigious Jesuit school under the Restoration) joked in 1817 that the accumulation of illustrious names among his pupils would soon give him 'almost the history of France in medallions, in miniatures'.[14] Legitimism, as well as religious and pedagogical scruples, inspired families under the July Monarchy to send their sons across the border to receive their schooling from the Jesuits at Fribourg in Switzerland or Brugelette in Belgium.[15] Under subsequent

---

[13] Comte de Damas d'Anlezy, 'L'Éducation du duc de Bordeaux', *Revue des deux mondes*, 5th ser. 11 (1902), 608–24; Delattre (ed.), *Les Établissements*, ii. 630–4 (Frohsdorf).

[14] Quoted in A. Henrion, *Vie du Révérend Père Loriquet, de la Compagnie de Jésus, d'après sa correspondance et ses ouvrages inédits* (Paris, 1845), 161–2.

[15] The image of the faithful Fribourg alumnus, according to the school's modern historian (basing her remarks on a study of its *livre d'or* and the speeches at annual reunions), was 'unmistakably that of an "homme de droite"—of the legitimist

regimes, significant numbers of Jesuit pupils continued to come from politically disaffected homes. In 1857, noting the disciplinary action taken against two pupils of the *collège* of Mongré who, on finding an image of the Emperor in a New Year's Day bon-bon, had stuck it on a door and spat on it, the Jesuit Provincial could only add: 'but what a problem with children whose parents are themselves so imprudent!'[16] How far the Jesuits could be held responsible for the political prejudices of their clientele was, no doubt, a complex question, but their own attitudes certainly did little to dent them. Most Jesuits, like most other Catholic clergy, were deeply hostile to what they took to be the prevailing values in modern French society, and even those who were not legitimist saw little call to go beyond what prudence demanded in the way of public respect for the secular authorities of Second Empire or Third Republic.[17] The obvious demand for the order's services among those who seemed, by social interest and by political conviction, to have most to lose from the triumph of Revolutionary principles could only enhance its sinister standing in the eyes of the Revolution's admirers.

THE JESUITS AND ECCLESIASTICAL POLITICS

A combination of their supporters' claims and their own dispositions thus helped to draw the Jesuits to the attention of secular politicians and thinkers accustomed to see a struggle between old and new worlds, between Revolutionary and counter-revolutionary principles, as the mainspring of contemporary history. To see the significance assigned to them purely in social and political terms, however, would be to ignore the extent to which religious and ecclesiastical issues impinged on secular politics and polemic. The secular perspective was not, in the nineteenth century, the only one from which the Jesuits might be attacked, or within which

branch'. Five such alumni were in attendance at the death of the comte de Chambord, and forty-one ex-pupils or their sons attended his funeral (Ashe, *The Jesuit Academy*, 120–1, 129–30).

[16] Quoted in Delattre (ed.), *Les Établissements*, v. 174 (Villefranche-sur-Saône).

[17] Sometimes they seem to have done rather less: police spies confirmed in 1861 that the Jesuits of Poitiers no longer bothered with the 'Domine salvum fac imperatorem' at mass, if they had ever done so: AN F[19] 6288 (Jésuites, extension dans les diocèses: Vienne), Prefect to *Ministre des Cultes*, 17 July 1861.

conspiracy theories about them could take shape. For some, within and on the borders of the Catholic Church, Jesuitism was essentially a religious evil. A detailed study of their attitudes is beyond the scope of this book.[18] The lessons which liberals, republicans, and anticlericals drew from religious anti-jesuitism, however, are not. Its ingredients, and the tensions within nineteenth-century French Catholicism that nurtured it, must therefore be considered.

Though each nineteenth-century wave of political aggression against the Jesuits was met by an impressive display of Catholic solidarity, and though the incidence of anti-jesuit feelings among clergy and faithful laity is impossible (thanks to the social and moral pressures militating against its public expression[19]) to determine with any accuracy, it is clear that unreserved enthusiasm for the Jesuits was not universal in French Catholic circles. An inability to transcend its own sectional interest or to adapt to progress, a misguided pedagogy, a monopolistic attitude to good works, confession, and religious vocations, were all (in Brou's early twentieth-century Jesuit view) defects attributed to the Society of Jesus by many sincere Catholics who would not have attacked it in print.[20] The parish clergy had other possible reasons for lukewarmness: resentment at the Jesuits' greater glamour and social standing, fear of a usurpation of their own authority in their parishes, a feeling that, in the periodic rushes to praise and defend the Jesuits, their own claims to recognition were unjustly neglected. Though the normal tenor of their complaints is no doubt exaggerated in virulently anti-jesuit works like abbé Brébion's *Épîtres populaires anti-jésuitiques*[21] or the anonymous novels of abbé Michon, it shows through more plausibly in abbé Clavel's *Le Bien social*, a journal which articulated the grievances of the lower clergy in the mid-1840s. As bishops hastened to identify themselves with the threatened Jesuits, Clavel urged the parish clergy not to do so; some prelates, he pointedly remarked, 'affect not to appreciate that the Church of France is not composed solely of the bishops and the

---

[18] For a fuller treatment, see G. T. Cubitt, 'The Myth of a Jesuit Conspiracy in France, 1814–1880', Ph.D. thesis (Cambridge, 1984), ch. 5.

[19] 'Fully convinced as I may be of the harm that the Jesuits do and have done, I would not like to denounce them at a moment when the Commune is shooting them,' declared the marquise de Forbin d'Oppède, quoted in A. Houtin, *Le Père Hyacinthe*, 3 vols. (Paris, 1920–4), ii. 85–6.

[20] Brou, *Les Jésuites de la légende*, ii. 529–30.

[21] See Cubitt, 'The Myth of a Jesuit Conspiracy', 366.

Jesuits'.[22] There was no guarantee, though, that bishops themselves would always be on the best of terms with an organization whose prestige could occasionally rival that of the episcopate, and whose status as a regular order (in the eyes of the Roman Church, though not of the French State) placed its establishments for most purposes outside their jurisdiction. A few, like Belmas of Cambrai, Thibault of Montpellier, and Sola of Nice, were distinctly unsympathetic.[23] Clearly, though, there is a difference between the coolness towards Jesuits which professional jealousies, personal resentments, or local tensions over jurisdiction might promote and the presence of anti-jesuitism as a major systematic element in a religious or ecclesiastical mentality. Doctrinal divisions provide the obvious bridge between the two. Here, the struggle between Gallicans and Ultramontanes in the French Church is crucial.[24]

Unlike the Gallicanism of secular politicians and jurists (which was essentially a theory giving the civil power extensive rights and jurisdiction in ecclesiastical matters), ecclesiastical Gallicanism was a theory concerning the distribution of authority within the Church, which insisted firstly on a substantial degree of episcopal independence from papal control, and secondly on the superiority of General Councils over papal decisions in the definition of doctrine. During the first half of the nineteenth century, this Gallicanism, as interpreted by men like Frayssinous and Emery, reigned supreme in the French Church; it enjoyed the assent of the great majority of bishops and, largely through the Sulpicians, dominated the seminaries. French Ultramontanism was, in one historian's words, 'essentially a dissident movement among student intellectuals';[25] its most notable exponent, Lamennais, condemned by Gregory XVI in 1832, left the Church two years later.

The third quarter of the century, however, witnessed two dramatic and related developments: the evolution of the Papacy in a

---

[22] *Le Bien social*, 1: 113, 122–3 (Apr. 1844). See J.-B. Duroselle, 'L'Abbé Clavel et les revendications du bas-clergé sous Louis-Philippe', *Études d'histoire moderne et contemporaine*, 1 (1947), 113–20.

[23] Delattre (ed.), *Les Établissements*, ii. 1300–1 (Lille), on Belmas; E. Appolis, 'Un évêque ennemi des jésuites sous la Monarchie de Juillet', *Actes du 81e congrès national des sociétés savantes: Section d'histoire moderne et contemporaine* (1956), 715–20, on Thibault; AN F[19] 6288 (Jésuites, extension dans les diocèses: Alpes-Maritimes), Bishop of Nice to *Ministre des Cultes*, 4 May 1862.

[24] My account of this struggle closely follows the excellent A. Gough, *Paris and Rome: The Gallican Church and the Ultramontane Campaign, 1848–1853* (Oxford, 1986).

[25] Ibid. 60.

direction directly opposed to that of Gallicanism, and the decisive destruction of the Gallican ascendancy in the French Church. Three symbolic dates mark the progress of the movement, presided over by Pius IX, to impose a centralized and absolutist order on the Church and to make the Pope the moral leader of European reaction: in 1854, effectively on his own authority, the Pope proclaimed the Immaculate Conception of the Virgin as Catholic dogma; in 1864, in the *Syllabus errorum* appended to the encyclical *Quanta cura*, he dealt a blow to the sort of understanding with civil governments on which Gallican hopes were pinned, by anathematizing virtually every assumption that made up the liberal conception of the modern world; in 1870, his apotheosis was completed, and Gallican hopes finally crushed, by the promulgation of the dogma of Papal Infallibility at the Vatican Council. The French Church, meanwhile, especially between 1848 and 1853, was ravaged by a determined Ultramontane offensive, co-ordinated by Louis Veuillot in the newspaper *L'Univers*, and connived in by the Pope and the Roman Congregations. The Ultramontanes harassed bishops into adopting the Roman liturgy, and wrought a profound rupture in French ecclesiastical education by securing the condemnation at Rome of a string of Gallican writings, stunningly including Bailly's *Theologia dogmatica et moralis*, the chief theological textbook in French seminaries for half a century. *L'Univers* openly encouraged priests to appeal to Rome against episcopal decisions. In 1853 a papal encyclical, *Inter multiplices*, effectively upheld Veuillot against the archbishop of Paris, Mgr. Sibour, and condemned a recent Sulpician summary of Gallican doctrine. With the aid of a sympathetic civil power, the Gallicans were able to stage a partial recovery in the remaining years of the Second Empire, but not to avoid final defeat in 1870, when their leading representatives withdrew from Rome rather than cause a scandal by voting against Papal Infallibility.

It is hard to exaggerate the bitterness generated in the conflict between Gallicans and Ultramontanes: each group considered the other to be in rebellion against the divinely instituted system of ecclesiastical authority, and thus, in effect, to be perverting the spirit of the eternal Church. There was no doubt which side in this battle the Jesuits were on. Bound to the Papacy both by their order's privileges and by their special vow of obedience to papal direction, they were involved in the Ultramontane cause both passively and actively. Their passive involvement arose from their position on the contested frontier between papal and episcopal authority. The checks suffered by the archbishops of Paris, Affre (in 1843 and 1845) and Darboy (in 1864), when they tried to treat the Jesuit establishments of the capital as falling under their jurisdiction, illustrate the point.[26] That more was at stake than merely local tensions is shown by papal intervention on the first and third occasions in support of the Jesuits' resistance, and by vociferous support for Darboy from secular Gallican politicians. Darboy claimed the right of visitation over Jesuit houses, on the grounds that the Jesuits' existence in his diocese did not fulfil the special conditions on which the exemption of regular orders from episcopal jurisdiction depended, an argument he based partly on the fact that the State did not recognize their order's legal existence. The Pope and the Jesuits denied the relevance of the State's attitude and rejected Darboy's other grounds; his claims, in their view, were an infringement not just of the order's privileges, but of the rights of the Holy See. The Pope informed the archbishop that his doctrine was 'altogether contrary to the divine primacy of the Roman pontiff over the whole universal Church', and that his determination to defend it amounted to a seditious Febronianism, by which 'you gravely offend the divine author of the constitution of the Church'.[27]

The Jesuits' active involvement in Infallibilist and anti-Gallican campaigns took various forms. At Rome the Jesuit newspaper *La civiltà cattolica* enjoyed close ties with Pius IX and functioned as the quasi-official organ of papalist ideology. Its French correspondence of 6 February 1869, which openly anticipated the proclamation of Infallibility by 'the unanimous explosion of the Holy Spirit' at the coming Vatican Council, lent apparent weight to suspicions of a Jesuit put-up job. Several Jesuits played an important part in preparing the work of the Council and steering it in the direction of Infallibility and of a confirmation of the doctrines implied in the *Syllabus*.[28] In France, too, Jesuits (especially in the 1870s those associated with the Jesuit periodical *Études*[29]) were active in the

---

[26] See Burnichon, *La Compagnie de Jésus en France*, ii. 543–9, iv. 272–88, 676–7; R. Limouzin-Lamothe and J. Leflon, *Mgr. Denys-Auguste Affre, archevêque de Paris (1793–1848)* (Paris, 1971), 247–53.

[27] Text in Burnichon, *La Compagnie de Jésus en France*, iv. 676–7.

[28] See R. Aubert, *Vatican I* (Paris, 1964), 56–9, 71, 261–9.

[29] On *Études* (which had itself been suspected of 'liberal' tendencies in the 1860s), see Linehan, 'The Society of Jesus', 40, 145–62.

struggle against Gallicanism and against Liberal Catholicism. Here the opposition between Ultramontane and Gallican conceptions of ecclesiastical authority overlapped (though it did not always precisely coincide) with two others. The first was that between the increasingly dominant probabilistic approach in moral theology (having as its common corollaries an uninquisitorial conception of the confessional and an encouragement of frequent communion) and the more forbidding rigorism—often stigmatized, with highly variable accuracy, as 'Jansenism'—inherited from the pre-Revolutionary French Church; the second, that between the affective, demonstrative, often sentimental style of piety most notably expressed in devotions to the Sacred Heart and to the Virgin, and the austerer, more intellectual style associated with the Gallican tradition. Besides their traditional fidelity to the Pope, the Jesuits had a long *ancien régime* record both as scourges of rigorism and as propagators of special devotions (having a particular association with that of the Sacred Heart). Their nineteenth-century conduct belied neither reputation: Jesuits like Gautrelet, Ramière, and Drévon were among the leading promoters of the cult of the Sacred Heart, and, though nineteenth-century probabilism owed more to Liguori than to any specifically Jesuit source, the Jesuits were among its earliest adherents and contributed, in J.-P. Gury's *Compendium theologiae moralis* (1850), one of its more influential exemplars.[30] The Jesuits were thus associated with a package of ideas, practices, and devotions to which many clergy and Catholic laity took stubborn and motivated exception. Those who welcomed or invited them into French dioceses (especially those bishops who entrusted their diocesan seminaries to them under the Second Empire) often meant by doing so to advance the extirpation of Gallicanism or 'Jansenism' among the local clergy and laity; even

---

[30] On the debate in moral theology, see J. Guerber, *Le Ralliement du clergé français à la morale liguorienne; L'Abbé Gousset et ses précurseurs (1785–1832)* (Rome, 1973); T. Zeldin, 'The Conflict of Moralities: Confession, Sin and Pleasure in the Nineteenth Century', in T. Zeldin (ed.), *Conflicts in French Society: Anticlericalism, Education and Morals in the Nineteenth Century* (London, 1970), 21–35; R. Gibson, *A Social History of French Catholicism, 1789–1914* (London, 1989), 260–5. On the various aspects of 'Ultramontane piety', see G. Cholvy and Y.-M. Hilaire, *Histoire religieuse de la France contemporaine*, 2 vols. (Toulouse, 1985–6), i. 153–96. On 19th-century Jesuit spirituality, see J. de Guibert, *The Jesuits, their Spiritual Doctrine and Practice: A Historical Study*, 2nd edn. (St Louis, 1972), ch. 12, esp. 496–501; P. Vallin, 'La Nouvelle Compagnie en France', in *Les Jésuites, spiritualité et activités: Jalons d'une histoire* (Paris, 1974), 155–96.

where this was less clearly the purpose, friction could arise. A chronicler of the early years of the Jesuit residence at Vannes, established in 1828, wrote that 'the Jansenist contagion' had left many traces in the diocese, and that 'many priests, including some of the most influential, distrust our ideas, to such an extent that they would fear to be contaminated by frequenting us'. In the late 1830s, the Vannes Jesuits were suspected (perhaps wrongly) by the Bishop of stirring up an anti-Jansenist witch-hunt. In 1832, the Jesuits of Avignon were banned from preaching by the diocesan authorities, after hostile local reaction to a sermon in which one of them had preached devotion to the Sacred Heart of Mary. Similar instances of conflict or suspicion could be cited from other dioceses.[31]

It was where the thinking of religious opponents of the Jesuits was streaked with the bitterness of defeat or an acute sense of crisis that some of them crossed the line between mere antipathy and full-fledged conspiracy theory, so that, instead of attacking the Jesuits simply as representatives of Ultramontanism, probabilism, or new-fangled devotions, they came to see these things as so many manifestations of a systematic Jesuit corruption of all aspects of Church life. Throughout the first three quarters of the nineteenth century, there were men who placed themselves within the Catholic tradition, but whose sense of religious struggle was dominated by this anti-jesuit vision. They fall roughly into two groups, corresponding equally roughly to two periods.

The first and more tightly knit group consisted of the last polemically active Port-Royalists (or, to use a label they themselves rejected as a Jesuitical slur, 'Jansenists').[32] By the nineteenth

---

[31] See Delattre (ed.), *Les Établissements*, on the orientation of the Jesuit-run seminaries at Mende (iii. 221), Montauban (iii. 459, 463), and Périgueux (iii. 1558–60), on the tensions at Vannes (v. 37, quoting chronicle), Castres (i. 1170), Dijon (ii. 113–14), and Nancy (iii. 769); Orhand, *Le Révérend Père Pillon de la Compagnie de Jésus et les Collèges de Brugelette, Vannes, Sainte-Geneviève, Amiens, Lille* (Lille, 1888), 116–29; A. Canron, *Les Jésuites à Avignon: Esquisse historique* (Avignon, 1875), 112.

[32] For a detailed discussion of this group, see Cubitt, 'The Myth of a Jesuit Conspiracy', 305–63; also vol. ii of Gazier, *Histoire générale du mouvement janséniste*; L. Séché, *Les Derniers Jansénistes, depuis la ruine de Port-Royal jusqu'à nos jours (1710–1870)*, 3 vols. (Paris, 1891); J. Gadille, 'Le Jansénisme populaire: Ses prolongements au XIXe siècle: Le Cas du Forez', *Études foréziennes*, 7 (1975), 157–67; R. Taveneaux, 'Permanences jansénistes au XIXe siècle', *XVIIe siècle*, 32 (1980), 397–414. A valuable insight into the mental and social world of early 19th-century Port-Royalism is provided by the published collection of abbé Jacquemont's letters: E. Jacquemont, *Une âme de janséniste: François Jacquemont, curé de Saint-Médard-en-Forez, 1757–1835: Sa vie et sa correspondance d'après des documents inédits* (Lyons, 1914).

century they were a small and scattered remnant in France, completely at odds with the prevailing ecclesiastical trends, yet bound together by a fierce devotion to the pious memory of the nuns and *solitaires* of Port-Royal, by a determination to perpetuate their witness to the Truth in the face of persecution and corruption, and often by a continued adherence to the miraculous and prophetic tradition of the *œuvre des convulsions*, the ecstatic movement launched on the tomb of the deacon Pâris in 1730.[33] A semi-clandestine network of contacts still, in the first half of the century, linked together Port-Royalist groups in the Paris region (where the *réunion catholique* of the rue Saint-Jacques—known from 1845 as the Société Saint-Augustin—provided an organizational centre of sorts), in Forez, in the neighbourhoods of Troyes and Auxerre, and elsewhere. A succession of periodicals—the *Chronique religieuse* (1818–21), the *Revue ecclésiastique* (1838–48), and, in its early years, the *Observateur catholique* (1855–67)—helped preserve these contacts and, together with the writings of men like Louis Silvy, Pierre-Jean Agier, and the abbés Jacquemont and Tabaraud under the Restoration, and the early works of abbé Guettée in the 1850s, represent the contribution of French Port-Royalism to nineteenth-century religious and political polemic. Port-Royalism's efforts to cling to the inside of a Catholic Church whose leaders and increasing numbers of whose lower clergy regarded it as heretical became increasingly forlorn as the Ultramontane flood swelled, and it finally dissolved as an effective force in the early 1860s, in an acrimonious feud between Guettée (who controlled the *Observateur catholique* but by 1864 had become an ordained priest in the Orthodox Church) and the members of the Société Saint-Augustin. For much of the half-century following the Jesuits' reintroduction to France, however, Port-Royalists were among their most uncompromising opponents.

Anti-jesuitism, in fact, was an integral part of the Port-Royalist tradition: the sole and persistent aim of Port-Royal itself was held to have been the defence of pure Christian doctrine against the Jesuits' scandalous innovations. In the nineteenth century Port-Royalist anti-jesuitism remained resolutely theological in its concerns, accusing the Jesuits of 'a sort of plot whose aim is to introduce a new body of religion in place of the old faith'. The

[33] On the earlier history of the *œuvre*, see B. R. Kreiser, *Miracles, Convulsions, and Ecclesiastical Politics in Early Eighteenth-Century Paris* (Princeton, NJ, 1978).

Revue ecclésiastique charged them with undermining 'the whole economy of God's plans for the human race' by their relegation of divine grace to an auxiliary role in producing salvation, and with softening 'the HOLY SEVERITY OF THE FAITH' to mould it to human pride, by disguising such essential dogmas as 'original sin and its consequences, the damnation of children dead without baptism, the absolute necessity of faith in Jesus Christ, and above all that terrifying maxim against schismatics, heretics, and infidels: *There is no salvation outside the Church*.'[34] The Port-Royalists' insistence on these forbidding dogmas led them to reject, usually in no uncertain terms, any idea of an alliance with anti-jesuits whose theological views were either different or non-existent. Jacquemont devoted an entire work to demonstrating that the Jesuits and the *philosophes* (whom he regarded as the mentors of Restoration Liberals) were 'two offshoots from the same family'.[35] The *Revue ecclésiastique* in the 1840s denounced what it saw as a 'real consanguinity of doctrine' or a 'treaty of offensive and defensive alliance' between the Jesuits and such prominent anti-jesuit champions as Michelet, Quinet, and Victor Cousin.[36]

The strong eschatological element in Port-Royalist thought could heighten both the intensity and the exclusiveness of its anti-jesuitism. This effect was most striking among adherents of the *œuvre des convulsions*, some of whose eighteenth-century prophets, in predicting troubles which could easily be identified with the French Revolution, had assigned an important role in them to their traditional enemy, while others had warned of the Jesuits' inevitable restoration and of the persecution and seduction which would then befall the *amis de la Vérité* (as *convulsionnaires* called themselves), as part of the pre-ordained apocalyptic progression.[37] A text

[34] *Revue ecclésiastique*, 4: 5–7.
[35] F. Jacquemont, *Examen impartial du jésuitisme ancien et moderne, par un ami sincère de la religion et du roi* (Lyons, 1828), quotation 77.
[36] *Revue ecclésiastique*, 6: 188, 7: 302; see also the *Revue*'s vehement rejection of Michelet's praise for its own anti-jesuit struggle, as coming from one who himself went 'well beyond the Jesuits, when they teach, with the *philosophes* and the Pelagians, that men are saved less by Jesus Christ than by their free will' (ibid. 7: 288).
[37] See Cubitt, 'The Myth of a Jesuit Conspiracy', 336–43, for the anti-jesuit revelations and interpretations contained in a *convulsionnaire* text of the 1790s, the 'Précis des annonces des événements et révolutions temporelles et spirituelles qui doivent s'opérer dans toute la gentilité mais plus particulièrement en France' (manuscript in BNMS NAF 4261).

like Agier's *Commentaire sur l'Apocalypse*, however, showed how prophecies that were part of a broader Christian tradition could also receive an anti-jesuit sense. In a detailed discussion, Agier identified the Jesuits with the plague of locusts unleashed by the fifth angel in the ninth chapter of the Book of Revelation. Their commander in this role was Satan, a suggestion Agier took quite literally. Their work prepared the ground for the next plague—the Revolutionary 'sect of the impious'—whose ravages, in Agier's view, were at once the logical conclusion of Jesuitical tendencies and the divine punishment for the civil and ecclesiastical authorities' long connivance in the Jesuit war on Port-Royal. In the end only the men of Sardis, who had not soiled their garments, and whose identity with the Port-Royalists was transparent, were destined to regenerate a Church the rest of which was 'counted for nothing in the eyes of the Truth'.[38]

Port-Royalism was not calculated to entice the nineteenth-century secular intellect: its theological assertiveness, its exclusiveness, its apocalyptic speculations, its fatalism, its narrowly partisan view of history, combined to give it a dauntingly sectarian aspect. This did not necessarily deprive its anti-jesuitism of all exemplary value, or even of occasional influence, outside its own tradition. The obsessive quality and improbable historical assessments that characterize the anti-jesuitism of François-Vincent Raspail may well, beneath the secular republican surface, owe something to the influence of his old 'Jansenist' teacher.[39] The periodical *L'Album*, distinguished by its anti-jesuit stance in the 1820s, was edited by Magalon, another who had learnt hostility to the Jesuits from a Port-Royalist teacher; according to him, some of its articles on the Jesuits came from the pen of 'a celebrated abbé, very *ultra*, but very Jansenist'.[40] Mortonval's *Le Tartufe moderne* (1825)—a novel as much about anti-jesuitism as about Jesuitism—treated 'Jansenism' with sympathy as a living anti-jesuit tradition, two representatives of which, the aged and somewhat fanatical Mme de Paranges and the good and moderate *curé* Le Noir, took their place alongside the

---

[38] [P.-J. Agier], *Commentaire sur l'Apocalypse*, 2 vols. (Paris, 1823), i. 78–82, 176–228, 235, 241, 280–1. Agier also identified the Jesuits with the seductress Jezebel in Revelation 2: 20.

[39] See D. B. Weiner, *Raspail: Scientist and Reformer* (New York, 1968), 34–5.

[40] J.-D. Magalon, *Ma translation; ou La Force, Sainte-Pélagie et Poissy* (Paris, 1824), 3–6, 15–16.

conservative aristocrat Valbains and the liberal Lierville among those resisting the intrigues of the Jesuit Laurent.[41] On the whole, though, the survival of Port-Royalism showed the diversity of anti-jesuit opinion, while doing little directly to affect the framework within which other anti-jesuits argued.

The version of religious anti-jesuitism that emerged among dissident Catholics in the third quarter of the century, however, was considerably more accessible to secular minds. Its roots lay not in an exclusive and backward-looking tradition, but in a common reaction to a contemporary experience—the capture of the Catholic Church by authoritarian Ultramontanism—whose consequences also impinged on secular politics; the essence of its objection to Jesuitism had to do not with the recondite intricacies of the theology of grace and salvation, but with the ostensibly less specialist issue of authority. While Gallican leaders struggled against the Ultramontane challenge with one hand tied behind their backs by their unwillingness openly to take issue with the Pope, a number of Gallican intellectuals developed a sweeping interpretation of the Church's plight and divisions, in which the Jesuits were assigned a central role. Their shared conviction that Catholicism had come under the control of a highly organized and aggressive but radically unchristian force did not lead all these men in the same direction. Guettée, who provides a bridge between Port-Royalism and this dissident Gallicanism, took the road to Orthodoxy.[42] The year 1864, however, which saw his admission to its priesthood, also witnessed the controversy over *Le Maudit*, the first of a stream of novels published, under closely guarded anonymity, by abbé Michon, a liberal Gallican remaining within the Catholic Church.[43] The novel was a trenchant denunciation of ecclesiastical tyranny, but it was also a plea to priests wishing to work for religious regeneration not to abandon their priestly calling, and the author paid no heed to the possibility of pursuing that calling within a rival

---

[41] Mortonval, *Le Tartufe moderne*, 3 vols. (Paris, 1825), *passim*, esp. i. 248, ii. 271–80, iii. 107–8, 135–6. See also the figures of abbés Chélan and Pirard in Stendhal's *Le Rouge et le noir* (Paris, 1830).

[42] See his autobiography, R.-F.-W. Guettée, *Souvenirs d'un prêtre romain devenu prêtre orthodoxe* (Paris, 1889).

[43] See C. Savart, *L'Abbé Jean-Hippolyte Michon, 1806–81: Contribution à l'étude du libéralisme catholique au XIXe siècle* (Paris, 1971), esp. part iii, ch. 2; P. H. Spencer, *Politics of Belief in Nineteenth-Century France: Lacordaire, Michon, Veuillot* (London, 1954), 182–91.

Church. The book's hero, abbé Julio, is disgraced, placed under interdiction, and harried to an early grave by the Jesuits and their allies, but his fate is presented as a worthwhile martyrdom, and contrasted with the moral failure or loss of faith that overtakes two other characters, Verdelon and Loubaire, who allow disgust or disillusionment to divert them from the priesthood.[44]

Especially after 1870, however, Julio's road to the martyr's crown was bound to strike many as the path of defeatism. In 1872, when canon Mouls and abbé Junqua, two Bordeaux clergymen with whom Michon had relations, published their own novel *Les Mystères d'un évêché*, libellously critical of the episcopate and hostile to the Jesuits, they portrayed the anonymous author of *Le Maudit* as a sympathetic but over-cautious member of a committee of radical reforming clergy. When their own anonymity was punctured, they broke publicly with Rome and joined with the ex-Benedictine Pierre des Pilliers (a future editor of the supposed Jesuit world-domination plan, the *Monita secreta*) in founding a schismatic chapel in Brussels.[45] By this time, increasing numbers of French Catholic dissidents were finding their way into the loose-knit Vieux-Catholique movement. Among them were some, like abbé Michaud (till 1872 the *curé* of the prestigious Parisian parish of La Madeleine), who hoped to see the utter dissolution of the structure presided over by Pius IX; others, like the Gallican journalist Jean Wallon, still saw themselves as participants in a movement to reform it.[46] The interdicted *curé* of Saint-Jean de Gaillac (Tarn), abbé Laurens, proposed a series of contingency plans: ideally, the bishops and government should persuade the Pope to renounce Infallibility and restrain the Jesuits; failing this, the bishops and their clergy should declare their opposition to Infallibility; if the bishops refused, the lower clergy should elect new ones; if the bulk

[44] Savart, *L'Abbé Jean-Hippolyte Michon*, 184–6; Cubitt, 'The Myth of a Jesuit Conspiracy', 371–6.

[45] Savart, *L'Abbé Jean-Hippolyte Michon*, 242–50; X. Mouls, *Les Mystères d'un évêché: Scènes du jésuitisme et de la rénovation chrétienne*, 2 vols. (Brussels, 1872), ii. 126, 141–2, 300–9.

[46] See R. Dederen, *Un réformateur catholique au XIXe siècle: E. Michaud, 1839–1917: Vieux-Catholicisme, œcuménisme* (Geneva, 1963); and, on Wallon, L. Séché, *Les Derniers Jansénistes*, iii. 301–9; J.-R. Palanque, *Catholiques libéraux et gallicans en France face au Concile du Vatican, 1867–1870* (Gap, 1962), 19–20, 184; J. Wallon, *La Vérité sur le Concile* (Paris, 1872), esp. 238.

of the clergy refused, the Catholic laity should take the lead and call on priests 'of the old faith' to join them.[47] Only one group, it seemed, was to be considered constitutionally incapable of joining in reform: the Jesuits.

Whatever their differences, these dissident critics of the Church of Pius IX were agreed that the Society of Jesus lay at the heart of its sickness. Without necessarily using the same labels, they all in practice accepted the distinction which Guetteé drew in 1860, between 'Catholicism'—Christianity properly understood, and compatible with modern liberal and nationalist aspirations—and 'Jesuitism'—'an anti-Christian theory' based on a false conception of the Church as an absolute monarchy.[48] The stages by which this conception had become dominant were regarded as stages in a carefully planned Jesuit triumph. Thus Guettée saw in *Quanta cura* and the *Syllabus* 'the application on a vast scale of the legislation of that Society of Jesus', intended to produce 'an immense army of Jesuits', capable of preserving the power of 'the black Pope' (the Jesuit General) despite a flood of desertions from Rome. Before long, he wrote, 'the Roman Church will have disappeared, there will remain only a *Company of Jesuits*'.[49] Shortly before the Vatican Council, he returned to the theme: 'The history of the Company of Loyola is nothing but a series of conspiracies against the episcopate, against the doctrines and the ecclesiastical institutions which could have posed an obstacle to it. On the one hand, it destroys; on the other, it relentlessly pursues the exaltation of the Papacy.' Having fuelled papal ambitions for three centuries, the Jesuits were now 'on the point of carrying off a complete victory by the conciliar definition of the infallibility of the Pope'.[50] Michaud, after the event, saw it in the same light: 'if the Jesuits wished to assure the Pope of Infallibility and of universal domination, it was so that, having become the masters of one man, they would be masters of all. Their ultimate cunning is to have performed the confiscation of the Papacy while seeming to work its apotheosis.'

---

[47] J. Laurens, *Le Cas d'un curé gallican; ou Explication de l'infaillibilité du pape et de l'Église ultramontaine: Deuxième lettre* (Paris, 1879). See E. Appolis, 'Une tentative de schisme vieux-catholique dans le Tarn en 1879', *Bulletin de la Société des Sciences, Arts et Belles-Lettres du Tarn*, NS 12 (1951), 197–209.

[48] *Observateur catholique*, 11: 119–24, 141–5.   [49] Ibid. 16: 202–4, 280.

[50] *L'Union chrétienne*, 10: 482–3 (Nov. 1869).

The identification of Romanism with Jesuitism was now 'an accomplished, official, undeniable fact'.[51]

Jesuit domination was described in social and organizational as well as doctrinal terms. The Church which Michon depicted in *Le Maudit* was contorted and corrupted at every level by Jesuit influence. The Jesuit General was its 'effective king', the Jesuit bureaucracy, rather than the outmoded papal one, its real administration. The bishops were humble servants of the Society of Jesus, to which they were bound by a mixture of fear and self-interest, and the lower clergy, victims of episcopal tyranny, lacked the courage to resist the Jesuitical current.[52] 'Only the fanatics, and fanaticism is a force, speak out loud in the Church. Instruments of the religious orders, and above all of that of the Jesuits, it is they who create these currents of ideas whose aim is to draw us back to the Middle Ages and to establish universal theocracy.'[53] Michaud, for his part, dwelt on the detail of Jesuit control: Jesuit textbooks in the seminaries, the *Civiltà cattolica* dominating the Catholic press, bishops sending their bright young men to the Jesuit college in Rome. The Jesuits' influence over bishops and 'great ladies', he claimed, permitted them to control ecclesiastical appointments and diocesan administration, to be the masters of clerical education and the clergy's mentors on all major issues.[54]

On the precise nature and implications of the relationship between Jesuitism and Romanism, views differed. Arguing from Church history, Michaud, following Guettée, saw nothing accidental here: the seed of Jesuitism had been present in the Church, and destined to flourish, from the moment that the false conception of papal authority supported by the pseudo-Isidorean decretals had become established. Religious renovation could come only through a return to the status quo of the first eight Christian centuries; it could never be achieved within an ecclesiastical structure of whose whole spirit Jesuit omnipotence was simply the fullest expression.[55] Michon, though he too envisaged a return to the purity of the early Church,[56] presumably took a less extreme view, but it was Wallon

---

[51] E. Michaud, *Le Mouvement contemporain des églises: Études religieuses et politiques* (Paris, 1874), 11.

[52] [J.-H. Michon], *Le Maudit*, 3 vols. (Paris, 1864), i. 51–2, ii. 310.

[53] Ibid. i. 57.   [54] Michaud, *Le Mouvement contemporain*, 11–12.

[55] Ibid. 13.   [56] [Michon], *Le Maudit*, i. 153.

who most explicitly contested the notion that Jesuitism was the revealed reality of a millennium of Catholic history. His declared aim in *Jésus et les jésuites* was 'to expose to view the source of the contemporary fanaticism, so that it will be clearly seen that it lies neither in the doctrine of the Church properly so called, nor even in any doctrine whatsoever'.[57] By showing that it lay instead in the Jesuits' *Spiritual Exercises*, he hoped to persuade secular politicians to develop a new and constructive sensitivity to ecclesiastical politics. They were too prone to believe themselves faced with a 'clerical problem' whose resolution required a sweeping alteration in Church–State relations.[58] 'In reality, it is neither the regime of Separation nor the regime of the Concordats which makes peace or war between the Church and the world. The Jesuits were three hundred in 1844, they are more than three thousand today: that is the evil. There is no other.'[59] The Jesuits dominated because the ecclesiastical forces which might have resisted them were in no position to do so, and this was not because of the pseudo-Isidorean decretals, but because the State had failed both to protect the lower clergy from episcopal domination and to support the bishops themselves against Jesuit and Roman pressure. Such solidarity as existed between Catholics and Jesuits was not intrinsic; it was a reaction to the way in which polemicists like Michelet and Quinet had used the weapons of anti-jesuitism against the Church in general. Statesmen should strive instead to create conditions in which a non-Jesuitical Church might re-emerge. This meant purging the State's own apparatus of Jesuit influence, securing reforms in favour of the lower clergy, and coming to the sort of terms with the bishops that would give the latter the strength and independence to keep their own house in order.[60] It meant, in other words, recognizing the anti-jesuit potential, and sponsoring the revival, of a liberal version of ecclesiastical Gallicanism.

The message that anti-jesuitism was as much a religious as a political matter, and that any onslaught on the Jesuits that failed to cater for legitimate religious aspirations was likely to be counterproductive, was one which secular politicians might also have derived from Guettée, Michon, Michaud, and others. Though

[57] J. Wallon, *Jésus et les jésuites: Moïse—Jésus—Loyola, les jésuites dans l'histoire* (Paris, 1879), 17–18.　　　[58] Ibid., pp. v–vii, xi.
[59] Ibid. 167–8.　　[60] Ibid., pp. ix–xi, 4–5, 160, 285.

Wallon was unusual in this company in addressing his remarks
explicitly to a secular audience, he was much less so in delivering
them in a liberal and progressive language which such an audience
could readily understand. In *Le Maudit*, Julio was made to confront
'this grave problem of the flagrant contradiction between the
generous and emancipatory social theory of Christianity and the
clergy's spirit of domination', and to strive for a Christian religion
'in touch with the mankind of our times'. He summarized his
differences with his Jesuitical opponents thus: 'I wanted to prepare the Christian for the slow and successive transformations of
Christianity; and they, turning their followers' faces towards the
past, offered them as an ideal the epochs of profound darkness
when the priest, ruling over souls by terror, held them trembling
under gross superstitions which he himself often shared.'[61] Though
Michon, writing anonymously, made his overtures to secular anticlericalism more forcefully than did a more theologically minded
writer like Guettée (referring, for example, to 'the revolution which
Christ made for the first time in the thirty-third year of the present
era, and which France made for a second time in the year 1789'[62]),
it was characteristic of this whole wave of anti-jesuit Catholic dis-
sidence that, even while it criticized some of the preconceptions of
liberal or republican anti-jesuits, it made clear its own assumption
that the causes of religious revival and of secular freedom and
progress—the causes of Christianity and of modern civilization
which both Pius IX and conservative Port-Royalists considered
incompatible—could be made to harmonize. The crime perpetrated
through the sinister novelties of Jesuitism was not (as Port-
Royalists maintained) to have sold out Christianity to human
vanity, but to have tied it down in despotic immobilism in defiance
of human liberty. Politicians and secular writers who had their own
reasons to deplore the directions taken by the Catholic Church
under Pius IX could find much in this analysis to chime with their
own reactions.

It seems fair to suggest that the Jesuits' involvement in conflicts
and tensions within the nineteenth-century Church, and the sometimes intense hostility felt for them among Catholic dissidents and
renegades, significantly enhanced their eligibility for a prominent
place in liberal and moderate republican demonologies. Hostile

[61] [Michon], *Le Maudit*, i. 38, ii. 216, iii. 290.   [62] Ibid. ii. 420–1.

though liberals and moderate republicans were to the reactionary and theocratic postures to which the Church too often seemed committed, few of them were eager to draw the line of battle between the modern world and its foes in a way that would deny all possibility of an understanding with the living forces of modern Catholicism; many appreciated the contribution that religion could make to public order, and almost all could see the political dangerousness of open war with the Church, even had they supposed it philosophically desirable. Their declared quarrel was with what came to be called 'clericalism', not with Catholicism in what they took to be its proper sense. In sustaining this distinction between acceptable and unacceptable versions of Catholicism, however, secular politicians and commentators—many of them unlearned in the technical points at issue in ecclesiastical disputes—were drawn into taking sides, vicariously at least, in the Catholic Church's more obvious internal conflicts. Their need was for an account of these conflicts that would accord with the model of binary struggle between progressive and reactionary forces that informed their broader view of the post-Revolutionary world. The formulation of such an account presented difficulties. It was easy enough to be for Gallicanism against Ultramontanism, for those who tried to reconcile Catholicism with freedom and progress against those who made it the pillar of reaction, for the oppressed lower clergy against their oppressors. It was harder, however, to reduce these three antagonisms to one: there were too many Gallicans whose outlook on the world was staunchly reactionary, too many religious intellectuals who (in the wake of Lamennais) believed it possible to reconcile Ultramontanism with faith in liberty, too many lower clergy who resorted to Rome for protection against their Gallican bishops. The Jesuits, however, seemed to offer a fixed point in this shifting picture; they, at least, were marked by reputation with a triple brand, as foes of Gallicanism and of liberalism and haughty rivals of the humble *curé*. A writer like Michon showed how, without denying the surface complexity of ecclesiastical politics (the existence of oppressive Gallican bishops, for example), one could symbolize those politics as a conflict between the Jesuits and their diametrical opposites, the abbé Julios. By concentrating on the Jesuits, and by appropriating the criticisms (and even perhaps the conspiracy theories) of their Catholic opponents, liberals and republicans might hope to integrate an account of ecclesiastical affairs into their more general reading of modern politics.

THE JESUITS AND THE LAW

If it is hard, in exploring the background to political anti-jesuitism, wholly to separate political from religious issues, it would be harder still to divorce them from legal ones. This is not only because moments of legal dispute over the Jesuits provided obvious occasions for the expression of more general anti-jesuit sentiments; it is also because the terms in which the legal dispute was conducted promoted a broader critique. Had the points at issue been merely legal technicalities, this could scarcely have been so. Instead, however, the question of the legality of the Society of Jesus and of other unauthorized religious orders was a battleground for competing conceptions on some of the crucial issues of nineteenth-century political thinking: the nature and limits of individual freedom and of state authority, the relationship of associations both to their members and to the state structure, the balance between spiritual and temporal jurisdictions in a secularized political system. Because the legal arguments concerning it raised these issues, the mere existence of the Society of Jesus in France took on, in some people's thinking, a powerful symbolic charge, which in turn influenced the way in which Jesuit actions were perceived.

For most of the nineteenth century, the Jesuits and other unauthorized religious *congrégations* enjoyed a limited *de facto* toleration on French territory, and the question of their legality remained a genuinely contested one. Neither their defenders nor their opponents could claim a total victory in debate, though both could point to short-term triumphs either in parliament or in the law courts. Even the two decrees of March 1880, which finally subjected the unauthorized *congrégations* to a formal dissolution, did so in a manner that struck many on both sides as incoherent: if the *congrégations* were already illegal, it was argued, special decrees were not needed to destroy them; if they were not, such decrees could be no substitute for parliamentary legislation.

Prior to 1880 the conditions of debate on the legality of the Society of Jesus' existence in France had not changed substantially since 1814. The structure of the debate itself and the broad lines of

legal argument both for and against the Jesuits had been compar-
ably consistent.[63] Fundamentally, the debate revolved around two
questions. First, was the Society of Jesus illegal by virtue of legislation directed against it in particular? Second, was it illegal by
virtue simply of being an unauthorized religious order?

The body of French law which explicitly envisaged the Society
of Jesus dated from the *ancien régime*. Nineteenth-century anti-jesuits
never tired of quoting the *arrêt* of 6 August 1762, in which the
Parlement of Paris

declares the institute of the Jesuits inadmissible by its nature in any
organized State [*État policé*], as contrary to natural right, contemptuous of
[*attentatoire à*] all spiritual and temporal authority, tending to introduce
into the Church and into every State, under the veil of a religious institute,
a political *corps*, whose essence consists in a continual activity in order
to arrive by every sort of route, direct or indirect, secret or public, first
at an absolute independence, and successively at the usurpation of all
authority.[64]

On these grounds, the Parlement dissolved the Society of Jesus
in the area under its jurisdiction, declaring the Jesuits' vows to be
an abuse, and commanding them to live separately and to accept
normal episcopal authority. This *arrêt*, and similar ones issued by
other Parlements, were followed by a royal edict in November
1764, which formally abolished the Jesuit order in France. A
further edict, in May 1777, finally established the terms under
which ex-Jesuits were permitted to remain in France. On the eve of
the French Revolution, then, the Society of Jesus had been clearly

---

[63] The arguments summarized in the following pages were developed and
rehearsed in numerous legal treatises and speeches. My account is based particularly
on what were probably the two most influential works, anti- and pro-Jesuit respectively: A.-M.-J.-J. Dupin, *Libertés de l'Église gallicane: Manuel du droit public
ecclésiastique français*, 5th edn. (Paris, 1860), 263–98, 519–34; A. F. de Vatimesnil,
*Lettre au R.P. de Ravignan, suivie d'un extrait d'un mémoire sur l'état légal en France des
associations religieuses non autorisées* (Paris, 1844). See also A. Ravelet, *Traité des
congrégations religieuses: Commentaire des lois et de la jurisprudence, précédé d'une introduction
historique et économique* (Paris, 1869), and E. Rousse, *Consultations sur les décrets du 29
mars 1880 et sur les mesures annoncées contre les associations religieuses* (Paris, 1880). For
historical accounts, see C. de Rochemonteix, *Les Congrégations religieuses non reconnues
en France, 1789–1881*, 2 vols. (Cairo, 1901); M. Rimbault, *Histoire politique des
congrégations religieuses françaises, 1790–1914* (Paris, 1926); P. Nourrisson, *Histoire
légale des congrégations religieuses en France depuis 1789*, 3 vols. (Paris, 1928–30).
[64] Quoted e.g. by Dupin, in *Moniteur*, CD 2 May 1845: 1171.

and explicitly illegal in France. The legislation which made it so
had never been subsequently repealed, and most of the Jesuits'
nineteenth-century opponents considered it to be still in force.
Since the order had been restored in 1814 with the same statutes
that the *arrêts* and edicts had condemned, they argued, its existence was as illegal now as it had been before. If confirmation of
this illegality had been necessary, the Revolutionary laws of 17
February 1790 and 18 August 1792, which had accomplished the
abolition of *all* religious orders, had surely supplied it.

The Jesuits' supporters contested this line of argument. Far from
reinforcing the pre-existing legislation against the Jesuits, they
argued, the laws of 1790 and 1792 had replaced it: the ban on all
religious orders made the specific prohibition of one of them re-
dundant. Having gone out of force in this way, the specifically
anti-jesuit dispositions of the old *arrêts* and edicts could not be
revived except by a fresh law, even if the laws of 1790 and 1792
went out of force themselves. Since no such new law had been
enacted, the Jesuits' defenders argued, the legal position of the
Society of Jesus was at present no different from that of other unauthorized *congrégations*. What that position was, however, remained
a matter of bitter dispute. To understand this, it is necessary to
explore some of the shifts and cleavages that had developed since
the late eighteenth century in thinking both about associations and
about the relationship between the individual and the State.

The corporate system of the *ancien régime* had had no conceptual
room for such a thing as an unauthorized *congrégation*. The freedom
to form durable associations within society had been regarded not
as a general right but as a privilege which the State accorded
sparingly and must necessarily regulate. Any such association was
either officially recognized as a *corps*, in which case its hierarchy,
discipline, and privileges were both approved and guaranteed by
the public authority, or it had no legal basis for existence. There
could be no question of a *congrégation*, whose corporate existence
had not been formally authorized, claiming a right to toleration
as an unofficial association of private individuals. When applied to
religious orders instituted or approved by Rome, this insistence on
authorization by the civil power was part of the tissue not only of
corporatism but also of secular Gallicanism.

The Revolution dismantled the *ancien régime*'s corporative
structure. There was no intention, however, to replace it with an

uncontrolled freedom of association. Revolutionary ideology postulated a society of individual citizens whose coalescence into an indivisible sovereign nation took place directly, and not through membership of intermediate groups; as Le Chapelier declared, 'there is no longer anything but the particular interest of each individual, and the general interest'.[65] Associations which sustained groups of citizens in a collective identity which other citizens did not share, or which organized them for the pursuit of ends not common to all, were a danger to the nation; it was self-evident to men like Mirabeau that 'particular societies placed within the general society break the unity of its principles and the equilibrium of its forces'.[66] Such principles inspired the Le Chapelier law of 1791, forbidding craftsmen of the same trade to combine together in defence of 'their supposed common interests'; it was in a similar spirit (though one also coloured with anticlericalism) that the law of 18 August 1792 completed the abolition of religious orders.

The total prohibition of the *congrégations* was, however, relatively short-lived. France's nineteenth-century rulers, beginning with Napoleon, were readier than their Revolutionary predecessors to recognize the possible usefulness of religious orders in the fields of education and sick-care. A handful of male orders and a larger number of female ones, all subject to French rather than Roman superiors, received official authorization, the legitimacy of which was contested only by the more radically anticlerical commentators. Many orders existing on French soil, however, never obtained (and never formally sought) this recognition by the civil power; these included such active or well-known orders as the Jesuits, the Dominicans, the Benedictines, the Trappists, the Marists, and the various branches of the Franciscan family.

Most of the opponents of these unauthorized *congrégations* considered them illegal. Against them, they cited the law of 1792 (which they took to be still in force except where a *congrégation* had been explicitly authorized) and a decree-law of 3 messidor an XII (22 June 1804), dissolving the Pères de la Foi and other unauthorized religious groupings, which stated that in future no '*agrégation* or *association*' of men or women was to be formed 'under the pretext of religion' without prior authorization after an

[65] *AP*, Ass. N. 14 June 1791: 210.   [66] Ibid., Ass. N. 2 Nov. 1789: 640.

examination of its proposed statutes and regulations. They also referred to Articles 291–2 of the Penal Code, which provided for the dissolution of any unauthorized association of more than twenty persons whose purpose was to meet daily or on appointed days 'pour s'occuper d'objets religieux, littéraires, politiques ou autres'.

Behind the invocation of these texts lay an attitude of mind which owed much both to the Gallican traditions of the *ancien régime* and to the Revolutionary concern with the protection of national unity against sectional interest, and which dwelt especially on the role of the State both as the embodiment of national sovereignty and as the guarantor of public order. The State's right and duty to regulate the associative life of its citizenry was presented as an indispensable protection for the national integrity both against external threat (from Rome) and against fragmentation from within. The basic argument was put by Dupin *aîné* in his influential *Manuel du droit publique ecclésiastique français*: 'Where indeed is the people, where is the government that has ever accorded its citizens the unlimited faculty of organizing themselves in secret as the fancy takes them, and of creating within the bosom of the great society secondary societies capable of counterbalancing by their influence the operation of the public powers?'[67] According to men like Dupin, the danger of societies within society or 'states within the State'[68] could only be withstood if the right to form associations was firmly recognized as being conditional on informed approval by public authority. The principle that no society could be formed in a state without the approval of 'the great powers of the nation' was, baron Pasquier argued in debate over the Jesuits in 1827, 'more than a law'; it was 'an eternal principle and one independent of positive laws'.[69] In changed circumstances, then, jurists like Dupin and Pasquier reached the same conclusion as their *ancien régime* predecessors: there was no generally acceptable middle position for associations, between illegality and authorization. Only where the law itself clearly created an exception (as Article 291 of

[67] Dupin, *Libertés*, 263.
[68] The theme of the subversive 'state within the State' is, of course, not peculiar to the anti-jesuit tradition: see J. Katz, 'A State within the State: The History of an Anti-Semitic Slogan', in J. Katz, *Emancipation and Assimilation: Studies in Modern Jewish History* (Farnborough, 1972), 47–76.
[69] Quoted in Dupin, *Libertés*, 291.

the Penal Code did for associations with no more than twenty members) could unauthorized associations claim a right to toleration. In all other circumstances, while there might be dispute over whether the government was duty-bound to dissolve them or had some discretion to tolerate them, there could be no disputing its absolute right to dissolve them if it chose.

The statist and secular Gallican principles professed by men like Dupin were a major ingredient in the reasoning of Restoration Liberals, July Monarchy Orleanists, and moderate republicans of the Third Republic on the Jesuit question. The prevalence of this way of viewing the question of associations helps to explain a common feature of anti-jesuit polemic: the ease with which it slides from proofs of Jesuit illegality to allegations of subversive intent. It was hard, from this standpoint, to see why the members of any association would shun the process of authorization unless they had something to hide. If the very fact of existence as an unauthorized association defied an incontrovertible principle of political organization, on which both the legitimate authority of the State and the moral unity of the nation depended, it was hard to see compelling reasons to distinguish between the pretension to such an existence, the aspiration to political autonomy, and outright and deliberate subversion—subversion that was likely to seem doubly sinister when the evasive association was one instituted by Rome, and doubly contemptuous when (like the Society of Jesus) it was one which many believed to be explicitly rejected by French law.

The arguments for the unauthorized orders' illegality did not go unchallenged. The terms in which the challenge was posed, however, may themselves have influenced or reinforced anti-jesuit attitudes. The legal defence of the orders rested on an invocation of individual, as distinct from corporate, rights. Their defenders accused their opponents of failing to appreciate how radically the Revolution had transformed France's general system of legality. Men like Dupin and Pasquier, it was suggested, continued to reason as if the system in force was one of privilege, such as had pertained before 1789; in such a system, legal rights to enjoy civic freedoms existed only where the law had explicitly created them, exclusion from them being the general rule. In fact, however, France now lived under a regime of liberty, in which the reverse was true: the crucial civic freedoms were held to be enjoyed as of right, and hence implicitly protected by law, except where the law

explicitly limited or withheld them. The two freedoms relevant
in the case of religious *congrégations* were those of association and
of religion. The present extent and conditions of the former were
fixed by Articles 291–4 of the Penal Code, and the latter was proclaimed in Article 5 of the *Charte* of 1814 (identically reproduced
in that of 1830): 'Everyone professes his religion with an equal
liberty and obtains for his cult the same protection.' Neither the
Charte nor the Code, it was argued, could properly be interpreted
as opposing unauthorized religious *congrégations*. The *Charte* must be
assumed to have recognized the right of Catholics to join religious
orders, since it would be an infringement of religious liberty to
prevent them from following a way of life which their Church
recommended for those called to seek a fuller perfection in the
Christian life; nor did it give any reason to distinguish unauthorized orders from others in this respect. Article 291 of the Code
had been designed to prevent the development of secret societies,
not to stop people living together under a shared monastic or
religious rule—a purpose for which it could not, in fact, be used,
since the figure of twenty members, by exceeding which an association incurred the need for authorization, explicitly excluded
'those domiciled in the house where the association meets'. As for
the other props in the case against the unauthorized orders—the
law of 1792 and the decree-law of 1804—these were at odds both
with the *Charte* and with the Code, and could thus no longer be
in force.

It followed, the defenders of the unauthorized orders claimed,
that French citizens were perfectly within their rights in forming
associations for the purpose of leading a communal life governed
by the rules of a religious order. The legality of such an order as an
association was thus derived not from any process of authorization,
but from the rights which its individual members possessed as
citizens. What distinguished authorized from unauthorized orders,
then, was not their legal permissibility, but their official status.
Authorization established a *congrégation* as a *personne civile*—a body
legally empowered to receive, own, and transmit property, and to
enter into contracts and legal proceedings, as if it were an individual. An unauthorized *congrégation* had no such corporate existence in the eyes of the law, which could therefore only regard it as
the aggregate of its members, and only envisage them as ordinary
citizens. In a legal *mémoire* originally written in defence of the

Trappists in 1831 (and revived for the Jesuits in 1844), Vatimesnil made this clear:

In that case the civil power disregards the religious bonds which exist between these individuals, and it sees in them only private persons making use of the right of association naturally belonging to all citizens. If the members of the group [*réunion*] have signed a contract of partnership [*contrat de société*] between themselves, this contract is performed as if it had been made between laymen. The religious character of the group adds nothing to the force of this contract, but it takes nothing away from it either.[70]

In other words, although an unauthorized *congrégation* had no rights or powers itself, its members were fully entitled to exercise jointly or in common the rights which each of them possessed individually. Thus, it was argued, if French law permitted citizens, subject to the fulfilment of certain specified conditions, to teach in or to run schools, then *religieux* who fulfilled these conditions as individuals were entitled to run and staff schools together; the fact that those who joined together for this purpose were also joined together as members of an unauthorized *congrégation* made no difference. Nor, as Vatimesnil implied and as Armand Ravelet argued in detail in his *Traité des congrégations religieuses* (1869), did it affect their right to engage with each other in any of the forms of contract or convention—*contrat de société, contrat de communauté, convention tontinière*—available to ordinary citizens for the joint management of their resources. Legacies or gifts made with the intention of benefiting an unauthorized order or community in itself were no doubt invalid (whether made directly or through third parties); but, argued Ravelet, the same was not true of ones made for the purpose of benefiting its members in common.[71] In short, while the aggregation of their individual members' rights could not give unauthorized orders the power of holding property in mortmain, it provided, in their defenders' view, an adequate legal basis for the development of a communal life and a range of activities not dissimilar to those open to authorized orders.

In other words, the Jesuits' opponents could be forgiven for thinking, now you saw the Society of Jesus, now you didn't. If you

---

[70] Vatimesnil, in the *Extrait d'un mémoire* appended to (but separately paginated from) his *Lettre au R.P. de Ravignan* (p. 6).

[71] Ravelet, *Traité*, 239–302.

looked for a social organization, whose members pursued a communal life, accepted a highly demanding discipline, and considered themselves bound to do so by solemn vows, it was there; the moment, however, that you tried to determine its place in the State, it dissolved into a collection of private individuals. To men whose conception of citizenship was tied up with the notion of personal independence, and who saw the State not merely as an apparatus for the exercise of personal rights but as the supreme co-ordinator of personal loyalties, this was a disturbing piece of prestidigitation. Liberals found the rhetoric of individual rights turning in their hands, threatening to subvert its own anti-corporatist purpose. They were confronted by a fundamental dilemma: how to reconcile an abstract commitment to individual freedom with a rejection of the powerfully group-orientated nature of some individual self-images. Men like Dupin responded by trying to de-legitimize their opponents' choices: they argued that, unlike the members of ordinary *associations* (meeting only occasionally and for limited purposes), the members of *congrégations* simply could not be considered as individuals: their vows, their obedience, their total immersion in a common life, amounted to an abdication of individuality, and hence of individual rights.[72]

In two ways, the impressions created by the arguments and strategies of the unauthorized orders' defenders may have been reflected in liberals' receptivity to traditional or stereotypical images of Jesuit villainy. First, the arguments themselves were ones which might well seem, to those who rejected them, to reinforce the Jesuits' antecedent reputation for hypocritical, devious, or equivocal reasoning. Since when, sceptics asked, had the freedoms of the individual been so dear to the Jesuit heart? Opponents may indeed have seen, in the fine distinctions which the lawyers used to minimize the inconveniences to an order of remaining unauthorized, something to remind them of the legendary prowess of Jesuit casuists in securing to their penitents the benefits of sin without the costs of damnation. Such observations were no doubt unjust, but the position of an unauthorized order was one which made a degree of equivocation hard to avoid. For the Jesuits, this was nothing new. A tale long established in the anti-jesuit repertory

---

[72] On the difference between an *association* and a *congrégation*, see Dupin *aîné* in *Moniteur*, CD 25 Jan. 1844: 157.

told how, in 1565, when the early French Jesuits had been pressed by the Sorbonne to declare whether they were monks or seculars, they had replied only that they were such as (*tales quales*) the Parlement had named them.[73] The phrase *tales quales* (often misleadingly rendered as 'tels quels'—'just as we are') figured as a standard reference in nineteenth-century anti-jesuit literature,[74] alluding both to the Jesuits' talents for verbal evasion and to their resistance to the sort of official classification which would have facilitated surveillance and limitation of their activities. Their modern existence as an unauthorized *congrégation*, and the tactical reticence about their collective identity which this encouraged,[75] could easily appear to confirm these subversive traits.

Second, as will be seen in more detail later, the mythology of anti-jesuitism was well suited to express in dramatic form the apprehensions which the defence of the unauthorized orders in terms of individual rights provoked among liberals and republicans. Beliefs about the Jesuits' sinister ability (through their *Spiritual Exercises* or through their educational system) to annihilate and replace the individual personality, rumours about the unperceived proliferation of *jésuites de robe courte* in civil society, and above all the stereotypical image of the Jesuit himself as a man capable of playing any outward role but inwardly totally devoted to his order, all reflect the same fascination with camouflaged corporatism and sham individuality. The prominence of these elements in nineteenth-century presentations of the anti-jesuit case suggests

[73] See C. Sutto, introd. to E. Pasquier, *Le Catéchisme des jésuites* (Sherbrooke, 1982), 55–6.

[74] This was noted, disapprovingly, by one of the more moderate anti-jesuit historians: C. Laumier, *Résumé de l'histoire des jésuites, depuis l'origine jusqu'à la destruction de leur société* (Paris, 1826), 210.

[75] This is reflected, for example, in the careful wording of the draft replies concerning the Jesuit-run *petit séminaire* of Bordeaux, in response to a ministerial questionnaire in 1828, quoted in L. Bertrand, *Histoire des séminaires de Bordeaux et de Bazas*, 3 vols. (Bordeaux, 1894), ii. 283. The Jesuit superior suggested that the Bishop answer the question of whether the priests running the *petit séminaire* were members of a religious *congrégation* by stating: 'No external act announces that they are part of a *congrégation*.' The answer actually given (proposed by the vicar-general) admitted that they followed a common rule internally. The question of which *congrégation* they belonged to was then answered (the Bishop having been warned by the Minister that their Jesuit membership was publicly notorious): 'Notoriety regards them as Jesuits, but of the various names they have been given, PÈRES DE LA FOI, JESUITS, they have adopted none openly, appearing as simple ecclesiastics, following, for their internal conduct, the rule of Saint Ignatius, and living under the authority of the bishops.'

that the Jesuits owed their eminence in nineteenth-century liberal and republican demonologies in part to the way in which the controversy over their existence as an unauthorized order provided a focus for the insecurities of liberal individualism.

Neither as enemies of Revolution, nor as Ultramontanes, nor even as unauthorized *religieux*, did the Jesuits stand alone. Their casting in these roles does not, on its own, explain the special hatred and mistrust reserved for their order in the demonologies of the secular Left. The roles do, however, reveal a set of overlapping contexts —political, religious, and juridical—within which the old growths of anti-jesuit suspicion could root themselves in the sort of modern ground that might make them seem relevant to the preoccupations of secular thinkers and politicians. Had there been no substance to the Jesuits' performance of these roles, it is unlikely that the anti-jesuit myth could have been a potent nineteenth-century force; equally, however, the prior existence of the myth helped to make the roles look more definite, more portentous, and more exclusive to the Jesuits than they would otherwise have appeared. These facets of the Jesuit reputation remained fairly constant throughout the century and their durability helps, at a general level, to explain why a susceptibility to anti-jesuit conspiracy theories proved so persistent a feature of certain political mentalities. A fuller understanding of how and why anti-jesuit analyses were formulated, however, must depend both on a detailed study of the political functions of anti-jesuitism during the periods of its greatest influence, and on an exploration of the structures and themes of anti-jesuit myth.

2

The Restoration

In April 1826, as the Chambre des Députés took heed of the public controversy generated by the recent publication of the comte de Montlosier's *Mémoire à consulter sur un système religieux et politique tendant à renverser la religion, la société et le trône*, one of its members, the comte de Saint-Chamans, remarked dismissively that 'one has seen, after sixty years, the remnant of the Jesuits still pursued by the remnant of the Jansenists, to the joyful cries of the sad remnant of our self-styled *philosophes*'.[1] Saint-Chamans's intention, of course, was to discredit the anti-jesuitism of the 1820s by presenting it both as an anachronism and as a product of sectarian fanaticism of the most suspect sort. In the ideological climate of the Restoration, *philosophes* and Jansenists—the two mental tribes whose adherents had combined against the Jesuits in the mid-eighteenth century—both stood compromised by perceived connections with the Revolution.

The great majority of Restoration anti-jesuits were understandably unwilling to recognize the dubious ideological parentage which men like Saint-Chamans sought to foist upon them. They were far, however, from rejecting all connection with the anti-jesuitism of the pre-Revolutionary age. On the contrary, the need to establish the conservative and monarchist respectability of their cause led them back in argument to the governmental, corporative, and institutional traditions of the *ancien régime*—to the resistance repeatedly (though sporadically) mounted to Jesuit encroachments by the Parlements, the Gallican Church, the Sorbonne, even the Bourbon dynasty itself. Frequent invocation of such anti-jesuit traditions, however, did not indicate their untroubled persistence. There were still men, like the duc de Choiseul (a relation of Louis XV's chief minister), for whom anti-jesuitism was a matter of family tradition,[2] and the anti-jesuit spirit of the Parlements was

---

[1] *AP*, CD 8 Apr. 1826: 43.   [2] See Choiseul in *AP*, CP 18 Jan. 1827: 183.

often reported to live on among Restoration magistrates, but the Revolutionary and Napoleonic upheavals had left many anti-jesuit traditions without obvious or willing heirs. Post-Revolutionary Bourbons had to be constantly reminded that, as descendants of Henri IV, they could not have forgotten the antagonism between the founder of their dynasty and the Society of Jesus.[3] More seriously, the corporate and institutional barriers to Jesuit encroachment under the *ancien régime* had been dismantled, and not replaced to the satisfaction of anti-jesuits. The Sorbonne no longer existed in its old form, and the Napoleonic Université, placed under ecclesiastical control in 1821, was not yet the focus for resistance to the Jesuits it was to become in the 1840s. The Parlements had been swept away, and their faculty of receiving and judging *appels comme d'abus*, widely acclaimed as the most effective of the *ancien régime*'s safeguards against Jesuitism, was now vested in the Conseil d'État, in whose vigilance and effectiveness anti-jesuits had little confidence.[4] In the course of the Restoration, anti-jesuits would begin to seek a new kind of protection against Jesuitism, in an active public opinion enlightened and articulated by the Liberal press. In the meantime, however, there were frequent lamentations over the vulnerability of a France stripped of her traditional defences against Jesuit attack, and frequent attempts to inspire Restoration Frenchmen to imitate ancient anti-jesuit examples. The *député* Gilbert de Voisins published the documents of the Paris Parlement's proceedings against the Jesuits,[5] and leading *parlementaire* opponents of the Jesuits, like La Chalotais and Ripert de Monclar, were widely invoked and quoted. Anti-jesuits tried hard to persuade themselves, the public, and the members of the relevant bodies that the Parlements' anti-jesuit traditions had or ought to have devolved upon some modern institution, either the

---

[3] See D. Baillot's introd. to P. de Landerset, *Opinions prononcées dans le Grand Conseil de Fribourg, les 16 janvier 1817 et 15 septembre 1818, au sujet de l'admission des ligoriens et des jésuites* (Paris, 1819), p. iv.

[4] See notably P.-P.-A. Gilbert de Voisins (ed.), *Procédure contre l'Institut et les Constitutions des jésuites, suivie au Parlement de Paris, sur l'appel comme d'abus, interjeté par le procureur-général du roi* (Paris, 1823), p. xiii; also Lally-Tolendal in *AP*, CP 14 July 1824: 264: 'Where will be the Joly de Fleurys, the Omer Talons, the Monclars, the La Chalotais? Far be it from me to insinuate in the least that we lack the men for the post; we lack the post for the men.'

[5] Gilbert de Voisins (ed.), *Procédure*.

two Chambers (together or separately) or, more usually, the Cours Royales.[6]

A defence of Gallican traditions was central to the respectable face of Restoration anti-jesuitism. This, again, was not because anti-jesuits had much confidence in the current anti-jesuit potential of the French Church and official ecclesiastical Gallicanism; the former, in its post-Concordatory form, lacked the corporate strength and independent spirit of the old Gallican Church, and the latter struck many as a watered-down Ultramontanism (whose chief Restoration theorist, Frayssinous, was to seem fatally compromised as a protector of the Jesuits). Anti-jesuitism took a Gallican form because the general ideological climate of the Restoration encouraged all moderate opposition to counter-revolutionary politics to do so.[7] Though Restoration political debate revolved around questions of Revolution and counter-revolution—how much of the Revolution's work must be accepted? how much of the *ancien régime* could or should be restored, and how?—it was not, in any clear sense, a debate or dialogue between the forces of Revolution and those of counter-revolution. For public purposes, the Revolution was a discredited political cause. The touchstone for Liberal arguments was the *Charte* of 1814, not the *Déclaration des droits de l'homme et du citoyen*. Political dispute took place within the bounds of monarchism, religious dispute within those of Catholicism; the *Charte*'s recognition of Catholicism as state religion soldered the two spheres. Unless they were prepared openly to challenge the regime's ideological basis, those who wished to combat the prevailing current of theocratic reaction—be they Liberals, or conservatives who believed the aggressive tactics of the Ultras were more likely to provoke than to prevent a resurgence of Revolution—thus had to offer an alternative account of the Throne–Altar alliance. In practice, this meant taking their stand on some

[6] See, among others, Bernard in *Recueil complet du procès intenté par les héritiers de M. de La Chalotais, ancien procureur-général au Parlement de Bretagne, contre les éditeurs du journal dit l'Étoile* (Paris, 1826), part I, p. 43 (on the Chambre des Députés); comte de Montlosier, *Pétition à la Chambre des Pairs, précédée de quelques observations sur les calamités, objet de la pétition* (Paris, 1827), 5 (on the upper Chamber); I. Lebrun, *La Bonne Ville; ou Le Maire et le jésuite*, 2 vols. (Paris, 1826), ii. 226 (on the Cours Royales).

[7] On the use made of Gallicanism in the Liberal campaigns of the Restoration, see Mellon, *The Political Uses of History*, ch. 5.

conception or other of Gallican monarchy. The posture, though politically necessary, was not necessarily insincere. Some no doubt did seek to undermine Throne and Altar under cover of an 'acceptable' politico-religious rhetoric. But others (including Liberals as well as conservatives) who used the same rhetoric to attack the Ultras or the Jesuits genuinely sought a way to defeat theocratic trends in Church and State while exculpating Monarchy and Church as institutions.

THE REIGN OF LOUIS XVIII

These general characteristics of Restoration anti-jesuitism—the Gallican framework, the emphasis on past traditions and present vulnerability, the desire to combat a certain style of counter-revolution—were already present during the reign of Louis XVIII, though anti-jesuitism had yet to attain the popularity, the stridency, and the political influence it was to have under Charles X. During the opening years of the Restoration, only a few 'Jansenistic' writers, most notably Louis Silvy, deeply conservative but primarily religious in their concerns, found the Jesuit menace worth more than occasional passing mention.[8] The volume and variety of anti-jesuit literature increased from around 1818, but remained a trickle by the standards of the later 1820s. Yet the reign of Louis XVIII has its importance in the history of anti-jesuitism. It saw the appearance of a number of significant anti-jesuit works: Béranger's much-quoted song 'Les Révérends Pères' (1819); the first nineteenth-century publication of the so-called *Monita secreta* (1820); the first large-scale attempt to invoke pre-suppression Jesuit history against the restored Society of Jesus, by Goubeau de la Bilennerie (1820); and Gilbert de Voisins's influential collections of documents in the eighteenth-century case against the Jesuits (1823 and 1824).[9] More generally, some examination of expressions of anxiety about the Jesuits at this time helps us both to observe the

---

[8] See the anonymous works by Silvy and by abbé Tabaraud listed in the Bibliography.
[9] P. J. de Béranger, *Œuvres complètes* (Brussels, 1844), 236–8; *Le Citateur politique, moral et littéraire*, 1: 144–257 (for the *Monita secreta*); [J.-F. Goubeau de la Bilennerie], *Histoire abrégée des jésuites et des missionnaires pères de la foi*, 2 vols. (Paris, 1820); Gilbert de Voisins (ed.), *Procédure* and *Nouvelles Pièces pour servir de complément à la Procédure contre les jésuites* (Paris, 1824).

transition of anti-jesuitism from the eighteenth to the nineteenth century, and to appreciate what, if anything, was new in the anti-jesuit polemic of the later 1820s.

According to some contemporary observers and subsequent historians, the figure of the Jesuit took over, around 1824, the central place in anticlerical polemic previously occupied by the missionary.[10] This is an over-simplification, inasmuch as it ignores the extent to which 'Jesuit' and 'missionary' were entangled categories in the thinking and polemic of their opponents. It was in reaction to the internal missionary campaign that penetrated much of France in the years either side of 1820 that Restoration anti-jesuitism first took wing. The mid-1820s saw not so much a simple shift from one bogy to another as a diversification of the anti-jesuit vision of contemporary Jesuit activity, in which the attention previously focused on the missionary aspect of that activity was to some extent shifted on to the sinister 'Congrégation' and the Jesuit threat in education.

The missions were the fruit of a mentality that saw impiety as the root of all evil, especially Revolution.[11] France was to be re-Christianized, in the interests not just of individual salvation, but of social order, and not just of God, but of the Bourbon dynasty. The best known of missionary canticles proclaimed the intimate connection between 'the Bourbons and the Faith'. Some critics of the missions saw them as a cynical attempt to use religion as a vehicle of counter-revolutionary politics. Others, while accepting the missionaries' sincerity, deplored their fatal tendency to compromise both Christianity and monarchism by associating each with an extravagant and emotional version of the other. Frenchmen of various religious and political persuasions reacted against the violence and intolerance of the missionaries' language, and resented the implication that the nation was a gang of impious reprobates whose salvation required extraordinary measures. In the missionaries' emphasis on the histrionic aspects of evangelization—hell-fire preaching with special effects, processions, mass conversions, ostentatious lamentation—they saw at best a dangerous

[10] Duc de Fitz-James in *AP*, CP 14 Feb. 1825: 150; Bertier de Sauvigny, *Le Comte Ferdinand de Bertier*, 372.

[11] On the missions, see E. Sevrin, *Les Missions religieuses en France sous la Restauration, 1815–1830*, 2 vols. (Paris, 1948–59).

neglect of the development of solid piety and Christian conduct, and at worst a deliberate excitation to fanaticism.

The renascent Society of Jesus participated enthusiastically in the missionary campaign, and several of its members, most notably Père Guyon, were among the most active and notorious missionaries.[12] Critics of the missions, however, seldom had clear information about who was and who was not a Jesuit. Some simply assumed that the missionaries were all Jesuits,[13] or, as Béranger would have it, 'commercial travellers' in the Jesuits' service;[14] others accepted, in theory or in practice, the existence of non-Jesuit missionaries. Some knew that certain missionaries were Pères de la Foi, but were unsure whether Pères de la Foi were Jesuits.[15] Such variations do not obscure the central point: it was in the missions that many Restoration Frenchmen first saw the signs of a revived Jesuit menace. For the most part, it was the style, the rhetoric, and the presumed implications of the missions that suggested this, rather than personal detail about the missionaries. 'It is torch in hand that the children of the visionary Ignatius return to a kingdom which rejected them and which still rejects them,' wrote Édouard Corbière in 1819, in a pamphlet celebrating the hostile reception accorded to 'these evangelical marauders' by his hometown of Brest.[16] It was because Goubeau de la Bilennerie perceived a resemblance between the principles and actions of the 'missionnaires pères de la foi' and those of the pre-suppression Jesuits that he felt it urgent to publish the latter's history; the rapid spread of the missionaries, their rapaciousness, ambition, divisive conduct, and provocative anti-Gallicanism, were among the most suggestive signs.[17] The missions provided what passed for many as the first decisive proof that the Jesuits, with all their old faults, were back in France.

[12] Ibid. i. 67–74, ii. 76–88.
[13] e.g. A.-M. Barthélemy and J. Méry, *Les Jésuites: Épître à M. le président Séguier* (Paris, 1826), 40–1 n.
[14] Béranger, *Œuvres complètes*, 238.
[15] For rather vague remarks on this relationship between missionaries, Pères de la Foi, and Jesuits, see L. Magnier, *Considérations sur les jésuites* (Paris, 1819), 1–2; *Les Jésuites marchands, usuriers et usurpateurs: Par G****** de N****, volontaire royal en 1815* (Paris, 1824), 1.
[16] E. Corbière, *Trois jours d'une mission à Brest* (Paris, 1819), 1–2. On this incident see Sevrin, *Les Missions religieuses*, ii. 429–54.
[17] Goubeau de la Bilennerie, *Histoire abrégée*, vol. i, p. iii.

This in turn suggested that the aggressions of the missionaries were but the tip of the age-old iceberg of Jesuit ambition; its other ramifications were no less to be feared for being at present invisible. Any sign of Jesuit activity, however apparently innocuous, was cause for alarm. This was the case with a letter written by the Jesuit General, Fortis, in 1823, which figured prominently in anti-jesuit literature. In it Fortis turned down a request for a Jesuit school at Chambéry, in French-speaking Savoy, on the grounds that the number of French-speaking Jesuit teachers was inadequate to meet demands in France itself. Far from being reassured by such an admission of insufficiency, the anti-jesuits who quoted it saw only the documentary proof that the Jesuits were established, recruiting, teaching, and hoping to expand, on French soil. When one knew, as Gilbert de Voisins did, that 'wherever the Jesuits have established themselves, their society has been a public calamity, a hotbed of intrigues, of agitation and of troubles', such proof was enough to warrant the deepest anxiety.[18] The typical tone of anti-jesuitism under Louis XVIII was conditional but urgent; on the basis of the Jesuits' past record, it asserted the inevitability of calamity if preventive measures were not adopted. As one anti-jesuit warned: 'Let them take a few steps, these destructive men, and it's all up with us.'[19]

If the missions were the form of current Jesuit activity on which anti-jesuit attention was initially concentrated, the chief spectre dredged up from the past to stand as a menace over the future was that of regicide. A long-established staple of anti-jesuit polemic, this theme was doubly useful to Restoration Liberals. It provided not just a direct line of attack on the monarchist credentials of the Jesuits and their supporters, but also a way of refuting the implication, derived from the Revolution and freshly dangerous after the assassination of the duc de Berry in 1820, that the shedding of royal blood was somehow a distinctively Liberal political expedient. Strings of allegedly Jesuit-inspired attacks on monarchs were recalled, with special emphasis on those against Bourbons like Henri IV and Louis XV. 'It is against the principal members of

---

[18] Gilbert de Voisins, *Nouvelles Pièces*, 78–9 (and Fortis letter printed on 110–15); for other references to the letter, see e.g. *Constitutionnel*, 21 May 1824 and 19 Dec. 1824.

[19] *Du rétablissement des jésuites en France sous le nom de Pères de la Foi: Par M.G., avocat* (Paris, 1819), 43.

the Bourbon family that the Jesuits turned the daggers of their fanatical pupils, and it is under the rule of the Bourbons that these regicides dare to reappear in France,' remarked one indignant author.[20] A history of Jesuit regicidal plots, published early in the reign of Charles X, asserted unequivocally, once at its beginning and again in conclusion: 'The dagger which struck down the best of our kings threatens his children.'[21]

The Jesuits' enemies at this time were by no means all men of Liberal outlook; after all, Gallicanism, fear of regicide, hostility to the excesses of the missions, could all fit with a conservative, or even a reactionary, attitude. 'Jansenist' writers like Silvy and Jacquemont provide one example of a counter-revolutionary anti-jesuitism. Another can be found in a number of works like Lombard de Langres's *Des sociétés secrètes en Allemagne* (1819), and the anonymous introduction and conclusion to the 1824 edition of the pamphlet *Les Jésuites marchands, usuriers et usurpateurs* (originally published in 1759). These works continued a tradition, developed by men like Bonneville and Cadet-Gassicourt in the 1780s and 1790s, of speculation about parallels and connections between the Jesuits and revolutionary secret societies.[22] Believing in the necessity for strong political, religious, and social authority, these authors discerned two parallel forms of subversion, both leading to anarchy, and each attributable to a secret society. The Jacobin or revolutionary sort was the fault of the Illuminati, working through Freemasonry; the Ultramontane sort (most visible in the missions) was that of the Jesuits. The difference between the two societies was minimized. Both, according to Lombard, aspired to world domination; both sought to restrict power, wealth, and

[20] Flocon, in F. Flocon and A. Beckhaus, *Dictionnaire de morale jésuitique* (Paris, 1824), p. xi.

[21] E. de Monglave and P. Chalas, *Histoire des conspirations des jésuites contre la maison de Bourbon en France* (Paris, 1825), 1, 423.

[22] R. Le Forestier, *La Franc-maçonnerie templière et occultiste aux XVIIIe et XIXe siècles* (Louvain, 1970), 719–22, surveys the different versions of the theory of secret Jesuit influence in Freemasonry advanced during the 1780s; for further detail and discussion, see Roberts, *The Mythology of the Secret Societies*, 154–5, 193–5, 327–8, and Lemaire, *Les Origines françaises de l'antimaçonnisme*, 75–9. The duc de Fitz-James (*AP*, CP 18 Jan. 1827: 186) testified to the persistence of the belief that the Jesuits were 'the promoters and chiefs of the secret societies'. A Restoration Liberal version of the Jesuit–Illuminati parallel was offered by the masonic writer E.-F. d'Hénin de Cuvillers in his introduction to another reissued anti-jesuit tract, *La Monarchie des solipses* (Paris, 1824), 29–31, 68.

honour to their own partisans; both placed religion at the service of politics; both had their spies, oaths, and impenetrable secrets.[23] The anonymous author of 1824 put regicide at the centre of the comparison. 'These two famous societies wish to arrive at the same end, but by different means: they are equally determined to seize power, to overthrow thrones, and finally to rule after having slaughtered the kings,' he explained.[24] This author was content to indicate the 'exact parity' of Jesuit and Illuminist political doctrines,[25] but Lombard followed the English author George Smith (as used earlier by Bonneville) in drawing attention to coincidences between the initial letters and numerical values of words referring to grades in the masonic and Jesuit hierarchies. Just what was to be made of such 'singular relations which cannot be absolutely the effect of chance', however, was left unstated.[26] The drift of both authors' arguments, though, was clear enough: contemporary history was largely the record of conspiracies to cast legitimate authority down into anarchy, and there was little to choose between the two forms of conspiracy—Ultramontane or Liberal for the exterior, Illuminist or Jesuit for the interior—that presented themselves.

The standpoint from which Liberal organs like *Le Constitutionnel* and especially *La Minerve française*[27] attacked the Jesuits was quite different. For them, there were not two enemies (however similar), but only one. 'Jacobinism' in the present was not a real threat, but a malicious Jesuit invention.[28] France had not rejected religion and morality, but only fanaticism and Jesuitism.[29] The danger which the

---

[23] [V. Lombard de Langres], *Des sociétés secrètes en Allemagne et en d'autres contrées, de la secte des illuminés, du tribunal secret, de l'assassinat de Kotzebue, etc.* (Paris, 1819), 70–1, 76–7.   [24] *Les Jésuites marchands*, 11–12.

[25] Ibid. 41 (references on 28 and 396 to the '*illuminés* of the Vatican' and to the 'high-*Illuminés* of Rome' appear to be meant metaphorically).

[26] [Lombard de Langres], *Des sociétés secrètes*, 78–9, which closely resembles N. de Bonneville, *Les Jésuites chassés de la maçonnerie, et leur poignard brisé par les maçons* (London, 1788), esp. 6–9. The original source (translated into French by Bonneville in 1783) was G. Smith, *The Use and Abuse of Free-Masonry: A Work of the Greatest Utility to the Brethren of the Society* (London, 1783). An example of the type of coincidence with which these writers were concerned is the fact that the final letter of the word 'mason' is the initial letter of the Jesuit grade 'Noster', which is attained at the age of 45, the very number which is obtained by adding up the numerical values of the other four letters in the word.

[27] A. Harpaz, *L'École libérale sous la Restauration: Le Mercure et La Minerve, 1817–20* (Geneva, 1968), 58, lists *La Minerve*'s main anti-jesuit articles of this period.

[28] *Minerve*, 7: 217.   [29] Ibid. 598–9.

Jesuits posed at present was not anarchy, as men like Lombard implied, but civil and religious tyranny. Their lust for domination predisposed them to hate modern institutions, and their present interest bound them to the party of blind reaction. 'He who says Jesuits, says despotism,' affirmed *Le Constitutionnel*.[30]

To identify the Jesuits with the governmental vice of despotism, rather than the revolutionary one of anarchism, was to open room for speculation about complicity between the Jesuits and the governments of the day. Liberals were firing anti-jesuit shots across governmental bows well before the triumph of reaction in 1820 or the advent of Villèle to power in 1822. The following passage, whose implications for Restoration France are thinly disguised by its ostensible reference to eighteenth-century Portugal, was penned by Tissot in *La Minerve* in May 1818:

Could, or should, a minister conscious of his duties, and devoted to his prince, have suffered the shameful abasement of royal authority before a religious order, and abandoned the reins of the State to greedy and ambitious monks? It may be said that he should have moderated their power and restrained them within the bounds of their ministry; this is to say that he should have allowed them the time to divide the court, to sow trouble in the royal family, to manœuvre in the shadows, to clasp the government in the shackles of a vast conspiracy which would have embraced the whole of Portugal, to seduce or intimidate the great, to stir up the fury of the people, to dethrone the monarch, if they did not succeed in having him killed in the midst of a revolt which would have had religion for its pretext.[31]

By late 1819 *La Minerve* was going significantly further than such veiled reminders of the ministerial duty to stamp out the Jesuits: several ministers, Decazes in particular, were accused of actively advancing the Jesuit cause. In September it was suggested that Decazes and Fontanes were plotting to hand French education over to Jesuit control, and in early November Étienne asserted that 'the Jesuits march with their heads held high, and authority openly protects them, both in their cloisters and in their triumphant excursions'; this protection allegedly exceeded any they had received from the three previous Ministers of the Interior.[32] 'You are far richer in Jesuits than you believe,' affirmed a Jesuit character in

---

[30] *Constitutionnel*, 8 Jan. 1823.   [31] *Minerve*, 2: 459–60.
[32] Ibid. 7: 333–4, 8: 25 (and similar insinuations in other articles).

a fictional dialogue by Jouy in February 1820; among the neglected varieties were opportunistic officials and ministers.[33] Under
Decazes's relatively liberal government, the polemical assimilation
of government to Jesuitism was already well under way in Liberal
journalistic practice. Those who encouraged it could scarcely agree
with the counter-revolutionary anti-jesuits who saw the remedy for
Jesuitism in authority; this remedy lay in defence of the *Charte*,[34]
and support for the vehicles of active resistance identified by Jouy:
'mutual teaching, freedom of the press, the right of petition, the
Liberal *députés*.'[35]

Great though their differences were, counter-revolutionaries like
Lombard and Liberals like the journalists of *La Minerve* both
interpreted the Jesuit threat in essentially political terms. Not all
anti-jesuitism, however, can be so tidily squeezed into political
categories. The case of Alexis Dumesnil, once best known in his
native Normandy as a swaggerer and duellist, then as a disorderly
leader of *volontaires royaux*, but who became in the early 1820s a
moderately successful polemicist and a persistent denouncer of
Jesuit influence, illustrates this point. Dumesnil's attacks on the
Jesuits and on government ministers, in his articles in *L'Album*
from 1822 onwards, had much in common with those of political
Liberals.[36] Yet, as his 1824 pamphlet *Considérations sur les causes et les
progrès de la corruption en France* most clearly showed, his conception
of France's ills was not political but moral. His most vehement
denunciations were reserved not for despotism but for what he
called 'corruption', the absence of moral standards in public life.
This he regarded not as the work of any particular political group,
but as the cumulative product of the successive phases of recent
French history: 'it is the inevitable result of that *fervour* which broke
everything, of that Empire which soiled everything, finally of
Jesuitism which sanctifies everything.'[37] Jesuitism, in short, was the
prevalent Restoration form of a wider moral evil. The cure for this

---

[33] Ibid. 9: 21.
[34] The Jesuits' war on the *Charte* was the subject of another of Jouy's dialogues
(Ibid. 9: 14–15).   [35] Ibid. 8: 448.
[36] On Dumesnil, see G. Lavalley, 'Les Duellistes de Caen de l'an IV à 1848: Le
Bretteur Alexis Dumesnil', *Mémoires de l'Académie Nationale des Sciences, Arts et
Belles-Lettres de Caen* (1913), 325–96; on *L'Album*, Magalon, *Ma translation*, esp. 13–
14.
[37] A. Dumesnil, *Considérations sur les causes et les progrès de la corruption en France*
(Paris, 1824), 76–7.

evil could not lie in the triumph of a particular party—Dumesnil thought Liberal politicians about as corrupt as the rest—but in the revival of religious sentiment and the return of men of all parties to the principles of honour and probity.[38]

On the whole, anti-jesuitism under Louis XVIII was a secondary, though persistent, concern of mainstream Liberal opinion, and a primary preoccupation only of occasional, generally minor, figures like Silvy or Dumesnil. There were a few signs, by the end of the reign, that this might be beginning to change. The volume of anti-jesuit literature increased slightly, and prosecuted polemicists took to defending themselves in court by attacking the Jesuits.[39] Anti-jesuit opinion made itself felt during the Chambre des Pairs' repeated debates (in 1823, 1824, and 1825) on bills proposing to permit the authorization of female religious communities by royal *ordonnance* without the need for a law debated in parliament; the bills' opponents, notably Lanjuinais, feared an extension of this mode of authorization to male communities, and warned of an invasion of 'jésuites' and 'jésuitesses'.[40] Anti-jesuitism's impact, however, was still sporadic. It had not yet become either a prevailing passion among large sectors of the politically minded, or the ideological focus of a political movement.

THE REIGN OF CHARLES X

The beginnings of an increase in anti-jesuitism reflected growing anxiety not only at the progress of the Jesuits, but at the strengthening hold of ultra-royalism on national politics, confirmed by the election of February 1824, which returned 410 royalist and only nineteen Liberal *députés*. Its sharp intensification early in the reign of Charles X had less to do with the new monarch, earlier

[38] Ibid. 63–70.

[39] See the remarks of Dumesnil at his trial in 1823 (*L'Album*, 8: 333) and of Santo-Domingo in 1824, turning his appeal against the sentence imposed for his scandalous *Tablettes romaines* into an all-out attack on the Jesuits and their alleged system of venality: J.-H. de Santo-Domingo, *Plaidoirie . . . devant la Cour Royale* (Paris, 1824), 24–8.

[40] Lanjuinais in *AP*, CP 2 Apr. 1823: 88–9; CP 13 July 1824: 226; CP 4 Feb. 1825: 4; also Lally-Tolendal, CP 14 July 1824: 264–5.

suspected of harbouring Jesuit sympathies[41] but currently popular thanks to his abolition of censorship, than with the legislative work of the parliamentary session which began at the end of 1824. The missions had seemed to bear the stigmata of Jesuit revival, but had occupied the margins rather than the centre of politics. Now, however, the 'Jesuitical' values that allegedly inspired them seemed to have migrated to the core. The string of projects that occupied the Chambers in 1825—the law indemnifying the *émigrés*, the law finally passed on the authorization of female religious communities, the sacrilege law, the bill to restore primogeniture—constituted just such a comprehensive counter-revolutionary and pro-clerical programme as anti-jesuits had long claimed would be produced if ever the Jesuits acquired a ruling interest in the nation; Liberal commentators were quick to find a Jesuit influence in all these measures.[42] The notion of a hidden hand in affairs of state could only be bolstered by the dimly perceived but real part which the ultra-monarchist secret society the Chevaliers de la Foi played in inspiring and passing this legislation.[43] It is not surprising either that long-standing anti-jesuits became increasingly insistent and alarmist, or that increasing numbers of people found their analyses persuasive.

Whatever the causes, anti-jesuitism escalated during the first half of the reign of Charles X. The quantity of anti-jesuit literature rose to a peak in 1826 and remained high till June 1828, before declining until a partial revival under the regime of Polignac from August 1829 onwards. Liberal and opposition papers like *Le Constitutionnel, Le Courrier français*, and *Le Journal des débats* returned constantly to the Jesuit theme. Early in 1827 the Minister for Ecclesiastical Affairs, Mgr. Frayssinous, could remark that the Society of Jesus seemed nowadays to inspire only hatred or enthusiasm, never indifference: 'for the past two years above all, the name of Jesuit has reverberated around the whole of France, blessed by some, cursed

---

[41] See e.g. Kératry's remark in 1820 concerning the return of the Jesuits: 'I know no one in the kingdom who has the right to authorize such things, be he the heir presumptive to the crown!' (quoted in *Minerve*, 9: 73–4).

[42] See e.g. *Constitutionnel*, 12 Jan. 1825, 6 Feb. 1825, 9 Feb. 1825, 9 Apr. 1825 (all on the sacrilege bill), 16 Feb. 1825 (on the indemnity), and General Sébastiani's denunciation of the primogeniture bill as a device for creating 'a poor and disinherited youth', who would be susceptible to Jesuit control (quoted ibid. 10 Feb. 1826).

[43] See Bertier de Sauvigny, *Le Comte Ferdinand de Bertier*, 353–68.

by the others, presented sometimes as a lantern of salvation, sometimes as a sign of ruin and calamity.'[44] Reports by government officials bore the Minister out. In the Moselle, the Prefect reported in April 1827, hostile public opinion pursued the Jesuits in the towns they visited. An ex-prefect of the Seine-Inférieure wrote in 1828 that his old *département* had suffered an 'inexpressible irritation' over the Jesuit question during the previous two years.[45] Anti-jesuit feeling seems also to have played a part in the disorders in the *collèges royaux* in 1827; it was reported that pupils of the Lycée Louis-le-Grand in Paris 'always take the Jesuits as the subject of their conversations'.[46]

What happened to French anti-jesuitism during these years amounts to more than an escalation in scale and intensity. Already, by the time Frayssinous made his remarks, three things had happened: anti-jesuitism had become a major public passion, prominently and extensively aired in law courts and parliamentary Chambers, as well as in newspapers; it had launched proceedings against the Jesuits themselves that were eventually to lead to their defeat in 1828; and it had become a system of political opposition. This triple change had taken place quite quickly, in the course of a series of episodes between late 1825 and late 1826.[47]

The first of these was the trial, or more accurately the two trials in tandem, of *Le Constitutionnel* and *Le Courrier français*, before the Cour Royale de Paris in late November and early December 1825, for their alleged 'tendency to undermine the respect due to the religion of the State'. The Jesuits were barely mentioned in the articles from the papers which the prosecution cited as the basis for its accusation, and were not referred to at all in the *acte d'accusation* drawn up by *procureur-général* Bellart in July.[48] This had the air of a

---

[44] *AP*, CP 19 Jan. 1827: 200.

[45] AN F^7 6770 (Moselle), Prefect to *Ministre de l'Intérieur*, 2 Apr. 1827, forwarding an 'anti-jesuit acrostic' circulating in large numbers in Metz; ibid. (Loire-Inférieure), Prefect (previously of Seine-Inférieure) to *Ministre de l'Intérieur*, 23 Sept. 1828. In Aug. 1826 Guizot wrote to Barante from Bois-Milet that the anti-jesuit mood, imported with the *Journal des débats*, was spreading 'like the most rapid contagion' in the neighbourhood: baron de Barante, *Souvenirs, 1782–1866*, 8 vols. (Paris, 1890–1901), iii. 345.

[46] Brugerette, *Le Comte de Montlosier*, 217 n., quoting a report by the *recteur d'académie*.

[47] There is another account of these episodes in Mellon, *The Political Uses of History*, 151–81.

[48] The fullest published version of the trial proceedings is *Procès du Constitutionnel et du Courrier, accusés de tendance à porter atteinte au respect dû à la religion de l'État*

deliberate omission: if the two papers had an irreverent tendency, anti-jesuitism was certainly by this stage a more important component in it than scurrility about Trappists, Frères de la Doctrine Chrétienne, and other groups mentioned in the accusation. In an open but anonymous letter to Bellart, abbé Tabaraud suggested reasons for this 'strange discretion'. If Bellart denounced the Jesuits, Tabaraud argued, he would offend a powerful party which he had no wish to cross; if he defended them, he would contradict the anti-jesuit rulings of a host of *ancien régime* magistrates, whose successors he was trying to win over. His silence was therefore understandable, but it was likely the defence would use it against him.[49]

This proved an accurate apprehension. Opening for the prosecution in November, *avocat-général* de Broë tried hard to keep the Jesuit question out of the case, arguing that the court had to consider not the particular assertions of the two papers, but the general spirit of their articles, so that there was no occasion to reopen 'a famous trial'.[50] He also prudently refrained from taking up the defence of religious orders offered in Bellart's *réquisitoire*. But the two defence lawyers, Dupin *aîné* for *Le Constitutionnel* and Mérilhou for *Le Courrier*, were not so easily put off.

Dupin presented his client as a defender of the Gallican Church and liberties, the attacker only of priestly abuses and Ultramontane corruptions. Homing in on the weak point Tabaraud had identified, he criticized Bellart for suggesting that *Le Constitutionnel* accused religious institutions in general of trying to interfere in politics; only one such institution had been accused, and this was the only one Bellart had omitted to name, no doubt for fear of dissenting embarrassingly from the judgements of the old magistracy by approving it. Nevertheless, Dupin asserted, the name could not be avoided, for 'those whom it denotes are present in everyone's

(Paris, 1826); this reproduces Bellart's text, but not that of the passages incriminated. The relevant extracts from *Le Constitutionnel* are included in *Réquisitoire de M. le procureur général près la Cour Royale de Paris, contre le Constitutionnel, suivi des articles incriminés dans le Constitutionnel, à la suite du réquisitoire, ainsi que de l'ordonnance de M. le premier président, et de l'exploit de signification* (n.p., 1825).

[49] M.-M. Tabaraud, *Lettre à M. Bellart, procureur-général à la Cour Royale de Paris, sur son réquisitoire du 30 juillet contre les journaux de l'opposition* (Paris, 1825), 15–16.

[50] *Procès du Constitutionnel et du Courrier* (Plaidoyer de M. de Broé), 57–9 (each document in this collection is paginated separately).

thoughts'.[51] Having thus ensured that this was so, Dupin titillated his audience with a string of insinuations in which he himself left the Jesuit name tantalizingly unmentioned. The Liberal threat to religion, he concluded, was a red herring, but the current religious agitation in Catholic Europe was a real threat to the State. His suggestion of its cause, though it still did not name the Jesuits, rapidly became a classic anti-jesuit quotation: 'recognize the striving of the Pharisees of today; feel the blows of this sword whose hilt is in Rome and whose point is everywhere.'[52] Two days later, Mérilhou ungloved the defence's anti-jesuitism. 'It is visible to all eyes that the Jesuits' interest alone has dictated this suit,' he affirmed. The prosecution's affected preoccupation with Trappists and *ignorantins* was a mere diversion; the two papers would not have been prosecuted had they not consistently opposed the revival of the Jesuits, whom Mérilhou, in his conclusion, denounced as foreign agents and as the crucial force in a league for the ecclesiastical subjugation of the civil power. The latter was no longer protected by the vigilance of anti-jesuit corporations; indeed the Jesuits had affiliates among precisely those whose duty it was to maintain law and royal authority. A 'civil Jesuitism' was usurping power, wealth, and honour. It was the citizen's duty to sound the alarm.[53]

The two papers were acquitted, with mild reprimands for their irreverent tone. The ruling on *Le Constitutionnel* stated that no offence to the state religion was involved in combatting the establishment of unauthorized associations or the spread of doctrines which threatened royal sovereignty and public liberty. The court found a few articles in *Le Courrier* reprehensible in substance, but saw an attenuating circumstance in the fact that these had been provoked by the introduction of 'religious corporations forbidden by the law' and the public profession of Ultramontanism among the clergy.[54] Anxiously awaited and widely publicized because of the case's general importance for freedom of the press, these rulings were readily taken as endorsing the anti-jesuit premisses of the defence. They confirmed the Liberal press in its

---

[51] Ibid. (Plaidoyer de M. Dupin *aîné*), 42.   [52] Ibid. 127–9.

[53] Ibid. (Plaidoyer de M. Mérilhou), 5, 84–91.

[54] Ibid.: the judgements on *Le Constitutionnel* and *Le Courrier* are reproduced on p. 34 of 'Réplique de M. Dupin *aîné*' and pp. 94–5 of 'Plaidoyer de M. Mérilhou', respectively.

self-appointed sentryship against Jesuitism, and encouraged the hope that the Restoration courts would live up to the anti-jesuit traditions of their predecessors.

The effort to cast the modern magistracy in an inherited anti-jesuit leading role was continued in the La Chalotais case early in 1826. In January, taking advantage of the emotions aroused by the recent trial of the *Constitutionnel* and *Courrier*, a Parisian printmaker issued a portrait of one of the heroes of the Parlements' campaigns against the Jesuits, the *procureur-général* of the Breton Parlement, La Chalotais. This provoked a sharp exchange of views between the *Courrier* and the semi-ministerial paper *L'Étoile*, in the course of which the latter described La Chalotais as a felonious magistrate, whose attacks on the Jesuits had been motivated by personal animosity, in contempt of duty and impartiality.[55] For such insults to their ancestor's memory, *L'Étoile* was promptly sued by two groups of La Chalotais's descendants. When the case came before the Cour Royale at the end of March, the Catholic lawyer Berryer, acting for one group of descendants, strove to rescue it from the prevailing current of anti-jesuitism. The court, he argued, had simply to decide whether *L'Étoile*'s journalist had written as a serious historian or as an irresponsible *libelliste*, and whether, in the latter case, La Chalotais's descendants were empowered to sue; to rekindle old passions by discussing the rights and wrongs of La Chalotais's *comptes-rendus* on the Jesuits or of the order's expulsion would be both unnecessary and reprehensible.[56] This attempt to separate the cause of the dead anti-jesuit's honour from that of his anti-jesuitism was, however, directly challenged by the lawyer representing the second group of La Chalotais's descendants, Bernard.

'La Chalotais accused, the Jesuits accusers':[57] this, according to Bernard, was the essence of the case, and La Chalotais could be defended only by showing that his pursuit of the Jesuits had been justified. This, Bernard argued, was beyond doubt. The Society of Jesus' megalomaniacal spirit, which had made it the absolute ruler of the eighteenth-century world, would on its own have justified the condemnation which a stream of irrecusable authorities had heaped upon it; the Jesuits' religious, political, and moral doctrines were

---

[55] *L'Étoile*, 2 Feb. 1826, quoted in *Recueil complet du procès intenté par les héritiers de M. de la Chalotais*, part I, pp. vi–vii.

[56] *Recueil complet*, part I, pp. 10–14.   [57] Ibid. 28.

equally pernicious. All this was so obvious, indeed, that one could
only attribute sinister intentions to a paper which strove to call it
into question just when alarming rumours were circulating of
a Jesuit revival. With characteristic Liberal double-edged punctili-
ousness, Bernard hastened to reassure his listeners that Charles X,
favouring the *Charte* and the happiness of his people, would never
tolerate the Jesuits.[58] At the end of his *plaidoyer*, the rest of which
dealt with other matters, he returned to the Jesuit menace: 'Their
name alone is enough to agitate France: before they have appeared,
their influence makes itself felt. A thousand concealed intrigues
embrace and divide families. What inconceivable vertigo, then, calls
down new tempests on our heads?'[59]

According to Bernard, the court faced a simple choice, 'between
the family of La Chalotais, illustrious over six centuries, and the
Jesuits, driven thirty-eight times from the states of Europe, and
whose history is nothing but a succession of outrages'.[60] The readiness of Hennequin, *L'Étoile*'s lawyer, to trade blows with Bernard
in defence of the eighteenth-century Jesuits and in denigration of
their opponents[61] did nothing to discourage the Liberal press from
accepting this view. In such circumstances, it mattered little that
the court itself agreed with Berryer that the Jesuit question was
irrelevant to the legal points at issue, and that its ruling, though
critical of *L'Étoile*'s attacks on La Chalotais, dismissed the case on
the grounds that the law did not enable the dead man's descendants to receive legal satisfaction on his behalf.[62] Since the ruling
contained nothing which contradicted Bernard's attacks on the
Jesuits, it still left room for anti-jesuit triumphalism. *Le Courrier
français* openly affirmed what Bernard had implied: the Jesuits
had deliberately provoked the trial in the hope that, by discredit-
ing La Chalotais, they could overturn in the public mind the
verdict against their order, and prepare the ground for its legal
recognition.[63] Viewed in this light, the court's ruling confirmed
an anti-jesuit status quo. La Chalotais was considered triumphantly
vindicated, and his expositions of Jesuit viciousness, reissued in
small format, enjoyed a brisk success.[64] The La Chalotais case

---

[58] Ibid. 47–67.   [59] Ibid. 80.   [60] Ibid. 82.
[61] Ibid., part ii, pp. 25–47.   [62] Ibid. 114–19.
[63] *Courrier*, 23 Apr. 1826.
[64] L.-R. de Caradeuc de La Chalotais, *Résumé de la doctrine des jésuites* and *Résumé des Constitutions des jésuites*, both presented by J.-A.-S. Collin de Plancy (Paris, 1826).

served to publicize and to nourish two increasingly tenacious convictions in the Liberal mind. The first was the belief that the crust of Restoration affairs concealed a powerful Jesuit push towards ascendancy, which was now increasingly breaking to the surface. The second was the view that nothing new had been added to the Jesuit question since the eighteenth century: the old condemnation of the order still condemned it; its old victims were its victims still, and the wisdom of its old opponents was sufficient for their successors.

If the *plaidoyers* of Dupin, Mérilhou, and Bernard in late 1825 and early 1826 raised anti-jesuitism to new public prominence, the man who did most to transform its significance in Restoration politics and to keep the Jesuit question in the public eye for the last two years of the Villèle administration was the comte de Montlosier.[65] Montlosier's onslaught began with five articles in the ministerial paper *Le Drapeau blanc* in October 1825.[66] These, however, were no more than a preview of his *Mémoire à consulter sur un système religieux et politique, tendant à renverser la religion et le trône*, which appeared, with the La Chalotais trial imminent, on 25 February 1826, causing an immediate stir in the press and the Chamber, and going on to sell 10,000 copies in three months.[67] Though the Jesuits were only part of the 'system' or 'conspiracy' the *Mémoire* denounced—one of four 'scourges', the other three being the Congrégation, Ultramontanism, and the clerical spirit of encroachment ('l'esprit d'envahissement chez les prêtres')—the book was to exercise an important influence on the subsequent fortunes of Restoration anti-jesuitism, both by its ideological orientation and by its demonological development.

In the first place, Montlosier gave a new prominence and a new, albeit contested, respectability to anti-jesuitism of an essentially conservative, monarchist kind. He did not do so single-handedly; men like the magistrate Charles Cottu and the journalist Jacques-Barthélemy Salgues wrote in similar vein.[68] No work of theirs,

---

[65] On Montlosier and his writings, see R. Casanova, *Montlosier et le parti prêtre: Étude, suivie d'un choix de textes* (Paris, 1970); A. Bardoux, *Le Comte de Montlosier et le gallicanisme* (Paris, 1881); Brugerette, *Le Comte de Montlosier*; Bertier de Sauvigny, *Le Comte Ferdinand de Bertier*, 386–402.   [66] On 2, 5, 8, 13, and 20 Oct.

[67] Mellon, *The Political Uses of History*, 168. For parliamentary reaction, see *AP*, CD 8 Apr. 1826: 42–3; CD 15 May 1826: 40.

[68] The most notably anti-jesuit works of these two authors are listed in the Bibliography.

however, had the impact of the *Mémoire* or did as much to stimulate and publicize conservative resentments. Hitherto best known for his annual treatises *De la monarchie française*, Montlosier wrote as an established champion of the aristocratic and monarchical order. His book provided the first full-scale statement of reasons why defenders of that order in the Restoration should oppose the Jesuits and their allies.

Furthermore, these reasons were now defined, as they had not been by men like Silvy and Lombard de Langres earlier, in a way which left room for understanding of a sort with anti-jesuits of a Liberal stamp.[69] This is impossible to understand if we dismiss the *Mémoire*, as it sometimes is dismissed, as a *tour de force* of idiosyncratic anachronism, executed by an aristocratico-Gallican fossil mentally embedded in the *ancien régime*.[70] Montlosier may have been bizarre, but it was not this that permitted Barante to consider the *Mémoire* 'in complete harmony with the public disposition'.[71] He was certainly Gallican, but no more so than was normal among Restoration anti-jesuits.[72] The *Mémoire* itself did bear strong marks of aristocratic class interest, but it cannot be read as an unthinking plea for a return to the *ancien régime*. Montlosier was the most noted of Restoration critics of the Jesuits, and deserves to be remembered as such, not because he provided an exotic reincarnation of outmoded prejudices, but because his critique was in fact rooted in an analysis of specifically Restoration problems that was bold and able to appeal even to men more likely to be repelled than attracted by a feudal emphasis. The nature of Christianity, its relationship to morality, that of morals to institutions, the function of the priesthood, the causes and effects of the Revolution: all these were questions of major importance in the theory and practice of Restoration politics, and Montlosier's discussion of them, in part III of the *Mémoire* (often neglected by commentators), was not alien to his work's importance.

Essentially, the *Mémoire* set out to refute a whole counter-revolutionary way of thought, in the name of its own catch-words:

[69] The need for such an understanding had been a theme of Mortonval's novel *Le Tartufe moderne*, published in 1825 (see esp. ii. 218–19).

[70] For such a view of Montlosier, see Mellor, *Histoire de l'anticléricalisme français*, 246.   [71] Barante, *Souvenirs*, iii. 321–2.

[72] Indeed Barante commended him 'for not having gone in for all the humbug about the liberties of the Gallican Church' (ibid.).

monarchy, religion, public order. The need for Restoration was taken seriously, but the fashionable obsession with the threat of Revolution scorned. Montlosier rejected the sharp distinction which Ultras insisted on between 'royalists' and 'liberals': the *parti libéral*, he was later to write, had 'a monarchical tint', while the *parti monarchique* had a liberal one.[73] This rejection rested on a similar rejection of the notion that the Revolution had been an outbreak of pure evil engineered by the sheer malice of men whose direct spiritual descendants were to be found on the Liberal benches in the Chamber and in the offices of *Le Constitutionnel*. The suggestion that only Jesuit education could have prevented the Revolution or could now forestall its repetition was likewise attacked: the Jesuits had themselves educated the most impious *philosophes*, and won notoriety by their regicidal tendencies.[74] Neither Montlosier nor Salgues (who stressed the role of Jesuit theological fanaticism in provoking Revolutionary fanaticism in politics[75]), however, meant their undermining of the Jesuits' counter-revolutionary credentials to imply acceptance of the thesis advanced by Lombard and the anonymous author of 1824, namely that the Jesuit and Revolutionary threats were fundamentally the same. Such a thesis left the view of the Revolution as the work of absolute malice intact, whereas both Montlosier and Salgues regarded it as the product of specific and analysable historical circumstances: in Salgues's view a general revulsion against tyranny and persecution; in Montlosier's, a disparity between feudal institutions and anti-feudal sentiments in society.[76]

Montlosier's disinclination for the moral absolutism so common in right-wing writing at this time is equally clear in his assessment of the Revolution's consequences. In destroying the old institutions, he argued, the Revolution had created a vacuum in French society. None of the various groups which had since sought to impose their own domination had been able to enshrine it in institutions; France remained in a state of political chaos and corresponding moral fragility.[77] Nevertheless—and this was the

[73] Montlosier, *Pétition*, 10.

[74] Comte de Montlosier, *Mémoire à consulter sur un système religieux et politique tendant à renverser la religion, la société et le trône*, 4th edn. (Paris, 1826), 119–22.

[75] J.-B. Salgues, *Pétition sur l'exécution des lois ecclésiastiques relatives à la Compagnie de Jésus, présentée à la Chambre des Députés* (Paris, 1828), 6–7.

[76] Ibid. 6–7; Montlosier, *Mémoire*, 244–5.

[77] Montlosier, *Mémoire*, 169–71, 246–56.

crucial point—the Revolution's work of destruction had not been total. 'Indeed, while losing her social institutions, that is to say the visible and sometimes worn-out forms in which her old spirit was enclosed, it is a fact that France did not lose that spirit': from her upper classes she had derived noble sentiments which proved capable of surviving even the furies of middle-class tyranny. Justice, honour, and religion persisted in French minds, despite the disappearance of the institutions that had given them body. Restoration was thus a matter of conservation as well as of recovery, and in the latter respect, '*to have had* offers a great facility for having again. It is astonishing with what facility *mœurs* which have merely been effaced or bent down by events can re-establish themselves.'[78]

Montlosier's argument directly challenged the rationale of the mission movement, which rested on the assumption that France was in a state of religious apostasy and moral degradation from which only intensive evangelization could rescue her. He warned against 'those who, to obtain domination, first tell you softly that morality makes society, to tell you afterwards more boldly that religion makes morality'.[79] In his view, neither stage in this argument was strictly true, and the second in particular was dangerously misleading. *Mœurs*—the amalgam of sentiments and habits that cemented a society—did not derive from religion, and religion could not force good *mœurs* into existence. Where it clashed with those that existed, 'it is always religion which succumbs'. Religion could achieve a great good, when it was able to endorse and support society's moral habits, but it committed great damage when it engaged with them 'not to correct them gently, as they sometimes need, but to subjugate them and dominate them'. The error was compounded when religion invaded civil life, substituting religious *mœurs* for civil ones, 'from which it results that bit by bit the civil laws merge into the religious laws, that the priest as religious legislator is induced to become at the same time legislator and sovereign of society: a thing which prepares the downfall of religion and of society'.[80]

All Montlosier's offensives in the *Mémoire*—against Ultramontanism, against the intrusion of the clergy into worldly affairs on various levels, against the efforts made to impose the life-style of full-time pious devotion (*la vie dévote*) on a population the great

---

[78] Ibid. 248–9.   [79] Ibid. 252.   [80] Ibid. 240–1.

majority of whose members were suited only to the much less demanding life of unspectacular rectitude and conventional observance (*la vie chrétienne*)—reflected this rejection of the view that religion was the sole and ultimate basis for viable society, and of its corollary that every aspect of civil, political, and private life ought therefore to be brought under overt religious regulation. To act on such assumptions, Montlosier believed, was to risk compromising religion and the priesthood, and weakening everything—society, morality, monarchy—that the strategy was intended to strengthen. There was a real and urgent work of Restoration to be undertaken in the France of the 1820s, but effort must be concentrated in the realm of institutions and of constitutional doctrine, not in that of religion, and must assume a certain resilience in moral and religious instincts rather than their total annihilation. A counter-revolutionary campaign proceeding on the contrary assumption could only be counter-productive and, inasmuch as it claimed royal approval, provide pretexts for revolt.[81] It was in this sense that the 'religious and political system' denounced in the *Mémoire* was subversive of religion, society, and the throne.

It was only because argument along these lines established theoretical conditions in which conservatives and Liberals were not automatically each other's demons that the demonology Montlosier proposed to his readers—that of the four 'scourges', especially the Congrégation and the Jesuits—could become the rallying-point for oppositions of differing political hues. In practice, by late 1826 the Jesuits were to be firmly established as senior demons. Montlosier had not intended this: he himself always insisted that the other 'scourges' were equally important and that the Jesuits themselves were simply a visible indicator of the 'general encroachment of the *parti prêtre*'.[82] The eventual focus on the Jesuits owed something to the Minister for Ecclesiastical Affairs, Mgr. Frayssinous, who fixed attention on them in May by

---

[81] Ibid. 163. [J.-B. Salgues], *Courtes Observations sur la congrégation, les jésuites, et les trois discours de M. le ministre des affaires ecclésiastiques, prononcés à la Chambre des Députés, les 25, 26, et 27 mai 1826* (Paris, 1826), 144, issued a similar warning.

[82] Letter by Montlosier (Mar. 1828), quoted by Bardoux, *Le Comte de Montlosier*, 283; other letters quoted by Bardoux (291–2) make a similar point. The term *parti prêtre* was coined by Montlosier to denote 'those who, at whatever risk and whatever danger, wish to hand over society to the priesthood' (*Mémoire*, 34). He used it sometimes to refer to a section of the upper clergy to whom he attributed this aim, but more usually as a loose label to describe the whole ensemble of clerical forces.

openly admitting their existence in France; arguably it also reflected
the long-term effects of the disbanding of the Chevaliers de la Foi,
whose activities were misattributed to the Jesuits' main rival in the
demonology, the Congrégation.[83] Finally, it resulted from the way
in which Montlosier's own efforts to press home his broad-fronted
attack on the subversive 'system', by a harrying pursuit through
legal and political channels, which commanded considerable public
attention, were transformed by legal practicalities into a narrow
thrust against the Jesuits.

Montlosier's own view, in the *Mémoire*, had been first that each
of the four 'scourges' was illegal in itself, and secondly that, even
had this not been so, each of them would still have been pursuable
in law by virtue of its participation in a joint tendency towards a
criminal end, namely the destruction of State, religion, and society.[84] The lawyers, whom he consulted in large numbers, were less
sure. The idea that the different elements of clerical aggression
might be caught together in the net of a *procès de tendance* resembling
those too often cast to catch alleged revolutionary conspirators (not
a suggestion with a guaranteed appeal to Liberal lawyers) was omitted from the *Dénonciation*[85] which Montlosier submitted to the Cour
Royale de Paris in July, and only one of the legal consultations
subsequently published in his support, that of Isambert, showed
any inclination to revive it.[86] Nor were sympathetic lawyers confident that, taken separately, all four 'scourges' could be brought
under the hammer of the law. In Dupin's view, subscribed to
by forty-one other lawyers of the Parisian bar, it was doubtful
whether Ultramontanism and the ecclesiastical *esprit d'envahissement*,
in the forms which Montlosier had pinpointed, could be made
the subjects of a successful judicial denunciation; the legal attack
should therefore concentrate on the Jesuits and the *congrégations*
(now put in the plural).[87] Devaux and others of the Bourges bar

---

[83] See Bertier de Sauvigny, *Le Comte Ferdinand de Bertier*, 398. The Chevaliers
de la Foi had in fact disbanded before the publication of Montlosier's book (ibid.
378–9).   [84] Montlosier, *Mémoire*, 295–6.
[85] Text in Montlosier, *Dénonciation aux Cours Royales, relativement au système
religieux et politique signalé dans le Mémoire à consulter; précédée de nouvelles observations sur
ce système, et sur les apologies qu'on en a récemment publiées* (Paris, 1826), 275–85.
[86] F.-A. Isambert, *Consultation sur la dénonciation adressée à la Cour Royale par M. de
Montlosier* (Paris, 1826), esp. 2–7, 91.
[87] A.-M.-J.-J. Dupin *et al.*, *Consultation sur la dénonciation adressée à la Cour Royale
par M. le comte de Montlosier* (Paris, 1826), 51–64.

preferred to focus exclusively on the Jesuits, so as not to risk compromising the case against them by seeming to link it to an attack on institutions whose standing in law and public esteem was more secure. Unlike Montlosier, the Bourges lawyers considered that only the Jesuits ultimately mattered: without them 'nothing of what M. de Montlosier complains of would take place'.[88] The Cour Royale, on 18 August, dismissed, as not constituting legal offences, all the evils Montlosier had denounced except one: the re-establishment of the Society of Jesus was formally declared to be contrary to standing French law, founded 'on the recognized incompatibility between the principles professed by this society and the independence of all governments; principles yet more incompatible with the constitutional *Charte*, which today forms the public law of the French'.[89] Since the court, reasoning that the legislation it had invoked entrusted the responsibility for dissolving Jesuit establishments to the *haute police*, promptly declared itself incompetent to act, its ruling served only to fortify anti-jesuit feeling. Montlosier forwarded his denunciation to the Minister of the Interior; when this predictably brought no response, he converted it into a petition to the Chambre des Pairs.[90] On 18 January 1827 the *rapporteur*, Portalis, told the Chamber that requests for action against Ultramontanism and the *esprit d'envahissement* were inadmissible in a petition, since they amounted to calls for fresh legislation, and that Article 291 of the Penal Code protected lay *congrégations* from dissolution:[91] Montlosier's quadruple attack was again mortifyingly boiled down to a narrow anti-jesuitism. Debate raged over the Jesuits for two days, before the Chamber, accepting Portalis's suggestions and ignoring Montlosier's own call for an address to the king, voted by a large majority to forward to the *Président du Conseil* those parts of the petition which related to 'the establishment in France of various houses of a monastic order not authorized by the law'.[92]

If attention came to focus more narrowly on a blackened image

[88] H. Devaux *et al.*, *Consultation sur la dénonciation adressée à la Cour Royale par M. le comte de Montlosier* (Paris, 1826), 2.

[89] Text in Dupin, *Libertés*, 288–9.

[90] The petition itself is on pp. 171–84 of Montlosier, *Pétition*. Montlosier followed this with *Les Jésuites, les congrégations et le parti prêtre en 1827: Mémoire à M. le comte de Villèle, Président du Conseil des Ministres* (Paris, 1827).

[91] *AP*, CP 18 Jan. 1827.

[92] For a summary of the debate, see Mellon, *The Political Uses of History*, 175–80.

of the Jesuits than Montlosier would have wished, that image was nevertheless one enriched and ramified by associations which he, by placing the Jesuits in a broader conspiratorial context, had done more than anyone to establish. These associations, rather than his fairly conventional hostile remarks on the Jesuits themselves, were his principal contribution to anti-jesuit mythology. They did not rest on any clear demonstration by Montlosier of organizational connections between different elements in the conspiracy; indeed his definition of a conspiracy—'a concerted aspiration on the part of a certain number of individuals to arrive at an end'[93]—was loose enough to leave it unclear how far he really believed such connections existed. Nevertheless, his bold statement and stubborn repetition of an argument in which the four 'scourges' were associated made it hard for many Frenchmen thereafter to think of them as separate phenomena.

The most important of the associations which thus became current among anti-jesuits was that between the Jesuits and the Congrégation. As Bertier de Sauvigny has convincingly shown, the myth of the Congrégation rested on a confused conflation of the real Congrégation, a pious and charitable confraternity directed by the Jesuit Père Ronsin, with the genuinely influential ultra-royalist secret society the Chevaliers de la Foi.[94] Montlosier did not initiate the jumbling-up of Congrégation, Chevaliers de la Foi, and Jesuits, which was already a feature of Dumesnil's pronouncements early in 1823,[95] but it was he who did most to develop the spectre which resulted and to establish its place in the polemical arsenal. The

---

[93] Montlosier, *Mémoire*, 294–5.

[94] Bertier de Sauvigny, *Le Comte Ferdinand de Bertier*, 369–74, 402–7.

[95] Bertier de Sauvigny (ibid. 373) cites Dumesnil's *Considérations* (1824) as the first published instance of this confusion. It can, however, already be found in his 'Examen de conscience', in *L'Album*, 15 Jan. 1823: 205–6: 'Life will fail me, sooner than the courage to point out to the prince and to the whole nation a menacing league, formed in the shadows, and which, under the pretext of combatting the Imperial tyranny, lately threw out roots all over the kingdom. I know what this mysterious association wants, I am acquainted with it, and I refused from the beginning to be part of it, because it was under the influence of Rome and the Jesuits. . . . But let there be no mistake! This *congrégation*, which has become so famous, is just the Ligue again, poorly disguised, which is reborn more dangerous and more implacable than ever.' At his trial shortly afterwards Dumesnil stated that this association had been formed under Jesuit auspices, and that its chief object was to re-establish the Jesuits in France (ibid. 10 Feb. 1823: 333). The Jesuit nature of the Congrégation was again dwelt on in his article 'Chapitre des analogies' (ibid. 15 Feb. 1823).

Congrégation figured in the *Mémoire* as a wide-ranging but flexible and elusive power with a membership of 48,000, well organized in both Paris and the provinces, and capable of functioning at one moment as a network of piety, at the next as one of intrigue and espionage. Its affiliates, who included 130–50 *députés*, riddled the realms of politics and administration; meanwhile, it marshalled the lower orders in front-organizations like the Association de Saint-Joseph.[96] Its connection with the Society of Jesus was suggested by the involvement of particular Jesuits (or so-called 'secret Jesuits' like the organizer of the Association de Saint-Joseph[97]), but above all by its structural complexity, in which Montlosier saw the clear mark of Jesuit organizational cunning, and continuity with the Jesuit sodalities of past centuries.[98]

Given such a suggestion, it is not surprising that many of Montlosier's readers, though not he himself, tended to regard the Congrégation as simply a form or an extension of the Society of Jesus. *Le Constitutionnel* had already expressed the view that the Jesuits' cause and that of the Congrégation were 'intimately linked, or rather amount to one: Jesuits, *congréganistes*, it is the same thing.'[99] Now, reviewing Montlosier, the *Journal des débats* remarked that the Congrégation 'is to Jesuitism what the pioneers are to an army: it prepares the way.'[100] The myth of the Congrégation laicized the Jesuit menace, and multiplied the instances in which it could be detected. Lay 'affiliation' replaced the missions as the chief vehicle of Jesuit subversion denounced by anti-jesuits. It retained this place for the rest of the 1820s, even though the Congrégation itself lost its pre-eminence in Liberal demonology after 1826. In retrospect, the emphasis on Congrégation and affiliation marks a transitional phase in the evolution of the political conceptions underpinning the anti-Jesuit view of subversion. Earlier anti-jesuits, in portraying regicide as the gravest subversive act, by implication located power narrowly in and around the monarch. Those of the July Monarchy and Third Republic, adapting their fears to a more broadly based political system, would stress more 'social' forces of subversion, especially Jesuit education. For the time being, in the later 1820s, it was on a 'social' form of political

---

[96] Montlosier, *Mémoire*, 17–37, 118.   [97] Ibid. 31.
[98] Ibid. 18–19.   [99] *Constitutionnel*, 29 Oct. 1825.
[100] *Débats*, 13 Mar. 1826.

subversion—the corruption and manipulation of political institutions by Jesuit-controlled personnel—that attention was focused.

This idea of a politically active Jesuitical Congrégation greatly facilitated the transformation of anti-jesuitism from a warning of as yet not fully realized political disaster into a denunciation of occult government. The suggestion that acts of government sometimes reflected a sinister Jesuit influence was not new: indeed *Le Constitutionnel* had already, early in 1825, announced that the government 'already exists only by the protection of the Jesuits and in submitting to their laws'.[101] By prompting people imaginatively to convert politicians or officials of whose politics they disapproved into men motivated by a secret but formal Jesuit loyalty, however, Montlosier and other hounders of the Congrégation set this conception of occult influence on a clearer, firmer, more persuasively alarming basis. No longer were the Jesuits conceived to be besieging power from without, with varying degrees of success; in the persons of their affiliates, they were entrenched within. If Montlosier exaggerated when he wrote that 'all France is imbued with the opinion that she is governed today not by her king and by her statesmen, but, like the England of the Stuarts, by Jesuits and by *congrégations*',[102] his *Mémoire* certainly helped promote such a view.

Such statements clearly posed the question of complicity: to what extent were the ostensible political authorities, whether willingly or not, collaborators in the circumvention or perversion of their own power? In 1826, it was still conventional as well as prudent to present the monarchy as the natural victim, rather than the ally, of Jesuitism. Outwardly at least, Liberal anti-jesuits chose with Montlosier to find the cause of the current decline in royal popularity —arising partly from the king's apparent self-abasement before the Church during the recent Jubilee celebrations—not in the king himself, but 'in the things which beset him and in the personages who surround him'.[103] Increasingly ambiguous ways of remaining outwardly respectful were being found, however. References to the sad fate of the Stuart dynasty, doomed by its Jesuitical associations, could, according to context, be taken to imply anything from the most obsequious recommendation that the king take care to distance himself from the Jesuits to the most barely veiled threat of

---

[101] *Constitutionnel*, 6 Feb. 1825.   [102] Montlosier, *Mémoire*, 116.
[103] Ibid. 153.

insurrection if he did not. Long a stand-by of anti-jesuit rhetoric, they enjoyed a new vogue, which would culminate in the dubious loyalism of Dupin *aîné*'s exhortation to the *députés* in 1828: '*Messieurs*, the Jesuits ruined the Stuarts, let us prevent the Jesuits from compromising the Bourbons.'[104]

The ambiguity of the Liberals' public posture on the question of relations between Jesuitism and the monarchy may be observed in the reaction of *Le Constitutionnel* to the nomination in April 1826 of Mgr. Tharin as tutor to the young duc de Bordeaux. In the paper's expressions of outrage at the handing over of responsibility for the education of a future monarch to a known apologist for the Society of Jesus two elements were combined, each of which qualified the other. On the one hand, grave warnings of the dangers which a Jesuitical monarch would pose both to the nation and to the survival of the monarchy itself were couched in terms which, while ostensibly envisaging only the future Henri V, might well be taken obliquely to refer to, and even to threaten, the present king: Tharin, it was feared, would produce 'a king for the Jesuits, and not for France', a prince who would rule in accord with the Jesuitical doctrine that anything, including perjury, was permissible in the service of intolerance and despotism. If this were to happen, 'what would become of France, what would become of the prince himself?'[105] On the other hand, *Le Constitutionnel* covered itself against allegations of disloyalty, not only by the familiar expedient of blaming the king's advisers rather than the king for Tharin's appointment, but also by loudly proclaiming the historical incompatibility between the regicidal Society of Jesus and the Bourbon dynasty. It cited Monglave and Chalas's recent history of Jesuit sedition against Bourbon rulers to show that the appointment could only have been suggested by persons either ignorant of history or hostile both to king and to country.[106] Returning six months later to the subject of the prince's sinister educational prospects, it expressed the hope that his hereditary virtue would protect him from the Jesuit poison: 'Is not his name a sort of

[104] *AP*, CD 21 June 1828: 235. Among many other instances, see Barante (ibid., CP 19 Jan. 1827: 199): 'You have noticed, messieurs, that the word Jesuits cannot be pronounced without England and the fall of the Stuarts coming instantly to mind.'
[105] *Constitutionnel*, 4 May 1826 (and articles in similar vein on 20, 22, 23 Apr. 1826). The reference to perjury contained an obvious allusion to the royal coronation oath.   [106] Ibid. 23 Apr. 1826.

talisman? Yes, yes, when he has gained his reason, he will know that he is called Henri.'[107]

For the time being, then, the free-floating clouds of anti-jesuit suspicion were permitted to gather around the head of monarchy in only a thin and fleeting mist. They settled in all the denser a fog upon Villèle and his colleagues. Nothing did more to crystallize this suspicion into dogmatic anti-governmental certainty than the effort which Mgr. Frayssinous made to dispel it, in a speech during the budget debate in the Chambre des Députés on 26 May. The previous day Frayssinous had tried to deflate the Congrégation myth: his assurances that the pious Congrégation was unrelated to any shadowy political organization, and that he as Minister experienced no occult influence from such a quarter, failed to convince those who believed otherwise, but at least gave them no fresh reason for so believing. Now, however, to the probable horror of Villèle, whom he seems not to have consulted,[108] he tried to take the wind out of anti-jesuit sails by revealing that the Jesuit presence in France, subject of so much speculation, amounted to a mere seven *petits séminaires* under episcopal control.[109] Anti-jesuits, insisting that any Jesuit presence, however small, was both illegal and poisonous, were quick to interpret this revelation as a shameless admission of the Minister's own felony in knowingly permitting one.[110] The impression of governmental complicity in Jesuit designs — deepened by Frayssinous's subsequent statement that the government, regarding the Jesuits simply as individuals, 'believes it possible to tolerate them'[111] — made it possible to detect a sinister Jesuit purpose behind the revelation itself: casting off the secrecy in which it had previously shrouded itself, the Society of Jesus no doubt hoped, by having its *de facto* existence publicly recognized by the Minister, to prepare the ground for its official re-establishment in France in the near future.[112] Everything

---

[107] Ibid. 15 Oct. 1826.

[108] G. de Grandmaison, *La Congrégation (1801–1830)* (Paris, 1889), 317.

[109] *AP*, CD 26 May 1826: 271.

[110] See e.g. *Débats*, 28 May 1826; *Constitutionnel*, 14 Aug. 1826 (accusing Frayssinous of treason); Bertier de Sauvigny, *Le Comte Ferdinand de Bertier*, 396–8.

[111] Frayssinous in CP 4 July 1826, quoted in Burnichon, *La Compagnie de Jésus en France*, i. 365. The government made matters worse by removing this phrase from the version of the speech published in the *Moniteur*.

[112] *Courrier*, 31 May 1826.

the government did, according to Salgues, seemed to lead in this direction.[113]

Frayssinous's speech, and the reaction to it, consolidated and aggravated the double process whereby anti-government feeling rebounded on the Jesuits, and anti-jesuit feeling on the government. The two were by now hardly distinguishable, as Liberal journalists explaining the significance of Montlosier's campaign to readers abroad made clear. 'To denounce the Jesuits in 1826, in France, is neither more nor less than to demand a complete change in the internal administration of the country,' Stendhal told the British in October, while Thiers in January informed the Germans: 'The word Jesuit today characterizes the whole system of the government.'[114] The government was damned for its failure to stamp out the Jesuits (especially after the Chambre des Pairs' adoption of the anti-jesuit part of Montlosier's petition); the Jesuits were damned because general antipathy to the government's politics was constantly expressed as denunciation of Jesuit domination. Thus, the most resented legislative proposal of the 1827 session, Peyronnet's press bill (the notorious 'loi de justice et d'amour'), was represented by the hostile press as purely and simply a Jesuit measure: 'dictated by Montrouge',[115] drafted with the assistance of Jesuit casuists, and vetted by the Jesuit General, it constituted,

[113] Salgues, *Courtes Observations*, 91.
[114] Stendhal in *New Monthly Magazine*, 17: 303; Thiers in *Augsburger Allgemeine Zeitung*, 30 Jan. 1827, repr. in R. Marquant, *Thiers et le baron Cotta: Étude sur la collaboration de Thiers à la Gazette d'Augsbourg* (Paris, 1959), 392.
[115] Montrouge was in reality the home of the French Jesuit noviciate during the Restoration years, but it had a far larger significance in the anti-jesuit imagination. Situated on the southern threshold of Paris, and in a region riddled with catacombs, and thus well suited to serve as a symbol of imminent threat and occult influence, it became the focus for an outlandish mythology of secret passages (to the Tuileries), hidden armaments, and subterranean ceremonies; for details, see A. Lirac [C. Clair], *Les Jésuites et la liberté religieuse sous la Restauration* (Paris, 1879), 46–7; Delattre (ed.), *Les Établissements*, iii. 616–19. Thanks in part to the writings of a former inmate, the one-time Jesuit novice Marcet (*soi-disant* abbé Martial Marcet de la Roche-Arnaud), it also came to be regarded as the principal centre of Jesuit intrigue and occult government for France, and even perhaps for other countries. Its superior, Père Gury, was presented by Marcet, in *Les Jésuites modernes, pour faire suite au Mémoire de M. le comte de Montlosier* (Paris, 1826), 81, as a secret despot, whose slightest glance could mobilize a thousand daggers to assassinate princes and destroy empires. Constant usage turned 'Montrouge' into frequent shorthand for Jesuitism envisaged as occult government (even in 1825, *Le Constitutionnel* routinely used terms like 'the police of Mont-Rouge' and 'the newspaper of Mont-Rouge'). Like 'the Kremlin' or 'Wall Street' in other polemical traditions, it lent an often spurious air of geographical unity and precision to the vision of conspiracy.

according to *Le Constitutionnel*, 'the pledge of this holy union' between government and Jesuits.[116] Lacretelle, in a letter published in both *Le Constitutionnel* and the *Journal des débats*, denied the government paternity of its own bill, which he described as a watered-down version of a more ferocious Jesuit draft. 'It is thus no longer the government that tolerates Jesuits,' he added, 'it is the Jesuits who tolerate the government. They say to it: *Sign*, and the government signs. They say to it: *Get angry*, and the government gets angry.'[117] By early 1827 a certain view of France's predicament must have become deeply familiar to readers of the opposition press. Two short passages, coincidentally taken from different Liberal papers on the same day in January, reveal its terms: 'the Jesuits, proscripts in law, are our masters in fact'; 'don't delude yourselves that Jesuits will deliver us from the Jesuits.'[118]

The main steps by which the Jesuit question became a central political issue in Restoration France, and anti-jesuitism a major feature or vehicle of political opposition, have now been traced. It has been shown, apropos of Montlosier, how anti-jesuitism could form part of a conservative view of Restoration politics. Baron de Frénilly, an Ultra, later recalled that the Jesuit question had been 'an apple of discord thrown into our ranks by the Liberals'; he had to admit that it 'divided the best royalists'.[119] Prefects' reports from several *départements* in 1827 told a similar story. From the Moselle, in February, it was reported that men of sincere religious and monarchist sympathies saw in the government's toleration of the Jesuits evidence either of its inability to act against them or of its secret desire to re-establish them. 'All the royalists who are in this frame of mind are drawing away from the government,' warned the Prefect, 'and I would be concealing the truth if I did not say that the number of these new dissidents increases daily.'[120] At Amiens, though 'the so-called royalist opposition' was stated to be small and uninfluential, the Prefect declared that 'opinion is divided on the

---

[116] *Constitutionnel*, 30 Oct. 1826, 18, 23 Jan. 1827.

[117] *Constitutionnel* and *Débats*, 31 Jan. 1827.

[118] *Constitutionnel*, 21 Jan. 1827; *Courrier*, 21 Jan. 1827.

[119] Baron de Frénilly, *Souvenirs*, ed. A. Chuquet, new edn. (Paris, 1909), 522.

[120] AN F⁷ 6770 (Moselle), Prefect to *Ministre de l'Intérieur*, 28 Feb. 1827. Ibid. (Loire), Prefect to *Directeur-général de police*, 4 Mar. 1827, reported that a number of local royalists had picked up fears about the Jesuits and the Congrégation in Parisian salons.

question of the Jesuits'.[121] The propensity of a section of royalist opinion to believe the worst of the Jesuits, and of the government for tolerating the Jesuits, undoubtedly enhanced anti-jesuitism's political significance; it prevented the consolidation of conservative forces in a front against Liberalism. It was among Liberals themselves, however, that anti-jesuit beliefs gained the widest currency and met with least contradiction, and in the columns of the Liberal press that the perspective of anti-jesuitism was most incessantly imposed on the reporting and interpretation of current affairs.

A sense of what anti-jesuitism meant within the framework of Liberal attitudes may be obtained by taking *Le Constitutionnel* as an example. This was both France's leading newspaper (with a circulation of 20,000 and a much higher readership) and the one which attained the most lasting reputation as (in the Jesuit bibliographer Carayon's phrase) 'the model of the anti-jesuit genre'.[122] In 1825–7 its columns were sometimes almost saturated with the Jesuit question: in the issue of 20 August 1826, for example, the first three items under the 'Interior' rubric were an approving comment on the Cour Royale's judgement on Montlosier's *Dénonciation*, an extract from a letter exposing the existence of a Jesuit school, and a contribution to a running polemic about Jesuit regicidal doctrine. *Le Constitutionnel* was always alert for fresh evidence or rumour of Jesuit establishments; it printed details of legal proceedings that were of interest only because foul play by Jesuits was suspected; it blamed those it called 'the Jesuits', among much else, for the shortcomings of French industry and for the sentiments of Pierrot, the blind street-singer of Nantes.[123] Its horizons were broad, for it believed that 'the *congréganistes* and the Jesuits of all countries'

[121] AN F⁷ 6772 (Somme), Prefect to *Ministre de l'Intérieur*, 1 Mar. 1827.

[122] A. Carayon, *Bibliographie historique de la Compagnie de Jésus; ou Catalogue des ouvrages relatifs à l'histoire des jésuites depuis leur origine jusqu'à nos jours* (Paris, 1864), 537. In the pamphlet and *brochure* press, no single Liberal work had the impact of Montlosier's *Mémoire*, perhaps partly because none so successfully combined theoretical discussion with scandalous revelation. For the former, Liberals could turn to abbé de Pradt's *Du jésuitisme ancien et moderne* (Paris, 1825); for the latter, to the works of Marcet, especially *Les Jésuites modernes, Mémoires d'un jeune jésuite; ou Conjuration de Mont-Rouge, développée par des faits* (Paris, 1828), and *Nouveau Mémoire à consulter du jeune jésuite sur l'état actuel des jésuites en France, des évêques et des prêtres, suivi de la pétition à la Chambre des Députés* (Paris, 1829).

[123] *Constitutionnel*, 13 Jan. 1827 (industry), 15 Jan. 1828 (Pierrot).

were in concert to dominate peoples and kings.[124] Its vigilant eye
extended to London (where it found a Jesuit agent distributing
pamphlets on Waterloo Bridge[125]), to Ireland, Galicia, and (in 1830)
Naxos, but especially to countries geographically or dynastically
close to France, Jesuit encroachments in which might have repercussions at home: Switzerland, Portugal (after Dom Miguel's coup
of 1828), the Low Countries, Savoy, parts of Italy, and above all
Spain.[126]

Le Constitutionnel publicized and supported works written against
the Jesuits by conservatives like Montlosier, Salgues, and Silvy, as
well as by Liberals like abbé de Pradt. The theoretical bases of its
own anti-jesuitism were most clearly stated in two articles published on 23 and 24 September 1826. On 23, the paper proclaimed:

If France is appalled at the new apparition of the Jesuits, one need not
be astonished; she sees in it the counter-revolution in its entirety, a war
to the death against her institutions, against her laws, her *mœurs*, her enlightenment and her prosperity; the ruination of the liberty which she only
obtained through so many efforts and sacrifices, and the return of the bloody
regime of theocracy.

The Jesuits, the article continued, had constantly striven to 'arrest
the soaring of the human spirit, to stifle civilization, and to rob
man of the enjoyment of the faculties which he holds from the
author of his being'; their mission in France in the 1820s was to
restore theocracy and feudalism.[127] Here was one recurrent strand
in *Le Constitutionnel*'s anti-jesuitism: the familiar Liberal identification of the Society of Jesus with counter-revolution, conceived in
a broad cultural as well as a narrow political sense, accompanied
by the attribution of France's present decadence (often implicitly
contrasted with her Revolutionary and Napoleonic glories[128]) to
Jesuit influence. 'Europe is marching with great strides towards a

---

[124] Ibid. 27 June 1826.   [125] Ibid. 28 July 1826.
[126] Specific references are listed in Cubitt, 'The Myth of a Jesuit Conspiracy',
107 n.   [127] *Constitutionnel*, 23 Sept. 1826.
[128] For an explicit statement of the contrast, see AN F[7] 6706 (Seine 1823–6) for
the song 'Les Belges à leurs voisins', circulating in the *département* of the Seine
(forwarded by the *Directeur-général des postes* to the *Directeur-général de police*, 8 July
1826). Recalling their period under Napoleonic rule, the Belgians taunted the
French: 'Nous étions fiers d'être Français... | ... Illusions détruites !!! | Vos
aigles seront désormais, | Les croix de vos Jésuites.' They concluded by asking the
French to instruct their frontier officials 'De laisser pénétrer vos vins, | Mais gardez
vos Jésuites.'

new system; everywhere civilization is uneasily acquainting itself
with the new destinies which await it; and we, passive spectators
at these great events, we are sleeping on the edge of a precipice,'
lamented the author of a slightly earlier article. 'Delivered to the
Jesuits, invaded on all sides by the *parti prêtre* . . . France resembles
a vast cloister closed to the century.'[129]

The article of 24 September brought out a quite different face of
Liberal anti-jesuitism: an anti-pluralist emphasis on national unity,
affecting to place itself above the standpoint of particular political
interest. The argument is stated in general terms:

The principle of association, excellent and conservative when it is applied
to the great human societies, becomes the most active of dissolvents when
it gives rise to particular affiliations in a state; then *esprit de corps* takes the
place of love of the *patrie*; the ties which are closer, and which seem to
present more immediate advantages, cause one to renounce the general
bond of all citizens with society; the interests are shifted, and soon, instead
of a close-knit population, united by the same sentiments, there is nothing
in a country but isolated, rival, antagonistic little associations; anarchy is
organized; and this is how a principle applied without discernment becomes for nations a germ of decadence and death.

Religious orders under foreign leadership were a particularly intolerable species of sectarian grouping, *Le Constitutionnel* went on
to explain, and the Jesuits, by virtue of their unbridled ambition,
deplorable doctrine, 'system of domination', and record of criminal
fanaticism, were the worst of them.[130] Other articles placed the
Jesuits and their allies in a similar perspective, as agents, beneficiaries, and symbols of national disintegration. The Jesuits themselves were repeatedly represented either as a rival and usurping
nation—'a nation apart which has taken over the soil, which
arranges it for its own use, exploits it for its own profit'[131]—or as
the disruptive agents of a conspiracy against France by foreign
powers jealous of her prosperity and enlightenment but unable to
destroy her by military means.[132] The type of public spirit in which
Le Constitutionnel (in an article published early in 1828) sought a
barrier against such anti-national intrigues was described in explicitly anti-pluralist terms:

---

[129] *Constitutionnel*, 12 Sept. 1826.
[130] Ibid. 24 Sept. 1826.   [131] Ibid. 11 June 1826.
[132] Ibid. 19 July 1825, 12 May, 9, 13 July, 25 Aug., 29 Nov. 1826, 13 Nov. 1827,
all offer variations on this xenophobic theme.

Family affections, personal sentiments must disappear before the general interest; this is the only way to foil once again the ever-flagrant conspiracies of the Jesuits, the *congréganistes*, the *parti prêtre*, and the irreconcilable enemies of order, of the country's prosperity, and hence of constitutional monarchy.[133]

Liberalism itself had accordingly to be defended against any imputation of sectarianism: *Le Constitutionnel* was at pains to dismiss the alleged Jacobin threat to political and religious authority as a diversionary Jesuit fabrication. It even went so far as to hint at Jesuit responsibility for the excesses of the Revolution,[134] and to accuse the Jesuits of secretly publishing immoral books in order to establish grounds for abolishing the freedom of the press.[135]

The two sets of professed values which ran together in *Le Constitutionnel*'s anti-jesuitism—those of faith in progress and liberty and those of concern with unity and order—did so in Restoration Liberalism more generally. The potential divergence between them was kept in check so long as Liberals remained out of power and uniformly convinced of the government's unacceptability. When this consensus broke down, as it did to a limited extent in 1828–9, and more clearly after 1830, a split would appear in Liberal opinion, and be reflected in anti-jesuit polemic, between those satisfied with the status quo, who emphasized the importance of unity, and the disenchanted, who stressed the priority of further progress. In 1825–7, however, the Liberal anti-governmental front was intact; *Le Constitutionnel*'s anti-jesuitism during this period expressed the conviction that the rulership of France was in the hands of a usurping, reactionary, anti-national sect.

Thus all branches of public administration were deemed to be riddled with Jesuit agents and *congréganistes*. Complaining that the sons and nephews of high state functionaries were always sent to Jesuit schools, *Le Constitutionnel* demanded: 'Is it not from this nursery that have already emerged men who have only left the school bench to occupy great posts in the administration, who

[133] Ibid. 12 Mar. 1828.
[134] Ibid. 20 July 1825: 'Doesn't one find the Jesuits everywhere? Doesn't one find one of them in the celebrated affair of the necklace [in 1785]? Didn't they have their revenge to take on the House of Bourbon? One knows how far Jesuit revenge can go. If they remained strangers to the Revolution, why does one recognize among their most fanatical affiliates so many *bonnets rouges* and men of 1793?'
[135] Ibid. 30 Aug. 1826.

surround the ministers and command them?'[136] The police, under the control of the Chevaliers de la Foi Franchet d'Esperey and Delavau—both simply 'Jesuits' in *Le Constitutionnel*'s parlance[137] —were considered especially subject to Jesuit management. Their sins both of omission (failure to deal with mad dogs) and of commission (cruelty to political prisoners, violence towards mourners at the funeral of the duc de la Rochefoucauld-Liancourt) were ascribed to their preoccupation with serving the Jesuits, or their docility to Jesuit orders, or their inspiration by the Jesuits' fanatical spirit.[138] In November 1826 *Le Constitutionnel* voiced the suspicion that the police were neglecting their duty to suppress violent crime as part of a Jesuit plot to distract attention from attacks on the Constitution, or alternatively to provide a pretext for recruiting 500 more Jesuitical gendarmes.[139]

The Jesuits' most prominent accomplices, in *Le Constitutionnel*'s eyes, were, of course, to be found in Villèle's government. In an article of October 1826 two groups of ministers were distinguished: those who actively 'protected' the Jesuits (Frayssinous, Damas, Clermont-Tonnerre, Doudeauville) and those who more passively 'tolerated' them (Villèle, Corbière, Peyronnet, Chabrol).[140] Frayssinous, after his speech on 25 May, was widely regarded, by both Liberal and conservative anti-jesuits, as the Jesuits' most active agent in the government.[141] Villèle, on the other hand, sometimes emerged as a victim as well as an accomplice of Jesuitism, a man not wholly in sympathy with the Jesuits but hopelessly bound to them. In October 1825 *Le Constitutionnel* claimed that Villèle had incurred Jesuit displeasure, and should listen to Montlosier; a year later it reported his inability to break loose from the Jesuits and the Congrégation.[142] The pathetic dependence of 'the head clerk of Montrouge' (as *Le Constitutionnel* called him[143]) illustrated in

[136] Ibid. 10 Dec. 1825 (also 9 Nov. 1826: 'Montrouge is the *école normale* of constitutional France').   [137] Ibid. 12 Nov. 1827.
[138] Ibid. Apr. 1825 (mad dogs), 9 June 1826 (political prisoners), 5 Apr. 1827 (violence at funeral).
[139] Ibid. 9, 22 Nov. 1826.   [140] Ibid. 5 Oct. 1826.
[141] See e.g. Montlosier, *Dénonciation*, 222; L.-A.-F. Cauchois-Lemaire, *Lettres historiques adressées à Sa Grandeur Monseigneur le Cte de Peyronnet, Garde des Sceaux, Ministre de la Justice* (Paris, 1827), 42.
[142] *Constitutionnel*, 13 Oct. 1825, 30 Oct. 1826; Stendhal in *New Monthly Magazine*, 17: 280 (Oct. 1826), claimed that Villèle's private secretary was a Jesuit and that he was unable to sack him.   [143] *Constitutionnel*, 24 Jan. 1827.

miniature what Liberals saw as the moral bankruptcy of his Jesuit-dominated administration. 'The RR.PP. of the Company of Jesus have offered their mysterious support to an ageing power, and the best has had to be made of it, though certain ministers sometimes permit themselves blasphemies against the turbulent disciples of Loyola,' wrote Lacretelle.[144] Another writer suggested a deeper spiritual affinity between the Jesuits and the government:

From the moment that it became necessary to falsify principles by consequences, to spoil the nature of things by the choice of men, to set the constitution and the laws at war with each other, Jesuitism entered the administration. From then on, the door was open again to the Jesuits; this was the militia necessary to the system.[145]

Clearly, the convergence and intertwining of anti-jesuit and anti-governmental themes which had become familiar in disgruntled polemic by 1827 could translate a variety of perceptions of the actual relationship between the government and the Society of Jesus, ranging from a total identification at one extreme to a loose analogy at the other, passing through various degrees of alliance, connivance, and affinity. When the government, its supporters, or its acts were attacked in the idiom of anti-jesuitism, it was not always clear which, or which combination, of these possible relationships was meant to be conveyed. Nevertheless, the cumulative effect of such attacks was certainly to corrode respect for Villèle and his colleagues, by levelling against them a triple imputation: of neglect of duty (in tolerating the Jesuits), of treason (in collaborating with them), and of deep 'Jesuitism' of spirit. The various sins and failings of the government and its agents were marshalled under a single heading—Jesuit orientation—which made each one a sign of fundamental illegitimacy. Anti-jesuitism gave a common colouring, a perceived underlying sameness, to the numerous different reasons for detesting the government; it reinforced the intensity with which each one was felt, and made it harder to remove. In this way, it contributed to the government's downfall.

The complexity of the connections that had grown up in the public mind between the Jesuits, the spirit of Jesuitism, and the

---

[144] Ibid. 31 Jan. 1827.   [145] Ibid. 31 Aug. 1826.

Villèle government can best be observed in the way they unravelled
in the aftermath of the government's decisive defeat in the elections of November 1827. Shortly before the eventual change of
government on 5 January 1828 the *Journal des débats* summarized
the position. Since the Jesuits were basically a faction conspiring
against the *Charte*, it declared, the Jesuit question was properly
a political rather than a judicial one, but it had been impossible
to treat it as such so long as the government and Chambre des
Députés were in the Jesuit camp. Now, however, deliverance from
the Jesuits need no longer be sought from the *Code pénal* and the
Bulletin des lois; it could be exacted as a duty from the new, non-
Jesuitical Chamber. The Jesuit faction consisted of men and doctrines. To get rid of the men, all the Chamber had to do was get rid
of the Villèle government. Whatever their differences when in
power, Villèle and the 'men of Jesuitism' would fall together, for
both were fatally implicated in 'the system of these last five years'.
Jesuitical doctrines should then be fought not by persecution, but
by constructive legislation in the spirit of the *Charte*. Jesuitism,
after all, was essentially 'the last attempt of absolute power'. It
followed that 'everything done for liberty will be done against the
Jesuits', but it was not so certain that 'everything done against
Jesuitism would be done for liberty'.[146]

The natural connection which the *Journal des débats* perceived
between triumphant Liberal statesmanship and the diminution of
Jesuit influence, seemingly making specific measures against the
Society of Jesus unnecessary, might seem plausible to the erstwhile
opposition in the first flush of victory. The emergence of the
compromise government unofficially headed by Martignac, however, diluted, without entirely destroying, anti-jesuit confidence.
What were people who had just spent two years denouncing men
like Frayssinous and Vaulchier as Jesuit agents to make of a
government which retained the former as Minister for Ecclesiastical
Affairs and continued to employ the latter as *directeur-général des
postes*? Anti-jesuits quickly came to regard a willingness to take
concrete measures against the Jesuits as an indispensable guarantee of the government's own un-Jesuitical character. Noting on
21 January that no such measures had yet been set afoot, *Le
Constitutionnel* was suspicious that the Jesuits had merely switched

[146] *Débats*, 2 Jan. 1828.

allies. In February, it reasserted that the Jesuit question was
France's most important problem, and warned the government: 'if
it does not openly separate itself from the Jesuitical influence, it
will be subject to it, it will be regarded as Jesuit, and however
constitutional its words, they will not be believed, for the sole principle of Jesuitism is falsehood.'[147] In parts of provincial France, fear
of the Jesuits ran as high as, or higher than, before.[148]

The steps the government did take in the matter of the Jesuits
irritated many anti-jesuits by their circuitousness. What France
wanted, according to *Le Courrier français* in January, was simply the
execution of the laws against the Jesuits;[149] what she got, at the end
of the month, was the appointment of a commission to investigate
the *petits séminaires*. Worse still, though the commission's members
were unanimous in indicating abuses in the *petit séminaire* system,
they ended up divided over the Jesuits: four found their position
in the *petits séminaires* illegal, but the other five accepted them as
priests subject to episcopal authority.[150] Though the commission's
report was not published till late June, this defeat for the anti-jesuit
opinion was known by rumour by mid-May. *Le Courrier français*
was outraged that the government's timorous failure to take the
straightforward path should have produced such a result: 'Thus
a Chamber nominated in hatred of Jesuitism will have assembled
only to see a sort of legal sanction given to the Jesuits' public existence.' Nevertheless, it hastened to point out, the government was
not bound by the commission's decision; its conduct now would
show whether it was the guardian of the law or the defender of the
Jesuits.[151] In the Chamber itself, various *députés* voiced their indignation, or their suspicion of the government's liability to Jesuit

[147] *Constitutionnel*, 21 Jan., 2, 5 Feb. 1828. J. Desmalis, *Le Cri d'alarme; ou La
France aux prises avec l'hydre jésuitique* (Paris, 1828), captures the mood of the moment, trusting the *députés* rather than the government to strike down the Jesuitical
monster.

[148] AN F^7 6771 (Basses-Pyrénées), Prefect to *Ministre de l'Intérieur*, 2 June 1828,
reported: 'The words Congrégation and Jesuit, scarcely pronounced in this region
six months before the dissolution of the Chamber, are today on everyone's lips.
The most timid are afraid of them, as they would be of an enemy army advancing
to invade the territory, to burn and lay waste its properties.' Ibid. (Saône-et-Loire),
Prefect to *Ministre de l'Intérieur*, 1 July 1828, stated that the inhabitants, before the
recent *ordonnances*, 'were crying out against the invasion of Jesuitism, whose influence was ridiculously exaggerated'.   [149] *Courrier*, 7 Jan. 1828.

[150] A. Garnier, *Les Ordonnances du 16 juin 1828, d'après des documents inédits tirés des
Archives du Vatican et des Archives Nationales* (Paris, 1929), 64.

[151] *Courrier*, 12, 13 May 1828.

influence.[152] Mgr. Feutrier, who had replaced Frayssinous as Minister for Ecclesiastical Affairs in March, tried on 30 May to allay these suspicions. However, any calming effect that might have been achieved by his denial that the Jesuits were influencing ministers and bishops, or by his indication that their case was shortly to occupy the Conseil du Roi, was squandered by his insistence that 'as individuals, they have a right to public esteem, and I take pleasure in bearing witness to their virtues, to their probity, to their unselfishness'.[153] To anti-jesuits this sounded altogether too much like the 'tolerant' Frayssinous of 1826. The Chamber's mood was such that Dupin *aîné* could plunge it into momentary disarray by claiming to have found the Jesuit monogram displayed above a temporary altar in front of its own building.[154] Finally, on 14 June, Labbey de Pompières moved the *mise en accusation* of Villèle and his colleagues for transgressions among which their toleration of the Jesuits figured prominently, to the obvious embarrassment of their successors, who had still to end it.

Under this pressure, anxious to safeguard its majority, the government finally secured from the king two *ordonnances*, dated 16 June. The first, countersigned by Portalis, the *Garde des Sceaux*, dealt with the Jesuits: one article placed their eight existing schools under Université control; the next established that in future no one was to direct or teach in either a Université school or a *petit séminaire* unless he had affirmed in writing that he did not belong to any 'religious congregation not legally established in France'. The second *ordonnance*, countersigned by Feutrier, imposed restrictions designed to confine the remaining *petits séminaires* to the narrow function of educating future clergy, but also ordained the funding of 8,000 *demi-bourses* to assist in this.[155] For the time being, the *ordonnances* killed the Jesuit system of secondary education in France. The calming of anti-jesuit apprehensions was slower and

[152] *AP*, CD 16 May 1828 (Petou and Viennet), 29 May 1828 (de Corcelles).
[153] *AP*, CD 30 May 1828: 403. On the political ill-effects of this speech, see the remarks of Thiers, reproduced in Marquant, *Thiers et le baron Cotta*, 449.
[154] *AP*, CD 7 June 1828: 576–7. The incident arose from the presence on the altar of the monogram IHS. Catholics maintained that this was not peculiar to the Jesuits, but in general use in churches. *Courrier*, 9 June 1828, remained unconvinced: 'if it is everywhere nowadays, it is because nowadays the Jesuits are everywhere.'
[155] The *Ordonnances* are reprinted in A. Debidour, *Histoire des rapports de l'Église et de l'État en France de 1789 à 1870* (Paris, 1898), 699–701. On their political and diplomatic circumstances, see Garnier, *Les Ordonnances*.

more partial. Some, like the *député* Petou, suspected a governmental
manœuvre to secure the budget, and declined to give thanks till
they saw the *ordonnances* put into effect.[156] Others questioned the
adequacy of a measure which did not even name the Society of
Jesus, let alone suppress it. How sure a safeguard was an oath
of non-membership, applied to an order whose theologians were
notoriously casual about the sanctity of oaths? What was the point
of shutting eight schools, when the other *petits séminaires*, probably
equally Jesuit in spirit if not in personnel, were actively supported?
What good would a closure of Jesuit schools do, if the Congrégation remained the fountainhead of honours and employment?
Anti-jesuits asked all these questions, more or less rhetorically. *Le
Constitutionnel* held that the trial of Villèle and his associates would
have thwarted the Jesuits much more effectively.[157] 'I hope you are
not dupes of the two *ordonnances*,' Montlosier wrote to Barante, 'the
Jesuits are better anchored than ever'.[158] Nevertheless, whatever
their doubts about its efficacy, most anti-jesuits seemed willing
to be convinced that the government's measure marked a defeat of
sorts for the Jesuits, and a severing of whatever links might have
existed between them and the government. On 21 June the Chambre des Députés voted, on the advice of the *rapporteur* de Sade,
to forward petitions by Salgues and Dutasta (for the expulsion
of the Jesuits) and by Marcet (for a new anti-jesuit law) to the
relevant ministers. A week earlier, this would have implied sharp
criticism of government neglect; now it was presented as support
for the government's resolution to enforce legality. In this debate
and that on the budget the following month, anti-jesuit orators like
the Dupin brothers welcomed the *ordonnances* and defended them
against the charge of persecution.[159] The evident dismay of the
Jesuits' supporters ('this sorrowing of iniquity, disappointed in its
covetous hopes', as Charles Dupin called the feelings of the parents
of Jesuit pupils[160]) helped reassure anti-jesuits that the government
had not pulled its punch. The close connection between anti-
jesuitism and political opposition was broken. Unlike the Villèle
administration, Martignac's government had incurred the charge
of 'Jesuitism' not as a comment on and explanation of its whole
perceived political direction, but largely for its simple failure to

[156] *AP*, CD 7 July 1828.   [157] *Constitutionnel*, 20 June 1828.
[158] Quoted in Bardoux, *Le Comte de Montlosier*, 291–2.
[159] *AP*, CD 21 June, 7 July, 8 Aug. 1828.   [160] *AP*, CD 8 July 1828: 640.

take steps against the Jesuits; now that it was seen to have taken them, it ceased to incur it to any great extent, and anti-jesuitism therefore became less urgent and less politically significant. The *ordonnances* themselves achieved a place in the affections of Gallican jurists that the subsequent branding of their royal signatory as a Jesuit puppet did nothing to shake.

For the remaining duration of the Martignac regime, mainstream Liberal papers like *Le Constitutionnel* made relatively little play with the Jesuit theme. The practice of some of those further to the left, however, shows that the perceived recession of the Jesuit threat opened the way for further experiments in the use of 'Jesuit' as a derogatory term. *L'Ancien Album*, the revived version of *L'Album*, launched in November 1828, provides an example. Its view of contemporary political alignments is well illustrated by a cartoon it published in January, showing three men in a *cabinet littéraire*: a Jesuit, reading of the doings of past and prospective Ultra ministers in the pages of the *Gazette* and the *Quotidienne*; an 'enormous *fusionnaire* or *ventru* of the new regime' (wearing the insignia of monarchy but also, hidden from view, those of Republic and Empire), reading the *Débats* and the *Constitutionnel*; finally, a young man immersed in literature fit only for 'true friends of liberty', namely the *Courrier français* and the *Ancien Album*.[161] Here, as in the conventional Liberal view, the Jesuit was identified with Ultra reaction, the political orientation of the previous government. Another cartoon, which reproduced the same three categories, added the dynamic relationship between them: a similar young man was shown kicking a 'false patriot', who simultaneously kicked 'an *affiliée* of Montrouge'.[162] This could well have served to illustrate Alexis Dumesnil's article in the journal's opening issue in November. Dumesnil recalled *L'Album*'s earlier anti-jesuit record, but declared that the Jesuits had now been defeated. It was therefore proper to leave Jesuit-baiting to such cowardly hypocrites as found it a painless way of striking an opposition pose with which to cover their own treachery.[163]

Yet Dumesnil seemed reluctant to discard good abusive terminology just because its object had disappeared, for these hypocritical anti-jesuits instantly became Jesuits themselves: 'I have said it and I

[161] *L'Ancien Album*, 30 Jan. 1829: 304–5.   [162] Ibid. 20 May 1829: 401–2.
[163] Ibid. 25 Nov. 1828: 1–2.

repeat it, not all the Jesuits are at Montrouge. How many so-called liberals, ostentatious protectors of the poor people, are at bottom bigger Jesuits than P. Loriquet and P. Ronsin!'[164] Dumesnil's articles set an example which was followed in the months ahead. Occasionally *L'Ancien Album* dealt with the real Society of Jesus, but more usually anti-jesuit language was used to describe *Le Constitutionnel* ('jésuitique' or at best 'jésuitico-libérale'), or men like Portalis ('Jesuit's looks, Jesuit's clothes, Jesuit's heart, he is all Jesuit, though a Jansenist'), Lacretelle (one of the 'Escobars of liberalism'), or Dupin *aîné* (chided repeatedly for his appearances as an honoured guest at Saint-Acheul in 1825).[165] Such men were champions of Liberal or Gallican anti-jesuitism, the equivalents not of the Jesuit in the *cabinet littéraire* cartoon, but of the *fusionnaire*. Their 'jesuitism', in their critics' eyes, seems to have consisted of two things: firstly, their display of a deviousness and deceitfulness traditionally associated with the Society of Jesus; secondly, an inner resemblance between their supposedly treacherous, anti-national politics and that of the other 'Jesuits', of Montrouge and Villèlism. And this resemblance could be seen as a likely basis for collaboration: ashamed of their rivalry, the *Ancien Album* sarcastically reported, the two 'Jesuit' camps had agreed to join hands 'for the greater prosperity of the country'.[166]

The diverging attitudes of different shades of Liberal or left-wing opinion under the Martignac regime were thus reflected in different ways of using anti-jesuit vocabulary. This was to happen again under the July Monarchy. The advent of the Polignac administration in August 1829, however, put an end to the divergence for the time being. Faced with a new onslaught of Ultra government, *L'Ancien Album* returned to old ways: suddenly the Jesuits, dismissed as a broken force by Dumesnil less than a year before, emerged again as 'the greatest enemies whom we have to fight';[167] the Jesuitism of bloated Liberals was forgotten. *Le Constitutionnel*, for its part, was busy detecting the Jesuit interest in the re-combination of the Ministries of Education and Ecclesiastical

---

[164] Ibid. 3.
[165] Ibid. 5 July 1829: 174, and 20 June 1829: 119 (*Le Constitutionnel*); 25 Apr. 1829: 279 (Portalis); 15 Dec. 1828: 74 (Lacretelle); 30 Dec. 1828: 156, 20 Mar. 1829: 116, and 15 Apr. 1829: 217–21 (Dupin). On Dupin's visits, see his *Mémoires*, 4 vols. (Paris, 1855–61), i. 220–7, 487–505; also P. Bliard, *Le Père Loriquet: La Légende et l'histoire*, 2nd edn. (Paris, 1922), 83–90.
[166] *L'Ancien Album*, 15 Feb. 1829: 376–7.   [167] Ibid. 15 Aug. 1829: 13–15.

Affairs and the suspension of Liberal professors.[168] After a ministerial reshuffle in November, it denounced 'a government entirely
and exclusively devoted to the Jesuits', a puppet administration
ready to be manipulated by the masters 'behind the curtain'. The
fate of this government, it remarked in February, would finally
determine whether or not France could be bent to the Jesuit
yoke.[169]

Le Constitutionnel was soon able to offer its readers a 'great revelation' of the Polignac regime's origins in a 'vast conspiracy which
menaces the freedom of peoples and the progress of civilization'.
A correspondent in Munich supplied a purported account of the
experiences of a young German naturalist who had chanced, while
taking refuge at the Mont-Saint-Bernard hospice early the previous
summer, to overhear an animated conversation, in which plans for
'the prince' to take over the administration were outlined. 'Villèle
was too politic,' remarked one speaker; 'we needed a man who
would risk all to gain all; happily we have found him.' Another
ominously remarked that counter-revolutions could only be made
by violence and terror. A few dropped names and references
revealed the Jesuit or Jesuitical nature of the plotters, who thereafter said little that readers of *Le Constitutionnel* would not have
expected. News from various parts of Europe was commented
on, orders exchanged, the importance of controlling the education
of future monarchs was stressed. Dining in company with the
conspirators later, the naturalist gained information on some of
the conspiracy's agents, most notably an ex-minister who acted as
'lieutenant-general of the chief of the Jesuits for the Province of
France'. A subsequent encounter, at Brigg, convinced him that:

there existed in that part of Europe a sovereign committee which hides
itself in the shadows, dictating the orders of the counter-revolution, full of
contempt for kings and of hatred for free institutions, which works night
and day for their downfall, and whose power, if it is not contained by the
vigilance and the patriotism of the peoples, will raise itself one day on the
ruins of civilization and of liberty.[170]

Though most French anti-jesuits continued to see Rome or
Montrouge, rather than the Swiss Alps, as the likely centre of
conspiracy, the purported revelations from the Mont-Saint-Bernard

---

[168] *Constitutionnel*, 12 Aug., 25 Sept. 1829.
[169] Ibid. 24 Nov. 1829, 4 Feb. 1830.   [170] Ibid. 24 Feb. 1830.

no doubt encouraged a tendency to see the coming of Polignac as part of a Jesuit-orchestrated scheme of counter-revolution on a European scale.

Despite the crucial role of Charles X in the creation of Polignac's ministry, *Le Constitutionnel* would still go no further in the direction of implicating the throne in the Jesuit conspiracy than the usual cryptic but not openly disrespectful solemn reminder of the fate of the Jesuit-compromised Stuarts.[171] For others, however, royal Jesuitism was no longer a matter for erudite hinting, especially after Charles X nailed his colours even more firmly to Polignac's mast by his menacing remarks about opposition, in the speech from the throne in March 1830. Coins representing the king as a Jesuit had circulated in parts of France as early as 1826 and 1827, apparently amusing even some royalists.[172] This hitherto surreptitious iconographic tradition came into the open on 3 May, when *La Silhouette* published perhaps the simplest yet most damaging political cartoon of the Restoration. Drawn by Philipon, this was a head-and-shoulders portrait of Charles (clearly recognizable by his large teeth and hanging lower lip) wearing ecclesiastical bands and skull-cap, entitled simply *Un jésuite*.[173] *La Silhouette*'s editor and printer were charged with offending the royal person, and sentenced to a fine and six months' imprisonment. Their defence (apart from the implausible claim that the resemblance was unintended) was to argue that the prosecution's suspicions were 'inopportune' (and by implication themselves risked offending royal dignity) unless it was shameful to be called a Jesuit, in which case the condemnation of *La Silhouette* would be a judgement on the Jesuits themselves.[174] This fooled no one; the cartoon's purpose was clearly to brand the monarch as a docile creature (merely 'a Jesuit', not a Jesuit leader) of the anti-national power the struggle against which had absorbed the recent history of France. It followed that the struggle could no longer be fought as a defence of *Charte* and Throne; it must be for *Charte* alone.

---

[171] Ibid. 18 Sept. 1829.

[172] Such coins, or rumours of them, were reported in AN F^7 6769 (Haute-Garonne), Prefect to *Ministre de l'Intérieur*, ? Mar. 1826, and F^7 6770 (Loire-Inférieure), Prefect to *Ministre de l'Intérieur*, 1 Mar. 1827; see also de Frénilly, *Souvenirs*, 522.

[173] *La Silhouette*, 2: 12. See J. Cuno, 'The Business and Politics of Caricature: Charles Philipon and La Maison Aubert', *Gazette des beaux-arts*, 106 (1985), 97–8.

[174] *La Silhouette*, 3: 1–3 (26 July 1830).

The four *ordonnances* which the king signed on 25 July—suspending freedom of the press, dissolving the freshly elected and anti-governmental Chamber, modifying the franchise, and calling new elections—could be fitted all too neatly into such a perspective. In the revolutionary days that followed, hostility to both the Jesuits and the political regime was intensified by the intimate association supposed to exist between them. To many, at the time and after, the July Revolution was as much an anti-jesuit as an anti-governmental revolt. The iconography of late 1830 and early 1831 bears this out strikingly. From the mass of cartoons and caricatures with an anti-jesuit theme, two motifs emerge with particular persistence.

The first was the Jesuit king. *La Silhouette* reissued *Un jésuite* with the caption: 'Portrait déclaré ressemblant à Charles X par jugement du tribunal de police correctionnelle'.[175] What had been a seditious novelty in May now became a caricaturist's convention: it was almost as rare after July to portray the fallen monarch without Jesuit trappings as without the distinctive teeth and lip. Even as the 'roi des veaux' or the royal 'cornichon', he still appeared *en jésuite*.[176] It was Charles's docile subservience to the Jesuit interest, and not any share in the proverbial Jesuit cunning, that the cartoonists meant to convey. He was portrayed either as a mere utensil—a candle-snuffer or a *'cruche* which the Jesuits used for their provisioning'[177]—or as a superstitious or infantile idiot. *L'Éducation jésuitique* showed the Jesuits teaching him to walk.[178] Other cartoons showed him as a penitent, submitting to the criminal and anti-constitutional demands of his Jesuit confessors.[179]

The second persistent theme was that of expulsion. Some cartoons simply showed Jesuits in flight or creeping away. *La Silhouette*, for example, portrayed a hideous semi-human 'bête

[175] Copies in BN Est.: Tf 57 (pp. 12–13), Tf 530, de Vinck (90) 11501, Hennin (165) 14468. Another cartoon, Tf 57 (pp. 16–17), showed Charles before, during, and after transformation into a Jesuit.

[176] BN Est.: de Vinck (90) 11418 and 11546 ('des veaux' was a pun for *dévot*; 'cornichon' had the double meaning gherkin/clot).

[177] BN Est.: Tf 57 (pp. 36–81), de Vinck (90) 11456 and 11507, for candle-snuffers; de Vinck (90) 11502 for the 'cruche' (jug/idiot).

[178] BN Est.: Tf 57 (p. 78).

[179] BN Est.: 57 (pp. 73–4). Hennin (164) 14388 is unusual in showing the king in a more active role, trying to leap across a river from a bank cluttered with constitutional emblems to one piled with emblems of despotism and Jesuitism, and clinging on to a breaking branch marked 'Jesuits'.

malfaisante', to illustrate a passage of macabre fantasy in which a group of such creatures celebrated a bloodthirsty sabbath before fleeing from the dawn, leaving the narrator startled to discover that they had not been beasts after all, but Jesuits.[180] More remarkable, however, are the numerous cartoons which showed the Jesuits being positively driven or herded out of France either by allegorical figures (as in *La Religion et la Charte expulsant les Jésuites*[181]), or by *gardes nationales* or revolutionary citizens. In *Départ forcé des bons Jésuites pour Holyrood*, one of the *gardes* held a paper with the legend: '*Charte* 1830. The present *Charte* and the rights which it consecrates are entrusted to the patriotism of the *gardes nationales*.' The caption recalled previous expulsions of the Society of Jesus, and affirmed: 'The latest revolution delivers us from them for ever.'[182] When one considers first that the 1828 *ordonnance* had substantially diminished the Jesuits' role in French affairs, and secondly that the July Revolution in reality entailed no new measures against them, the cartoonists' insistence on presenting that Revolution's achievement as an act of Jesuit-expulsion is significant. It bears striking witness to the way in which the Jesuits had come to symbolize the whole system in politics and religion that those who rebelled in 1830 believed themselves to be sweeping away.

To this general association of the Jesuits with the abhorred regime was added a wave of rumours assigning them a sinister role in the violence of the moment. Cartoons reflected this too. *Serment des braves* showed Jesuits with daggers swearing 'to uphold our good Frère Charlot and to massacre the stupid Parisian'.[183] There were also pictures of Jesuits doing arms-drill; the caption to one claimed that passers-by had witnessed such exercises taking place in their establishments ever since 1817. 'With what intentions did monks learn the art of war?' it asked rhetorically.[184] In August the Jesuit Provincial, Père Druilhet, summarized the rumours: 'It is they [the Jesuits] who managed the fatal *journées*, gunned down the good people; it is they who now stir up the workers, set fires in the countryside, etc.'[185] The charge of arson was bolstered in October

---

[180] *La Silhouette*, 3: 93 and facing 89. 'Un monsieur qui fuit le grand jour', in BN Est.: Tf 58 (p. 46), has a similar theme.   [181] BN Est.: Hennin (165) 14490.

[182] BN Est.: Tf 58 (p. 39). Similar expulsion images can be found in Tf 57 (p. 125), Tf 58 (p. 34), and *La Caricature*, 11 Nov. 1830.

[183] BN Est.: Tf 58 (p. 40).   [184] BN Est.: de Vinck (89) 11324.

[185] Quoted in Burnichon, *La Compagnie de Jésus en France*, i. 516. Several cartoons depicted Jesuits either as counter-revolutionary rabble-rousers or as (unsuccessful)

by a petty criminal, Berrié, who tried to convince the Chambre des Pairs that he had started fires in Normandy under orders from Polignac, relayed through 'the Congrégation of Montrouge'.[186]

Not surprisingly, given this background of long-term hostility and immediate fears, Jesuit communities faced deep suspicion and sometimes physical violence during the July Days and their aftermath. The Jesuits evacuated their establishments and abandoned ecclesiastical costume. Montrouge was invaded and pillaged on 28 July and again in the riots of February 1831. Saint-Acheul, attacked in the night of 29 July, was saved by the mob's timely discovery of its wine cellar and the equally timely arrival of troops. Armed men searched for hidden weapons in the Parisian *résidence* of the rue de Sèvres; at Dôle, the mayor carried out a similar search to allay public suspicions. There were similar alarms at other establishments.[187]

It was not a good time to be mistakenly identified as a Jesuit either. Priests venturing into the streets of Paris in *soutanes* were likely to be beaten or thrown in the river as Jesuits, according to Druilhet in October; the Austrian ambassador claimed that the same would have happened to anyone who tried to stop the sack of the *archévêché* in February.[188] A poster in Versailles, the same month, denounced a 'gathering of Jesuits' shortly to be held in the town, and urged local patriots to take arms 'so as to destroy all that *canaille*'; the gathering was actually one of Saint-Simonians.[189] At Rochefort, in March, the *garde nationale* was called on to disperse a crowd who were shouting anti-jesuit slogans outside the house of the officer commanding the artillery park.[190]

instigators of machine-breaking: see BN Est.: Tf 58 (p. 32), Hennin (165) 14488. In the latter cartoon, and in Hennin (165) 14489, Luddism rebounded on the Jesuits: they turned out to be the 'machines' that the revolutionary populace were intent on breaking.

[186] Crétineau-Joly, *Histoire religieuse*, vi. 272 n., also describing another hoax, in which a murderer, on trial before the Cour d'Assises of the Seine in Mar. 1831, sought to implicate three Jesuits by claiming that they had given him a chest of treasure to hide at the time of the July Revolution.

[187] Burnichon, *La Compagnie de Jésus en France*, i. 517–21; A. Rosette, *La Compagnie de Jésus à Dôle après sa rétablissement: Un siècle de labeur, 1823–1920* (Paris, 1945), 67–9.

[188] Druilhet quoted in Rosette, *La Compagnie de Jésus à Dôle*, 66; R. Apponyi, *Vingt-cinq ans à Paris (1826–1850)*, ed. E. Daudet, 4 vols. (Paris, 1913–26), i. 422.

[189] Burnichon, *La Compagnie de Jésus en France*, i. 516.

[190] AN F⁷ 6779, *Lieutenant de gendarmerie départementale de Rochefort* to *Ministre de l'Intérieur*, 8 Mar. 1831.

The word 'Jesuit', in the mouths of the crowd, may not always have meant anything very precise, and attacks on Jesuits or their establishments did not necessarily take place for specifically anti-jesuit reasons. Nevertheless, to many of those that made it, and most of those that approvingly rationalized it, the anti-jesuit significance of the July Revolution was scarcely in doubt. It had closed a new chapter—which historians like Lacretelle were already writing up,[191] systematizing the insights of the Liberal press into a coherent conspiracy theory—in the history of Jesuit intrigue in France. It had closed it in the standard manner, with a resounding defeat for Jesuitism by the forces of national vigilance finally awakened. What gave the chapter novelty was the fact that these forces, represented in previous episodes by kings and Parlements, were now embodied in the nation itself, under Liberal guidance. What gave it urgency was the gap in Jesuit history that had preceded it. The subversive traditions of the pre-suppression Jesuit order were shown to have survived in the restored one, and the crucial anti-jesuit assumption, that the Society of Jesus was innately incorrigible, was re-emphasized. The Liberal historians had a triumph to celebrate, but a warning to deliver: that the Jesuits were as resilient, as turbulent, as devious, and as power-mad in the nineteenth century as ever.

---

[191] See the third and fourth vols. (published in 1830—shortly before the July Days—and 1835 respectively) of C. de Lacretelle, *Histoire de France depuis la Restauration*, 4 vols. (Paris, 1829–35).

3
The July Monarchy

THE July Revolution affected the political development of French anti-jesuitism in several important ways. Men like Montlosier faded from the scene: their fears that 'Jesuitical' counter-revolution would provoke another Revolution were seemingly confirmed, but the very confirmation made it hard to go on seeing the Jesuits as the chief threat to aristocracy and legitimate monarchy. The Liberals—men whose ideas and reputations had in many cases been moulded in the *chasse aux jésuites* of the 1820s—triumphed, and their success meant that anti-jesuitism was a style of thinking acceptable in the ruling circles of the July Monarchy. Within these circles, its conservative implications were developed and its radical edge corroded, though the shift was partly masked by a change in quasi-official rhetoric which opened the way for new developments of a more radical style of anti-jesuitism as well. Liberty and nation replaced monarchy and religion as the publicly acceptable touchstones of anti-jesuit argument. The Jesuits ceased to be the hereditary enemies of the House of Bourbon, and became those against whom the responsible national rebellion of July had been directed.

Once the initial fears of counter-revolution had receded, however, anti-jesuitism was not to be the passion or the language of the 1830s. The Chambers received a number of petitions for the Jesuits' expulsion in the early months of the new regime,[1] but then worried little about the Jesuit question for over a decade. In 1834, the Minister of the Interior tried to justify his expulsion of a certain Wolfrüm from French territory by reading to the *députés* a letter, allegedly written by a Jesuit in October 1830, summoning 'the affiliated member Wolfrüm' to attend at a confessional in a Munich church at six o'clock one November morning, where, on giving the password 'Ignatius Loyola and Capet', he would receive money and a passport for a voyage under a false name. His audience greeted

---

[1] *AP*, CP 23 Sept. 1830: 639; CD 4 Oct. 1830: 24–5; CD 20 Nov. 1830: 518.

the revelation with hilarity.[2] A rather greater anti-jesuit vigilance in 1837 secured the passage of the Schauenbourg amendment (requiring aspiring directors of secondary schools to swear that they were not members of an unauthorized association) to Guizot's secondary education bill,[3] but this remained an isolated episode. Where Jesuit establishments existed, they might well still encounter suspicion and hostility, and be subject to unsympathetic government surveillance; indeed the Prefect of Police boasted in 1839 that France was the country in which such surveillance kept the Jesuits in 'the most passive situation'.[4] There was no sign, however, of any sustained mobilization of public opinion on the Jesuit issue. Charles de Lacretelle, a veteran of the anti-jesuit offensive of the 1820s, could write in 1840 that in 1829 he and his friends had been 'strongly obsessed with the fear of the reign of the Jesuits'.[5] The obsession seemed firmly in the past.

THE JESUITS AND THE FREEDOM OF EDUCATION

Those who heard the same Lacretelle, in November 1843, returning to his chair at the Sorbonne after a five-year absence, rail against the Jesuits as 'pitiless persecutors of all those who do not submit to their laws and who retain a citizen's heart, a French heart', would have formed a different impression.[6] The professor's motive was to defend the Université against the slanders of its enemies. The anti-jesuitism of the 1840s, like that of the 1820s, first gained

[2] Ibid., CD 25 Jan. 1834: 751–2.

[3] L. Grimaud, *Histoire de la liberté d'enseignement en France*, new edn., 6 vols. (Grenoble, 1944–54), vi. 261–70, summarizes the debates on this occasion; see *AP*, CD 15 Mar. 1837: 393; CD 16 Mar. 1837: 419–20, 429, 437–9.

[4] AN F^{17} 8828 (Jésuites 1837–42), Prefect of Police to *Ministre de l'Instruction publique*, 8 Jan. 1839. Documents relating to government surveillance of the Jesuits in the 1830s and early 1840s can be found in this dossier; in F^{17} 6830 (Clergé-Université) files for Aix, Angers, Clermont, and Dijon; in F^{19} 6252 (Dissolution des jésuites); and in F^{19} 6287 (Police 1837–9), (Jésuites 1843), (Jésuites et l'Université), (Circulaires relatives aux jésuites 1843–5), (Surveillance et dispersion 1845). See also Burnichon, *La Compagnie de Jésus en France*, ii. 236–54.

[5] C. de Lacretelle, *Testament philosophique et littéraire*, 2 vols. (Paris, 1840), ii. 342 n.

[6] C. de Lacretelle, *Discours prononcé à la Faculté des Lettres, le 29 novembre 1843, suivi d'une lettre à M. de Lamartine sur les rapports de l'Église et de l'État* (Paris, 1843), 26.

momentum as a reaction to a wave of Catholic agitation: not now the internal missions, but the campaign against the Université's so-called 'monopoly' over secondary education.[7] Since the frustration in 1828 of efforts to establish independent Catholic secondary schools in the guise of *petits séminaires*, and the ending in 1830 of hopes that the Université (the State's agency of control over education) could be kept under ecclesiastical domination, freedom of education (*la liberté de l'enseignement*) had become a familiar Catholic demand. The *Charte* of 1830 had promised laws to establish it in both primary and secondary sectors, and the Loi Guizot of 1833 had kept the promise for the former. A decade later, however, secondary education—the education of the élite—remained subject to the regime widely though misleadingly known as the *monopole universitaire*. Private secondary schools needed prior authorization (*autorisation préalable*) by the Université's Grand Master, renewable every ten years, and were subject not only to inspection but to the annual payment of a *retribution universitaire* proportionate to the number of their pupils. Their ability to compete with their rivals in the state system was restricted by two rules which, though sometimes laxly enforced, established a clear inferiority of status: first, in towns possessing a *collège royal* or *communal*, private schools were obliged to send their older pupils to follow its classes, rather than provide an alternative; secondly, candidates for the *baccalauréat* (necessary for access to the medical or legal professions) were required to produce a *certificat d'études* stating that their two final years' study had taken place in an establishment of the Université or at home or in one of a small number of private schools specially empowered to prepare students for the exam (the right of *plein exercice*). Supporters of the *monopole universitaire* saw it as a guarantee of academic standards and ideological rectitude; its critics regarded it as a legacy of Napoleonic despotism. Many Catholic parents considered that the restrictions on private schools, combined with the continued disqualification of members of unauthorized orders from teaching, and the ascendancy of Victor Cousin's allegedly 'godless' Eclectic philosophy within the Université, prevented their children from receiving a proper Christian schooling.

[7] For a detailed account of this campaign, see Grimaud, *Histoire de la liberté d'enseignement*, vi. 332–503; more briefly, D. Johnson, *Guizot: Aspects of French History, 1787–1874* (London, 1963), 206–10.

The efforts of education ministers in successive Orleanist governments to introduce the promised freedom of secondary education,
when not non-existent or palpably insincere, had been unsuccessful:
three schemes (those of Guizot in 1836–7, of Cousin in 1840, of
Villemain in 1841) had come to nothing, the last after being
criticized on all sides and mutilated in committee. When Villemain,
despite a public commitment to introduce a new bill, showed no
signs of urgency, Catholic frustration began to take more vehement
and organized forms. A stream of petitions, episcopal pronouncements, resolutions by *conseils généraux*, and pamphlets by clergy
and laity denounced the *monopole*. In late 1843 Montalembert, one
of the leading organizers of the campaign, urged his co-religionists
to behave as a party in defence of their rights, to be Catholics
'avant tout', to make themselves 'a serious embarrassment'.[8] By
then, the elements of a co-ordinated movement on a national scale
were in place: Louis Veuillot and *L'Univers* provided a journalistic
spearhead, bishops like Clausel de Montals of Chartres and Parisis
of Langres participated vociferously, national committees gave a
degree of order to the work of propaganda and the preparation of
petitions, and local committees agitated in the provinces.

The campaign for *liberté de l'enseignement* turned liberal rhetoric
against its habitual exponents and customary beneficiaries, and
showed a new face of French Catholic militancy: a Catholicism
refitted for operations as a political force within a constitutional,
pluralistic, ostensibly liberal system. To many this was a disconcerting spectacle. The effect was somewhat marred, however, by
the tendency of the more vehement Catholic polemicists to mix
their attacks on the Université's *monopole* with denigration of its
teaching and personal insults to its professors. The most notorious
of anti-*universitaire* tracts (and the first of several from the anonymous pen of the Lyons Jesuit Nicolas Deschamps), *Le Monopole
universitaire destructeur de la religion et des lois*, published in March
1843, accused members of the Université of 'a vast conspiracy of
irreligion and immorality'. The *monopole*, Deschamps claimed, was
the most monstrous despotism ever known: 'it is the death of a
people in a sewer, it is degradation to the level of the beasts.'[9]

---

[8] Comte de Montalembert, *Œuvres*, 9 vols. (Paris, 1860–8), iv. 352 (*Du devoir des
catholiques dans la question de la liberté d'enseignement*).

[9] [N. Deschamps], *Le Monopole universitaire destructeur de la religion et des lois; ou La
Charte et la liberté de l'enseignement* (Lyons, 1843), 431, 553. A canon of Lyons,
Desgarets, accepted public responsibility for Deschamps's tract.

The suddenness with which the apparent religious peace of the 1830s, in which it had seemed possible to believe that a Church cured of its theocratic passions and a secular State mindful of religion's contribution to social order were approaching a harmonious relationship, had given way to a bitter and concerted attack, involving prominent members of the clergy, on the State's apparatus of control in the crucial area of education, struck many as suspicious. Those who argued that the Jesuits were to blame did so for three reasons especially.

First, they noted that *liberté de l'enseignement*, as defined by its partisans, not only stood to benefit the Jesuits, but often seemed to be desired at least partly for that reason. This was undoubtedly true. Montalembert made his position clear: only the religious orders had the resources of men, material, and energy to rival the Université and regenerate French education, and it was appropriate that among them the Jesuits, saviours of Catholicism in the sixteenth century, should hold a certain pride of place; not until their exclusion was ended would 'the tyranny of unbelief' be dismantled.[10] Such arguments received an instant anti-jesuit translation: a freedom that was inadequate unless it extended to the Jesuits meant one that was desired only in order to include them. Catholic invocations of liberal principles were a smoke-screen, behind which (if *Le Constitutionnel* was to be believed) lurked forty-seven ready-made Jesuit *collèges*, disguised as *petits séminaires*, waiting to swoop on French youth once *liberté de l'enseignement* became law.[11]

Secondly, the target of Catholic attack was the Université, and this, it was claimed, was the 'eternal object of the Jesuits' hatred, vengeance and ambition'.[12] Its ruin would satisfy 'an immense need of vengeance' in the Jesuit breast.[13] Such claims rested on an identification of the secular, administrative Université established by Napoleon with the ancient ecclesiastical University of Paris, which had obstructed the Jesuits' progress in the sixteenth century. This was at least as tenuous a link as that drawn in the

[10] Montalembert, *Œuvres*, iv. 344–6 (*Du devoir des catholiques dans la question de la liberté de l'enseignement*).

[11] *Constitutionnel*, 12 Nov. 1843. Politically, Montalembert offered France a simple but meaningless choice, according to F. Génin, *Les Jésuites et l'Université* (Paris, 1844): 'the Jesuits and the elder branch [of the Bourbons], or the younger branch and the Jesuits, which amounts to exactly the same.'

[12] Lacretelle, *Discours prononcé . . . le 29 novembre 1843*, 18.

[13] Génin, *Les Jésuites et l'Université*, 152.

1820s between the Cours Royales and the Parlements, but it
appealed to a similar type of corporate vanity. Believers in the
Université's hegemony, especially among its own personnel, were
naturally attracted by the suggestion that attacks on it were merely
the vindictive assaults of a traditional and self-interested enemy.

Finally, the sheer virulence of the polemic was held to betray the
Jesuit hand. The common attribution of the *Monopole . . . destructeur*
and other works (some by Deschamps, some by non-Jesuits like
abbé Védrine) to 'the Jesuits of Lyons' or the Jesuits *tout court*
rested not on precise knowledge of the authors' identities or of
the Jesuits' publishing arrangements,[14] but on a combination of the
tracts' pro-Jesuit remarks and their injurious tone. It was impossible, asserted *Le Siècle*, not to recognize the Jesuits 'by these
perfidious attacks, by this rising tide of denunciations and calum-
nies'.[15] Of course, the Jesuits knew another tone, revealed, for
example, in Père de Ravignan's passionate gasp for the common
freedom of all citizens—'I ask only to breathe like you the free
air of the *patrie*.'[16] But one had only to juxtapose these two registers of Catholic complaint, as *Le Constitutionnel* did, to have one's
suspicions confirmed: the Jesuits were recognizable by their double
face.[17]

The revival of anti-jesuit feeling, of which there were signs in
1842, and which developed rapidly in the spring of 1843, fed on
two kinds of reference: allusions to the Jesuit past (often focusing
on the antagonism between Jesuits and Université) and renewed
denunciations of the order's contemporary presence. The traditional references were the first to appear: first Arnauld, before
the Parlement in the 1590s, speaking 'against the Jesuits, in the

[14] *Constitutionnel*, 22 May 1843, did provide some details about the Jesuit establishment in the rue de Sala in Lyons, but these did not in themselves substantiate
its claim that the Lyons Jesuits were responsible for the *Monopole . . . destructeur*.

[15] *Siècle*, 22 May 1843.

[16] X. de Ravignan, *De l'existence et de l'institut des jésuites* (Paris, 1844), 12. By
publicly proclaiming his Jesuit membership in this book, Ravignan laid both his
eloquence and his public reputation (as a widely acclaimed preacher at Notre-
Dame) at his order's service. Anti-jesuit reactions to this brave attempt to face
down anti-jesuit opinion varied, and sometimes involved recognition of Ravignan's
admirable personal qualities. Nevertheless, Cuvillier-Fleury's response was not un-
typical: 'What does it matter if the monks of the rue des Postes or the rue Sala are
saints, if they hide in the folds of their robe of innocence the scourge which must
trouble the state? What good are your virtues to me, if you give me the plague?'
(*Débats*, 10 Mar. 1845).   [17] *Constitutionnel*, 20 May 1843.

name of the Université' (a topic set as a rhetorical exercise by students of the École Normale doing teaching practice in Parisian schools in April 1842); then Pascal, whose eulogy Villemain himself set as the subject of a competition of the Académie Française the same year. Villemain's report made the intended reference clear: 'What memory could be more instructive even today, and what polemic more intelligible to our times, than the passionate resistance of so many enlightened and virtuous men, of whom Pascal was the soul and the voice, against that turbulent and imperious society, which the spirit of government and the spirit of liberty reject with equal mistrust?'[18] Similar allusions were made by other orators at the Académie, and by Dupin *aîné* in his *discours de rentrée* at the Cour de Cassation the following year.[19]

It was at the Collège de France, however, that this scholarly version of anti-jesuit combat was practised most sensationally and protractedly.[20] There, on 27 April 1843, the historian Jules Michelet, leaving unfinished his course on the Middle Ages, embarked on a scathing polemic against the Jesuits, in which he was joined a fortnight later (after a false start when a large and expectant audience were disappointed to hear their professor lecture on Columbus) by his colleague Edgar Quinet. For the next few weeks, they waged 'la guerre aux jésuites'[21] in tandem, Quinet on Wednesdays, Michelet on Thursdays, dissecting and denouncing the Jesuit spirit (as revealed in the order's history and fundamental writings) to an enthusiastic, and largely youthful and anticlerical, audience. The scenes of disorder, frantic applause, and heckling which marked some of the earlier lectures (but which later hagiography exaggerated[22]) helped give the occasions an odour of the

---

[18] Crétineau-Joly, *Histoire religieuse*, vi. 471–2.

[19] J.-B. Bordas-Demoulin, *Mélanges philosophiques et religieux* (Paris, 1846), 538–9 ('Éloge de Pascal'); *Institut royal de France: Discours prononcés à l'Académie Française pour la réception de M. le baron Pasquier, le 8 décembre 1842* (Paris, 1842), 34 (speech by Mignet); A.-M.-J.-J. Dupin, *Éloge d'Étienne Pasquier: Discours prononcé à l'audience de rentrée de la Cour de Cassation, le 6 novembre 1843* (Paris, 1843).

[20] See G. Monod, *La Vie et la pensée de Jules Michelet, 1798–1852*, 2 vols. (Paris, 1923), ii. 118–30; J. Pochon, 'Edgar Quinet et les luttes du Collège de France, 1843–1847', *Revue d'histoire littéraire de la France*, 120 (1970), 619–27; P. Viallaneix, introd. to the abridged edn. (Pauvert: Libertés 35) of J. Michelet and E. Quinet, *Des jésuites* (Paris, 1966), 16–25.

[21] The expression is Michelet's (*Journal*, i. 505).

[22] G. Monod, 'Les Troubles du Collège de France en 1843', *Séances et travaux de l'Académie des Sciences Morales et Politiques (Institut de France)*, 172 (1909), 407–23,

polemical front line. The lectures were reproduced *in extenso*, the morning after delivery, in *Le Siècle*, France's highest-selling daily, and were much discussed; when the two courses were published jointly in book form, in July, the first edition sold out almost immediately.

The content of Michelet and Quinet's remarks on the Jesuits, and their contribution to the longer-term development of anti-jesuit polemic, will be discussed shortly. Their more immediate impact is equally important. Undoubtedly, the lectures lent themselves to varied interpretations: as the resurgence of repressed revolutionary spirit, as the essay of a new religious faith, or merely as a high-flown presentation of traditional liberal anticlericalism. As the two professors developed their thinking with increasing boldness in 1844 and 1845, many of their initial admirers would draw back. In 1843, however, they enjoyed the support of a strikingly broad spectrum of the press (from the pro-governmental *Journal des débats* to organs of the Republican Left) and of many respected members of the Orleanist establishment.[23] This breadth of support is explicable chiefly in terms of the general tendency to see their lectures—an attack on the Université's supposedly traditional enemy, delivered from the eminence of prestigious State-endowed chairs, by professors who themselves had been repeatedly abused and denounced by clerical polemicists—as first and foremost a campaign of retaliation on behalf of the State's slandered educational community.[24] The phalanx of distinguished scholars (including Ranke, Mickiewicz, and Geoffroy Saint-Hilaire) which ostentatiously deployed itself around Michelet at his third lecture could only encourage the impression that the assailed honour of secular learning and teaching was at stake.[25]

downplays the disturbances; R. H. Powers, *Edgar Quinet: A Study in French Patriotism* (Dallas, 1957), 110–11, 185 n., takes them more seriously. For hagiographical excess, see notably Mme H. Quinet, *Edgar Quinet avant l'éxil*, 2nd edn. (Paris, 1888), 322.

[23] For details and analysis of the press response, see E. Brisson, 'Le Tribun du Collège de France devant la presse', in P. Viallaneix (ed.), *Michelet cent ans après* (Grenoble, 1975), 166–95; E. Brisson, 'L'Enseignement de Quinet au Collège de France d'après la presse parisienne, 1842–1845', in S. Bernard-Griffiths and P. Viallaneix (eds.), *Edgar Quinet, ce juif errant* (Clermont-Ferrand, 1978), 89–108. See also Monod, *La Vie et la pensée de Jules Michelet*, ii. 132–8.

[24] See e.g. *Siècle*, 15 May 1843; *Constitutionnel*, 2 Aug. 1843.

[25] Monod, 'Les Troubles', 421.

While the two professors at the Collège de France were delivering their critique of the Jesuits' spiritual heritage, a professor of the Faculté des Sciences, the mathematician Libri, was setting out the logic of detection of their present influence, in two 'Lettres sur le clergé' in the *Revue des deux mondes*. Not only could the Jesuits' presence in France be deduced from their own assertions, he wrote,

but one recognizes them by their works, by the violence of their polemic, by the agitation which they spread through the country, by the oppression which they cause to weigh upon the clergy, by their moral doctrine, so often stigmatized yet never abandoned by them, by [their] probabilism, by their famous mental reservations, by their aversion to the liberties of the Gallican Church. Yes, they are in our midst, all around us; they are still the same men, they have the same doctrines, and they bring the same dangers.[26]

Similar arguments and similar conclusions were already becoming a commonplace in the press:[27] increasingly free use was made of the anti-jesuit idiom in describing and denigrating the agitations of bishops, clergy, and Catholic laity. The fullest, clearest, and most influential expression of the new application of anti-jesuit conspiracy theory was provided by the professor-cum-journalist François Génin, in his book *Les Jésuites et l'Université*, published in February 1844. Génin described the Jesuits, after their defeat in 1830, pursuing a broad conspiratorial plan aimed at the seduction of all classes of French society. As under the Restoration, they had covered France with *confréries* and subjected the populace to 'a system of popular *abêtissement*'. The intended centrepiece of the conspiracy, however, was the invasion of education:

This will be the final blow to our liberties, so dearly won by two revolutions. When the Jesuits have the children, they will have the fathers and mothers, in other words everyone: the present and the future. Therefore their war-cry in this expedition which they have undertaken against the State is *Death to the Université*. They thus conceal, beneath the appearance of a particular quarrel, the extent and temerity of a general attack.

Each major attack on the Université, from abbé Garot in 1840 to the recent 'manifeste carlo-jésuite' of 'le comte de Montalembert,

---

[26] G. Libri, 'Lettres sur le clergé, II: Y a-t-il encore des jésuites', *Revue des deux mondes*, 2nd ser. 2 (1843), 977.

[27] A good example is the article 'Existence contestée des jésuites' in *Constitutionnel*, 29 May 1843.

pair de France et jésuite', and including several episcopal pronouncements, took its place, in the second part of Génin's book, in this grand and unfolding Jesuit design.[28]

'Woe to the Jesuits! Death to those who want to bring trouble and disunity to France! Death to those who want to rise up against the Université!' began a placard, signed 'J.C. défenseur des libertés nationales,' affixed to the door of the Jesuit residence in the rue des Postes in late December 1843. A second placard, from the same hand, threatened: 'If the Jesuits go on playing the rebel [*faire la mauvaise tête*], we'll make them dance, them and their whole works. They'll roast within a week: they'll be sent up to heaven as martyrs. An example's got to be made which frightens this rabble a bit, and the students undertake to avenge the Université, since the government doesn't want to. Let them watch out!'[29] Though most defenders of the national liberties expressed themselves less violently, there is no doubt that for many, by early 1844, the question of *liberté de l'enseignement* had been rephrased as, or subsumed by, the question of whether the Jesuits were to be permitted to triumph over the Université. The Université, wrote Génin, was the sole barrier to the 'parti jésuite': with it, France would be free; with the Jesuits, she would be enslaved.[30]

The strength of anti-jesuit feeling in parliament, hinted at during the Chambre des Pairs' discussion of petitions for *liberté de l'enseignement* the previous May, showed itself again when the *députés* responded in January to the announcement that a new secondary education bill would shortly be introduced. Both Chambers pointedly welcomed the government's promise that the bill would maintain 'the authority and the action of the State' in the educational field.[31] There was little doubt that its success in doing so would be judged primarily by the perceived strength of its safeguards against the Jesuits.

Villemain's bill, when introduced, had something to anger everyone.[32] It removed some of the disabilities on private schools, yet kept intact the double barrier to Jesuit education: the *déclaration de*

---

[28] Génin, *Les Jésuites et l'Université, passim* (quotations on 44, 108, 151, 327, 329). The book was compiled from Génin's articles in *Le National*.

[29] Delattre (ed.), *Les Établissements*, iii. 1329–30 (Paris).

[30] Génin, *Les Jésuites et l'Université*, 469–71.

[31] *Moniteur*, CP 15 May 1843, 8 Jan. 1844; CD 28 Jan. 1844.

[32] See Grimaud, *Histoire de la liberté d'enseignement*, vi. 603–37.

non-appartenance (preventing members of unauthorized orders from teaching in France) and the *certificat d'études* (preventing those they taught outside France from proceeding to the *baccalauréat*). In an effort to woo the bishops, however, it effectively extended the right of *plein exercice* to their *petits séminaires*, a concession which (though somewhat diminished in committee) was seen by some as opening a back door to the Jesuits. The report on the bill, read to the Chambre des Pairs by de Broglie on 12 April, made no specific mention of the Jesuits, though it affirmed the impossibility of yielding ground to the unauthorized orders in general. Once debate opened on 22 April, however, the champions of the Université and of secular Gallicanism—the two sacred cows of Orleanist statism —were quick to come to the point. Victor Cousin led for the Université, prefacing his account of its importance with a comparison between the educational traditions of the Oratorians and the Jesuits, to the latter's discredit; he was followed by the comte de Saint-Priest, who stressed the order's incompatibility with the proper principles of a national education. Charles Dupin (now baron Dupin) then launched the Gallican attack, rounding off his acclamation of 'the indivisible liberties of the king, the Church, and the Catholic people' with a xenophobic challenge to the Jesuits: 'Make yourselves citizens, become Frenchmen again, stop being foreigners, henchmen of the foreigner, propagators for the foreigner, enslavers in the name and to the profit of the foreigner; then we will have no further objection to you, and will fear you no longer, for then you will no longer be Jesuits.'[33]

These speeches introduced the main anti-jesuit themes (going well beyond a narrow attack on Jesuit education) that were to be embellished by a stream of orators during the two months the debate lasted. It is a mark of the prevalence of anti-jesuit sentiments in high political circles that only one orator—Montalembert—was prepared openly to praise the order; others, like Beugnot, preferred to resist the anti-jesuit offensive by arguing that the Society of Jesus posed no real threat under modern conditions and that anti-jesuitism was merely a rhetorical device for protecting the

[33] *Moniteur*, CP 12 Apr. 1844 (de Broglie); CP 22 Apr. 1844 (Cousin); CP 23 Apr. 1844 (Saint-Priest and baron Dupin), quotations p. 1061. For summaries of the debate, see Burnichon, *La Compagnie de Jésus en France*, ii. 580–601; P. Thureau-Dangin, *Histoire de la Monarchie de Juillet*, 7 vols. (Paris, 1884–92), v. 533–43.

Université from competition.[34] Such men joined Montalembert in
attacking the bill's restrictive clauses (especially those obviously
aimed against the Jesuits) as fundamentally illiberal. The anti-
jesuits' reply was that they loved liberty in what baron Dupin called
'an enlightened manner': to preserve it, not to lose it. For men like
Dupin and Kératry, the *Charte* of 1830, to which Catholics now
appealed, was not a statement of abstract principle; it was a
formalization of the achievements of the July Revolution. Since
that Revolution had been fought precisely to defend liberty against
the Jesuits, it was absurd to invoke the *Charte* on the Jesuits'
behalf. True liberty required the guarantees that only legal definition and regulation by the enlightened State could provide; it was
not meant to permit licence to 'men who do not want to ask for
and receive rights, who want to filch them, who want to slip
fraudulently under the barriers of a legitimate government, instead
of presenting themselves openly at the constitutional gates of the
State'. For both historical and constitutional reasons, then, there
could be no question of accepting 'the enthronement of the Jesuits
in the name of liberty'.[35]

Government ministers seemed divided in their attitude to the
peers' anti-jesuit passions. The *Garde des Sceaux*, Martin *du Nord*,
was criticized for playing down the Jesuits' influence.[36] Villemain,
on the other hand, boasted that his bill did 'what was legally possible for the bishops, and nothing for the Jesuits'. By openly
accusing Montalembert of serving the Jesuit interest (before the
Catholic champion himself had mentioned the Jesuits in the debate), he did as much as anyone to keep the focus on the Jesuit
issue.[37] The main aim of the government's effective head, Guizot,
was to keep the issue under control; he sought to show, on the one
hand, that the government knew how to be firm with the Jesuits,
and on the other, that it knew how to rise above the prejudice and
intolerance of their more aggressive opponents. The government's
aim, he insisted, was to give France an educational system that
would reflect the basic character of modern society by balancing
public power with individual liberty. The Jesuits could find a place

---

[34] Ibid., CP 8 May 1844 (Montalembert); CP 24 Feb. 1844 (Beugnot).
[35] Ibid., CP 8 May 1844 (baron Dupin), quotations 1278–9. For Kératry's views,
see CP 27 Apr. 1844: 1125.
[36] Ibid., CP 14 May 1844 (Saint-Priest); CP 22 May 1844 (Martin).
[37] Ibid., CP 26 Apr. 1844, quotation 1108.

in this system only if they could abandon their old absolutist purposes and corporate ambition, and present themselves as ordinary citizens. Unlike most anti-jesuits, Guizot did not suggest that they could never do so, but he claimed that the public had strong reasons to believe they had not done so yet. It therefore remained the government's duty to protect society against them.[38]

Towards the end of the debate, a peer remarked with some justice that the Society of Jesus would find it hard to resist the temptation of pride, 'so great is the place which it has occupied in our debates'.[39] Much of the discussion of particular articles, like the general discussion, seemed to bear out the *Journal des débats*' view that 'the question which dominates the whole bill' was that of whether or not the Jesuits were to be the masters of French education.[40] A provisional answer, to the Jesuits' disadvantage, was given when Article 4, requiring a *déclaration de non-appartenance* from prospective openers of secondary schools, was passed with minor modifications on 9 May. For anti-jesuits, however, the bill would still have been 'altogether in the Jesuits' interest' (as an ex-minister, Persil, put it[41]) without Article 18's insistence on the *certificat d'études*. This, however, was passed (amended so as to exempt *baccalauréat* candidates aged 25 or over) on 15 May. Some anti-jesuits still sought further safeguards. The unsuccessful Franck-Carré amendment to Article 25, which would have made heads of secondary schools liable to prosecution 'in the event of teaching contrary to public and religious morality, or to the laws of the kingdom', was recommended by one speaker as protection against members of unauthorized orders who falsely made the *déclaration de non-appartenance*.[42] More serious was Cousin's resistance to Article 30, which embodied Villemain's concessions to the *petits séminaires*. If the latter were allowed to function as *collèges* in competition with the Université, he argued, it was bound to be the Jesuits who would run them; such a concession might well sow the seeds of future 'civil wars of religion'.[43] Cousin was opposed, however, not only by the government, but also by a prestigious exponent of conservative Gallicanism, Portalis, who deplored the tendency to extend the mistrust due to the Jesuit order to the whole Gallican

---

[38] Ibid., CP 9 May 1844. [39] Ibid., CP 23 May 1844 (Rossi), 1484.
[40] *Débats*, 9 May 1844. [41] *Moniteur*, CP 14 May 1844: 1360.
[42] Ibid., CP 21 May 1844 (Bussière), 1443.
[43] Ibid., CP 22 May 1844: 1470–1.

Church.[44] Article 30 (renumbered 31) was adopted unamended. The bill as a whole was passed on 24 May, by eighty-five votes to fifty-one.

The slenderness of this majority cast doubt on the bill's prospects of weathering intact the combined onslaughts of Catholics and pro-*universitaires* in the lower Chamber. The fortunes of anti-jesuitism and of M. Thiers now meshed felicitously. Seeing an opportunity to re-establish himself in the parliamentary foreground at the expense of the government, the former head of government secured nomination as *rapporteur* of the committee to consider the bill.[45] His voluminous report, delivered on 13 July, made an ostentatious defence of the State's right to control education. On the Jesuits, Thiers said nothing new, except that the possibility of schools like Saint-Acheul reappearing in France made it necessary to allow the Université authorities the right to suppress them, but he clearly associated himself with the anti-jesuit attitudes aired in the upper Chamber.[46] The report left the government in an unpromising position: the bill was less likely than ever to emerge in a form that would appeal to Catholic opinion, and if it survived at all, it would seem to do so under Thiers's patronage. In the end, however, Guizot was saved from the embarrassment of the bill by the embarrassment of its author. The Chambers went into recess at the beginning of August and had barely reassembled at the end of December when Villemain was reported mad.[47] Though his recovery—from, among other things, hallucinatory fantasies in which he was menaced by Jesuits—proved swift, Guizot was swifter still in replacing him with a minister more acceptable to the clergy, Salvandy. No attempt was made to revive the bill in the next session.

GOVERNMENT, OPPOSITION, AND THE JESUIT QUESTION

By the summer of 1844 it was clear that the Jesuits would not be permitted to teach in France. That anti-jesuit agitation, instead of

[44] Ibid., CP 23 May 1844: 1482.
[45] My account of Thiers's motives here follows that of Johnson, *Guizot*, 212 (following contemporary assessments); J. P. T. Bury and R. P. Tombs, *Thiers, 1797–1877: A Political Life* (London, 1986), 87, are more charitable.
[46] *Moniteur*, CD 13 July 1844: 2193–4.
[47] See Thureau-Dangin, *Histoire de la Monarchie de Juillet*, v. 546–7; C.-A. Sainte-Beuve, *Les Cahiers* (Paris, 1876), 30; C. de Rémusat, *Mémoires de ma vie*, ed. C. Pouthas, 5 vols. (Paris, 1958–67), v. 73–5.

slackening, remained to play an important part in French politics for another year was due in part to continuing clerical agitation, and in part to the impetus of anti-jesuit arguments which, even in the context of a primarily educational debate, had gone far beyond the point of merely wishing to exclude the Jesuits from education. It was also, however, partly due to the political usefulness of anti-jesuitism to an opposition eager for issues on which to overcome its own divisions and to put pressure on ministers who, though entrenched in power since 1840, were always anxiously protective of their parliamentary majority.[48] Even in 1843, complaints at Jesuit aggression had sometimes been coupled with criticisms of ministerial weakness or complicity,[49] and the opposition press had begun to try out unkind 'analogies' between present circumstances and those experienced under Villèle and Polignac.[50] So long, however, as attention had focused on the educational bill, something resembling a common anti-jesuit front between supporters and opponents of the government had persisted. When the focus shifted to the whole question of the Jesuits' existence, the issue developed a new political significance.

This does not mean that anti-jesuitism came to function again, as it had done in the 1820s, as an effective opposition monopoly. The alignment of forces was different. Unlike its Restoration predecessors, the Soult–Guizot government, thanks to its failure to satisfy Catholic educational aspirations, did not attract the compromising friendship of the Jesuits' most obvious sympathizers. Its members, furthermore, like those of other Orleanist governments, were drawn from the same frequently reshuffled political circles as were their principal political opponents, from whom they were not divided by any clear ideological rift, nor indeed by any fundamental difference in attitude to the Jesuits. Though Villemain's breakdown removed the most vehement anti-jesuit from the ministerial ranks, the reluctance of Guizot and Martin to enforce laws against the Jesuits stemmed from a pragmatic concern not to appear as persecutors of the church, not from doubt as to the laws' validity or belief in the Jesuits' usefulness; Thiers, in power, had not

---

[48] Johnson, *Guizot*, 200–1.
[49] Thus *Constitutionnel*, 31 Aug. 1843 ('Never has Jesuitism more audaciously raised its head; never has the government shown greater weakness and complicity') and 9 Jan. 1844.   [50] Ibid. 30 Oct. 1843; *Siècle*, 21 Dec. 1843.

behaved very differently.[51] The police and Université officials who
kept a suspicious eye on Jesuit establishments often encouraged
their political masters to see the inmates as instigators of the clerical
attacks on state education, and of legitimist intrigues.[52] Nor were
the government's supporters in the press willing to be outbid in
anti-jesuitism; the *Journal des débats* had supported Michelet and
Quinet in 1843, and was quick to defend itself and the government
from charges of inadequate anti-jesuit zeal.[53] The 1820s had seen an
anti-jesuit campaign by those excluded from power against those
holding it; what developed through late 1844 and early 1845 is
better described as a struggle between government and opposition
factions for control of the Jesuit question.

By loudly pressing Guizot and Martin to enforce the laws against
the Jesuits, Thiers and his friends could hope to present themselves
as protectors of the national interest and spokesmen for a powerful
current of public concern, and to drive the government, hampered
by its desire not to alienate the Church, into a corner from which it
could not emerge with dignity: if it resisted the pressure, it would
seem culpably negligent; if it accepted it, the opposition would get
the credit. Guizot, however, hoped to escape this dilemma, and to
restore a measure of religious peace, by diplomacy: towards the end
of 1844, his envoy Pellegrino Rossi left France *en route* for Rome,
to negotiate for the dissolution of the French Jesuits.[54] In the later
months of 1844, however, the working-out of these manœuvres lay

---

[51] See *La Commission extraparlementaire de 1849: Texte intégral des procès-verbaux*,
ed. G. Chenesseau (Paris, 1937), 214, for Thiers's admission that, as a minister, he
had advised the Jesuits to conceal their identity, so that he could turn a blind eye to
their presence.

[52] See AN F^{19} 6252 (Dissolution des jésuites), police report (copy) on the Jesuits
of the rue des Postes (Paris), 31 Dec. 1843; F^{19} 6287 (Jésuites et l'Université), police
report (copy) on the Jesuits of Lyons, 15 Feb. 1844; F^{17} 6830 (Clergé-Université:
Clermont), *Recteur de l'Académie* to *Ministre de l'Instruction publique*, 17 June 1844.
The same dossier also contains a notable exercise in the logic of prejudice, in a
confidential report (28 July 1844) to the Minister concerning the Jesuits of Vals: by
a combination of *ad hominem* remarks and rhetorical or leading questions, *inspecteur-
général* Artaud succeeds in passing, without producing any further evidence, from
the fact that the Jesuits had erected new buildings, locally rumoured to be for a
noviciate or secondary school, to the conclusion that 'at Walss [*sic*], as at Avignon,
as at Toulouse, as at Bordeaux, the Jesuits' establishments are hotbeds of political
intrigue, of legitimist opposition, and perhaps one day of revolution'.

[53] e.g. *Débats*, 24, 31 Dec. 1843.

[54] F. Guizot, *Mémoires pour servir à l'histoire de mon temps*, 8 vols. (Paris, 1858–67),
vii. 391–449, gives an account of these negotiations.

in the future: Rossi would not effectively commence his mission till March 1845 (and not enter negotiations in earnest till late May), and the opposition would not revive the Jesuit issue in parliament till mid-April. A combination of other matters—literary, foreign, and legal—kept interest in the Jesuits burning through the winter.

The best remembered of these is the long march (from June 1844 to June 1845) of *Le Juif errant*, Eugène Sue's epic novel of Jesuit intrigue, serialized in *Le Constitutionnel*, a paper now politically at the service of Thiers. The paper's owner, Dr Véron, paid Sue 100,000 francs; his reward (to which a bold slashing of subscription rates, and the author's reputation as the author of *Les Mystères de Paris*, as well as the topicality of the Jesuit theme, contributed) was to see subscriptions rise from 3,600 at the beginning of 1844 to 20,000 fifteen months later.[55] This success, and Sue's skilful cross-breeding of the conventions of anti-jesuit polemic with those of cloak-and-dagger fiction, introduced anti-jesuitism to an audience significantly broader than that which is likely to have followed debates on secondary education. Elements and echoes of the attack on Jesuit education found a place in *Le Juif errant*, but it was as part of a much more varied mythology of Jesuit devilry in which murder and the fanatical pursuit of wealth had as major a place, and in which conspiracy was the organizing theme; Sue showed the Society of Jesus as a secret society bent on world domination by all available means. One does not have to suppose that readers of *Le Constitutionnel* invariably believed all this, to appreciate Sue's contri-bution to the popularization of anti-jesuit belief. It would be doing him too much honour, however, to hold him primarily responsible for the fact that the Jesuit question seemed as topical and exploit-able in the spring of 1845 as it had done in that of 1844. For this, news was needed. It came from two sources: Switzerland and the Cour d'Assises de la Seine.

It was not to the news which their paper reported from the Swiss cantons that *Le Constitutionnel*'s new-found readers could turn for relief from Sue's tale of Jesuit intrigue. The train of events that captured French attention began on 24 October 1844, when the Grand Council of Lucerne invited the Society of Jesus to take over in the following year the canton's seminary and theological

[55] L.-D. Véron, *Mémoires d'un bourgeois de Paris*, 6 vols. (Paris, 1853–5), iv. 272–4. On the popular reception of *Le Juif errant*, see J.-L. Bory, *Eugène Sue: Le Roi du roman populaire* (Paris, 1962), 300–8.

institutions.[56] Coming at a time when Lucerne was discharging the functions of *Vorort* (presiding canton), and barely two months after the Federal Diet had rejected a motion to expel the Jesuits from Switzerland entirely, its invitation was perceived by radicals, in Lucerne and throughout the Confederation, as a provocative escalation of clerical aggression. The first stage in resistance to it culminated in a rising in Lucerne, with armed support from outside, on 8 December, which was harshly suppressed. In the following months, bands of irregular volunteers (Free Corps) mobilized openly in a number of cantons with a view to armed intervention, and popular pressure mounted for Federal action to secure the expulsion of the Jesuits not just from Lucerne but from the whole Confederation. Political repercussions were felt in several cantons, notably in Vaud, where the government's inadequate response to the anti-jesuit campaign led to its overthrow. With the Jesuit question thus the pretext for increasing turbulence and for controversy over the respective limits of federal and cantonal sovereignty, hopes for a solution were placed in the Federal Diet, which assembled at the end of February. The Diet, however, though it condemned the Free Corps, failed to determine a course of action on the Jesuits. This left the initiative to the Free Corps, who promptly invaded Lucerne, but were decisively defeated on 31 March. The first Jesuits reached Lucerne in July.

These events, which in Swiss history form part of the prelude to the *Sonderbund* crisis and war of 1847, were extensively reported in France. Papers like *Le Siècle* and *Le Constitutionnel* left no doubt as to whom they held responsible for Switzerland's disorders. 'Let all Switzerland perish, rather than the Jesuits' ambition suffer a check!' was *Le Constitutionnel*'s comment on the events of December.[57] 'Guerre des jésuites', the heading under which it reported them, meant a war not simply over the Jesuits, but caused and waged by them: 'The Jesuits' war continues in Switzerland, and soon perhaps

[56] There seems to be no detailed modern account of these events in French or English, though their diplomatic aspects are briefly considered in A. G. Imlah, *Britain and Switzerland, 1845–60: A Study of Anglo-Swiss Relations during some Critical Years for Swiss Neutrality* (London, 1966), 13–17. The contemporary account in M. J. Mayers, *The Jesuit and Sonderbund Contest in Switzerland* (London, 1847), 10–20, remains useful.

[57] *Constitutionnel*, 15 Dec. 1844. The paper's Berne correspondent called for the Bernese government to take the lead in driving the Jesuits not only from Lucerne, but from all Switzerland (ibid. 21 Dec. 1844).

blood will flow thanks to the good Fathers. Their presence gives birth to and sustains discord everywhere.'[58] Reports were repeatedly phrased so that the Jesuits appeared as active participants in the political and military struggle: the crushing of the Lucerne rising was 'the bloody victory of the Jesuits at Lucerne'; the prisoners taken were the 'unhappy victims of Jesuitical ambition': Lucerne in May, over a month before any Jesuits arrived, was already 'the Jesuit-canton of Lucerne'.[59] Even as they happened, the Swiss events became an anti-jesuit example, a fresh illustration of the Jesuits' affinity with bloodshed, repression, and anarchy, to add to the list stretching back, through the Revocation of the Edict of Nantes, to St Bartholomew's Eve[60]—and a warning to France. For the Society of Jesus through whose intrigues and obstinacy, *Le Siècle* reported in early April, 'rivers of blood have just flowed in Switzerland, and the tranquillity of Europe might have been disturbed', was the same 'which presents itself here in so cautious a form'.[61] The Jesuits' actions abroad, *Le Constitutionnel* had remarked in November, 'give us the measure of what they are disposed to do here, the moment they can unmask their batteries'.[62]

Swiss affairs also gave the opposition in France a chance to turn anti-jesuitism against the government and its conservative supporters. For the latter, though not approving Lucerne's invitation to the Jesuits, took a view of Swiss politics which by February and March 1845 was clearly shaped primarily by the desire to protect public order and cantonal sovereignty, and to prevent the crisis being used by those seeking a revision of the 1815 Federal Pact: 'the debate is no longer between the partisans and the opponents of the Jesuits,' wrote the *Journal des débats*, 'it is between the revolutionaries and the conservatives.'[63] The *Débats* insisted that its refusal to support the anti-jesuit movement in Switzerland in no way contradicted its earlier attacks on the Jesuits in France, where the constitutional position was quite different and the Jesuits plainly illegal.[64] To show that no domestic volte-face had occurred, it published a two-part review article by Cuvillier-Fleury, which emphasized the collaboration of all responsible forces in resistance to Jesuit encroachments in France, and which yielded nothing in

---

[58] Ibid. 12 Dec. 1844 (before news of 8 Dec.).
[59] Ibid. 13, 20 Dec. 1844; *Siècle*, 25 May 1845.   [60] *Siècle*, 15 Dec. 1844.
[61] Ibid. 5 Apr. 1844.   [62] *Constitutionnel*, 1 Nov. 1844.
[63] *Débats*, 20 Feb. 1845.   [64] Ibid. 15 Mar. 1845.

anti-jesuit trenchancy to the polemicists of the opposition.[65] But such denials of the government's solidarity with the Jesuits had to vie with the impressions created by the vigorously worded diplomatic note which Guizot caused to be conveyed to the Federal authorities and the Diet in early March, in which he said nothing about the Jesuits, while insisting on the need for firm action to suppress the Free Corps. Highly critical of this intervention, the anti-government press argued that if the Free Corps were problematic, it was as part of the Jesuit problem: the appropriate way to get rid of them was to get rid of the Jesuits, who had provoked their formation. Guizot was accused of trying to prevent the Diet from taking action against the Jesuits; this, it was argued (skating over the question of Lucerne's own cantonal rights of sovereignty), was tantamount to denying a sovereign state, the majority of whose inhabitants opposed the Jesuits, the right to reject them. In short, in contempt of the broader interests of global liberalism and of state sovereignty, Guizot had made himself the protector and 'the auxiliary of the Jesuits in Switzerland'.[66] This made hard-line anti-jesuits, for whom the Jesuit question was fundamentally the same wherever it was posed, all the more alert for signs of ministerial softness towards the Jesuits in France.

Switzerland, it was argued, showed what horrors the Jesuits held in store for France; the Affenäer case, heard at the Cour d'Assises de la Seine on 8 and 9 April, revealed what their presence in France already amounted to.[67] Louis Affenäer, a Belgian layman, had entered the employment of the Jesuits of the rue des Postes in Paris in 1841, as an assistant to the *père économe* responsible for the establishment's external financial dealings. To his employers, he seems to have professed piety and disenchantment with the world; to the world itself, he presented a different face, maintaining a

[65] Ibid. 10 and 11 Mar. 1845.

[66] *Constitutionnel*, 12 Mar. 1845 (quoted), 14 Mar. 1845; *Siècle*, 25 Mar., 1 Apr. 1845. For Guizot's attitude (and the text of the diplomatic note), see his *Mémoires*, viii. 429–36.

[67] The most complete published version of the trial proceedings is *Procès d'Affenaer: Vol de 333,000 francs, au préjudice des jésuites* (Paris, 1845), published from a standpoint sympathetic to Affenäer and hostile to the Jesuits; this includes the cross-examinations of defendant and witnesses. Fuller or slightly different versions of certain speeches (and a small amount of additional material) are contained in *Procès Affnaer, Cours d'Assises de la Seine, audience des 8 et 9 avril 1845* (Paris, 1845), which is hostile to Affenäer. An account of the case is contained in Burnichon, *La Compagnie de Jésus en France*, ii. 558–62.

lavish apartment and at least one mistress (three, the prosecution was to claim), and carrying on a life of affluent dissipation. In May 1844, deceived by false friends into believing that he was about to be arrested in connection with charges of commercial forgery and fraudulent bankruptcy of which he had been convicted by a Belgian court, he fled to England with his mistress, leaving the embarrassed Jesuits to discover the embezzlement by which this unsuitable life-style had been sustained. He rashly returned to Paris the following month, and was arrested. In August, the *procureur-général* of the Cour Royale de Paris, Hébert, warned the government that the case was likely to have an unfortunate effect on public opinion: the revelations that were bound to be made of the Jesuits' organization and activities would make it hard to dismiss warnings of their increasing influence as chimerical, and might well lead many people—already alarmed by publications and legal consultations in the Jesuits' favour, and by the recent tendency of prominent Jesuits (presumably Ravignan) to declare themselves openly—to call for firm action against them.[68] The moment at which Affenäer came to trial—a week after 'the Jesuit-canton of Lucerne' repelled anti-jesuit invasion—made this all the more likely.

Affenäer and his lawyer Nogent Saint-Laurent did their best to exploit the anti-jesuit mood. The accused denied the charges against him and insisted that he had been the Jesuits' general business agent, not the humble book-keeper that they claimed. Each weak point in his story was covered by deflecting suspicion on to his former employers: if transactions to which he alluded were not shown in the account-books submitted to the court, it was because there were other books that the Jesuits had kept secret; if he had sought to escape extradition to Belgium, it was because the Jesuits, for mysterious reasons of their own, had paid him to do so; if he had rented a larger than necessary apartment, it was because the Jesuits themselves wanted to be able to use it if their establishments were closed.[69] Far from having concealed his departure for England from his employers, he had returned his keys and 'several copies of the book *Maria Stella*' (a notoriously subversive book) which the

---

[68] AN F¹⁹ 6252 (Dissolution des jésuites), *Procureur-général* of Cour Royale de Paris to *Garde des Sceaux*, 20 Aug. 1844.

[69] *Procès d'Affenäer*, 24, 28–30, 37, 39–40.

Jesuit librarian had entrusted to him in order not to be found in possession of them.[70]

Nogent made a more systematic effort to put the Jesuits on informal trial. He called a succession of them as witnesses,[71] and then, in his *plaidoirie*, made much of their different functions and offices, and of the wide range of transactions that appeared to be carried on in this 'immense business centre' (as he called it) in the rue des Postes. Having emphasized that the court was confronted not with a few private individuals, but with a full-fledged and unauthorized *congrégation*, he went on, in a speech peppered with anti-jesuit insinuations, to imply that the Jesuits had paid Affenäer to flee because they feared the scandalous evidence of their own illegal existence and activities that his trial for earlier offences would have brought to light. To discredit the Jesuits' own testimony, he reminded his listeners of the notorious doctrines on perjury and dissimulation for which the casuists of their order had been condemned by the Parlement. He concluded by defying the jury to reject his arguments: 'Well then, in that case, gentlemen of the jury, proclaim it loud and clear, open your ranks, take courage — Let the Jesuits through.'[72]

Nogent's blatant appeal to anti-jesuit sentiment did not save Affenäer from conviction (he was sentenced to five years in prison and ten under surveillance), but his outcry over proof of the Jesuits' corporate existence found a ready echo outside the court. Information about genuine Jesuit establishments in France, including that of the rue des Postes,[73] had been presented in the press before, but the trial gave an unprecedented glimpse within the walls. Journalists seized the opportunity to be scandalized at the spectacle of French priests paraded and exposed not just as Jesuits, but as holders of offices within the Jesuit organization, and at the mass of impressionistic detail on Jesuit financial operations that had bubbled to the surface during the legal proceedings. Nor was the opportunity lost to scold the government: *Le Constitutionnel* reported the rumour that Martin had caused the *avocat-général*

---

[70] Ibid. 31–2. Forced to admit the accuracy of this detail, the librarian was sternly rebuked by the court for not having destroyed the book (52–3).

[71] As the prosecution pointed out, these did not include the most celebrated of the Parisian Jesuits (Ravignan), whose eloquence and legal experience would have been a threat to the defence (ibid. 62).

[72] Ibid. 66–7, 79, 85, 96–100, 103–6. A more elaborate version of the final challenge is in *Procès Affnaer*, 52.   [73] See *Constitutionnel*, 9 Jan. 1844.

originally entrusted with the prosecution to be withdrawn on pretext of illness after reading the anti-jesuit remarks in the draft of his *plaidoirie*; the replacement, it claimed, had delivered 'a pompous eulogy of the Jesuits', thanks to which the order had been 'as it were officially recognized, in contempt of jurisprudence and of legislation'.[74]

In mid-April, the Jesuit question returned to parliamentary politics. On 14 April, as the Chambre des Pairs debated a petition for disciplinary action against Michelet and Quinet (whose courses had become increasingly polemical and extreme), both baron Dupin (invoking the Swiss anarchy) and Cousin (invoking the Affenäer revelations) raised the issue of the Jesuits' suppression. Cousin declared himself sure that the government would take no 'severe measure' at the Collège de France till it had enforced the law against the Society of Jesus. When Martin, in reply, insisted on the government's right of discretion over whether and when to do this, *Le Siècle* applauded Cousin for having forced him to reveal his 'shameful complicity' in the Jesuits' revival.[75] Well might Guizot, on 17 April, warn Rossi that 'here the question is hotting up'.[76] A week later, it became known that Thiers would interpellate the government concerning the Jesuits in the Chambre des Députés on 2 May.

The debate of 2 and 3 May bore witness, once again, to the widespread acceptance of anti-jesuit arguments in parliamentary circles. Those who challenged the basic premisses of these arguments (here Carné and Berryer, and more ambiguously Lamartine) spoke for a small minority. Thiers's speech reflected this: it was geared not to a trial of strength between entrenched factions but to the provocation of a display of anti-jesuit consensus, which the government could not refuse to accept, but which would put it under pressure and magnify the loss of face and support it would sustain if, as was commonly expected, Rossi's negotiations failed. In a somewhat slightingly phrased advertisement of political generosity, Thiers insisted that his object in interpellating the government was to give it the strength it needed if its actions were to conform to the

---

[74] Ibid. 11, 13 Apr. 1845 (and the earlier speculations in *Siècle*, 11 Jan. 1845). Nothing really describable as a eulogy of the Jesuits is contained in the published versions of *avocat-général* de Thorigny's speeches at the trial.

[75] *Moniteur*, CP 14 Apr. 1845; *Siècle*, 15 Apr. 1845.

[76] Guizot, *Mémoires*, vii. 411.

opinions he was sure it shared with him. The facts revealed by the Affenäer case, he argued, made it impossible any longer to turn a blind eye to the Jesuits' presence. If, once both Chambers had discussed the matter, nothing was done, 'you will have done more than tolerate the Society of Jesus, you will have rescinded the laws and royal edicts which prosecuted it; you will, in 1845, have pronounced the Jesuits' recall to France!' The question was of great importance, for France stood at a point of 'collision' in Church–State relations, to which she had been brought by the turbulence and disrespect for law shown not by the clergy as a whole, but by a domineering faction within it. 'Where do we find this faction? As to that, I tell you frankly, I believe that the primary impulse comes from the *congrégation* against which I am calling for the laws to be enforced.' In taking the necessary steps against the Jesuits, the government would be going 'straight to the cause of the evil', and could count on the Chamber's firm support.[77]

The enthusiastic response to Thiers's speech prevented Martin from replying for twenty minutes; even then, he faced frequent interruptions. His speech recognized that circumstances relating to the Jesuits gave cause for legitimate concern, but tried to dispel the dangerous impression that the government had needed to be pressed before attending to the matter. Rejecting Thiers's hints at the prospect of Swiss-style civil war, Martin insisted, as before, on the government's freedom of manœuvre: by seeking a diplomatic solution rather than peremptorily enforcing the law, it was following the most responsible course. In the ensuing debate, Dupin *aîné* and Hébert reaffirmed the political and juridical necessity of ending the Jesuits' illegal existence, but did not question the government's right to decide on the appropriate method. Only the leader of the *gauche dynastique*, Odilon Barrot, professed to find the approach to Rome humiliating and unjustified, and even he accepted the carefully worded *ordre du jour* which Thiers proposed: 'The Chamber, relying on the government to ensure the execution of the laws of the State, passes to the order of the day.' This motion—which, as Thiers made clear, left the government free to negotiate, but not to make the dissolution of the Jesuits dependent on the success of its negotiations—was adopted by a large majority.[78]

---

[77] *Moniteur*, CD 2 May 1845: 1166–8.   [78] Ibid., CD 2 and 3 May 1845.

Interpretations of the debate and the vote varied predictably. Where the *Journal des débats* saw 'rather a vote of confidence than a censure for the government', *Le Siècle* saw the government 'arraigned at the bar of the Chamber' by its own *procureur-général* (Hébert), and *Le Constitutionnel* saw it hustled along the path of duty by the opposition, its courage against the Jesuits that of 'the coward driven to the abyss'.[79] In the Chambre des Pairs, Montalembert accused the cabinet of yielding ignobly to the passions of its political rivals in order to preserve its precious majority. This stung Martin into abandoning his earlier restraint: reproducing, on the government's behalf, the familiar anti-jesuit account of the Jesuits' increasing audacity over the past year, culminating in their appearance in the Affenäer case, he added 'that all along, observing their conduct before any measure was taken against them, the government was able to convince itself that the agitation which exists was in large part provoked and maintained by them, and that the writings in which the country's institutions were audaciously attacked should be attributed to them'.[80] Little seemed now to separate the government's views on the Jesuits from those of the opposition.

Though the parliamentary campaign against the Jesuits put the government under pressure at home, it also, by spreading apprehension in Rome, helped Rossi to achieve the partial success which allowed Guizot to bring the Jesuit question back under control. A note in the *Moniteur* on 6 July announced that Rossi's mission had 'achieved its goal': 'The Congrégation of the Jesuits will cease to exist in France and is going to disperse itself of its own accord; its houses will be closed and its noviciates dissolved.' This message, on whose accuracy Guizot would insist, in fact concealed two circumstances which lessened the government's triumph. First, the decision in Rome had been taken not by the Pope, but by the General of the Jesuits; when this emerged, opposition journalists were quick to suggest that the government had bargained shamefully with the Jesuit order as an equal.[81] Secondly, the Jesuits did not accept the government's view of what had been conceded; their intention was simply (in Cardinal Lambruschini's phrase) 'to

[79] *Débats*, 4 May 1845; *Siècle*, 6 May 1845; *Constitutionnel*, 4 May 1845.
[80] *Moniteur*, CP 11 June 1845, quotation 1663.
[81] *Siècle*, 10 July 1845, alluded to the 'conditions imposed on M. Guizot by the General of the Jesuits', rumoured to include action against Michelet and Quinet.

arrange themselves in such a way as to permit the Government not to see them',[82] by dispersing their principal communities in Paris and Lyons and displacing or closing a few noviciates. Their stubborn avoidance of doing more left some of their enemies still suspicious or alarmed, but expressions of anti-jesuit concern during the final years of the July Monarchy were sporadic and posed little danger to the government.[83] Like the *ordonnance* of 1828, Rossi's success, for all its limitations, drained most of the wind from anti-jesuit sails; the Jesuit question ceased to hold a central place in French political discourse. Had Salvandy's secondary education bill of 1847 (which, when amended in committee, reproduced the anti-jesuit safeguards of that of 1844[84]) come to debate, some revival of pro- and anti-jesuit passions might have been expected, but the Revolution of February 1848 intervened.

RADICAL ANTI-JESUITISM

It was the common anti-jesuitism of the Orleanist political establishment that was mobilized in parliamentary debate over *liberté de l'enseignement* in 1844 and Thiers's interpellation in 1845, and in the polemics of the leading pro-government and opposition newspapers. This anti-jesuitism was, in many ways, defensive and authoritarian: its most obvious supports were a sense of the necessary authority of the State (represented in education by the Université), a profession of respect for the French secular clergy (despite the aberrations of bishops misled into serving the Jesuit interest) and of concern for the freedoms of the Gallican Church, and a rather self-congratulatory faith in the status of the victors of July 1830 as the connoisseurs, arbiters, and interpreters of liberty. The political and legal arguments of this style of anti-jesuitism should by now be familiar. It was not, however, the only one to exert an influence on French public opinion during these years. The myth of 1830 as an anti-jesuit revolution had different implications among those whose faith in revolution had not become wholly retrospective with the fall of Charles X.

---

[82] Quoted in Burnichon, *La Compagnie de Jésus en France*, ii. 658, 714.
[83] See *Moniteur*, CD 29 Jan. 1846: 227 (Lherbette); CD 10 Feb. 1847: 273 (de La Plesse).   [84] *Moniteur*, 11 Aug. 1847: 241–2.

Already, during the short but intense wave of anti-jesuit feeling after July 1830, the gap which had existed in 1828–9 between anti-jesuitism as retailed in *Le Constitutionnel* and as interpreted in *L'Ancien Album* had shown signs of reopening: Dumesnil had castigated Guizot and Broglie as 'the tricoloured Jesuits';[85] cartoons had shown Dupin *aîné* muttering Jesuitical mental reservations or consorting with the 'Jesuit' Charles X; the Jesuitical turkey had appeared (with the Napoleonic bee and the legitimist fleur-de-lis) on the coat of arms of the *juste milieu*, which a cartoon of May 1831 had contrasted with the arms of the People.[86] With the development of new and purpose-built anti-Orleanist symbols (notably Philipon's pear-shaped king), the Jesuit theme had then faded from the invective and iconography of unfulfilled revolution, as it had done from that of the fulfilled, until the 1840s. Then, however, anti-jesuit rhetoric and themes again became tools in the hands of men disposed to question the sharpness of the antithesis between Jesuitism and respectable Orleanism on which more conservative anti-jesuits insisted. Auguste Arnould saw a spiritual affinity between the Jesuits and the government: 'Yes, the impious doctrines of material interest, the demoralization which is invading each class of society successively like leprosy, the [cult of] success offered everywhere and always as the justification and excuse of every action, have served the Jesuits, just as the Jesuits, for their part, served the corruptors in power [*un pouvoir corrupteur*].'[87] Guizot and his colleagues were the target of this particular attack, but the opposition did not always escape. By no means all anti-jesuits could see anything heroic or purposeful in the parliamentary drama of May 1845; the *Almanach du mois*, whose contempt embraced the whole class of 'fossilized liberals', commented:

Here, one must admit, is a logical conclusion! That's to say, that the ministers do not enforce the laws; the *députés* complain and demand that the government be forced to respect the laws; and the Chamber relies for their enforcement on the ministers—precisely those who refuse to do it! It is easy to see that the discussion had to do with the Jesuits, for the spirit

---

[85] A. Dumesnil, *Les Jésuites tricolores: Un chapitre de mœurs politiques* (Paris, 1830).

[86] BN Est.: de Vinck (90) 11486–8 (Dupin cartoons); *La Caricature*, 26 May 1831 (coats of arms).

[87] A. Arnould, *Les Jésuites depuis leur origine jusqu'à nos jours: Histoire, types, mœurs, mystères*, 2 vols. (Paris, 1846), vol. i, p. iv.

of the order was clearly blowing on the assembly when it adopted such an equivocal and ridiculous measure.[88]

Nor did all anti-jesuits accept the conventional statist and Gallican pieties. The *Journal de la liberté religieuse* (whose leading figure was the lawyer and *député* F.-A. Isambert), for example, though it declared the protection of the Gallican liberties 'against the attacks of the Jesuitical party' as one of its aims,[89] argued both for the separation of Church and State and for the dismantling of the *monopole universitaire*. In this case, there was still a considerable rhetorical overlap with the anti-jesuitism that dominated parliamentary debates. This is much less evident, however, in the visions of Jesuitism propounded by Sue in *Le Juif errant* and by Michelet and Quinet at the Collège de France.

The quality of the Jesuits most repeatedly evoked by Sue, aside from their complete unscrupulousness, was their ability to reduce men 'to that mute and dejected obedience, to that submissiveness of the serf or the brute, which assures the peace of States through the immobility of the spirit'. The more conservative of *Le Constitutionnel*'s readers, who would have agreed about the stultifying effects of Jesuitism on the human psyche, might well have been startled at the suggestion that the peace of states stood to benefit. Père d'Aigrigny (the Jesuit character whose words these were) went on to criticize the rulers of the world for their failure to see that the Jesuits were their best allies in taming the people; at the end of the novel they were described as 'accomplices of every slavery, of every despotism'.[90] Sue said nothing openly disrespectful of the existing regime, but nor did he say anything to encourage his readers to distinguish the moral claims of the regime from those of despotical government, or to identify the cause of popular liberty with that of political stability as construed by rulers or ruling classes. That the Jesuits were the enemies of the people (a 'people' conceived in accord with Romantic notions of social harmony, and symbolized in the novel by the diverse members and friends of the scattered Rennepont family, who include a benevolent industrialist, an enlightened heiress, a saintly priest, and the daughters of a Napoleonic general, as well as male and female representatives of

---

[88] *L'Almanach du mois*, 3: 339–40 (June 1845).
[89] *Journal de la liberté religieuse*, 'Extrait du prospectus', 1.
[90] E. Sue, *Le Juif errant*, 5 vols. (Brussels, 1844–5), ii. 22, iv. 403.

the working classes) did not make them the enemies of states and governments; they were conspirators within rather than against the system. To ensure liberty did not mean (as the rhetoric of a Dupin or a Thiers or a Villemain implied) to preserve the system by keeping out the Jesuits, but to transform the system and destroy the Jesuits, by teaching the people to emancipate themselves. Here, as Sue's anti-jesuit patriarch Marius Rennepont made clear (in the seventeenth-century will around which the novel's plot revolved), the Jesuits themselves showed the great lesson to be learnt: that of the power of association. The Society of Jesus was the spirit of tyranny not just incarnate (a familiar anti-jesuit idea), but in its optimal social form. Rennepont urged his descendants to form a rival association, rooted in fraternity and dedicated to human happiness, work, enlightenment, and freedom; then 'the spirit of good' and 'the spirit of evil' would stand on a level footing, ready for battle, and 'God would protect the just'.[91] The way forward for anti-jesuitism, in short, lay not (as men like Dupin would have argued) in a rejection of the validity of associations capable of coming between the individual and the State, but precisely in their development: in the organization of labour and the banding together of the well-meaning.

This was one version of a radical anti-jesuitism. How seriously the majority of Sue's readers took the ideological dimension of his tale, and how much importance he himself attached to it, are open to question. There is less room to doubt the self-importance of the anti-jesuit crusade proposed and embraced at the Collège de France. 'What characterized the new teaching, as it appeared at the Collège de France (1840–1850)', Michelet later wrote, 'was the strength of its faith, the effort to draw from history, not simply a doctrine, but a *principle of action*.'[92] This ambition was much in evidence in the courses of 1843 to 1845, and the two professors' sense of mission was matched and encouraged by the passionate receptivity of the *jeunesse des écoles* and of others whose frustration at conventional parliamentarism made them eager for new tribunes. Michelet and Quinet aspired not simply to instruct, or even to lead, but to be the articulators of the vital word which would catalyse the inchoate ardours of their audience. Béranger, when students clamoured

---

[91] Ibid. iii. 36–40.

[92] J. Michelet, 'Le Collège de France', in *Paris-guide, par les principaux écrivains et artistes de la France*, 2 vols. (Paris, 1867), i. 139.

outside his house a few years later, would advise them to return to their studies.[93] Quinet's response to a deputation of them in 1844 was to speak proudly of his 'alliance with French youth in what must indeed be called the sacred war for religious and social liberty'.[94] Michelet, in 1843, had ended his course by summoning his listeners to 'the holy crusade we are beginning for God and liberty';[95] Quinet concluded his in 1844 with a kind of mystical swearing-in: 'I have but served as organ to the thought which, without our knowing how, was coming to everyone's lips. What has happened here, between us, is a stern bond. On your part, as on mine, it is a commitment.'[96] It was not through the social power of association, but through the spiritual one of heroic engagement, that Michelet and Quinet hoped to save France from Jesuitism.

Like Sue, Michelet and Quinet said much with which the proponents of a more conservative style of anti-jesuitism could agree —that the Society of Jesus was 'a foreign association, powerful, naturally and necessarily an enemy of France',[97] for example—but abandoned or reversed some of its more characteristic emphases. The Université's detractors were attacked without its importance and achievements being glorified (perhaps because Michelet and Quinet were privately contemptuous of the Eclectic philosophy Cousin had imposed on it), and Gallicanism was dismissed by Michelet as nonexistent and by Quinet as a dangerous chimera lacking the intellectual coherence of Ultramontanism.[98] Both men, as their courses developed, showed themselves increasingly disinclined to draw any practical distinction between Jesuitism and modern Catholicism. 'Jesuitism has compromised Catholicism,' warned Quinet in 1844; 'take care that Catholicism, thus committed, does not compromise Christianity.'[99] Michelet, in 1845, wrote of Jesuitism as 'the common spirit which the clergy now receives by a special

[93] E. Fage, *Souvenirs d'enfance et de la jeunesse* (Tulle, 1901), 273.

[94] E. Quinet, *Œuvres complètes*, 10 vols. (Paris, 1857–8), ii. 306 ('Réponse à une députation de la jeunesse des écoles', 20 June 1844).

[95] J. Michelet, *Des jésuites*, 116. For convenience, I refer to Michelet's and Quinet's lectures as separate works, though they were published together; in each case the reference is to the relevant part of J. Michelet and E. Quinet, *Des jésuites*, 7th edn. (Paris, 1845).

[96] Quinet, *Œuvres complètes*, ii. 301 (*L'Ultramontanisme; ou L'Église romaine et la société moderne*).　　　　　　　　　　　　　　　[97] Quinet, *Des jésuites*, 220.

[98] Michelet, *Des jésuites*, 16–17 (preface); Quinet, *Des jésuites*, 269–70; Quinet, *Œuvres complètes*, iii. 209 (*Le Christianisme et la Révolution française*).

[99] Quinet, *Œuvres complètes*, ii. 130–1 (*L'Ultramontanisme*).

education, and which its leaders make no difficulty about avowing'.[100]

The essence of Michelet and Quinet's anti-jesuitism, and its difference from that of the Orleanist political establishment, showed through its verbal style. The claim of both professors that the natural evolution of their courses had forced them in 1843 to speak of the Jesuits need not be taken at face value, but the terms in which it was couched are significant. 'The study of the death of peoples, if one seeks its cause, is as important as the study of their life,' Quinet affirmed: it was therefore necessary for him to consider the Jesuits, as cause of the decadence to which southern European culture and society (the legitimate subject of his course) had succumbed from the later sixteenth century onwards.[101] Michelet, whose startling leap from the Middle Ages seemed to call for more justification, explained that, having analysed 'life', as found in medieval civilization, he had naturally gone on to explore 'the false life, which counterfeits it', and which the Jesuits represented. 'The living organism' had had to be contrasted with 'the sterile mechanism'. To compare the two was to address 'the highest question of history and of morality'; as professor precisely *de morale et d'histoire*, he had both the right and the duty to confront it.[102] This repeated use of the imagery of life and death, of the organic and the mechanical, was typical of the anti-jesuitism propounded at the Collège de France; what was offered was not primarily a political or religious or social critique of Jesuitism, but a spiritual or moral one, based on a Romantic celebration of the authentic and spontaneous, and disparagement of the artificial, the calculated, the automatic. It was the grandeur and universality of the Jesuit question, not its topicality, that, in Quinet's view, made it important to his audience: 'This question is that of reality and of appearance, of truth and falsehood, of life and of the letter.'[103]

Mistrust of the human spirit, in both men's view, lay at the heart of Jesuitism. The human soul, according to Michelet, could not survive the suspicious policing to which the Jesuits subjected it. In its place was left the machinery created by Loyola for generating the appearance of religious feeling, of morality, of human emotion.

---

[100] J. Michelet, *Du prêtre, de la femme, de la famille*, 3rd edn. (Paris, 1845), 46 (preface to 3rd edn.).   [101] Quinet, *Des jésuites*, 143.
[102] Michelet, *Des jésuites*, 39, 53.   [103] Quinet, *Des jésuites*, 207–12.

This explained the order's sterility, which Michelet considered indisputable. 'That which truly *is*, produces,' he declared: the Jesuits had produced no great men, and their principal achievements in 300 years had been their own mechanistic *Constitutions* and their development of the art of chicanery in the confessional.[104] Quinet expounded the same set of ideas in more detail. Because the Jesuits lacked faith in the spiritual powers both of Christ and of humanity, he argued, they knew no way to establish Christ's rule on earth except by 'calculations borrowed from the politics of cabinets': a discipline in which the spirit was kept in check by mutual espionage and blind obedience, *Spiritual Exercises* in which emotional effusions were performed to schedule, and a moral theology in which the divine law was reduced to written regulations and casuistical procedures were the results. In all things, the Jesuits experienced 'the systematic necessity of repressing the great instincts, and of developing the small ones'.[105]

This, then, was the profile of 'the spirit of death'. It was Quinet who most fully established its antithesis. He gave it three faces: true Christianity, the Revolution, and France. 'The first and last word of Christ is life. The first and last word of Loyola is the corpse,' he remarked, commenting on St Ignatius' last discourse on obedience.[106] Unlike Jesuitism, its degenerate form, true Christianity was a universal religion, which resisted the confinement in which particular churches sought to keep it.[107] The essence of the French Revolution, in Quinet's eyes, lay in its embracing of this universality—in the unprecedented initiative by which the French people had entered 'into communion with the God of all the Churches' and brought humanity into 'a universal communion'.[108] This made the Revolution 'more truly Christian than Ultramontanism', and ensured that the latter would never finally defeat it.[109]

Quinet demonstrated the incompatibility of Jesuitism and the Revolution by invoking history. By quite arbitrarily endowing Clement XIV with the Revolutionary spirit, he passed off the suppression of the Jesuits as a Revolutionary act: 'The spirit of 1789 and of the Constituent is entirely present in this pontifical bull of 1773. From that moment on, what happens? So long as the new

[104] Michelet, *Des jésuites*, 14, 46–9, 85–9.   [105] Quinet, *Des jésuites*, 207–12.
[106] Ibid. 198.   [107] Ibid. 154–5.
[108] Quinet, *Œuvres complètes*, ii. 298 (*L'Ultramontanisme*).
[109] Quinet, *des jésuites*, 135–7.

France remains victorious in the world, nothing more is heard of the Society of Jesus.' Only in 1814, with France forced to deny the Revolution, were the Jesuits able to recover. Now, in 1843, the two enemies faced each other: 'On the one side, the French Revolution with the development of religious and social life; on the other, hidden no one knows where, its natural contradictor, the order of Jesus, with its unshakeable attachment to the past. It is between these two things that one must choose.'[110]

France, as the land of the Revolution, was naturally opposed to Jesuitism. Their mutual antagonism, however, was a matter as much of character as of heritage:

If we [the French] are worth anything in the world, it is by our spontaneous *élan*; with it [Jesuitism], it is just the opposite. It is by our uprightness, even to the point of indiscretion, to the profit of our enemies; with it, it is just the opposite. It is by our rectitude of spirit: it, on the other hand, is nothing but subtlety and devious intentions. It is by a certain manner of inflaming ourselves in the cause of others; it is concerned only with its own. Finally, it is by the power of our heart, and it is precisely the heart that it mistrusts. What, then, are we to make of an institution which sets itself at every point to repudiate the character and mission that God himself has given to our country? I see well now that it is not a question only of the spirit of the Revolution, as I said before. Of what is it a question then? Of the very existence of the spirit of France, such as it has always been; of two incompatible things at grips with each other, one of which must necessarily stifle the other; either Jesuitism must abolish the spirit of France, or France abolish the spirit of Jesuitism.[111]

Michelet invited his readers to choose: 'If you have a Jesuit heart, pass that way, that is the side of Fribourg; if you are upright and straightforward [*loyal et net*], come here, this is France!'[112]

There were thus two oppositions in play: the first political and religious, between Jesuitism (Ultramontanism, intolerance) and the Revolution (universal religion, liberty); the second moral, between Jesuitism (insincerity, deviousness, artificiality) and the spirit of life (truth, authenticity, spontaneity), most notably exemplified in the French character. The latter opposition tended to absorb the former: the Revolution would triumph over Jesuitism politically, if Frenchmen reaffirmed by their example the spiritual characteristics for which they were famous. Quinet told his audience in 1844:

---

[110] Ibid. 175–6.   [111] Ibid. 216–17.
[112] Michelet, *Des jésuites*, 23.

Jesuitism, ultramontanism, are merely a symptom of an undoubtedly much deeper evil; these plants of the maremma show the state of the surrounding air. If we do not, in spite of the obstacles, reanimate the principle of our moral life, I hold it for certain that we are marching towards a downfall, or towards an irremediable abdication in the eyes of Europe.

The new generation must strive above all to establish 'the reign and religion of sincerity'.[113] The previous year, Quinet had urged them to vow 'to persevere right to the end, in all things, in sincerity, in truth, in liberty'—to promise, in other words, 'to remain faithful to the genius of France'.[114]

Anti-jesuitism, then, was to be a moral revolution. Michelet and Quinet could be criticized for permitting it to be nothing more: those most obviously enslaved to Jesuitism (women, lower clergy) were to be liberated, but their liberation was to be won by spiritual readjustment (women, Michelet made clear, were to be won back to the modern world by receiving intellectual nourishment and leadership from their husbands) rather than by social or political change. It was not, then, in immediate practical recommendations that the radicalism of Michelet and Quinet's anti-jesuitism lay, but in the more general implications of their rhetoric. By the terms of their spiritual critique of Jesuitism, they provided a dualist framework within which even quite conservative anxieties could be transferred to the realm of crusading fervour. Substitution of the rhetoric of spiritual conflict, of life and death, for the staider one of state surveillance and Orleanist liberalism (or the grafting of the former rhetoric on to the latter) could certainly give political conflicts over the Jesuits an air of higher significance, but it also made it harder to see how the Jesuit question could be politically resolved: the spirit of Death was scarcely likely to be extinguished by the mere closure of Jesuit establishments. Michelet and Quinet did not even bother to demand limited remedies of this sort. By seeming to place the Jesuit question in the timeless realm of fundamental spiritual issues, they created a perspective from which the style of anti-jesuitism favoured by most Orleanist politicians might well seem at best myopic, and at worst afflicted by the same vices of deadened formalism and mock vitality that the Society of Jesus was held to embody.

[113] Quinet, *Œuvres complètes*, ii. 130–2 (*L'Ultramontanisme*).
[114] Quinet, *Des jésuites*, 288.

Nor was it necessarily flattering to the Orleanist élite to have it bruited about that France's problems stemmed not so much from the sinister intrigues of a handful of malicious men against a basically sound political and social system as from the way in which society was blighted by spiritual corruption, by insincerity, calculation, and soulless materialism. Michelet and Quinet encouraged people to see these qualities not as vices more or less endemic in humanity, regardless of political or spiritual affiliation, but as the manifestations of a particular spirit, whose struggle with its polar opposite composed the central dynamic of modern history. On one level, of course, the association of these qualities with Jesuit influence helped to explain them away. It also, however, drew attention to them wherever (in the government, in the opposition, in bourgeois society at large) they might be found, and magnified their importance. Anti-jesuitism in the style of Michelet and Quinet was a medium well suited to articulating a sense of moral decadence which might reflect discredit on others besides the Jesuits themselves.

Finally, it was Michelet and above all Quinet who did most to establish the Revolution—conceived of not as a finished moment whose achievements had merely to be defended, but as a living force—as the enduring antithesis of Jesuitism, and vice versa. This would be of significance in the longer-term history both of anti-jesuitism and of the radical and republican traditions in France. The ideological coming-of-age of a radical anti-jesuitism that had previously been little more than a sarcastic commentary on the hypocrisies of its liberal counterpart offered the anti-jesuit tradition the sort of backbone it had threatened to lose with the decline, since the eighteenth century, of Jansenism and of forceful ecclesiastical Gallicanism. The Jesuits could once again be attacked in the name of a militant faith. And the style of Michelet and Quinet's polemic, whose influence could already be detected in the writings of Génin and others,[115] would make a significant contribution to the intransigence of that faith, in both its moderate and

---

[115] Thus e.g. F. Ducroix, *Les Frères, les jésuites, l'Université* (Thiers, 1843), a pamphlet which focused on purely local issues, still mentioned Michelet and Quinet, and echoed their message: 'On one side are the shadows, the falsehood, arbitrary power, and the grave; on the other, the light, the truth, independence, life. Let us hasten, then, to choose between the Society of Jesus and the Université of France' (p. 15).

its radical variants. For, in the end, the effect of taking a critique of insincerity and artificiality as one's guide to current affairs, of squaring up to 'l'esprit de mensonge' (Génin's term[116]), was not to divert attention from the political conflict, but to harden its lines, by heightening the conviction of one's enemies' bad faith, and by suggesting that victory was to be won not by manœuvre or compromise, but by forthright fidelity to doggedly held principles.

THE SECOND REPUBLIC

Thanks to the equivocal success of Rossi's mission in 1845, the anti-jesuit outcry of the 1840s, unlike that of the 1820s, ended with more of a whimper than a bang. For the Society of Jesus, the Revolution of February 1848 and its aftermath brought little of the suspicion or violence of 1830. There was a crowd attack on the Jesuit house at LaLouvesc, and the Jesuits of Lyons and Avignon were briefly dissolved or expelled by the local Republican *commissaires*; otherwise, however, neither the populace nor the new authorities seemed as interested in anti-jesuit action as the Jesuits had feared they might be. Few anti-jesuit tracts were published under the Second Republic. Equally remarkably, the General of the Society of Jesus, in flight from revolutionary developments in Rome, was able to live and travel secretly in France for over a year, beginning in April 1848, apparently without arousing the hostile attentions of police, press, or public—a fact which no doubt owes much to Jesuit precautions, but which certainly suggests a level of public and administrative vigilance markedly lower than under the Orleanist regime.[117]

If there was no new anti-jesuit revolution, however, there was an instructive coda to the struggles of 1843–5 in the debates which culminated in the Loi Falloux in 1850. The point at issue was the same as in 1844—*liberté de l'enseignement*, and behind it, the Jesuits' right to teach. The outcome, thanks to the prevailing mood of pro-religious and counter-revolutionary conservatism, was different: the omission of any clause excluding the unauthorized orders from secondary education reopened to them the door held shut since

---

[116] Génin, *Les Jésuites et l'Université*, 21.
[117] Burnichon, *La Compagnie de Jésus en France*, iii. 116–24.

1828. The arguments used concerning the Jesuits before and during the discussion of the law, however, reveal first the gap which the experience of 1848 had opened between some one-time exponents of Orleanist anti-jesuitism and their more radical counterparts, and secondly, the diversity of styles which was already part of the Republican anti-jesuit tradition.

Anyone who heard Thiers and Cousin airing their views as members of the extraparliamentary commission on secondary education set up in 1849 might have been forgiven for failing to recognize the anti-jesuit champions of four years before. Both men, admittedly, continued to oppose the admission of the Jesuits to the teaching profession, and to represent Catholic enthusiasm for them as a serious obstacle to agreement among conservatives. Neither, however, seemed willing to make his objections positive or passionate; Cousin implied that only respect for the law really held him back from accepting the Jesuits, and Thiers's resistance appeared to be little more than the by-product of his concern with the quite different threat of revolutionary socialism. 'God forbid that I should do the Jesuits the injury of comparing them with those associations dangerous to public peace,' he protested; it was simply unfortunate that one could not relax the law for the unauthorized orders without relaxing it for the 'clubs'.[118] In the parliamentary debate on the Loi Falloux the following year, Thiers expressed himself neither for nor against the Jesuits, but sought instead to put off discussion of them until the possible occasion of a proposed law of associations.[119]

Those who did attack the Jesuits during the debate included conservative figures like Flandin and Barthélemy-Saint-Hilaire as well as more radical ones like Victor Hugo and Bernard Lavergne. The four most notably anti-jesuit speeches, however, all came from firm Republicans (two of whom would go into exile, and two withdraw from public life, after Louis-Napoleon's *coup d'état*): between them, they display a spectrum of Republican anti-jesuit rhetoric. At the radical extreme lay Benjamin Raspail (son of a more famous radical father), whose anti-jesuitism was embellished by invocations of 1789, 1792, and February 1848, and whose professions of faith in progress and modernity were allied to a vision of universal religion.

---

[118] *La Commission extraparlementaire de 1849*, 209–14 (Thiers), 218–21 (Cousin), 237–40 (Thiers).   [119] *Moniteur*, Ass. N. 23 Feb. 1850: 622–3.

At the other end lay Bourzat, author of an unsuccessful amendment which would have continued the exclusion of the unauthorized orders. His speech reproduced the statist and socially conservative arguments familiar from the debates of 1844 and 1845: 'Jesuitism' was a danger to the State, to public order, to morality, family, and property (all represented as bases of the Republic); to unshackle it would be to open the way to 'independence and usurpation', two concepts seemingly as closely linked in Bourzat's mind as in those of the *parlementaires* of 1762. In mid-spectrum, the speeches of Emmanuel Arago (who had been the *commissaire* responsible for evicting the Jesuits from Lyons in 1848) and of Laurent *de l'Ardèche* stood for differing but qualified emphases within that dialectic of progress and order which Restoration Liberalism had bequeathed to its successors. Arago, supporting Bourzat, was less overtly conservative in his social views, and less emphatic on the rights of the State, but his rejection of the Jesuits as 'a foreign association, which comes to create a state within the State', and his analogy between accepting them and accepting an association of Cossacks under orders from St Petersburg, could have come from a speech by baron Dupin. Laurent (moving an amendment similar to Bourzat's) took a more progressive tone, denouncing the Jesuits as 'the last citadel of the old spiritual and temporal society', destined to crumble before the forward march of humanity. There were still, however, signs of more conservative instincts, both in Laurent's expressed preference for the anti-jesuit testimony of *ancien régime* authorities over that of 'those little word-mongers [*rhéteurs*] with whom the Université has peopled every career', and in his description of Jesuitism as the epitome of socialism and communism. The debate on the Loi Falloux showed, once again, the flexibility (and therefore the durability) of anti-jesuit conceptions; fears both old and new, and attitudes both defensive and aggressive, found expression through a complex of rhetoric whose tensions were at once traditional and suggestive of future divisions.[120]

[120] Ibid., Ass. N. 23 Feb. 1850: 660–1 (Bourzat), 664 (Arago); Ass. N. 25 Feb. 1850: 676–8 (Laurent); Ass. N. 11 Mar. 1850: 836–7 (Raspail).

4

The Road to Article 7

THE anti-jesuitism of the 1820s evolved from insignificance to its peak in around half a decade; that of the 1840s did so in a year or two. The third great public mooting of the Jesuit question, which came eventually to a head with the debate on Article 7 in 1879–80, had a far longer prologue. Anti-jesuitism left its traces, not overwhelming, but common and recurrent, in the political and religious polemic of the 1850s, 1860s, and 1870s. It had a more visible target during these decades than at any other time in the century. The freedom of secondary education finally granted in the Loi Falloux of 1850 permitted the Jesuits to open schools: they opened eleven by the end of the year, six more by 1854.[1] This thriving educational network provided an obvious focus for their enemies' attentions and meant that, unlike under the Restoration or the July Monarchy, little time was wasted on either side in proving or denying the Jesuits' existence. The scandalous revelations which anti-jesuits strove to exploit related not to this, but to supposedly sinister episodes or facets of the life and work of Jesuit *collèges*: the breaking of a plaster bust of Napoleon III in a playground incident which caused the temporary closure of the *collège* at Saint-Étienne in 1853, the scandal over corporal punishment at the *collège* of Tivoli (Bordeaux) in 1868, the allegations of foul play in public examinations levelled at the École Sainte-Geneviève (rue des Postes) in 1876.

FROM THE SECOND TO THE THIRD REPUBLIC

Though the Loi Falloux permitted the Jesuits to teach, it did nothing to alter their unauthorized status. The basis for the legalistic and statist arguments characteristic of conservative Orleanist

[1] Padberg, *Colleges in Controversy*, 102–4.

anti-jesuitism remained intact, and though some who had previously expounded them now abandoned the anti-jesuit colours
(baron Dupin, for example, could be found in 1869 defending the
Jesuits against a petition for their expulsion[2]), others did not.
Jurist-politicians like Bonjean and Troplong were the latest in the
line of Gallican magistrates who had figured so prominently in the
anti-jesuit tradition since the *ancien régime*.[3] Effectively, however,
they were to be the last.[4] Anti-jesuits in the 1870s would use many
of the same arguments, but they would look to education rather
than the law for protection, and view the magistrates of their own
time with mistrust. There was a poignant irony to the death of
Bonjean in 1871 at the hands of a Communard firing-squad, with
two Jesuits (as well as the Gallican archbishop Darboy) among his
last companions. One of them, Père Clerc, wrote from captivity
that, though he had long believed he would one day find himself in
prison, he had 'imagined that this would happen by the regular and
official means of some M. Bonjean or other, magistrate of the old
Parlements, while this poor M. Bonjean finds it less astonishing to
see himself in prison than to see himself there with the Jesuits'.[5]

Some of those active in government under the Second Empire
might have been equally surprised at the reputation for Jesuitism
which the regime they served was to enjoy in Republican hindsight.
In the 1850s and 1860s, the Jesuits were by no means generally
assured of the benevolence of a public authority many of whose
agents shared the statist and Gallican views so common among

---

[2] *ASCL*, Sénat 28 Apr. 1869: 81–3.

[3] See e.g. the anti-jesuit stance of Bonjean in the Sénat 15 Mar. 1865 (ibid. 123);
also references to his and Troplong's anti-jesuit arguments as members of the
commission considering Duruy's 1867 plans for freedom of higher education, in V.
Duruy, *Notes et souvenirs (1811–1894)*, 2 vols. (Paris, 1901), ii. 23–41.

[4] The author of the pamphlet *Du jésuitisme: Troisième annexe sur la justice et les
juges, par trois procureurs généraux, deux de l'ancienne monarchie, le troisième de la monarchie
constitutionnelle* (Paris, 1874) posed as an isolated continuer of the tradition, but his
anti-jesuitism was really in a different vein: after a brief summary of the anti-jesuit
pronouncements of La Chalotais and Monclar, and a rambling and self-glorifying
account of his own lifelong struggles against Jesuitism, he went on to propose
eccentric, draconian, and unprecedented legislation, aimed not against the Society
of Jesus, but against the undefined offence of 'Jesuitism', together with the establishment of a special 'section du jésuitisme' of the Cour de Cassation to judge cases
of it.

[5] Quoted in A. de Ponlevoy, *Actes de la captivité et de la mort des RR. PP. P.
Olivaint, L. Ducoudray, J. Caubert, A. Clerc, A. de Bengy, de la Compagnie de Jésus*
(Paris, 1871), 66–7.

their Orleanist predecessors, and which had reason to be wary of legitimist intrigue. The reasons given for closing the Saint-Étienne *collège* in 1853 included the Jesuits' alleged revival of memories of the Vendée, and their general hostility to existing laws and authority.[6] Earlier the same year, replying to a request by the Minister of Education, Fortoul, for information on the religious *congrégations*, several prefects had stressed either the Jesuits' *esprit d'envahissement* or their legitimist connections; later reports mentioned subversive preaching and underhand competition with state education.[7] In the old royalist heartland of Poitou, the *procureur-général* of Poitiers warned the government in 1854, the Jesuit school, 'with the secret struggles and subterranean domination that infallibly attach to it', would prove 'a nursery of generations hostile to the government' and 'a refuge for hopes of civil war'.[8] Warnings of this kind no doubt combined with the prior inclinations of Fortoul's successors, Rouland and Victor Duruy (the former a lawyer of Gallican bent, the latter a man of the Université) to generate a climate of official suspicion and a policy of vigilant containment. A decision taken in 1859, not to allow the opening of any further schools by unauthorized orders unless the government recognized their utility, remained in force till the end of the Empire.[9] Rouland several times reminded the Jesuits of their precarious legal position, and threatened particular establishments with closure in the event of misbehaviour.[10] In 1863 Duruy, obstructed in his efforts to inspect the École Sainte-Geneviève, painted it to the Emperor as a haven of conspiracy against the ruler and against French society. 'There', he warned, 'are the worst enemies of your son; they are preparing

---

[6] Padberg, *Colleges in Controversy*, 93. For Napoleon III's own misgivings about the Jesuits, see Ravignan's account of his interview with the Emperor on this occasion, in A. de Ponlevoy, *Vie du R.P. Xavier de Ravignan, de la Compagnie de Jésus*, 6th edn., 2 vols. (Paris, 1862), ii. 171–85. For an account of the whole episode, see Burnichon, *La Compagnie de Jésus en France*, iii. 402–8.

[7] AN F^{19} 6288 (Jésuites), extracts from prefects' replies to 1853 circular: Allier, Haute-Garonne, Rhône, Tarn-et-Garonne; (Dossiers Godichaux, Thomas/Husse, Tissier), correspondence between prefects and *Ministre des Cultes* concerning subversive preaching in Morbihan (1857, 1861) and Bouches-du-Rhône (1858); (Jésuites, extension dans les diocèses: Basses-Pyrénées), headmaster of Pau *lycée* to *Ministre des Cultes*, 2 May 1862.

[8] AN F^{19} 6288 (Jésuites, extension dans les diocèses: Vienne), *Procureur-général* of Poitiers to *Garde des Sceaux*, 2 Sept. 1854.

[9] C. de Rochemonteix, *Les Congrégations religieuses non reconnues*, i. 193–200; J. Maurain, *La Politique ecclésiastique du Second Empire de 1852 à 1869* (Paris, 1930), 463.

[10] For details, see Maurain, *La Politique ecclésiastique*, 568–74.

there a battle which the Emperor will win, [but] which the Prince Imperial would lose.'[11]

Though anti-jesuit opinions retained some force in the counsels of the government and of conservative supporters of the regime, it was among those on the left, whom the Empire excluded from honour and power, that they were most persistently in evidence and found the fullest development. The débâcle of 1848–51 rendered acute the Republicans' interpretative problem: how to reconcile belief in the inevitability of political and social progress with the fact that the history of French Republicanism seemed to be one of repeated defeat punctuated only by moments of false hope or bloody excess. By the accidents of its timing, one of the few French anti-jesuit texts of 1848 permits us to see how both the momentary joys and the disillusionment of a radical Republican could find expression within the framework of anti-jesuitism. The bulk of Victor Considérant's editorial introduction to abbé Leone's *Conjuration des jésuites*[12] was composed before the February Revolution: it is dated from London, 27 January 1848. It portrays Jesuitism as a powerful force, identified with reactionary Catholic theocracy, and opposed to the 'spiritualist and democratic Christianity of Jesus', in which Considérant saw the only hope of the Church's regeneration.[13] By the time this text appeared in print,

[11] Duruy, *Notes et souvenirs*, ii. 3.

[12] J. Leone, *Conjuration des jésuites: Publication authentique du plan secret de l'ordre*, ed. V. Considérant (Paris, 1848). This (coming after a pirated edition at Berne in 1847) was the authorized version of the revelations of Leone, an Italian *émigré* whom Considérant had met in 1846. The book's centrepiece (sandwiched between sections of autobiography and lengthy efforts to present the writings of European reactionaries and clericals as enactments of the 'secret plan') consisted of the alleged proceedings of a conference of leading Jesuits, which Leone claimed secretly to have overheard (and taken down verbatim) while himself a Jesuit novice at Chieri in Piedmont in 1824. Covering ninety-five pages (74–168), and involving twenty speeches by twelve Jesuits of varied nationality (including Fortis and Roothaan, the Generals in 1824 and in 1848 respectively), these proceedings amounted to a blueprint for world domination by a 'Jesuitized' Roman Catholicism. Ways of appealing to, and harnessing, both the people and 'les grands' were discussed, but the principal concerns were with intellectual subversion and the undercover struggle against Protestantism. Among the more curious features of the plan were schemes for turning to advantage the sexual yearnings of priests (by spreading the idea of a selective suspension of clerical celibacy) and the sexual indiscretions of nuns. The impact of Leone's book in France may well have been limited both by its appearance at a time of little anti-jesuit agitation, and by its un-French emphasis on Protestantism as Jesuitism's principal adversary, but it made one or two notable contributions to the fund of anti-jesuit mythology (see below, 195–6, 212–13).

[13] V. Considérant, 'Avertissement', in Leone, *Conjuration des jésuites*, a1–a21.

however, shifting political circumstances had caused two post-scripts to be added. The first, dated from Paris, 28 May, proclaimed the overthrow of oppression in the revolutionary days of February, and called on the Church to reject Jesuitical domination (by shedding the Papacy's temporal interests and giving the lower clergy a democratic constitution) and join in founding a society based on 'those three Christian words: Liberty, Equality, Fraternity!' Considérant persisted with his publication of Leone's exposure of the Jesuit conspiracy, in order to show the true nature of 'pseudo-Christianity, the Christianity of exploitation, of Theocracy, of Despotism', and prepare the final conflict between two irreconcilable parties: 'on the one hand the day, on the other the darkness.'[14] When the line between the parties of light and darkness was properly drawn, Considérant was clearly convinced, only the Jesuits would be on the wrong side. Anti-jesuitism helped reconcile the universalism appropriate to the construction of a new world with the dualism needed to sustain crusading revolution. By 19 July, when Considérant penned his second postscript, however, the confident hopes articulated in May had been dashed by the bloodshed of the June days and the repression of radical Republicanism. Far from envisaging the imminent isolation of the Jesuits, he now bitterly registered the latest in a seemingly inexorable series of defections to the Jesuit camp:

Under the Restoration, Jesuitism had on its side, in France, only the party of the emigration. Under the July Monarchy, it had, in reality, drawn up in alliance with it the official and satisfied bourgeoisie, which compacted with it in its retrograde tendencies. M. Guizot, and his rotten majority, upheld the general tendencies of Jesuitism and had formally harnessed themselves to its cause by committing French policy to the service of the Sonderbund.

Today, a new layer of French society has gone over to the enemy, to resistance, to fear of progress and of democratic and social principles, an unintelligent and fatal fear, for interests will only be saved through their alliance with sentiments and principles. This new retrogression is established by this sign, that M. Thiers . . . and *Le Constitutionnel*, his organ, have just shamelessly gone over to the party whose bogy-men they had for so long made themselves. This is the general coalition of all the fears, of all the egoisms, and of all the intrigues against the legitimate and regular development of Democracy.

[14] Ibid. a22–a25.

This is, word for word, the very aim of the Company of Jesus: and indeed the alliance with the *political* representatives of the Company has already been concluded.[15]

Considérant's tone was grim, yet anti-jesuitism still served, even in adversity, to protect the universalistic premises of his democratic thought from discredit. Though the multiplicity, as well as the growing strength, of counter-revolutionary forces was admitted, it was implied that only Jesuitism could hold the selfish coalition together, since a true realization and reconciliation of individual interests was possible only within a democratic framework.

In its usual forms, Republican anti-jesuitism under the Second Empire and in the first decade of the Third Republic was a variable mixture of elements drawn from several sources—Voltairean anti-clericalism, early nineteenth-century liberalism, the anti-jesuitism of Michelet and Quinet—and held to with varying degrees of intensity. Before following this mainstream, however, it is worth examining in detail an extreme case—one which shows how completely an anti-jesuit conspiracy theory might be integrated into, and come to express the convictions and frustrations which composed, the mentality of a radical democratic Republican. If the case of François-Vincent Raspail is not typical, even of the Republican Left (it bears, on the contrary the strong mark of personal idiosyncrasy), it nevertheless provides an unusually good opportunity to explore the workings of anti-jesuit obsession at a personal level, in the mind of one not without honour or popular influence in Republican circles.[16] Raspail, during these years, was a man thoroughly out of sympathy with, and often forcibly alienated from, the prevailing politics of his time. Imprisoned for his part in the Parisian demonstration of 15 May 1848 (while in prison he was elected *député* for Paris and received 36,000 votes in the presidential election won by Louis-Napoleon), he remained a prisoner till 1853, when his sentence was commuted to exile. He returned to France under an amnesty in 1863, but did not re-enter the political arena till May 1869, when he was elected *député* for Lyons, taking his place on the extreme left of the Chamber. Defeated in the

[15] Ibid. a26–a28.
[16] For biographical detail, see D. Ligou's preface to his collection of Raspail's writings, *François-Vincent Raspail; ou Le Bon Usage de la prison, précédé de l'Étude impartiale sur Jean Paul Marat* (Paris, 1968), and Weiner, *Raspail*.

conservative backlash of 1871 (and imprisoned again in 1874 for having praised the heroic death of the Communard leader Delescluze), he was re-elected in June 1876, and finally died in January 1878. Throughout the last three decades of his life, in and out of prison and exile, Raspail produced a constant stream of almanacs and periodicals, devoted both to the scientific and to the politico-social education of the people. It is in these that the traces of his anti-jesuitism may be found.[17]

These works, like their author's career, are heavily marked both by a profound identification with the causes of progress and popular education and by a highly developed sense of persecution. Raspail believed that the Jesuits had tried repeatedly to have him killed as long ago as 1815,[18] and had later organized a conspiracy of non-recognition around his scientific work.[19] Here their efforts and those of the scientific establishment had coincided. Sometimes Raspail referred to his scientific opponents (Orfila, Dumas, Ampère, and others) as the Jesuits' instruments; more usually, he simply spoke of them as Jesuits.[20] Similarly, in the political sphere, the 'Jesuits' he encountered were not on the whole monarchists or men of the Second Empire, but those with whom he had clashed personally in the Republican movement of the early 1830s or in 1848: the Cavaignac brothers, Trélat, Buchez, Marrast, Buonarroti, and others.[21]

In itself, Raspail's persecution complex is a curiosity; its significance lies in the way it nourished his more general conspiracy theory. Having learnt to see the Jesuit hand in his own troubles, he did not hesitate to expand the insight into a general theory of the sufferings of the righteous. 'When you happen to encounter a fine

---

[17] See principally the following of Raspail's works: *Revue élémentaire de médecine et pharmacie domestiques, ainsi que des sciences accessoires et usuelles mises à la portée de tout le monde*, 2 vols. (Paris, 1847–9); *La Lunette du donjon de Vincennes: Almanach démocratique et social de l'Ami du peuple, pour 1849* (Paris, 1848); *La Lunette de Doullens: Almanach démocratique et progressif de l'Ami du peuple, pour 1850* (Paris, 1849); *Revue complémentaire des sciences appliquées à la médecine et pharmacie, à l'agriculture, aux arts et à l'industrie*, 6 vols. (Paris, 1854–60); *Nouvelles Études scientifiques et philologiques* (Paris, 1864); *Prévision du temps: Almanach et calendrier météorologique pour l'année* ——(Paris, annually 1865–77, except 1871).

[18] See Weiner, *Raspail*, 50–2.

[19] Raspail, *Revue complémentaire*, i. 3, ii. 1, iv. 1–4, 307.

[20] Ibid. iii. 198, vi. 38–9; Raspail, *Revue élémentaire*, ii. 316; Raspail, *Almanach et calendrier* (1869), 171.

[21] Raspail, *Revue complémentaire*, iv. 4, 18, vi. 31, 378; Raspail, *Almanach et calendrier* (1872), 135–46; (1873), 76, 79.

soul exposed to all life's reverses, reader, I can vouch for it, think of these workers of evil and you will always have the key to the enigma; this key is written in letters of blood on the gates of Hell,' he wrote in 1870.[22] With the aid of this key, he saw the Jesuits behind the sufferings, and often the deaths, of numerous prominent servants of humanity; they were the definite or probable murderers, through subordinate agents, of Paul-Louis Courier, of Eugène Sue, of the scientist Straus-Durkheim, and of Raspail's three especial heroes: Rousseau, Voltaire, and Marat.[23]

The Jesuit conspiracy against Raspail's scientific achievement was likewise an instance of something more general. It went through three phases: an initial conspiracy of silence, followed by a concerted campaign of calumny and persecution, followed—most significantly—by wholesale plagiarism.[24] Raspail's obsession with plagiarism was notorious,[25] and reflected not just his private frustrations, but also his conception of obscurantist and reactionary tactics. It expressed one aspect of a more general fear that the traditional vehicles of progress—scientific and historical enlightenment, the free press—might somehow be kidnapped, in name and in fact, by its Jesuitical enemies. To serve humanity, scientific truth must remain in sympathetic hands. The same applied to historical truth; Raspail warned of malevolent tactical concessions in historical studies by Jesuit agents 'careful to fall into step with progress, so as to be able at every opportunity to trip it up in some way'.[26] Newspapers, for their part, were now controlled by the Jesuits, not through the open tyranny of censorship, but through the unseen pervasion of the Havas *entrefilet*: 'The instrument which for so long has served to spread enlightenment, the press, thus becomes a means to extinguish it when required or to dim its brilliance.'[27]

This vision of the traitorous abduction of progress emerges most strongly, however, from Raspail's account of recent history. This has to be pieced together from a host of scattered references in various

[22] Raspail, *Almanach et calendrier* (1870), 147–8.

[23] For a particularly good example of Raspail's logic in such matters, see his reasoning on the death of Voltaire in *Revue complémentaire*, iii. 187–8. See also ibid. ii. 125–8 (Rousseau), iii. 124–8, 152–9 (Voltaire), vi. 58–63 (Sue); Raspail, *Nouvelles Études*, 234–86 (Marat); Raspail, *Almanach et calendrier*, (1868), 84–106 (Marat); (1869), 168–72 (Straus-Durkheim); (1870), 142–68 (Rousseau); (1873), 74 (Courier).   [24] Raspail, *Revue complémentaire*, ii. 238–40.

[25] See Weiner, *Raspail*, 73–4.   [26] Raspail, *Almanach et calendrier* (1868), 87.

[27] Raspail, *Revue complémentaire*, iv. 19, 197–9.

works, especially in the *calendrier ou éphémérides des hommes et événements célèbres* contained in his annual almanacs from 1865 to 1877;[28] the references, however, deliver a single message with striking constancy, and no one who troubles to assemble them is likely to miss its relevance to Raspail's understanding of the débâcle of Republicanism in 1848. Modern French history, he maintained, was dotted with revolutions which violently overthrew or attempted to overthrow governments but which always left the Jesuit-packed administration standing; far from alarming the Jesuits, these violent outbreaks were engineered by them, and enabled them to get rid of their progressive enemies. Revolutionary and counter-revolutionary excesses were part of a single Jesuit plan to discredit and prevent progress.[29]

This account of Jesuit intervention in modern French history is worth setting out in detail. It begins in the 1790s, when, despite the vigilance of true revolutionaries like Marat, the Jesuits and their agents (Hébert and Robespierre among them) contrived to sponsor such atrocities as the prison massacres, the execution of the king, and the Terror. 'Rivarol had organized terrorism on their behalf; their agents pushed the chariot of the Revolution from behind into the mire and the gore; they steeped popular enthusiasm in blood; they pressed the theories of progress to extravagance [*extravaguaient les théories du progrès*]. Each mask of a ranter or a *corrompu* concealed a Jesuit.' (Thermidor was simply a Jesuit reshuffle: 'they sacrificed those among themselves who had placed themselves most in evidence.') The other horn of the plot emerged at the end of the Empire, with the Jesuit treason which twice delivered Paris to the Allies and which saved Wellington from defeat at Waterloo, and with the Jesuit-organized White Terror.[30] Thereafter, the

---

[28] The *calendrier* first appeared in an extended form in the *Almanach et calendrier* for 1866; details were added and altered in subsequent years. References below are to the first year in which a particular detail appeared.

[29] Raspail, *La Lunette de Doullens*, 107; Raspail, *Revue complémentaire*, vi. 58 (on how the Jesuits learnt 'to make revolutions serve counter-revolutions'); Raspail, *Almanach et calendrier* (1873), 165 (explaining that, since 1814, 'we have not had a scene of carnage which has not been their work').

[30] On the Terror: Raspail, *Revue complémentaire*, ii. 217–18 n. On revolutionaries as Jesuits/Jesuit agents: Raspail, *Almanach et calendrier* (1868), 86; (1869), 166; (1872), 129–38; on the prison massacres: (1866), 63; on the regicide: (1874), 166; on Thermidor: (1872), 135; on 1814 and 1815: (1866), 52, 57–8; on the White Terror: (1866), 49, 81. The entry on Waterloo (p. 57) declares: 'Wellington saved from complete ruin thanks to the treason organized by the occult association of the *pères de la foi* (Jesuits) in the French general staff (the gold of the English is not a chimera).'

manœuvre was repeated at regular intervals: '1830 and 1848 were merely the 3rd and 4th performances of 1794 and of 1815.'[31] The frustrations of Republicanism in the 1830s and in 1848 thus received an explanation. Having smuggled Louis-Philippe on to the throne,[32] the Jesuits had worked simultaneously through the government and through the secret societies ('The Jesuit G. Cavaignac and his band') to engineer hopeless uprisings and massacres of Republicans.[33] In 1848 they had momentarily lost control when the Republic was proclaimed, but had speedily regained it by rigging election results (deleting a zero from the end of Raspail's own tally) and setting up the 'clubs', which, behind their revolutionary façade, were actually 'one of the thousand disguises of the Société de Saint Vincent de Paul', enabling the forces of reaction to identify those they would later imprison or kill.[34] The disturbance of 15 May and the fighting of the June Days marked the Jesuits' accomplishment of their usual manœuvre.[35] In due course Raspail extended the analysis to the Commune of 1871: once again the Jesuits and their agents were behind the governmental provocation (the withdrawal to Versailles), the excesses of the revolutionaries (the arrest and execution of hostages, 'all excommunicated by the Pope and by the Jesuits'), and the final massacre of Republicans.[36] Their subversive control of ostensibly revolutionary organizations continued in the 1870s with that secret Jesuit agency, promoter of strikes as ruinous to workers as to employers, the International.[37]

The exposure of this repetitive history of generous impulses lured to destruction by Jesuit intrigue cleansed the image of Republicanism of its crimes and failures. It also bolstered Raspail's prestige, at least in his own eyes, as the clairvoyant, Marat-like, defender of the people against its worst enemies, false friends.[38]

[31] Raspail, *Revue complémentaire*, vi. 59.

[32] Raspail, *Almanach et calendrier* (1866), 60–1. On the July Monarchy as Jesuit instrument, see Raspail, *Nouvelles Études*, 212, and *Revue complémentaire*, iv. 228, 323–5.

[33] Raspail, *Almanach et calendrier* (1877), 79.

[34] Raspail, *Revue complémentaire*, vi. 28–31.

[35] Raspail, *La Lunette . . . de Vincennes*, 102; Raspail, *Almanach et calendrier* (1866), 55; (1873), 81.

[36] Raspail, *Almanach et calendrier* (1873), 73–4, 165; (1874), 166. Also (1872), 163, 170, on the disturbances of Oct. 1870 and Jan. 1871.

[37] Ibid. (1872), 153; (1873), 178–9.

[38] The contrast between his own steadfastness and the treachery of others (often seen as Jesuits) was central to Raspail's self-glorification. The theme of false

Most importantly, it offered confirmation of his view of how the Republic could be brought about and ought to operate. In 1848 he had written:

Republic! It is the public service [*la chose publique*] administered by public opinion, under the eyes of the public, and by the care of those whom [public] opinion has elected.

The Republic can therefore exist only on condition of overthrowing all the existing powers, and not replacing them by any other. For all power is a usurpation of the rights of everyone; it is a falsehood.[39]

What made Raspail's insistence on universal suffrage and on the charlatanry of imposed authority especially radical was its application not simply to politics narrowly construed, but to all areas of human activity. What was true of scientific learning, of curative medicine, and of criminal justice (to take three examples[40]) was certainly true of the Republican movement: the democratic Republic could not be achieved if people continued to abdicate judgement in favour of quasi-official spokesmen or parties. Above all, it would not be achieved by conspiracy: 'The good fathers are organized to oppose the spread of enlightenment; as for you, don't organize yourselves; it is with them that you would conspire, for they are artisans of occult conspiracies.'[41] To accept direction was to fall into a Jesuit trap, as each bloodstained tragedy of the revolutionary movement demonstrated. Only a true democracy—one practised as well as fought for—could defeat the Jesuits. Many anti-jesuits accused the Jesuits of usurping authority, or authority of favouring the Jesuits; Raspail was perhaps the one who saw least distinction between authority and Jesuitism in the first place.

Raspail's historical speculations and radical anti-authoritarianism were an extreme and intensely personal contribution to anti-jesuitism. The staple anti-jesuit fare on offer to a popular readership under the Empire and in the early 1870s—literature perhaps best

friendship was a veritable obsession: see *Revue complémentaire*, iv. 59–60, on how Jesuit agents disguised as admirers diverted Eugène Sue from his work, and *Almanach et calendrier* (1870), 152, for the general rule: 'Philosophers, remember what I tell you: whenever you see false friends assail you, your true friends desert you, those in your debt repay you with signal ingratitude, think of the men in black; it is among them that you will find all the keys to these enigmas.'

[39] Raspail, *La Lunette . . . de Vincennes*, 149–50.
[40] Raspail, *Almanach et calendrier* (1869), 132–4; Raspail, *Revue complémentaire*, iv. 358; Raspail, *Nouvelles Études*, 274.
[41] Raspail, *Revue complémentaire*, iv. 4.

exemplified by the numerous pamphlets of Charles Sauvestre and Jean-Mamert Cayla in the 1860s—was less original in its assertions. Anticlerical rather than anti-governmental in its broader orientation, and resorting frequently to scandal-mongering and anecdotal gossip, it displayed, before and after 1870, three fairly constant general characteristics. First, it described the Jesuit threat as a war of the past against modernity, of oppression against liberty, of obscurantism against enlightenment, of the *ancien régime* against the principles of the Revolution: in whatever terms the progress of the human spirit was described, Jesuitism served simultaneously as symbol, explanation, and index of the obstacles it encountered.[42] Second, it took it as more or less axiomatic that the contemporary Catholic Church was completely and perhaps irredeemably under Jesuit control, and that this accounted for its increasingly autocratic and anti-liberal complexion.[43] Men like Sauvestre, following Michelet, might find a place in their caustic anticlerical hearts to sympathize with the plight of the lower clergy under Jesuit tyranny (drawing sustenance for that sympathy from Michon's *Le Maudit*, an immediate success on its appearance at the end of 1863[44]), but they gave little sign of believing that forces within the Church—be they 'Jansenist', or Gallican, or Liberal Catholic—were still capable of regenerating it without drastic surgery from without. Cayla, in 1862, saw the struggle between legists and Jesuits as precursor and 'symbol' of that between Church and State: he called for a return to the Civil Constitution of the clergy, the abolition of religious orders and diocesan seminaries, and an end to clerical exemption from conscription.[45] For increasing numbers of its secular

---

[42] Eugène Pelletan put this forcefully (*Siècle*, 11 May 1854): 'Jesuitism is, by its nature, of its essence, the indefatigable enemy of the human spirit and of all progress brought about by the human spirit. It has as its natural auxiliary, as its *corps d'armée*, everything that believes itself humiliated by the fact of progress. There lies its *raison d'être*, there lies its strength, there also is its weakness and its downfall at a given moment. When Europe takes a step backward, as on the morrow of Waterloo, Jesuitism reappears; when she takes a step forward, under some new recrudescence of democracy, it vanishes over the horizon.'

[43] Thus Sauvestre in *Sur les genoux de l'Église* (Paris, 1868), 44: 'it is the Jesuits who command in the Church today; their doctrines have become the doctrines of the Church; their teaching, its teaching; their politics, its politics.'

[44] Sauvestre's sympathetic remarks in response to *Le Maudit* are in *Mes lundis* (Paris, 1864), 263; for other reactions to the novel, see Savart, *L'Abbé Jean-Hippolyte Michon*, 186–95. Sales of *Le Maudit* reached 17,000–20,000 within about a year (*L'Abbé Jean-Hippolyte Michon*, 174).

[45] J.-M. Cayla, *La Conspiration cléricale* (Paris, 1862), 29–32.

exponents, anti-jesuitism under the Second Empire and early Third Republic became openly what its Catholic critics had long claimed it was secretly: a weapon for use against the whole Catholic Church. Thirdly—and here the anti-jesuitism of the Left in the 1850s and 1860s resembled that of the 1820s—the Jesuits were presented as the *de facto* rulers of French society. Cayla restated and extended the Restoration myth of the Congrégation,[46] and another author explained France's decadence and lack of international influence by the fact that the Jesuits were as completely in control of the public mind as they had been in the Restoration years.[47] Sauvestre stated in 1867 that 'one feels their hand everywhere, from the top to the bottom of the social ladder, in public and private administrations, wherever there is an influence to exert, an authority to assume'.[48] In such remarks, criticism of the existing regime was certainly implied (especially when the Jesuits were also spoken of as the natural allies of despotism), yet the long perspective which references to the Restoration revealed made the Jesuits rather than the Second Empire seem the durable enemy. 'Ministers come and go, governments change, revolutions shake the country, laws are renewed,' Sauvestre gloomily remarked; 'only the Jesuits remain always and in spite of everything.'[49]

When the government did fall, and France again experienced an upsurge of revolutionary feeling, first with the Government of National Defence appointed on 4 September 1870, and then with the Paris Commune, the Jesuits, predictably, were among the sufferers. Manifestations of popular hostility towards Jesuit houses, which had begun early in the Franco-Prussian war, escalated after the Empire's fall: in Lyons, Marseilles, Poitiers, Périgueux, Bordeaux, and Lons-le-Saulnier, Jesuit premises were attacked, and in some cases Jesuits were imprisoned.[50] The requisitioning of establishments for military purposes was sometimes accompanied by the suggestion that public order required the Jesuits' removal. Garibaldi, evicting them from Dôle, described them as 'dangerous men whom the interest of my military operations commands me to

[46] See below, 220–1.

[47] *Les Jésuites et l'Inquisition: Histoire populaire et anecdotique des Compagnies de Jésus et de Saint Dominique* (Paris, 1869), 7.

[48] C. Sauvestre, *Les Congrégations religieuses: Enquête* (Paris, 1867), 148.

[49] C. Sauvestre (ed.), *Monita secreta Societatis Jesu: Instructions secrètes des jésuites, suivies de pièces justificatives* (Paris, 1861), 17.

[50] Burnichon, *La Compagnie de Jésus en France*, iv. 346–58.

distance from this town'. At Marseilles and Aix, the Prefect of the
Bouches-du-Rhône (Esquiros) and his deputy decreed the Jesuits'
expulsion from France, though this infringement of personal liberty
was hastily annulled by Gambetta.[51] It was in Communard Paris,
however, that the Jesuits faced the greatest danger. Garreau, the
officer who interrogated members of the order arrested in an early
morning raid on the rue des Postes on 4 April 1871, accused them
of complicity with Versailles and of corrupting their pupils, poisoning the wounded, and hiding weapons. Five Jesuits were held as
hostages; two met their deaths on 24 May, the other three in the
massacre of the rue Haxo two days later.[52] None of this prevented
the more imaginative anti-jesuits from speculating later about the
Jesuits' responsibility not just for the Commune, but specifically
for the murder of hostages.[53]

The conviction in some quarters that the Jesuits were to blame
for France's misfortunes in 1870–1 persisted through the 1870s.
Anti-jesuit literature commonly accused them of having used their
influence on the Empress Eugénie to bring about the war with
Prussia. The range of views on why they had done so was bewil-
dering: had it been (in the hope of a Prussian victory) to bring
down a regime in France which no longer served their purposes,
or to crush French liberal anti-jesuitism, or (counting instead on
a French victory) to harm Protestantism, or to cow the German
opponents of Papal Infallibility, or to rebuild the damaged fortunes
of Jesuitical Austria, or (simply seeking a diversion) to cover their
own manœuvres at the Vatican Council?[54] It was also suggested
that, whether or not they had caused the war, the Jesuits, and
Jesuit education particularly, had been to blame for France losing it. Erckmann-Chatrian's fictional *Histoire du plébiscite* attributed

[51] Rosette, *La Compagnie de Jésus à Dôle*, 138–45; J. P. T. Bury, *Gambetta and the National Defence: A Republican Dictatorship in France* (London, 1936), 230–1; L. Gambetta, *Dépêches, circulaires, décrets, proclamations et discours*, ed. J. Reinach, 2 vols. (Paris, 1886–91), i. 429–30.

[52] Ponlevoy, *Actes de la captivité* (pp. 36–7 for the Garreau interrogation).

[53] See A. Sirven and H. Le Verdier's novel *Le Jésuite rouge* (Paris, 1879), in which the Jesuits deliberately provoke first the Commune and then their own martyrdom; also A. Durantin, *Un élève des jésuites* (Paris, 1880), 85.

[54] See, among others, A. Andréï, *Les Jésuites* (Paris, 1872), 116; Michaud, *Le Mouvement contemporain*, 74–9; J.-M. Cayla, *L'Expulsion des jésuites* (Paris, 1876), 201–2; J. Laurens, *Le Cas d'un curé gallican* (Paris, 1879), 60–1; Sirven and Le Verdier, *Le Jésuite rouge*, 97–8.

defeat to the incompetence of Jesuit-trained officers. One of the novel's characters explained the civil strife of 1871 in similar terms:

Education is placed in the hands of the Jesuits, and the Jesuits have an interest in keeping the people in stupidity, in order to use them however they like. And all the divisions, all the internal agitations, the revolutions, the massacres in the streets, the deportations, the party hatred, the longings for vengeance stem from this as well: it is the treason of treasons![55]

Anti-jesuit terms were well suited to convey the deep sense of national decadence and yearning for regeneration that characterized many responses to the double débâcle of 1870–1. The analysis of the early modern decline of the peoples of southern Europe, worked out by Quinet thirty years before, was transposed to the France of the 1870s, by no one more bitterly or more scornfully than by the aged Quinet himself, in his 'Pensées intimes' of 1875: 'To make dead nations [*des nations cadavres*], *perinde ac cadaver*, peoples who are, in the hands of kings, like *the stick in the hand of the blind man*; that is what Jesuitism wants; and it reigns, it governs . . . All the efforts of political Jesuitism are concentrated at this moment on France.'[56] For those who thought in these terms, the form of national regeneration proposed by the conservative partisans of the *ordre moral*—one based (like that promoted by the Restoration missions) on repentance and atonement for the sins of France and reversal of a supposed national apostasy—was, of course, simply an indication of the depths of Jesuitical degradation to which France had sunk. The great symbol of this mode of spiritual reparation, the Basilica of the Sacré-Cœur, begun in 1876 and intended, when finished, to dominate Paris from the heights of Montmartre (the birthplace, coincidentally, of the Society of Jesus), signified, according to Jules-Antoine Castagnary, 'the apotheosis of Loyola'.[57] At a less symbolic level, too, the France of the early 1870s was considered at least as Jesuit-ridden as that of the Second Empire. 'The black legion covers and infests everything,' wrote Dionys Ordinaire in the *Petite République française* in 1876. 'Our

---

[55] Erckmann-Chatrian, *Histoire du plébiscite, racontée par un des 7,500,000 oui*, ed. 'Aux bureaux . . . du *Soir*' (Paris, 1872), 55, 81.

[56] BNMS NAF 15520 (Quinet, 'Pensées intimes'), 218, dated Feb. 1875.

[57] J.-A. Castagnary, *Les Jésuites devant la loi française* (Paris, 1877), 80.

Sénat, our Chambre des Députés, our civil service, even our army, alas, are peopled with Jesuits.'[58]

Set against such a background, the events which finally buried the period of *ordre moral*—the establishment of a Republican majority in the Chambre des Députés in March 1876; the mounting anticlerical pressure on the moderate government of Jules Simon in early 1877; the personal intervention of President MacMahon on 16 May to force Simon's resignation (the so-called coup of the Seize-Mai) and the formation, in defiance of the complexion of the lower house, of a right-wing cabinet under Broglie; the protest and vote of censure by 363 *députés*; the preservation of the Republican majority, despite the efforts of the government, in the elections of October, resulting in the fall of Broglie and his colleagues; the eventual consolidation of Republican ascendancy by the conquest of a majority in the Sénat and the resignation of MacMahon in January 1879 — seemed like a protracted and bloodless repetition of 1830. The Seize-Mai, in other words, entered Republican mythology as a *coup de main* attempted by the Jesuits in the hope of forestalling rising public resistance to their domination, and thwarted by the vigilant determination of the friends of progress, whose own accession to power followed. But whereas the Liberals of 1830 had considered the July Days sufficient to destroy the Jesuit threat for the present, the Republican victory, by its peaceable nature, left the work of anti-jesuitism to be completed. Article 7 in 1879 would draw much of its sense, in the eyes of its supporters, from this perceived need; for many, it was a response to what a pamphleteer of the day called 'the evident participation of the Jesuits in 24 and 16 May'.[59] Paul Bert, supporting it, argued that the elections of October 1877 constituted a public judgement on 'the clerical intrigues [*menées*], or rather the intrigues of the Jesuits, to call them by their proper name', and created a mandate for anti-jesuit legislation, regardless of the signatures of 1.5 million pro-Jesuit

---

[58] D. Ordinaire, *Seize lettres aux jésuites* (Paris 1879), 77 (originally in the *Petite République française* in 1876).

[59] Michel, *Les Jésuites*, 73 (24 May 1873 was the date of MacMahon's election to the presidency). The concept of 'evidence' could be flexible. When a speaker in the debate on Article 7 pointed out that the Broglie government's telegraphic correspondence revealed no trace of Jesuit influence, he was interrupted: 'They wouldn't be Jesuits if they had written.' Paul Bert likewise saw the absence of incriminating material as a reflection of Jesuit cunning (*ASCD*, CD 5 July 1879: 60, 65).

petitioners.[60] Dufaure, criticizing Article 7, deplored the 'permanent desire for reprisals against the conduct of the authorities [*pouvoir*] during the period of 16 May', and insisted that it was unfair to punish the Jesuits for what had been the offences of clerical politicians.[61] As Ferry had already made clear, however, it was precisely this distinction between the responsibilities of clerical politicians (and other Catholic activists) and those of the Jesuits that he, the proposer of Article 7, refused to draw:

Who then has given the clerical party in France this formidable organization? Who then has instituted, has grouped the *comités catholiques*, who has made them into a vast network extending over the whole of France? Who then has given the watchword? The Jesuits, they provoke, they preach this organization; it is their work, they are its soul, they are its leaders. And who then has joined together, so powerfully, so skilfully, with so energetic and so persistent an apostolate, all the *cercles catholiques ouvriers*, the *œuvre de Jésus* for example, if it is not the Jesuits and their pupils?[62]

Nevertheless, although the common belief that the Jesuits were the heart and soul of clerical and anti-Republican politics helps explain the determination of Republicans to be rid of them, what was actually proposed in 1879 was not a general measure against the Society of Jesus, but one specifically against Jesuit education. This reflected not only the crucial importance which Republican politicians assigned to education as a determinant of individual and social human destiny, and hence to educational organization as an ingredient of Republican stabilization, but also the fact that schools were the most visible and most notably successful branch of French Jesuit activity. When anti-jesuits alleged that the bureaucracy, the armed forces, or the magistracy were peopled with Jesuits, they tended to mean that they were peopled with products of Jesuit schools. The latest (and, since the Affenäer affair, the greatest) anti-jesuit scandal, whose exploitation formed part of the wave of anticlericalism which preceded the Seize-Mai, focused precisely on the means by which Jesuit pupils were launched on prestigious and strategically important civil and military careers. It concerned the most famous of Jesuit schools, the École Sainte-Geneviève in the

---

[60] *ASCD*, CD 21 June 1879: 62. The *sénateur* Foucher de Careil traced the mandate back to a supposed national verdict against Jesuit education after 1870 (ibid., Sénat 4 Mar. 1880: 169–75).
[61] Ibid., Sénat 9 Mar. 1880: 290.   [62] Ibid., Sénat 6 Mar. 1880: 244.

rue des Postes, whose specific function was to prepare pupils for entry to the various *grandes écoles* which were the gateways to such careers, and whose success in doing so had for some time been a source of pride to the Jesuits and of alarm to their enemies.[63]

On 29 June 1876, as Parisian candidates for admission to the École Polytechnique were about to begin their examination in geometrical drawing, a number of them protested that candidates from certain institutions had received prior knowledge of the problem set. Although it transpired that pupils from five schools (including three *lycées*) were involved, hostile rumour from the out-set focused on the École Sainte-Geneviève, and assumed that it was only through contacts with *postards* that information on the problem had filtered through to other schools. Conclusions were quickly drawn from the fact that the instructor at the Polytechnique who had set the question also held a teaching post at the Jesuit school. After this 'edifying revelation', remarked the *Petite République française*, one could no longer be astonished by the annual successes achieved by 'this factory of *jésuites de robe courte*', whose products were flooding the various branches of the public service, to such an extent that 'Republican France struggles in the clerical grip'. This was no isolated case, the paper continued, but one of a sort all too familiar, all over the country, in examinations for the *baccalauréat*; a thorough inquiry was needed to root out the Jesuit sympathizers in the State's own educational establishment who actively connived in such cheating.[64] It was now clear, the *République française* suggested, why clericals were so anxious to keep in force the provisions of the law of 1875 which had removed the State's monopoly over examining and awarding of degrees in higher education: these provisions protected their 'little ways of correcting the errors of fortune and of their pupils'.[65] Gambetta, in the Chamber, pre-empted the findings of an inquiry even as he called for one; the question to be confronted, he declared, was one which 'concerns the very future of this country', by placing at issue 'the influence of the Jesuitical spirit of domination'.[66] A

[63] See Burnichon, *La Compagnie de Jésus en France*, iv. 508–12; Langdon, 'The Jesuits and French Education'.

[64] *Petite République française*, 1 July 1876.

[65] *La République française*, 1 July 1876.

[66] *ASCD*, CD 3 July 1876: 212. Gambetta had an ulterior political purpose in exploiting the scandal: he hoped to divert the Chamber from a full-scale debate on

commission of inquiry, duly appointed, predictably reached no such conclusion. It reported that the prior knowledge which some candidates had had of the question had not been of a kind to give them a significant advantage, and that it might have originated in shrewd guesswork and sign-reading by pupils rather than in any 'indiscretion'; if one had been committed, it was not evident who was responsible. The report was critical of the state of affairs whereby some candidates (at two other schools besides Sainte-Geneviève) had been taught by the question's setter, but it stressed the probity of the officer concerned, and denied that there was any reason to suspect that an attempt had been made corruptly to advantage any particular set of candidates.[67] The response to the report in the anticlerical press was predictably sarcastic.

By the time it appeared, anyway, the focus of the scandal had shifted from the examination hall to the law court, where the superior of the École Sainte-Geneviève, Père du Lac, together with parents and pupils, was suing seven newspapers for their defamatory attacks.[68] As in the Affenäer case, the legal outcome of the proceedings—the papers were fined 2,000 francs each, and their subsequent appeal rejected—was overshadowed by the efforts of anti-jesuits to stage an unofficial trial of the Society of Jesus. Rejecting any distinction between du Lac and his order, the *Petite République française* took open pride in being the first newspaper to be sued by the Jesuits since the eighteenth century.[69] In court, the lawyer for *Le Bien public* cited the *Monita secreta* (the spurious Jesuit world-domination plan publicized by Charles Sauvestre).[70] Like the prosecution of Affenäer, du Lac's suit was denounced as a manœuvre whose true purpose was, as Castagnary put it in *Les Jésuites devant la loi française*, to allow the Society of Jesus 'to slip [*se faufiler*] into legality' by being recognized as a party in the case. Castagnary praised the judges for having thwarted this piece of insolent audacity by treating the Jesuit as a private individual.

the amnesty for the Communards, which might endanger the Dufaure government and threaten the Republic with crisis. See L. Gambetta, *Lettres, 1868–82*, 3rd edn. (Paris, 1938), letter 279 (to Léonie Léon, 2 July 1876).

[67] The report is reproduced in comte A. de Mun, *Nouvelle Réponse à une vieille accusation renouvelée contre l'École Sainte-Geneviève* (Paris, 1899), 44–50.

[68] See *Gazette des tribunaux*, 22, 29 July, 11, 18, 19 Nov. 1876, 18 Feb. 1877.

[69] *Petite République française*, 14 July 1876. It later (27 July 1876) ceded this honour to *Le Constitutionnel* in 1825.

[70] Burnichon, *La Compagnie de Jésus en France*, iv. 511.

(Others were more exacting: by failing to bundle du Lac and his colleagues into exile, *Les Droits de l'homme* argued, the court had shown that those whom even the old monarchy had condemned and expelled were now protected.) Dionys Ordinaire warned the Jesuits that their 'scandalous trial' would revive old hatreds, and cause all voices to be raised in defence of civil society and public education: 'At each of your enterprises against our institutions, we will cry: Jesuit!, as shepherds cry: Wolf!'[71]

There were signs here (and especially in Castagnary's book, published in January 1877) of a transition from the rhetoric of the excluded, denouncing the rule of Jesuitism, to that of Republican defence, stressing the need to protect French institutions from Jesuit attack; in this sense, the anti-jesuit polemic of 1876–7 foreshadows that of 1879–80, and reflects the evolution of the Republic towards Republicanism, which the experience of Seize-Mai would only temporarily interrupt. The implication of the Polytechnique scandal was not simply that the Jesuits and their pupils were dishonest and unscrupulous, but that Jesuit schools were in the forefront of what Gambetta would shortly describe as 'a regular siege' of the French State by clericalism and 'the Jesuitical spirit'.[72] To defend the State against this threat, to avenge and protect the Republic against the makers of the Seize-Mai and the *parti clérical*, to ensure the triumph of the modern spirit over the obscurantism enshrined in the Church of the Syllabus and of Papal Infallibility: these were the principal purposes that seemed, to many Republicans, to call for anti-jesuit action as soon as the distribution of political power allowed. As Castagnary explained, there were two reasons to single out the Jesuits: first, they were fundamental ('they form as it were the great general staff of the clerical army'); second, they were vulnerable (against them, unlike most others in that army, it was enough 'to apply the existing legislation').[73]

ARTICLE 7

In February 1879, with Grévy replacing MacMahon, and with a Republican government under Waddington at last backed by a

[71] Castagnary, *Les Jésuites*, 2–4; *Les Droits de l'homme*, 30 July 1876; Ordinaire, *Seize lettres*, 10.

[72] L. Gambetta, *Discours et plaidoyers politiques*, ed. J. Reinach, 11 vols. (Paris, 1881–5), viii. 243 (speech at Romans, 18 Sept. 1878).

[73] Castagnary, *Les Jésuites*, pp. iv–v.

Republican majority in both Chambers, the way seemed open. The government's initiative came (rather incongruously since its practical implications related essentially to secondary education) in Article 7 of the bill on higher education tabled on 15 March by the Education Minister Jules Ferry. This was effectively a resuscitation, and a generalization to all levels of education, of the prohibition originally contained in the *ordonnance* of 1828. It stated: 'No one is allowed to participate in public or private education [*l'enseignement public ou libre*], or to direct an educational establishment of any type, if he belongs to an unauthorized religious *congrégation*.' As in 1828 and in 1844, there was no doubt that the article, though applying to all unauthorized orders, was aimed primarily at the Jesuits. Ferry summarized his own argument for it by implying that its defeat would be tantamount to an official readmission of the Jesuit order. He also made clear that, if the article became law, the option of seeking authorization would be open to all unauthorized *congrégations* bar one: 'as for the Jesuits, it is another matter, their case has been heard.'[74]

From the start, Article 7 dominated the bill, taking up twice as much space in the government's *exposé des motifs* as all the other articles together.[75] It was also to dominate the whole anti-jesuit campaign of 1879–80. Governmental initiative and parliamentary debate were more central to this campaign than they had been in the 1820s or even the 1840s; no Montlosier, no Michelet and Quinet, arose to bring pressure on government or parliament from without, or to provide a rival attraction. The most famous anti-jesuit *brochure* of the moment, Paul Bert's *La Morale des jésuites*, was published by a leading *député* as a sort of illustrative appendix to his speeches in the debate on Article 7, and the vigorous anti-jesuit agitation which unfolded across the country—in which Republican educational societies and masonic lodges played a prominent part—was to a large extent the echo and extension of parliamentary polemics.

[74] *ASCD*, CD 27 June 1879: 198, 194. Paul Bert told his fellow *députés* that the Jesuit order was so notorious that 'it seems that the law is directed against it alone; so much so that, in the public mind, in the national opinion, among our constituents, the law which is submitted to you has as its aim to remove from the Jesuits the right to teach French youth, and that voting for or against this law will be equivalent to voting for or against recognition of the existence of the Society of Jesus and of its right to teach' (ibid., CD 21 June 1879: 53).
[75] *ASCD*, 1879 (III), annexes, 162–5.

The alignment of forces in the parliamentary battle over Article
7, and the main stages in that battle and its aftermath, are well
known to historians.[76] Broadly speaking, the article was opposed by
the royalists and Bonapartists of the Right, and by the bulk of the
Centre Gauche, the most conservative of the moderate Republican
groupings (and a powerful force in both the Waddington cabinet
and the Sénat), many of whose members, while no admirers of the
Jesuits, considered the measure against them sectarian and illiberal.
Its most enthusiastic support came from the ranks of the Gauche
Républicaine and the Union Républicaine, the two groups (associated respectively with Ferry and with Gambetta) which would
predominate in the Opportunist governments of the 1880s. Members of these groups did not necessarily expect Article 7 to be a
sufficient remedy for France's ills (Paul Bert, Gambetta's principal
lieutenant in educational matters, publicly declared his willingness
to apply 'a more energetic insecticide' to the clerical 'phylloxera' if
necessary[77]), but, on the whole, they thought it a coherent and
appropriate one. In this, they differed from the Radicals, who
considered it misconceived and over-timid, and were prepared to
support it only because (as Auguste Vacquerie later remarked) 'one
does not discuss tactics on the battlefield'.[78]

Thus supported and opposed, Article 7 encountered little serious
difficulty in the Chambre des Députés, where it was hotly debated
in June and July. The *députés* rejected, in both cases by a substantial
margin, on the one hand a moderate amendment by Bardoux,
which would have replaced it by a provision for stricter school
inspection, and on the other a Radical one by Madier de Montjau,
which would have extended the disqualification from teaching to
the entire clergy. They then, on 9 July, passed Article 7 by 333
votes to 164, and the bill as a whole by a slightly larger majority.
Energetic campaigns for and against the article were launched
throughout the country during the ensuing parliamentary recess,
with Ferry himself and Bert active among its champions. Ferry

---

[76] See L. Capéran, *Histoire contemporaine de la laïcité française*, 3 vols. (Paris, 1957–
61), i. 167–227; P. Chevallier, *La Séparation de l'Église et de l'école: Jules Ferry et Léon
XIII* (Paris, 1981), 126–250; E. Acomb, *The French Laic Laws, 1879–89: The First
Anticlerical Campaign of the Third French Republic* (New York, 1941), 136–46. The
diplomatic dimension of the events is covered by Y. Marchasson, *La Diplomatie
romaine et la République française à la recherche d'une conciliation, 1879–1880* (Paris,
1974.)   [77] Quoted in Capéran, *Histoire contemporaine de la laïcité*, i. 189.
[78] *Le Rappel*, 8 Apr. 1880.

enjoyed an intoxicating encounter with popular enthusiasm in the towns of the south; his arrival in Perpignan, he reported, 'was a triumphal march across a delirious flood of 20,000 enthusiasts and 20,000 fanatics for the Ferry laws, running, shouting joyfully, from their 20,000 chests, the name of Article 7. For henceforth, Article 7 is a popular saint. They say here "Long live Article 7!", as they have long said: Long live the Arago! To say: Long live the Republic!'[79] Canonized or not, however, Article 7 had still to face the Sénat, and its chances of survival were not improved by the change of government at the end of December, in which Waddington and his colleagues of the Centre Gauche gave way to Freycinet and others of the Union Républicaine. With their leaders out of office, members of the Centre Gauche no longer had cause to refrain from attacking Article 7. When the article came before the Sénat in late February and early March 1880, it was eloquently and decisively condemned in the name of liberal principles by two of the group's most illustrious and experienced members, Jules Simon (the bill's *rapporteur*) and Jules Dufaure. Despite the efforts of Ferry and Freycinet, it was defeated, by 148 to 129 at the first reading and by 149 to 132 at the second and final vote on 15 March.

This did not save the Jesuits. On the contrary, it merely switched the focus of attention from their right to teach to their right to exist, and forced the government to tread the executive rather than the legislative path. The day after the Sénat's vote, the presidents of the parliamentary groups which had comprised the anti-jesuit majority of the previous July interpellated the government in the Chambre des Députés, reminding it of the laws against the unauthorized orders, and the government, in the person of Freycinet, undertook, in return for a substantial vote of confidence, to apply these laws with the 'firmness' and 'prudence' which the task required. In the event, the firmness was for the Jesuits, and the prudence consisted of an attempt to avoid too sharp a confrontation with the Church by leaving an escape route for the other orders. On 29 March, on the advice of Gambetta, the government issued two decrees: while the second gave the other unauthorized *congrégations* three months in which to forestall the rigour of the law by submitting their statutes and ordinances with a view to authorization, the first flatly gave 'l'agrégation ou association non

[79] J. Ferry, *Lettres, 1846–1893* (Paris, 1914), 290.

autorisée, dite de Jésus' the same time (or six months in the case of its schools) in which to dissolve itself and evacuate its establishments. At the end of June, amidst scenes of emotion and in some cases tumult, the passively resisting Jesuits were removed by public force from their residences throughout France.[80] They and their supporters sought to preserve their schools by transferring the ownership or tenancy of the property to specially constituted *sociétés civiles* and appointing laymen or secular clergy as *directeurs*, the Jesuits themselves continuing to teach but ceasing to live together under one roof. The government, frustrated (by the failure of Article 7) in its desire to deny individual Jesuits the right to teach, proceeded to a similar end by a different route. Interpreting the Jesuits' continued presence in the schools as constituting a continuation or revival of their existence as a *congrégation*, it used the apparatus of academic discipline (school inspectors, *recteurs d'académie, conseils académiques*)—to pursue the non-Jesuit *directeurs* for misconduct (under Article 68 of the Loi Falloux) in conniving at such an illegality, and thus to secure the closure or thorough de-Jesuitization of the schools.[81] Since in practice the presence of even one or two Jesuits might be considered sufficient grounds for such a proceeding, the result resembled that which Article 7 had been designed to achieve. By early 1881, with its members barred both from cohabiting and from teaching, the Society of Jesus had again been driven underground in France.

Both Article 7 and the first decree of 29 March performed the traditional manœuvre of separating the Jesuits from the rest of the Catholic clergy. This tactic, always resisted by the Jesuits' friends, was now, to a much greater extent than in the 1820s or even the 1840s, controversial among their enemies. A study of the anti-jesuit arguments used in 1879–80, and especially of the tensions between keen and lukewarm supporters of Article 7, allows one not only to watch familiar polemical elements at play in changed political circumstances, but also to explore the questions which the development of the broader anticlerical current from mid-century onwards, and the nature of the anti-jesuit interpretation of the Church's

---

[80] See Duparc and Cochin (eds.), *Expulsions*, part I; Andrieux, *Souvenirs*, ii. 215–33; Burnichon, *La Compagnie de Jésus en France*, iv. 658–67.

[81] See J. Auffray and L. de Crousaz-Crétet, *Les Expulsés devant les tribunaux: Recueil des décisions judiciaires relatives à l'exécution des décrets du 29 mars 1880* (Paris, 1881); Chevallier, *La Séparation de l'Église et de l'école*, 235–43.

modern evolution which was common within that current, had tacitly raised about the status of Jesuitism as an analytical category and of anti-jesuitism as a practical policy.

The Radicals and the more moderate Republicans who made up Article 7's main parliamentary support agreed on certain important points. They shared the by now familiar sense of participation in a fundamental struggle between spiritually opposite historical forces: Ferry's summons to 'all those who proceed from the French Revolution' to join in 'this combat of the present hour, which is truly the good fight' was paralleled by the Radical *La Lanterne*'s recognition that beneath the 'petty quarrel' of Article 7 lay 'the great battle between the old world and the new world, between absolutism and liberty'.[82] They agreed, too, in assigning the chief responsibility for the reactionary and clerical direction imparted to both the Catholic Church and the political Right since 1848 (and especially since 1870) to Jesuit influence. They differed, however, in their perception of the Republic's present situation and security, and in the success they expected of narrowly anti-jesuit action. To some extent, the differences between them may be summarized as those between a Republican revamping of earlier governmental and statist traditions of anti-jesuitism on the one hand, and a style of anti-jesuitism owing more to the rhetoric of Michelet and Quinet and to the attitudes forged in the political wilderness since 1848 on the other.

In the arguments of Article 7's principal champions—above all Ferry himself, Bert, and Eugène Spuller (the bill's *rapporteur* in the Députés), but also *députés* like Émile Deschanel and Louis Janvier de la Motte, and *sénateurs* like Eugène Pelletan, Foucher de la Careil, Bertauld, and Ronjat—all the nationalist and statist clichés of Restoration and Orleanist anti-jesuitism reappeared: the Society of Jesus was an illegal order, a foreign body, and a secret society; its members were disqualified from citizenship by their vow of obedience; its teaching practices were corrosive of that national cohesiveness which it was the business of education to foster and of the State to protect. Though the framework within which these elements were assembled was now the ideology of 'Republican defence' which had taken shape in the 1870s,[83] the feeling of *déjà vu*

---

[82] *ASCD*, Sénat 6 Mar. 1880: 246; *La Lanterne*, 11 Mar. 1880.
[83] See J. Gadille, 'La Politique de la défense républicaine à l'égard de l'Église de France, 1876–1883', *Bulletin de la Société d'Histoire Moderne*, 4th ser. 1 (1967), 1–6.

which they provoke is no accident. Ferry and his colleagues insisted that, in attacking the Jesuits, they were conforming not just to the interest of the young and endangered Republic, but to juridical and statesmanly principles whose value was independent of particular governmental forms. Their reliance on the authority of earlier representatives of Gallican and statist legal and political thinking was heavy; a single speech by Ferry contained extensive extracts from Thiers, Fortoul, Bonjean, Troplong, Cuvier, Daunou, Guizot, Broglie, Villemain, and Rouland.[84] Freycinet later recalled how the Minister of Education, wishing to draw him into the debate on Article 7, had offered him 'a little volume of Dupin *aîné*', telling him it contained 'the whole question from the political and juridical point of view'.[85] When Jules Simon dismissed Ferry's protracted parade of authorities as an irrelevant substitute for real argument, he was attacking the substance as well as the style of his opponents' reasoning. When he denounced the legists of the past as servants of tyranny, Ferry and Bertauld rushed to defend them as 'the founders of modern society', and 'of French unity'.[86]

The remark which (in another debate early in 1880) Laboulaye levelled at Barthélemy-Saint-Hilaire—'that one might reproach him with having remained at the point reached by *Le Constitutionnel* in 1828, namely at a horror of the Jesuits and an unbridled love for the omnipotence of the State'[87]—might equally well have been applied to the leading advocates of Article 7. For them the State, properly understood, was the active embodiment, the political protector, and the moral guardian of society. Nothing was to be feared from its power, since it was simply 'the organ of social justice',[88] operating according to laws enacted by 'the totality of citizens consulted and as it were condensed in one or several Chambers'.[89] It was 'the true fulcrum' for a resistance to Ultramontanism and infallibilism within the traditions which the Gallican Church had established but was now itself incapable of defending.[90] Understanding its importance, the Revolution had been at pains to make the rights of the State unassailable, and neither Jesuits nor so-called

---

[84] *ASCD*, Sénat 5 and 6 Mar. 1880.
[85] C. de Freycinet, *Souvenirs 1878–1893*, 4th edn. (Paris, 1913), 119.
[86] *ASCD*, Sénat 8 Mar. 1880: 261–2.   [87] Ibid., Sénat 7 Jan. 1880: 161.
[88] *ASCD*, 1879 (VI), annexes, 20–1 (Spuller report).
[89] *ASCD*, CD 21 June 1879: 58 (Bert).
[90] Ibid., CD 24 June 1879: 128–9 (Spuller).

liberals (like Simon or Laboulaye) should be allowed to jeopardize them.[91]

For Republicans in the mould of Ferry and Spuller, in fact, the Republican State—the modern, secular, law-bound State finally endowed with Republican forms and brought under democratic control—was the decisive consummation of the Revolutionary achievement: its strength and security were the guarantees of liberty and equality in civil society. Once the State existed in this form, the proper and primary function of Republican politics was, both politically and socially, defensive. Further profound transformations were unnecessary, and if one might envisage an 'extension' or 'development' of the already realized 'conquests' (to use Spuller's careful terminology[92]), this could not be thought of till the essential protective work—notably the removal of the Jesuits from education—had been done. Anti-jesuitism in a Republican State was thus, fundamentally, a work of 'social defence'.[93] The society to be defended had various names—'the society in which we live', 'modern society', 'the secularized society', 'the society issued from the French Revolution', 'civil society freed by reason, by science, by law, by liberty'[94]—but each of them implied that it was a completed and coherent, if threatened, entity.

Radicals questioned most of these premises. Though they differed totally from Simon in their conclusions, they shared his simultaneous distaste for the legists' cult of the State and for the statesmen's cult of legists. They too were distressed to be offered Dupin *aîné* ('The Dupin of the *Châtiments*! The Dupin of 2 December!'[95]) as an object of Republican veneration; they too saw, in Ferry's assertion that the State, as arbiter of moral and political theory, was empowered to insist on the ideas of the Revolution as 'the state doctrine', a perversion of the Republican message and an ominous curtailment of the rights of Reason.[96] While they recognized that the State had duties and therefore rights in the

---

[91] *ASCD*, 1879 (VI), annexes, 20–1 (Spuller report).

[92] *ASCD*, CD 24 June 1879: 131.

[93] Both Bert and Émile Deschanel used this term to describe Article 7 (ibid., CD 21 June 1879: 52; CD 23 July 1879: 98).

[94] *ASCD*, Sénat 6 Mar. 1880: 235, 246 (Ferry); *ASCD*, 1879 (VI), annexes, 18, 16 (Spuller report); *ASCD*, CD 23 June 1879: 98 (E. Deschanel).

[95] A. Vacquerie in *Le Rappel*, 8 Apr. 1880.

[96] *ASCD*, CD 26 June 1879: 160 (Ferry), attacked by Camille Pelletan in *Le Rappel*, 29 June 1879.

educational field, they were impatient at the presumption with
which the rights of the State were invoked to justify the arbitrary
picking and choosing which seemed to characterize the government's policy on religious orders. In their view, French laws (good
Revolutionary ones) required the dissolution of unauthorized
orders (and perhaps even of authorized ones, since authorization
was an expedient of Monarchy and Empire); to promote a bill
which merely denied them the right to teach was superfluous, inadequate, and (since it might seem to recognize their right to exist)
dangerous and irresponsible.[97]

The Radicals' hopes for decisive victory over the Jesuitical
Church were pinned not on the tutelary State, but on the free
society, meaning one in which the Church's unfair advantage in the
struggle for social influence had been broken by the Separation of
Church and State, coupled with a law of associations. For them,
therefore, the political establishment of the Republic was not in
itself decisive. In Louis Blanc's view, the defensive timidities of
Article 7 showed that the government lacked the courage necessary
to clear away the obstacles to the real work of reform and to the
resolution of the 'great social question'.[98] The main Radical spokes-
man in the Députés' debate on Article 7, Madier de Montjau,
offered a more alarmist and more narrowly anticlerical vision.
Not until religious orders were suppressed and clerical education
banned, he argued, would the Republic truly exist and the Revolution cease to be in peril. At present, despite the constitutional
appearances, Republicans were 'still in a state of defeat'; France was
faced with a creeping substitution of 'the Jesuitical Republic' for
the Republican one. The members of religious orders were everywhere, 'acting, possessing, insinuating themselves, inveigling, teaching, directing', opposed only by the half-measures of a complacent
government.[99] In a later speech, interpellating the government
after the defeat of Article 7, Madier made free use of the vocabulary
of national humiliation and military occupation, raging against 'this
black army, which raises its forts and fortresses on every point of
our territory', and which, unchallenged, 'stations the posts of its

[97] See esp. Madier de Montjau in *ASCD*, CD 7 July 1879: 103–6, and CD 16
Mar. 1880: 130–3; also Louis Blanc's speeches at Troyes and at the Théâtre de
Cluny in May and June 1879, in L. Blanc, *Discours politiques (1847 à 1881)* (Paris,
1882), 338, 346.
[98] Blanc, *Discours politiques*, 335–9.   [99] *ASCD*, CD 7 July 1879: 106–9.

vanguard and rearguard amongst us, against us'. He described the Jesuits 'everywhere, like the hideous octopus, stretching out and positioning their ominous arms to entwine and stifle the *patrie*, drawing in with their suckers both its wealth and its intelligence, and its conscience!' Plainly, it was the duty of a Republican government 'to bring to an end this work of destruction, of gangrene, and of death to the nation'.[100] It is hard, however, to recognize in this desperate task of salvage the same work of preservation that more moderate Republicans like Ferry described in the self-confident rhetoric of Republican defence.

These differences in general political perspective between Radicals and men of Republican defence had implications for the conclusions which they drew from their notion of the relationship between the Jesuits and the Church. Neither group doubted that this was a relationship of domination, such as Spuller described in his report:

The Jesuits are already the masters of the spiritual power. The proclamation of the dogma of pontifical infallibility has confirmed the preponderance of their doctrines; the bishops are no longer anything but apostolic prefects. The other religious orders recognize the pre-eminence of the Society of Jesus. And as for the secular clergy, nobody talks about it any longer. One barely need mention it, except to say that, to use a well-known expression, it marches like a regiment, the moment the chief commands.[101]

Ferry explained that he pursued the Jesuits rather than the rest of the clergy

because they are the masters; because it is they who are the promoters of this religious revolution . . . of this attempt that is so dangerous for the civil power and for modern society; because they dominate in the Church, because they hold a great part of the clergy in servitude; because the clergy of France is their captive; because, in education, it is they who set the tone, it is they who furnish the example for the others, it is they who have the success, who are in fashion; because it is they who serve as models for all the ecclesiastical establishments; because it is to them that these establishments go to ask for books . . . and for travestied histories of France![102]

The differences between Ferry and his Radical critics were not over this analysis, but over what followed from it. The assumption

<hr>

[100] Ibid., CD 16 Mar. 1880: 130–3.   [101] *ASCD*, 1879 (VI), annexes, 27.
[102] *ASCD*, CD 27 June 1879: 192.

underlying Article 7 was that, since the Jesuits were responsible for what was wrong with the Church, action specifically against the Jesuits was the key to setting it right: in Ferry's wording, 'the particular role which the Company of Jesus plays in France' was not merely 'a new role', but one 'which will finish when she has disappeared'.[103] Once the Church was rid of this corrupting element, the affirmation of the State's rights, in accordance with traditional Gallican principles (as interpreted by the likes of Dupin *aîné*) would be enough to secure religious peace. There was no question of Article 7 obstructing the provision of a Christian education, and it would be 'the ultimate and most criminal madness' to 'go to war with the belief of the greater number of our fellow-citizens' by attacking Catholicism itself.[104]

Catholics attacked this position with two arguments. To the first—that, since the unauthorized orders were part of the Church, attacks on them were attacks on it—the defenders of Article 7 had a clear reply: the State recognized only the Concordatory Church, of which such orders were not part, and did not accept that Catholicism was incomplete without them.[105] The second argument was harder to answer, partly because Catholics and Radicals voiced it simultaneously. It held that the proponents of Article 7 were drawing an impossible line between the Jesuits and the rest of the clergy, since the doctrine and attitudes of which they accused the former were equally attributable to the latter. From this, Radicals concluded that Article 7 was the product of muddle-headedness or political cowardice, and Catholics that it was merely the deceitful opening to a campaign against the whole Church.

To argue, as Bert did, that the State already had institutional safeguards against misbehaviour by secular or authorized regular clergy which it lacked in the case of the unauthorized[106] seemed an inadequate reply. The very evidence which Ferry and Bert marshalled to prove the need for specifically anti-jesuit measures— massed citations from works of moral theology and textbooks in use in clerical schools—came, in many cases, from works by non-Jesuit writers. Radicals and Catholics alike can be forgiven for having found it hard to understand how such citations could be

---

[103] Ibid., CD 8 July 1879: 125.

[104] Ibid., CD 27 June 1879: 192 (Ferry); Sénat 5 Mar. 1880: 206 (Ferry).

[105] Ibid., CD 8 July 1879: 124 (Ferry); Sénat 4 Mar. 1880: 172–5 (Foucher de Careil).   [106] Ibid., CD 21 June 1879: 61.

used to justify legislation which attacked the Jesuits while leaving untouched those sections of the clergy and Catholic laity to which the incriminated authors actually belonged. Ferry and Bert's justifications of their use of such evidence are revealing. Challenged over one quotation, Ferry replied: 'No, it is not from a Jesuit, but from an author who professes the doctrines of the Society of Jesus.'[107] Bert argued in similar vein:

They [The Right] have told us—and it is the truth—that the whole Catholic Church has rallied to Jesuitical ideas and doctrines. Consequently, we have the right to say, when we find these doctrines expressed by a member of any *congrégation* or of the secular clergy, we have the right to say: These doctrines are Jesuitical doctrines, without needing to investigate anything else.[108]

In short, certain doctrines—whether the political doctrine of the Church's 'indirect power', attacked by Ferry, or the casuistical teachings denounced by Bert—were recognizably 'Jesuit' in provenance. If non-Jesuits expressed them, this was surely because, as Bert put it, the Jesuits now had 'the very great cunning to conceal themselves behind members of other *congrégations*, behind members of the secular clergy, and even behind laymen'.[109] Ferry was sure that, at heart, the vast majority of French Catholics, clergy included, were hostile to 'Jesuit doctrines'; their apparent solidarity with them was an illusion attributable to Jesuit tyranny. It was this that made Madier de Montjau's assimilation of the entire clergy and much of the Catholic laity 'to the elements of Jesuitism and Ultramontanism', in Ferry's view, 'inexact'.[110]

Radicals had little time for such analytical finesse. Madier told his fellow *députés* that they had been elected 'against the government of the *curés*—the people did not say only of the Jesuits'.[111] For some Radicals, the Jesuits were remarkable in the Church merely for their success. Édouard de Pompéry drew attention to 'the essential conformity' between their doctrines and those which the Church had always professed: 'The spirit of the Church is the blind submission of the faithful; the supreme virtue for the Jesuit is obedience. The one is no better than the other; or rather they are the same thing. But no religious order has preached and practised

---

[107] Ibid., Sénat 6 Mar. 1880: 247.   [108] Ibid., CD 5 July 1879: 70.
[109] Ibid.   [110] Ibid., CD 27 June 1879: 190–1.
[111] Ibid., CD 7 July 1879: 107.

the doctrine with such success as the children of Loyola.' This, in de Pompéry's view, was why the Jesuits had become 'the masters of the Church'.[112] Other Radicals were closer to Ferry in recognizing that a theoretical distinction between Jesuitism and Catholicism had once been possible, but considered that it was 'puerile' (Édouard Lockroy's word[113]) to try to apply it to the Church which had emerged from the Vatican Council. Whichever view was taken, the implication was the same. As Lockroy put it in the wake of the defeat of Article 7: 'The existing laws may well suppress the Jesuits. They do not rid us of Jesuitism.' The 'clerical peril' would remain.[114] Against such pervasive spirits there was little point in turning for protection to the State, as conceived by Ferry's Gallican imagination, for such a State could work only by discrimination and authorization—by distinguishing what was acceptable and controllable in the Church from what was not—and this was what had become impossible. If, as Radicals generally admitted, the clergy (to say nothing of the Catholic laity) were too numerous and socially entrenched to be banned as one might ban the Jesuits, there remained only one solution. Auguste Vacquerie summarized the Radical position: 'The separation which we desire is not the separation of the bishops and the Jesuits, it is the separation of the Church and the State.'[115]

Twenty-five years (and one further expulsion of religious orders) would elapse before such a Separation became a reality. In 1880, it was the older, secular Gallican, pro-Concordatory view of Church–State relations that still prevailed. Within this framework, the Jesuits continued to exert their power of fascination over Republican minds, to provide a focus for the analysis of France's and the Republic's problems, and a primary target for preventive or retributive action. But the extent to which anti-jesuitism had developed and merged into a wider anticlericalism is shown not just in the invective of the Radicals, but in the equivocations and complications to which the mainstream supporters of Article 7 were driven in their efforts to reconcile the breadth of their criticisms of the contemporary Church with the restricted nature of the anti-jesuit action they were proposing. The more numerous the aspects of ecclesiastical life and religious action that Jesuit influence was

---

[112] *La Semaine anti-cléricale*, 27 Mar. 1880: 411.

[113] *Le Rappel*, 29 Mar. 1880.   [114] Ibid. 26 Mar. 1880.

[115] Ibid. 14 Apr. 1880.

adduced to explain, the less likely it was that effective action against the Jesuits themselves would deflate the emotions mobilized in the anti-jesuit campaign. Both in 1828 and in 1845 it had to some extent done so. But then in the 1820s, and even in the 1840s (with men like Michelet, Quinet, and Génin the obvious exceptions), most secular anti-jesuits had confined themselves to blaming the Jesuits for clerical politics and displays of religious fanaticism; they had not (unlike the sternest religious critics of 'Jesuitized' Roman Catholicism) maintained that Jesuit domination extended to all areas of the Church's activity. They had continued to believe the Gallican Church capable of independent vitality, or at least to respect the clergy in the performance of its spiritual functions. By the time of Article 7, this had changed. It was commonly asserted that the Black rather than the White Pope ruled the Church, that the major event of modern Catholic history—the Vatican Council—had ratified the triumph of Jesuit principles and organization; that Jesuit doctrines were the staple nourishment of the French clergy; that Jesuit models and Jesuit books were the inspiration of Catholic education. In effect, the despairing conclusions of the embattled remnant of ecclesiastical Gallicans and Old Catholics had become the standard thinking of secular politicians and journalists. It was almost inevitable, then, that Republican opponents of Jesuitism, whether or not they considered Article 7 appropriate, would in practice find their task merely begun when the Jesuits had been dispersed. Republican defence would require a larger programme of laicization, especially in education; to this, the decrees of March 1880 would be merely the prelude. Republican anticlericalism might still find a place for anti-jesuit themes and mythology, but the Jesuit question, in its narrow definition, could no longer enjoy a special power to dominate French politics.

The polemics of the Dreyfus Affair, at the end of the 1890s, reflect both the durability of the anti-jesuit theme after 1880 and its altered and reduced significance. The Affair unleashed a grand free-for-all of conspiracy theories in French politics,[116] and the Jesuits (who had gradually returned to their establishments during the 1880s and 1890s) were prominent among those denounced, along

---

[116] For recent discussion, see R. Griffiths, *The Use of Abuse: The Polemics of the Dreyfus Affair and its Aftermath* (New York, 1991), esp. ch. 3.

with the Jews, the Freemasons, and the Protestants. In Dreyfusard pamphlets and journalism, the routine use of the anti-jesuit idiom re-emerged as a common feature of Republican polemic: confining oneself to Clemenceau's articles over a crucial few months, one finds references to 'the jesuitico-military madness', to the efforts of 'the whole *jésuitière*' against the Cour de Cassation, to the Henry memorial supported by 'the flower of French Jesuitism', to Dreyfus victimized by 'the great booted *jésuitière*' of the General Staff.[117] More explicit references to Jesuit conspiracy abounded also. In their emphasis they reflected the particular circumstances of the Affair: the subversion of the army by Jesuit-educated officers,[118] and the Jesuits' alleged responsibility for the anti-Semitic campaigns of Drumont (already denounced as 'Drumont-jésuite'[119]) and others, were the dominant themes. Anti-jesuit suspicions also now received a more personal focus than they had usually had before: Père du Lac ('the Jesuit of the General Staff',[120] on the table of whose humble cell an open and annotated copy of the *Annuaire militaire* was allegedly visible[121]), spiritual director of General Boisdeffre (the Chief of Staff) and close associate of the Catholic politician Albert de Mun, was regarded by many as the linchpin or presiding genius of the anti-Dreyfusard alliance.

Nevertheless, although all the old (and some new) elements of anti-jesuit conspiracy theory found a place in Dreyfusard polemic, they jostled with too many other elements to permit anti-jesuit discourse to dominate Republican perceptions as it had done earlier. Zola might, in his novel *Vérité*, place the Jesuits Philibin and Crabot at the heart of the clerical conspiracy to frame the Jewish schoolteacher Simon for murder (an obvious analogue for the

[117] G. Clemenceau, *Contre la justice* (Paris, 1900), 83, 146, 149, 380 (all quotations from articles between Dec. 1898 and Mar. 1899).

[118] Anti-jesuits were again particularly concerned with the success of the École Sainte-Geneviève in preparing pupils for the military *grandes écoles*. See de Mun, *Nouvelle Réponse*, on renewed allegations of cheating in exams directed against this school.

[119] H. Strauss, *Drumont-jésuite et ses complices démasqués A.M.D.G.* (Paris, 1892). A sinister link between the Jesuits and the anti-Semitic campaign was often detected in the fact that Odelin, the original administrator of the anti-Semitic paper *La Libre Parole*, had also administered the École Sainte-Geneviève. The Jesuits had also been blamed for the Catholic anti-masonic campaign of the 1880s: see L. Amiable, *L'Internationale noire et la francmaçonnerie* (Paris, 1884).

[120] Title of several articles in Clemenceau's paper *Le Bloc* in early 1901.

[121] J. Reinach, *Histoire de l'Affaire Dreyfus*, 6 vols. (Paris, 1901–8), iii. 26.

framing of Dreyfus for treason),[122] but in his most decisive intervention in the Affair itself, the famous open letter to President
Faure published in *L'Aurore* on 13 January 1898, he focused firmly
on the sinister figure of Lieutenant-Colonel du Paty de Clam, and
on other senior military figures; his passing reference to the
General Staff as a 'jésuitière' was not enough to switch attention
from the military to the Jesuits.[123] Urbain Gohier in *L'Armée contre
la nation* also had his anti-jesuit moment, when he claimed to draw
enlightenment about present politics from the suggestion that
Eugène Cavaignac, President of the Second Republic in 1848 and
father of the present Minister of War, had been influenced by the
Jesuit Ravignan: 'At fifty years' distance, the son takes up the
father's work, on the orders of the same powers.'[124] By the time
Gohier had finished, however, the Jesuits were merely part of a far
broader array of the nation's enemies: 'the men of Coblentz', 'the
Chouans', 'the men of Rome', 'the internationals of finance, Jewish
or Christian' (and other, still vaguer categories: 'the *cléricaille*', 'the
reactionaries of every hue').[125] In the midst of such a proliferation,
the Jesuits lost much of their significance. Like their opponents
(the denouncers of 'Judeo-Masonry', of the Dreyfusard 'Syndicat'),
the Dreyfusards built their conspiracy theories of disparate and
sometimes improvised materials; what they gained in flexibility,
they were apt to lose in clarity of outline.

The work which, more than any other, established a specifically
anti-jesuit view of the Affair was Joseph Reinach's massive *Histoire
de l'Affaire Dreyfus*, published in its immediate aftermath. Reinach's
message was clear enough: the Dreyfus Affair marked the cul-
mination of fifty years during which Jesuitism had identified itself
more and more closely with Catholicism and established a tighter
and tighter hold over France's ruling classes (and, during the final
decade, over the *classes populaires* as well). By exploiting the Dreyfus
case, the Jesuits hoped to forge an alliance with the military which
would permit them to complete their take-over of French society,
and their victory over every shade of heresy and free thought. They
were responsible for the anti-Semitic campaign, for the fabricated

---

[122] E. Zola, *Vérité* (Paris, 1903).
[123] E. Zola, *L'Affaire Dreyfus: La Vérité en marche* (Paris, 1901), 73–98
(quotation p. 88).
[124] U. Gohier, *L'Armée contre la nation* (Paris, 1899), 320–1.
[125] Ibid. 341, 355.

myth of the 'Syndicat', for the false crusade for the army's honour, and also for the educational formation of the upper classes which permitted such intellectual poisons to take a hold: their labour of 'intellectual subjugation' had produced the politics of anti-Dreyfusism at the end of the nineteenth century, just as it had produced the Ligue at the end of the sixteenth.[126] Such an argument, of course, placed Reinach in the mainstream of Third Republican anti-jesuitism, indebted to Michelet and Quinet and shaped in the 1870s. Yet it is noticeable how little of his book was taken up with its elaboration. For most of the six volumes, the focus was on the immediate actors of the Affair (of whom only du Lac—who emerges from Reinach's account more as a meddlesome mediocrity than as a truly dominant figure[127]—was a Jesuit); the Society of Jesus itself was absent from all but a few pages. On at least two of the occasions when it was invoked, furthermore, Reinach was careful to deny that the developments which he was explaining could be attributed to the Jesuits alone, though he insisted that they were the principal cause.[128] In Reinach's book, as in the day-to-day polemics of the Affair itself, the Jesuits appeared as part of a more general clerical (or clerico-military) complex of forces—no doubt the most conspiratorial part (whose manœuvres in the shadows contrasted with the cruder offensive methods of the Assumptionists[129]), perhaps the part which gave cohesion and direction to the whole, but no longer a part whose supposed activities filled the foreground of the anticlerical imagination to the exclusion of all others. At the end of the nineteenth century, the mythology surrounding the Jesuits still furnished Republican anticlericalism with its most influential images of conspiracy; it no longer supplied—as it had still done twenty years before—the central pivot around which anticlerical debate revolved.

The three major waves of political anti-jesuitism in France between 1814 and 1880 reveal, though with significant variations, a common pattern. In each case, anti-jesuitism first established itself as a polemical response to a wave of Catholic or clerical assertiveness—the internal missions of the Restoration, the

---

[126] Reinach, *Histoire*, i. 215–18, iii. 21–6, 267–72, 570–3, iv. 250–1.

[127] Ibid. iv. 240 ('the silliest of conspirators, because the most presumptuous'); v. 145–9 ('I found in him no trace of the famous cunning of his Company').

[128] Ibid. i. 215, iii. 25.   [129] Ibid. iii. 570–3.

campaign against the *monopole universitaire* in the 1840s, the politics of moral order and the development of Catholic social activism during the early Third Republic. In each case, once aroused, anti-jesuit energies expended themselves in two ways. On one level, they produced a tenacious pursuit of the Society of Jesus itself, involving revelations about Jesuit establishments, calls for action against them, and pressure resulting in legal or governmental action. On another, anti-jesuit rhetoric became available for broader political uses. These might begin with its deployment against those (clericals or monarchists) perceived to be most closely associated with the movements that had provoked the initial anti-jesuit outcry; they might by the end involve the denigration of anyone (including ministers or liberals with no stomach for intolerance) perceived to be lacking in the right sort of anti-jesuit ardour.

The political functions of the anti-jesuit conspiracy theory were varied: it could serve either as a discourse on occult government, fit to express the frustration of those who felt excluded from power, or as a discourse on subversion, expressing the fears of those uneasily ensconced within it. The political significance of the Jesuit question varied accordingly: the rallying-ground for opposition in the 1820s, it performed the same function for government-sponsored Republican defence at the end of the 1870s, and in the 1840s gave the competing factions of the Orleanist political class an arena for their rivalry. On each of these occasions, anti-jesuitism provided a *point de ralliement*, capable of bringing and holding disparate groups together in opposition to a common enemy. By the same token, however, it provided a point of tension: the collaboration of anti-jesuit factions did not exclude competition and could give way to mistrustful recrimination, sometimes couched in anti-jesuit terms. Restoration Liberals, conservative Orleanists, moderate Republicans, each in turn found themselves outflanked by more radical spirits, disposed (without rejecting the basic validity of anti-jesuit rhetoric) to question the solidity of moderate anti-jesuit credentials and the appropriateness of limited anti-jesuit goals. This tension or rivalry between moderate and radical was one of the recurrent features of anti-jesuitism's political history.

In seeking to explain the political importance of anti-jesuitism, it is to the moderates—to liberals rather than republicans early in the century, men of Republican defence rather than Radicals later on—that our attention is primarily drawn. It was their desire to

distinguish friend from foe in the Church, their commitment to a
strictly secular version of Gallican tradition and to a strong conception of the State's control over civil society, their need to balance a
practical conservatism with a theoretical commitment to the Revolutionary legacy, that made the Jesuit question a political sticking-
point and thus created space for anti-jesuitism to operate as a
distinctive political force. Radical anti-jesuitism, when not marked
by the idiosyncratic extremism of a Raspail, had a tendency either
to dissolve into a broader anticlericalism (as with Madier de
Montjau), or to operate as a satirical commentary on the hypocrisies of its moderate counterpart (as with L'Ancien Album), or to
expand into a spiritual critique so sweeping as to lose precise points
of contact with contemporary politics (as with Michelet); in all
three cases, it accentuated the rhetoric while eroding the program-
matic substance of a specifically anti-jesuit politics.

The differences between moderate and radical currents in
nineteenth-century French anti-jesuitism should not, however, be
exaggerated. Not only were 'moderation' and 'radicalism' matters
of degree, and variable with context; competition in anti-jesuitism
also presupposed a fund of common references. Anti-jesuits dis-
agreed openly in their assessment of the contemporary situation (of
how far the Jesuit take-over of Church or State had so far gone,
of which groups were favouring it, of how it might be overcome)
far more often than in their understanding of the Jesuits' basic characteristics, historical record, or distinctive modes of action. In their
analysis of these, moderates and radicals were joint beneficiaries
and joint continuers of a common anti-jesuit tradition. Forged in
the polemics of previous centuries, this was not a peculiarly liberal
or republican tradition; conservative monarchists like Montlosier,
Gallicans like Wallon, and even (though with some significant
reservations) reactionary 'Jansenists' like Silvy could appeal to it
also. Nor was it confined to the types of anti-jesuit literature with
which this study has so far been chiefly concerned—literature
generated in close proximity to high politics, or by men of public
prominence, or which demonstrates with particular clarity the
association of anti-jesuitism with a particular political or religious
stance. It was also passed on and elaborated (and its details often
most comprehensively set forth) in literature of a less individually
notable kind—in ephemeral pamphlets, obscure brochures, almanacs,
songs, and forgettable fiction. Between the anti-jesuitism of

eminent politicians, learned lawyers, and famous writers, and that of the pamphleteers and popular novelists, there were naturally differences of tone, of emphasis, and of presentation, but there was also much common ground; similar themes and motifs were developed in different (but not always very different) styles.

Tradition, then, provided the nineteenth century with an imagery and a mythology of Jesuit conspiracy whose appeal transcended a number of ideological and cultural boundaries, and whose peculiar combination of durability and flexibility were crucial in making anti-jesuitism a potent political force. It is with the nineteenth-century forms and transformations of this mythology, and with its salient themes and images, that the remaining chapters of this book are concerned.

5

Structures, Imagery, and Argument

THE notion of conspiracy was a crucial one in anti-jesuit mythology. It provided a framework within which each allegation against
the Jesuits could find a place and an enhanced significance. This
does not mean that all those who attacked the Jesuits believed in
the highly developed conspiracy theory, accusing the order of
consciously aspiring to world domination, that was advanced by
their most systematic detractors; some, no doubt, scarcely believed
in a formal Jesuit conspiracy at all. It was hard, however, in attacking the Jesuits, to find arguments to which the conspiracy theory
had not laid claim, and which could not be used to reinforce it. In
this sense, and in the absence of any substantial anti-jesuit critique
of its premises, the myth of Jesuit conspiracy dominated anti-jesuit
discourse. To a greater or lesser extent, most anti-jesuits accepted
this domination.

Imagination as well as reason was involved in this acceptance.
We need not suppose most anti-jesuits to have been as helplessly
suggestible as Sue's heroine Adrienne de Cardoville, who declared
herself unable to think of the Jesuits 'without ideas of darkness, of
venom and of nasty black reptiles being involuntarily aroused in
me'.[1] The imagery which anti-jesuits used does, however, provide
our best initial guide to the imaginative dispositions which under-
pinned their polemic. Four main families or complexes of imagery
figure especially prominently in the literature: images of light and
darkness, of ambush and trapping, of animality, and of disease.

The imagery of light and darkness conveyed, in stark terms, the
sense of irreducible binary opposition that informed the anti-jesuit
vision; it cast this opposition, often explicitly, in terms of a warfare
between 'enlightenment' and obscurantism. The struggle between
the Jesuits and their opponents appeared as 'a combat waged by the
darkness against the light', the Jesuits and their allies as 'legislators

---

[1] Sue, *Le Juif errant*, i. 406.

of darkness', who obstructed the light of the sun with 'all the eclipses of stupidity, all the clouds of error'.[2] But darkness had a further significance for anti-jesuits: it was the enemy's place of refuge, protective cover, and natural habitat. The Jesuits acted 'in the shadows', advanced 'silently in the night', emerged (in Béranger's famous verse) 'from below ground'. Their sorties from the gloom were rare, for Jesuitism 'only enjoys itself in the darkness; the light troubles and disconcerts it'.[3] The offensive of light against darkness accordingly took the form not only of a general enlightenment of humanity despite the Jesuits, but also of a specific exposure of Jesuit hiding-places. The Restoration *Constitutionnel* declared itself the first to have 'lit up' the underground regions where Jesuitism lay concealed, and to have 'forced it to appear in broad daylight'.[4] Paul Bert, similarly, boasted of having found the Jesuit theologian Gury 'in his lair', stripped him of the impure Latin 'behind which he was hiding', and brought him before the public 'in full daylight, ashamed of his nudity, and blinking in the sun'.[5]

With the attribution to the Jesuits of a subterranean existence, we pass from the first family of images, those of light and darkness, to the second, those of Jesuit ambush. Like darkness in general, the underground was both the Jesuits' refuge and the scene of their treacherous activity. Images of sapping and mining abound in anti-jesuit literature. *Le Constitutionnel* looked to freedom of the press to bring to light 'the mines where Loyola's labourers are sapping the new edifice of society in France', and baron Dupin warned of the dangers posed by 'these sappers of the intelligence, who advance underground, right beneath our ramparts, to arrive within the fortress, and to emerge there in force while we sleep'.[6] This was one version of the Jesuit ambush, in which society or the State or morality appeared as a fortress equipped to resist open assault, but vulnerable to secret undermining or penetration. Society could also,

[2] J.-B. Bouché, 'Préface appréciative sur l'état actuel de la Compagnie de Jésus', in J.-B. Salgues, *L'Antidote de Mont-Rouge*, new edn. (Paris, 1845), p. iii; *Constitutionnel*, 27 Oct. 1825.
[3] *Les Nihilistes de robe noire: Les Jésuites, leur enseignement: Par un professeur de l'Université* (Paris, 1879), 3; Wallon, *Jésus et les jésuites*, 266; Béranger, *Œuvres complètes*, 236 ('Les Révérends Pères'); Leone, *Conjuration des jésuites*, 296.
[4] *Constitutionnel*, 24 Feb. 1830.
[5] P. Bert, *La Morale des jésuites* (Paris, 1880), p. ii.
[6] *Constitutionnel*, 24 Jan. 1826; *Moniteur*, CP 23 Apr. 1844: 1061 (baron Dupin).

however, be conceived of as a collection of people, and here hidden danger received a different figuration: that of the trap. Jesuitical traps might be set for individuals, but they might also be set on a vast scale, to ensnare a whole society. The Jesuit Escobar, as imagined by Dinocourt, gloated that

We now guard all the exits from the arena into which we have lured society. Placed as if under an immense receptacle, the individuals may writhe, thrash about, and struggle perhaps for a while against the compressive force which is about to take hold of them; but none of them can cross or break the iron barrier we have erected all around them.[7]

The most common trap images, however, involved nets. Considérant described the Jesuits of Leone's secret conference knotting 'with an invincible perseverance' the net in which their order aimed 'to envelop kings and peoples, states and churches, the whole of humanity'; Ordinaire accused them of entangling society in 'a vast net, whose invisible meshes enchain our slightest movements'.[8] The net-image was flexible; it could simultaneously convey the idea of a society hopelessly caught up, a sense of the Jesuits' patient and calculating workmanship (even stronger in the similar image of the spider's web), and (especially where the word *réseau* was used) the notion of a tight-knit network of Jesuit organizations or agents.

The connotations of treachery and of deceitfulness with which the imagery of ambush was invested reappear, along with others, in the anti-jesuits' extensive repertoire of animal images. Four broad categories of animal made frequent appearances in anti-jesuit literature: beasts of prey (mainly wolves and foxes, but sometimes lions, tigers, or birds of prey); reptiles (generally snakes, sometimes chameleons); insects and arachnids (especially spiders, with a sprinkling of gnats, termites, scarabs, wood-lice, and others); mythical beasts (the hydra, or occasionally the phoenix). The intended analogies were usually obvious; what was meant when Jesuits were called chameleons, or Jesuitism an octopus or a hydra, seldom needed spelling out. In general, beasts of prey signified savagery (though foxes were noted primarily for cunning,[9] and wolves

---

[7] T. Dinocourt, *L'Ombre d'Escobar* (Paris, 1826), 57–8.

[8] Considérant, 'Avertissement', a9; Ordinaire, *Seize lettres*, 33.

[9] Thus, when Béranger wanted to indicate savagery as well, he described the Jesuits as 'half foxes, half wolves' (*Œuvres complètes*, 236).

were also famous for transvestism); reptiles represented subtlety, slitheriness, and venom; insects were meant to be stubborn and persistent;[10] and mythical beasts were noted for their abundance of heads, arms, or eyes, or their capacities of self-transformation or self-regeneration. On one level, then, animal imagery involved the imputation to the Jesuits of specific characteristics of this kind; on another, however, it involved their assimilation to a bestial and subhuman order of existence. So long as anti-jesuits dealt merely in emblems[11] or in simile ('the Jesuits . . . who are supple, insinuating, sharp, scheming, slide into jobs like reptiles'[12]) this assimilation might remain secondary, but imagination, verbal economy, and desire for forceful expression were permanent encouragements to slip into metaphor. One writer drew the attention of France to 'this pack of hungry wolves, concealed under sheepskins, prowling around you, enveloping you in a thousand nets [*réseaux*] in order to bind you. Draining your purest blood drop by drop, which they would like to drink in a single gulp; eating your flesh bit by bit and sucking your bones to the very marrow.'[13] The odd cross-fertilization of images notwithstanding, there is no doubting the bestial nature of these Jesuit-wolves. As important in establishing Jesuit animality as such lurid metaphoric set-pieces, however, was the routine use of words like *glisser* and *ramper* to describe Jesuit behaviour,[14] and the proliferation of ready-to-use phrases: 'les loups du jésuitisme', 'ces terribles pieuvres', 'ces reptiles d'Ignace'. The cumulative effect of such imagery was to reduce Jesuit behaviour to a comportment governed by animal instinct, uncurbable by

---

[10] Thus F. Génin, *Ou l'Église ou l'État* (Paris, 1847), 153: 'The Jesuits resemble the wood-louse or that little scarab that the people call *bête à bon Dieu*. It is the most cowardly of animals; at the slightest menacing sound, it hastily draws in its antennae and feet; it flattens itself in the dust, withdraws, concealed in its carapace. A child pushes it and rolls it over; it is dead. Has the noise gone away? Has the danger passed? Immediately, the dead creature unfolds again, and begins to hurry towards its goal. Accidents may delay it, but it will overcome the accidents, it will arrive.'

[11] See Hénin de Cuvillers's obliging explanation of the emblematic significance of the pictures of hydra, chameleon, serpent, etc. which decorate the pages of his *La Monarchie des solipses* (5–8).

[12] C. Guillaume, *1er pamphlet: Il ne faut point de sociétés dans la société* (Dôle, 1844), 5.   [13] Bouché, 'Préface appréciative', p. xiii.

[14] e.g. Génin, *Les Jésuites et l'Université*, 4: 'Ils glissent; ils rampent; ils escaladent'; V. Hugo, *Les Châtiments*, Gallimard edn. (Paris, 1977), 20: 'Nous, pareils au voleur qui se glisse et se rampe . . .'

morality and reason, unassimilable to human civilization, and fit only to be opposed by a facile intransigence:[15]

> Serpens hideux! il faut qu'on vous écrase
> Pour ne jamais vous laisser relever![16]

Such dehumanizing implications were taken even further by the anti-jesuits' imagery of malady or disease. In some cases, this conceived of society in organic terms, as a 'body social' exposed to the ravages of a Jesuitical ulcer, gangrene, or poison; in others, society appeared as a human collectivity, and the Jesuits or Jesuitism as a contagious or rapidly spreading disease—plague, yellow fever, or cholera. Such images (with the exception of some of those involving poison) left no room for a meaningful distinction between the Jesuits themselves and their action on society; the spread of both was reduced to the status of a mindless and automatic biological process. Nor does the distinction between cautious comparison and full-blown conflation ('cette hideuse lèpre jésuitique', 'une peste publique', 'cette gangrène morale') matter as much here as in the case of animal imagery; individual maladies seldom stood for different qualities in the way that animals did. Save that some of the 'body social' images also shared connotations with those of mining (alluding to the imperceptible destruction of the body from within[17]), the weight of most anti-jesuit images of malady fell on the same two points: Jesuitism's incessant, ravaging, uncontrollable expansion, and its ultimately fatal nature. There could be even less question of compromise with Jesuitism as disease than with Jesuits as wild animals. Malignancies in the body social must be cauterized, contagious diseases kept out by an unbreachable *cordon sanitaire*. Paul Bert reminded those who felt that their liberal principles required them to tolerate the Jesuits that 'freedom of trade is not violated because plague-ridden packages are stopped at our ports'.[18]

[15] The useful discussion of the workings of analogy and of animal imagery in anti-Communard literature in P. Lidsky, *Les Écrivains contre la Commune* (Paris, 1970), 153–6, provides numerous points of comparison.

[16] T. de Villeneuve and A. Bourgeois, *Le Congréganiste; ou Les Trois Educations: Comédie-vaudeville en 3 actes* (Paris, 1830), 71.

[17] As in the following image (strictly speaking an animal one) from E. de Pompéry, *Les Jésuites et le jésuitisme* (Paris, 1879), 10: 'The Jesuit is to the body social what the tapeworm is to the body of a man. Undetected, his action is incessant, mysterious; he swarms, he pullulates, soon he takes up and fills the whole space. The worm triumphs over the man and the Jesuit over society. Both die without suspecting the cause of their death.'

[18] Bert, *La Morale des jésuites*, p. xliv.

Imagery is a form of dramatization. This makes it a haphazard guide to likely behaviour. A man accustomed to talk, and to hear others talking, of the Jesuits as serpents to be crushed or an ulcer to be extirpated might, under certain circumstances, be more likely to perpetrate or to tolerate physical violence against them than a man not habituated to such talk, but he might equally well (and without feeling he was lacking the courage of his convictions) never do more than scowl at priests in the street and call for the Jesuits' expulsion. The imagery does, however, provide clues to the ways in which anti-jesuits viewed their social and political world. The prominence in anti-jesuit literature of the types of imagery just discussed suggests a concern with four supposed features of that world: the existence of an irreducible conflict between opposing forces; the ubiquity of hidden danger; the fundamentally alien and irrational character of opposition to the good; the unrelenting expansionism of evil. Conspiracy theory provided an analytical framework within which this complex of notions might be expressed. It postulated an entire strategy of hidden menace, and drew a sharp distinction between the agents of evil and the rest of humanity, reducing opposition to the good to a pursuit of unavowable ends by inadmissible means, and crediting the evil with such cunning, discipline, and energy that their triumph seemed assured unless militantly and unceasingly resisted.

Different conspiracy theories share a common explanatory logic, but their presentation may vary considerably. It is important, therefore, to look at the forms which the notion of Jesuit conspiracy actually took, at the ways in which it was alluded to, in anti-jesuit literature. Any conspiracy theory may be considered both as an interpretation of history—linking past events together, and present ones to the past—and as an analysis of contemporary reality, establishing connections between different aspects of current experience. The balance between diachronic and synchronic elements in particular cases clearly depends partly on the nature of the conspiracy theorists' dissatisfaction with the present—whether this is founded more on a sense of decadence or retardation or diversion from a true historical course, or rather on a feeling of the fragility of the status quo, its vulnerability to a range of simultaneous disturbing developments. The balance between elements may also, however, be affected by other factors, notably the age of the particular conspiracy theory tradition. The modern exponents of long-standing traditions often feel a strong temptation to recycle the findings and judgements of their predecessors, thereby lending the weight of authority to their own conclusions and the prestige of longevity to the denounced conspiracy.

Given the lengthy history of the anti-jesuit tradition, stretching back into the sixteenth century, it is not surprising that its diachronic element was pronounced. Lists of the expulsions and condemnations which the Jesuits had suffered at the hands of kings, Popes, Parlements, universities, assemblies of clergy, and other bodies were a common feature of anti-jesuit literature, both in pamphlet and in more developed forms; so were collections of 'témoignages historiques' critical of the order, drawn from the writings and utterances of long-dead bishops, lawyers, ambassadors, and others, most of them quite unknown to nineteenth-century readers except in this role of quotable anti-jesuit sages. Few anti-jesuit writings failed to include at least a brief summary of Jesuit history. On occasion—in Montlosier's tracts, for example, or (a more extreme case) in Wallon's *Un collège de jésuites*—the history took second place to synchronic analysis of present developments, but such cases were outnumbered by those in which the anti-jesuit argument was advanced largely in historical terms, often with little or no overt discussion of current affairs.

'The history of the Jesuits is the history of their crimes.'[19] Salgues's statement adequately summarizes the anti-jesuit approach. The Society of Jesus' internal history, its evolution, the divisions of opinion and struggles for ascendancy within it, had no place in anti-jesuit history. Only the Jesuits' action on society mattered, and this was discussed as if the order were entirely monolithic.[20] The record of intrigue and criminality which passed, in anti-jesuit eyes, for Jesuit history was in general highly standardized, at least as far as the period before the order's suppression was concerned. The assassinations of Henri III and Henri IV, the Gunpowder Plot, the Ligue, the Revocation of the Edict of Nantes, the persecution of Port-Royal, the downfall of the Stuarts, the misbehaviour of Jesuit missionaries in the Indies, the Orient, and Latin America (especially

[19] [J.-B. Salgues], *Étrennes aux jésuites, pour l'édification des personnes pieuses affectionnées à la société* (Paris, 1826), 128–9.

[20] Guettée, *Histoire des jésuites, composée sur documents authentiques en partie inédits*, 3 vols. (Paris, 1858–9), iii. 3: 'We have to consider the Company only in its external acts, for its inner existence reduces to nothing.'

Paraguay), the attempted assassination of Louis XV by Damiens, the Lavalette bankruptcy, the suspected poisoning of Clement XIV after his suppression of the Society of Jesus: these, among others, were the events which the readers of anti-jesuit histories could, and no doubt did, expect to hear about.

Anti-jesuits attached such importance to these past episodes not simply as ammunition to use against the modern Jesuits, but also as links in a chain of evidence which they believed would help to make sense of the present, by delivering a message like that discerned, early in the century, by Goubeau de la Bilennerie: 'that in all the disorders, all the misfortunes, that have occurred in Europe during their reign, these supposed apostles are no strangers, and that most often they play the most odious role in them.'[21] Jesuit history was here converted into general history, and the Jesuit criminal record became a myth with pretensions to resume whole tracts of modern history.

The mythical character of the great majority of anti-jesuit accounts of Jesuit history is evident both in their general presentation and in details of their composition. Both in the potted histories contained in pamphlets and almanacs and in the longer ones published in one or more volumes,[22] everything is done to preserve the clarity and simplicity with which the facts of myth, as distinct from those of critical history, are invested, and to free the historical record of anything that might prevent it yielding an uncomplicated message. Exclusion of contrary facts and testimonies was a crude aspect of this, but the arrangement of those facts and testimonies that were included is equally important.

The factors that might complicate the historical message were of two sorts: exceptions and contexts. The historical association between the Jesuits and certain types of crime or trouble could impress only if it appeared to be solid and uninterrupted. It would be weakened by the admission either of long periods of history without Jesuit villainy, or of villainy of the relevant sorts committed without Jesuit connivance. Anti-jesuits' ways of blaming the Jesuits for the crimes of others were sometimes (especially in the

[21] [Goubeau de la Bilennerie], *Histoire abrégée*, p. x.

[22] e.g. [Goubeau de la Bilennerie], *Histoire abrégée*; Monglave and Chalas, *Histoire des conspirations*; A. Boucher, *Histoire dramatique et pittoresque des jésuites, depuis la fondation de l'ordre jusqu'à nos jours*, 2 vols. (Paris, 1845–6); Arnould, *Les Jésuites depuis leur origine*; Guettée, *Histoire des jésuites*.

potted histories) crude: a simple transformation of a non-Jesuit assassin into 'the Jesuit Ravaillac',[23] for example. The authors of the longer histories, however, were usually less concerned to make out a supposedly watertight case against the Jesuits with regard to each real or suspected crime than to present Jesuit intrigue as constantly the most likely explanation for certain sorts of historical event, for example regicidal attempts. Careful detailing of circumstantial evidence against the Jesuits, coupled with neglect of comparable evidence against others, served to establish at least the possibility of Jesuit guilt in each particular case; the accumulation of such 'possibilities' then made it seem an ever more probable interpretation of each case arising. Thus Monglave and Chalas, in their history of Jesuit plotting against Bourbon kings, mentioned that Damiens came originally from Arras (a town 'known for the influence which the sons of Loyola exercised over the minds of the inhabitants'), that he had once been a Jesuit *pensionnaire*, that Jesuits had supposedly been seen in lay attire before his attack on Louis XV, and others observed leaving the rue Saint-Antoine by a back door at the moment of the crime; such facts were enough, when one took into account the allegedly definite (but actually equally uncertainly established) involvement of the Jesuits in the earlier regicidal efforts of Barrière, Châtel, Ravaillac, and others, to establish them as 'authors, to all appearances, of the regicide of Damiens'.[24] Once such a chain of interpretation had been set up, lack of positive evidence of Jesuit involvement posed few problems. If, for example, Clement XIV failed to mention regicide among his reasons for abolishing the Jesuits, this (according to Monglave and Chalas) was surely because he was 'surrounded by too many proofs not to tremble at them'.[25] As for the suggestion that Clement himself had fallen victim to Jesuit poisoning, Guettée could remark: 'They are too habituated to acts of that sort for one to reject these suspicions as ill founded, though the accusation was not juridically proved.'[26]

Exceptions weaken a historical myth by escaping from it; contexts do so more radically, by dissolving its constituent elements. Placed in historical context, each hard, bright, transparent fact becomes diffuse, elusive, unassertive. Historical myth and critical

[23] Durantin, *Un élève des jésuites*, 51–2.
[24] Monglave and Chalas, *Histoire des conspirations*, 305–6, 311.
[25] Ibid. 376.   [26] Guettée, *Histoire des jésuites*, iii. 303.

history must regard each other as impoverishing the event, critical history by draining it of its rich, uncomplicated significance, historical myth by thinning out its associations till it becomes one-dimensional. Guettée, in one of the fuller anti-jesuit histories, achieved the mythic evasion of context subtly, by an incorrigible use of generalizations—'as always', 'in accordance with the custom regularly followed in the Company'—to reduce specific offences to instances of universal Jesuit practice, so that the facts actually mentioned lost most of their historical peculiarity.[27] Most anti-jesuits were more blatant, simply suppressing contexts altogether. Pamphleteers sliced the events of Jesuit history into lists (of expulsions, of condemnations of various sorts, of casuistical excesses, of regicidal plots, etc.). Almanacs presented them as a calendar— 'containing one crime or one stupidity for each day of the year', as one declared[28]—with the original chronological order completely jumbled. The numerous potted histories appearing in pamphlets or as chapters in longer works respected the convention of chronology, but still presented the Jesuit past as a succession of separate facts, usually neatly dated, but without a trace of causal connection or unfolding narrative. A section of one such account runs as follows:

In 1619, they are banished from Moravia.
In 1643, Malta casts them away from her.
In 1723, Peter the Great finds security only in banishing them from his states.
In 1731, the Jesuit Girard fills the whole of France with scandal by his trial with Lacadière [*sic*], and escapes a just sentence only through [the intervention of] authority and money.
In 1755, the Jesuits of Paraguay arm the inhabitants, and lead them in open battle against their sovereign.
In 1757, a monster makes an attempt on the life of Louis XV, and that same year, the Jesuits reprint the abominable book of the Jesuit Busenbaum, which teaches one to kill kings . . .[29]

Multi-volume anti-jesuit histories gave more detail on particular episodes, but paid scarcely more attention to causal development.

[27] Ibid. 59 ('The Jesuits, as always, made common cause with vice against virtue'), 430 ('The Jesuits then resolved, in accordance with the custom regularly followed in the Company, to launch forlorn hopes in both directions').
[28] *Almanach des jésuites, contenant un crime ou une sottise pour chaque jour de l'année* (Paris, 1846). [29] [Salgues], *Courtes Observations*, 135–8.

In such 'histories', whether long or short, the links between events were ones of mythical significance, not of causality. The 'facts' of Jesuit history, as told by anti-jesuits, were essentially illustrations. As abbé Tabaraud put it: 'They differ from each other only by nuances which alter nothing at the heart of things.'[30] A single fatal theme, that of the perpetual struggle between the Jesuits and all responsible forces in society, was run like a skewer through a shish kebab of interchangeable historical facts.

Decontextualized and considered self-evident in their significance, the events of the Jesuit past were ever-immediate to anti-jesuit minds. The dates attached to them were fragile anchors, insufficient to keep them fixed at varying distances; three centuries of repetitive Jesuit infamy pressed together on the present. This radical compression of historical perspective made possible the sort of time-defying leap—part rhetorical but part mental—whereby Dionys Ordinaire could pause in an account of the role of Jesuit preachers in the Ligue to exclaim: 'After that, come and complain of the excesses of the Commune!'[31]

Anti-jesuits could hardly expect that a pattern so regularly and clearly established by the Jesuit past would fail to impose itself on any subsequent epoch in which the Jesuits were tolerated. Their historical myth carried within itself both an interpretation of the present and a conditional prediction of the future. 'From the moment of their institution, the Jesuits were what they have been since, what they are today, what they will always be so long as the slightest trace of them exists, that is to say the scourge of France.'[32] The particular manifestations of Jesuit iniquity, as well as the general fact of it, could be predicted, for the record of Jesuit history provided a sort of symptomatology. Though the detail of the supposedly infallible indicators of Jesuit activity might vary from writer to writer (and might in fact evolve over time), the style of argument remained constant. 'How have we felt the presence of the Jesuits?' asked one writer under the July Monarchy, 'who warned us they were there?—anti-revolutionary tendencies, ultra-montane systems, an indefinable malaise, and above all the division

---

[30] M.-M. Tabaraud, *Essai historique et critique sur l'état des jésuites en France depuis leur arrivée dans le royaume jusqu'au temps présent* (Paris, 1828), 293.

[31] Ordinaire, *Seize lettres*, 20.

[32] *Pièces historiques, rares ou inédites, pour servir à l'instruction du temps présent* (Paris, 1830), 120 (editor's note).

which was invading the hearth of the *père de famille*.'[33] The Prot-estant pastor Edmond de Pressensé argued in similar vein a quarter of a century later: 'If in any country one sees emerge a shady pol-itics, proceeding silently by undermining, organizing ambushes with a profound art, one can be assured that they are its inspirers.'[34]

The perceived plausibility of such arguments helps to explain the anti-jesuits' usual lack of interest in demonstrating actual links of or-ganization or personnel between the various contemporary manifes-tations of Jesuitism they denounced. For all the energy devoted to collecting information on Catholic lay associations, Jesuit schools, moral corruption, and clerical greed (for example), it was historical myth, not contemporary data, that supplied the connection between them. In short, anti-jesuits tended to regard conspiracy not as a novelty, whose agents had to be identified, and whose limits and ramifications ascertained, by painstaking and unprejudiced enquiry, but as the repetition of a familiar historical pattern, the precise detail of which might be varied or concealed by the conspirator's cunning, but the inevitable outlines of which were notorious.

Jesuit history, then, was not a tale of open-ended evolution, but a revelation of immutability. 'Everything progresses, except the Company of Jesus,' wrote the novelist Armand Durantin.[35] Others cited the defiant words attributed to the order's General Ricci, at the time of its suppression: *Sint ut sunt aut non sint*—words which they were apt to present as a general Jesuit motto, and as virtual proof of the order's exemption from historical change.[36] At the root of most elaborations on this theme of Jesuit immutability, however, lay a conviction of the importance of the order's *Constitu-tions*. As Montlosier put it, warning Frenchmen to expect the same from the Jesuits of the restored order as from those of old: 'it is evidently the same spirit, since it is the same institution.'[37]

---

[33] G. Dairnvaell, *Code des jésuites, d'après plus de trois cents ouvrages des casuistes jésuites, complément indispensable aux œuvres de MM. Michelet et Quinet* (Paris, 1845), 20.

[34] E. de Pressensé, *La Liberté religieuse en Europe depuis 1870* (Paris, 1874), 100–1.

[35] Durantin, *Un élève des jésuites*, 151.

[36] Thus *Constitutionnel*, 20 Sept. 1825: 'What they have done shows what they will do again, and the past is the guarantee of the future, for nothing is changed in the doctrines, the principles, the projects and the methods of this renascent society, and the *sint ut sunt, aut non sint* is still the order of the day for her.' Similarly Ferry in *ASCD*, Sénat 6 Mar. 1825: 235: 'Is their motto: *sint ut sunt, aut non sint*, not still the same? Have their doctrines changed? There lies the force and the greatness of that illustrious society; there is its power; there is the reason for its advances, for its successes.'   [37] Montlosier, *Mémoire*, 129–30.

Nowhere was the importance of the *Constitutions* to anti-jesuit argument more forcefully affirmed than in the preface to a new translation of the text published, with anti-jesuit intent, in 1843. The author argued that only a knowledge of the Jesuit order's laws could enable one to distinguish its fundamental 'spirit' from the behaviour of its individual members. It was only by virtue of these laws that the order itself existed, and only their consistency could explain why it had always and everywhere shown the same spirit and espoused the same principles, with the same deplorable results. 'It is thus not necessary, in order to have a thorough knowledge of the Society of Jesus, to follow it in its history; it is enough to consider the nature of its Institutions.' Whatever one might later learn about the Jesuits' actions and moral doctrines would merely confirm the conclusions of such a study: 'morality and history, means and end, inclinations and results, all that is in germ in the *Constitutions*.'[38]

According to such a view, the Jesuit *Constitutions* and the salient features of Jesuit history were each implicit in the other. They were different embodiments or enactments of the same fundamental Jesuit essence, and the same basic lesson was to be learnt from either of them, properly understood. Knowledge of the *Constitutions* supplied a key to Jesuit history, in part because the meaning of rules was more instantly apparent than that of conduct, and in part because, without the organizational framework which the rules established, the essential spirit of Jesuitism could not have issued in purposeful action, and perhaps could not even have existed. Jesuit history, in return, supplied the constant stream of examples which showed how constitutional continuity and consistency were reproduced as continuity and consistency in Jesuit misbehaviour.

What emerged when readings of Jesuit history and of the Jesuit *Constitutions* were linked together in this way was a sense of Jesuitism as at once a historical and an ahistorical force—one ceaselessly active in history yet immune to the normal conditioning and transforming effects of historical causality; a spirit frozen in the organizational forms established at a particular moment, yet capable of reproducing itself, with those forms, at any moment in history. It was on this conception of Jesuitism that the coherence of the

---

[38] *Les Constitutions des jésuites, avec les déclarations, texte latin, d'après l'édition de Prague* (Paris, 1843), pp. iii–iv. This edition is attributed to Athanase Cucheval-Clarigny in the Bibliothèque Nationale's *Catalogue des imprimés*.

anti-jesuit myth depended. It was, however, a conception which generated a significant tension in the nineteenth-century vision of Jesuit conspiracy. On the one hand, Jesuitism was considered to be, in its fundamentals, immutable, and this immutability was often seen as extending, in important ways, to its strategy and tactics. On the other, it was assumed to pose, whenever and wherever it appeared, the most dangerous conceivable conspiratorial threat to society, something which seemed to presuppose a formidable capacity for tactical adaptation. This tension between the notions of fixity and of flexibility, latent in earlier anti-jesuit literature, acquired particular significance in the nineteenth century, partly because the papal suppression and resuscitation of the Society of Jesus had posed with fresh acuteness the whole question of continuity and discontinuity in Jesuit history, but mainly because, in an age when social, economic, and political structures were undergoing rapid and startling change, it was natural enough to imagine corresponding adjustments in the strategy and tactics of conspiratorial world domination.[39] The nineteenth-century mythology of anti-jesuitism cannot successfully be reduced either to a straightforward repetition of inherited themes and motifs, or to the shallow registration of new perceptions in an old polemical vocabulary. Instead, the fabric of anti-jesuit myth strained and twisted to incorporate a shifting and sometimes clumsy amalgam of old and new (or newly emphasized) elements. Traditional themes like those of Jesuit regicide and *morale relâchée* retained a place in the repertory, and could still shape perceptions of the present in ways which may strike the historian as anachronistic. Some of the nineteenth-century additions to the mythology—the black legend of Montrouge under the Restoration, for example, or the bloodthirsty speech which abbé Leone claimed to have overheard in 1824, and which came to be attributed to the Jesuit General Roothaan[40]—did

[39] Strategic adaptation of this kind was the express purpose of the alleged Chieri conference, reported by Leone, *Conjuration des jésuites*, 22, 75.

[40] The original quotation was in Leone, *Conjuration des jésuites* (87): 'Truly, our century is strangely squeamish! Does it imagine, then, that the embers of the stake are totally extinguished? That not the smallest brand is left underneath to kindle a single torch?—The fools! All they know how to do is hate us: they are far from suspecting that we alone know how to prepare a revolution next to which all theirs have been, are, and will be no more than riots among pygmies. In calling us *Jesuits*, they think they cover us with opprobrium! But these Jesuits are reserving for them censorship, gag, and fire, and one day they will be the masters of their masters.' In Leone's account, these words were spoken at the Chieri conference, not by

little, in themselves, to modify the traditional emphases of anti-jesuit polemic. Others, however, whether (occasionally) by outright innovation or (more usually) by selective development of pre-existing themes, tended, despite frequent lip-service to the idea of Jesuit immutability, to adjust the image of Jesuit villainy in accord with evolving suppositions about the vulnerabilities of State and society.

This rough and ready dialectic of tradition and improvisation in anti-jesuit conspiracy theory is the unifying theme of the four following chapters, each of which explores in detail some of the major elements in nineteenth-century anti-jesuit mythology, and which between them trace in broad outline a shift in emphasis within the general account of Jesuit conspiracy. To attempt to draw a sharp line between old and new would, however, be foolish. Ancient themes were revamped, and novelties were disguised as timeless truths about Jesuit behaviour; perceptions derived from tradition and ones reflecting present circumstances constantly affected each other. Above all, anti-jesuits never renounced the belief that the diversity (and therefore the diversification or evolution) of Jesuit methods was but the product of a deep tenacity and uniformity of nefarious purpose. The tensions within the anti-jesuit myth found a resolution of sorts in the prevailing stereotype of the Jesuit personality, in which the extremes of single-minded fanaticism and of tactical flexibility were taken to be intimately connected; it is to this personified vision of Jesuitism that the final chapter will return.

Roothaan, but by an unnamed Irish Jesuit. However, when Victor Hugo (without citing Leone as his source) took the passage as epigraph to his anti-jesuit poem 'Ad majorem Dei gloriam', in *Les Châtiments* (published 1853), he attributed it to 'Le Père Roothaan, général des jésuites à la conférence de Chieri'. The attribution to Roothaan was repeated by other writers who quoted all or part of the passage; see *La Voix du peuple est la voix de Dieu: Plus d'abus dans la religion catholique, plus de jésuites, plus de couvents, et la France et l'Italie délivrées: Par un catholique* (Carouge, 1862), 103–4; C. Bouis, *Calottes et soutanes: Jésuites et jésuitesses* (Paris, 1870), 199; L. Taxil, *Calotte et calotins: Histoire illustrée du clergé et des congrégations*, 3 vols. (Paris, 1880), iii. 463.

6

Murder, Money, and Spies

THREE major generic figures from the blackened version of the
Jesuit past imposed themselves on nineteenth-century imaginations.
Each kept its place in the historical myth. Each, in the application
of that myth to present circumstances, appeared in modern forms
—changed, developed, interpreted, manipulated to reflect the new
conditions in which the Jesuits were at work. In each case, however, an awkwardness of fit remained: Jesuit villainy preserved the
manners of another age.

These three symbolic persons were the Jesuit regicide, the Jesuit
accapareur des héritages, and the Jesuit confessor as spy. Around them
may be ordered the accusations and speculations of anti-jesuits
concerning, respectively, Jesuit murder and terrorism, Jesuit accumulation of wealth, and the Jesuit intelligence system.

MURDER

Regicide remained, in the nineteenth century, the most salient
theme of anti-jesuit historiography.[1] Lists of the Jesuit theorists
of 'tyrannicide', and of the instances (including, besides French
examples, the Gunpowder Plot and a series of attacks on Elizabeth
I) in which their teachings had allegedly been put into practice,
were part of the standard repertoire of the anti-jesuit pamphleteer.
The names of the assassins or would-be assassins of French kings
—Barrière, Châtel, Clément, Ravaillac, Damiens—were graven on
anti-jesuit memories. It is unlikely, however, that many nineteenth-
century anti-jesuits seriously expected the Jesuits to continue their
supposedly impressive regicidal tradition in the modern age.
Suggestions that they might can certainly be found, and not only
in scurrilous fictions like those of Léo Taxil, who imagined a

---

[1] See esp. Monglave and Chalas, *Histoire des conspirations*.

Jesuit *mémoire* containing plans for the assassination of each European sovereign.[2] Rumours of a Jesuit plot to poison Louis-Philippe seem to have circulated in the Loire-Inférieure in 1844,[3] and Guettée's response to an assassination attempt on Alexander II in 1866 was to remark that the Tsar's enemies included 'a well-known aristocratic-clerical party, which is as one with the Society of Jesuits', famed for its 'tyrannicidal' doctrine.[4] There were even some who held the Jesuits responsible for the death of Louis XVI.[5] For the majority, however, the usual significance of references to Jesuit regicide had probably changed.

The case of one who still did believe in the reality of the threat to royalty helps show why this was so. In 1828, shortly after the *ordonnance* against the Jesuits, Martignac received a letter imploring him to take steps to protect the life of the young duc de Bordeaux. The Jesuits, his anonymous correspondent warned, would not hesitate to strike down any prince from whose death they expected to benefit. This had been the case in 1820, when the assassination of the child's father, the duc de Berry, had led to an anti-Liberal reaction. Now, with their own existence under threat (though not sent until after the *ordonnance*, the letter was written before it), the Jesuits might well seek to repeat the trick. By poisoning the young prince and throwing suspicion for the crime on their enemies, they could procure a *coup d'état* in their favour, or at least a dissolution of the Chamber followed by favourable elections.[6] What is striking here is not merely the letter-writer's readiness to believe the Jesuits capable of the effective dynasticide that the prince's murder would have represented, but the reasoning he attributes to them. Where once a prince might have feared for his life because his personal power obstructed Jesuit designs, he now (if the letter was to be believed) had to tremble because his death would enable the Jesuits to manipulate public opinion. Politics had changed; mere

---

[2] L. Taxil, *Les Amours secrètes de Pie IX, par un ancien camérier secret du pape* (Paris, 1881), 1626.

[3] Prefect's report, quoted in A. J. Tudesq, *Les Grands Notables en France, 1840–1849: Étude historique d'une psychologie sociale* (Paris, 1964), 725.

[4] *Observateur catholique*, 17: 383.

[5] See above, 151, for Raspail, and Cubitt, 'The Myth of a Jesuit Conspiracy', 338–9, for evidence of similar beliefs among Port-Royalist *convulsionnaires* in the 1790s.

[6] AN F[7] 6751: anonymous letter to Martignac, 10 June 1828 (with postscript dated 25 June 1828). The writer miscalls the prince 'duc de Berry'.

king-killing was unlikely to keep its central place in the political tactics of conspirators of the Jesuits' legendary astuteness. As the future Communard Casimir Bouis put it in 1870, after dwelling for several pages on the regicidal record, nowadays 'what has to be killed is the people'.[7] Most anti-jesuits probably agreed with Quinet and Bert, both of whom saw regicide as the typical tactic of Jesuitism in an earlier age, now abandoned for more modern methods.[8] Used as a historical reference, and sometimes as a perpetual prophecy, the regicidal theme served them (as has already been seen) as a charm against the compromising spectre of regicidal Revolution, and as a way of tarnishing the Jesuits' modern reputation as pillars of order and defenders of monarchy. They were shyer, however, about pinning their colours to it in the explanation of current affairs.

The attitude of the Liberal papers *La Minerve* and *Le Constitutionnel* in 1820 illustrates this. By striking down the duc de Berry outside the Opéra, and thus (it appeared) extinguishing the breeding hopes of the ruling Bourbon branch, Louvel's dagger called the bluff of those who presented regicide (defined here to include dynasticide) and the slaughter of Bourbons as virtual Jesuit monopolies. The Liberal papers responded somewhat ambiguously. Arnault, *La Minerve*'s theatre critic, pointedly choosing this moment to review Schiller's *Mary Stuart*, italicized everything that implied Jesuit involvement in plots against Queen Elizabeth.[9] His colleague Jay, however, recited the history of assaults on French kings in a way which sacrificed conventional anti-jesuit interpretations of several episodes in the interest of suggesting that Louvel was an isolated fanatic: the Jesuits were not mentioned in connection with Clément and Ravaillac, and it was declared probable that Châtel and Damiens had had no accomplices.[10] *Le Constitutionnel*, similarly, used the anti-jesuit reference to ward off attack,[11] but compared the present moment to that when Ravaillac had killed Henri IV, 'with no accomplices but his fanaticism and his fury.[12] When Louvel's crime was firmly in the past, some

---

[7] Bouis, *Calottes et soutanes*, 187–92.

[8] Quinet, *Des jésuites*, 258; Bert, *La Morale des jésuites*, 122–3 n.

[9] *Minerve*, 9: 292–304.   [10] Ibid. 151–60.

[11] *Constitutionnel*, 16 Feb. 1820.

[12] Ibid. 21 Feb. 1820 (also 28 Feb. 1820, summarizing Jay's article from *La Minerve*).

anti-jesuits would add it to their regicidal list;[13] most, however, did not. Nor did they annex the assassins Fieschi in 1835 or Orsini in 1858. These omissions weakened the myth of Jesuit regicide, and revealed the limitations of its influence on modern anti-jesuit thinking.

As a catalogue of illustrations of a more general unscrupulousness about political murder, however, the myth retained some force. Kings might no longer be the victims, but some anti-jesuits had their suspicions about the deaths of men like Mgr. Feutrier or the Liberal orator General Foy.[14] The illness of a Piedmontese minister in 1828 prompted one French newspaper to remark knowingly that 'For some time M. de Cholex had expressed himself strongly against the Jesuits'.[15] If some anti-jesuits were to be believed, murder was a routine Jesuit procedure, cold-blooded and almost bureaucratic. Hénin de Cuvillers remarked:

This army [*milice*], composed of regimented executioners, is always driven by vengeance and thirsty for human blood; but it likes to shed it without valour; and, fearing to fight in pitched battle, these intrepid soldiers of the faith prefer piecemeal assassinations, and they immolate at their leisure, mercilessly and without danger to themselves, the numerous victims indicated to them by secret lists of proscription.[16]

The ex-Jesuit Marcet (author of a series of anti-jesuit works during the Restoration) paraded a string of humble victims of Jesuit murder before the readers of his *Mémoires d'un jeune jésuite*: one of his own friends, struck down for rebelling against Jesuit discipline; some nuns; a Jesuit of Provence suspected of poisoning; a Brazilian murdered in Spain for reading *Le Constitutionnel*.[17] Raspail's numerous additions to the roll-call of anti-jesuit martyrs were matched by the revelations of another exile, Tapon Fougas, about the death of Eugène Sue. The author of *Le Juif errant*, it transpired, was the first casualty in a novel campaign by the Jesuits to rid themselves of hostile writers. The victims were followed around by mischievous

---

[13] See e.g. *Les Jésuites marchands*, 25–6; Marcet, *Mémoires d'un jeune jésuite*, 39–43.

[14] J.-H. Santo-Domingo, *Les Jésuites en action sous le ministère Villèle* (Paris, 1828), 138 (Foy); *Instructions secrètes des jésuites; ou Monita secreta Societatis Jesu, précédées de l'histoire et de la morale des jésuites depuis la fondation de leur société jusqu'à nos jours* (Blois, 1845), pp. xix–xx n. (Feutrier).

[15] *Le Précurseur* of Lyons (quoted in *Constitutionnel*, 29 July 1828).

[16] Hénin de Cuvillers, *La Monarchie des solipses*, 58–9.

[17] Marcet, *Mémoires d'un jeune jésuite*, 241–4.

gamins, who acted secretly as spotters for 'a swarm of *electro-galvanic* sharpshooters and artillerymen'. The latter were able, by means of 'an electro galvano-chemical current', to project morbid vapours into their victim's atmosphere from a distance, causing drowsiness, feebleness of will, and other debilitating symptoms. Repeated exposure produced imbecility and eventually death. Among those whose creative powers had already been impaired were Raspail, Michelet, Quinet, Victor Hugo, and Louis Blanc.[18]

Few people, probably, really believed in such systematic campaigns of extermination, though more may well have believed the Jesuits capable of the occasional murder when it suited them. Death, and the threat of it, was no doubt a potent weapon to command (and an order whose store-cupboard was believed to have held the lethal and undetectable poison *aqua tofana* could no doubt be expected to keep abreast of murderous technology), but most anti-jesuits could see that there was more to the control of the modern world than a taste and talent for homicide. At a crucial moment in the plot of *Le Juif errant*, leadership in the Jesuit campaign to capture the Rennepont fortune switches from Père d'Aigrigny to Père Rodin. Rodin criticizes the brutal methods of his predecessor as clumsy, compromising, and outmoded; he himself intends to triumph by the artful manipulation of human passions.[19] The impression of modern Jesuit methods that emerges from the mass of anti-jesuit literature reveals a similar tension and a similar shift: murder and violence retain a place, and reflect the basic inhumanity of the Jesuit character, but the emphasis is on subtler methods, which reflect its insidious cunning.

MONEY

The acquisition of wealth was one such gentler Jesuit art. 'Since your foundation', Guettée told the Jesuits, 'you have worked only to enrich yourselves; you have made of pious works themselves so many means to lucre: you have accumulated riches, by every means, even the most immoral; you have never done good for its own

---

[18] F. Tapon Fougas, *Sur la mort d'Eugène Sue: Humble Avis d'un démocrate* (Brussels, n.d.), 14–18, 22–5, 39–40 (drawing in places on an anonymous text, 'A un ami').   [19] Sue, *Le Juif errant*, iii. 81–8.

sake, but always for money.'[20] The Jesuits, it was claimed, would
even make money out of their own persons: a favourite anti-jesuit
anecdote of the Second Empire told how the pleasure of the
company of one of them, Père Lefebvre, had been offered as prize
in a lottery among the fawning aristocrats of the faubourg Saint-
Germain.[21] Three main supposed sources of Jesuit wealth, however, attracted the attention of anti-jesuit polemicists: mendicancy
disguised as charity; commerce and industry; and the capture of
family fortunes.

Anti-jesuit scepticism about charitable organizations was sometimes radical. Cayla, for example, attacked the Société de Saint
Vincent-de-Paul on the grounds that, since true charity was spontaneous, the truly charitable had no need to organize and regiment
themselves like Jesuits; centralized direction and communications
were necessary for Jesuit intrigue, not for philanthropy.[22] How
many anti-jesuits shared such a romantic conception of charity
is unclear, but there was certainly a widespread tendency to see
Catholic charitable or religious *œuvres* as mere fronts for Jesuit
greed. *Le Constitutionnel* feared in 1825 that collections from overseas missions were really financing the building of Jesuit schools in
France.[23] More than two million francs, according to Génin, passed
into Jesuit hands through the coffers of the Association pour la
Propagation de la Foi in one month in 1842.[24] The *Almanach du
mois*, in 1845, dismissed the Œuvre de la Sainte-Enfance (whose
purpose was to save Chinese children from slavery) as a 'pious joke'
which brought the Jesuits 120,000 francs a year.[25] A range of other
collections, appeals, and subscriptions, real and imaginary, were
suspected of feeding the fighting fund of Jesuit world domination.
The order was the recipient, according to *Le Constitutionnel*, of
financial tribute from every religious order in France, and of an
estimated net revenue of 2.5 million francs a year in French school
fees.[26] Marcet's revelations gave it 2,000 a year from pilgrims to
the Jesuit-controlled shrine at Lalouvesc, and 50,000–100,000 in
subscriptions to the Congrégation. Nor, he suggested, were the

[20] *Union chrétienne*, 18: 151.
[21] See e.g. *Observateur catholique*, 3: 112, 4: 140; F. Tapon Fougas, *Le Jésuite . . .
pour rire en loterie: Comédie en 1 acte et en vers* (Brussels, 1857).
[22] J.-M. Cayla, *Ces bons messieurs de Saint Vincent-de-Paul* (Paris, 1863), 30, 238.
[23] *Constitutionnel*, 28 Jan. 1825.   [24] Génin, *Les Jésuites et l'Université*, 114.
[25] *Almanach du mois*, 4: 116 (Aug. 1845).
[26] *Constitutionnel*, 28 Jan. 1825, 30 Sept. 1826.

Jesuits above disguising themselves as mendicant Trappists or Capuchins, for the sake of a little more.[27]

Such details amounted to an impressive picture of greed and pious fraudulence, but to a somewhat primitive conception of modern wealth-creation. Especially under the Second Empire and early Third Republic (though with the Affenäer affair's glimpse into Jesuit business dealings providing a foretaste), much anti-jesuit attention focused on an ostensibly more modern face of Jesuit avarice. In a passage whose details were repeated by several other writers, Sauvestre described the order's commercial and industrial activities:

At this very hour, the Company of Jesus is at the head of a host of counting-houses [*une foule de comptoirs*] in the two worlds; she possesses, alone or as principal partner, a veritable fleet of clippers, which ply the line to Brazil and whose home-port is Bordeaux. She has perhaps even more considerable interests at Le Havre, in the financing of the transportation of emigrants and of the shipyards. Finally, she possesses the finest ironworks in France: Bessèges, Alais, etc. In California she has gold-mines; and a whole street in San Francisco has become her property. It is there that she does her best lending business, at 30, 40, 50, 100, 200 per cent.[28]

When Père du Lac denied the existence of the Jesuits' supposedly large and lucrative fleet, Jean Wallon replied by invoking the personal backing given by the Jesuit Provincial to the Union Maritime steamship company, and by listing other trading, banking, and industrial ventures which he claimed the order controlled.[29] Other writers referred to Jesuit involvement in a humbler (but, Bouis claimed, perhaps equally lucrative) branch of commerce, 'that minuscule traffic in religious knick-knacks'—scapulars, miraculous medals, autographed letters from Christ, and so on.[30]

These visions of the Jesuits as merchants, financiers, or capitalists did something to modernize the image of Jesuit finance, but this should not be overemphasized. As the 1824 re-edition of *Les Jésuites marchands, usuriers, et usurpateurs* (a text first published in 1759), and the references to the bankruptcy of Père Lavalette in anti-jesuit historiography made clear, there was nothing especially

---

[27] Marcet, *Mémoires d'un jeune jésuite*, 131–2.

[28] Sauvestre (ed.), *Monita secreta*, 3rd edn. (Paris, 1863), 41–2.

[29] J. Wallon, *Un collège de jésuites, auquel on a joint le Jésus-ouvrier, le Jésus-roi, le Jésus-industriel, le Jésus-homme de lettres* (Paris, 1880), 185–206.

[30] Bouis, *Calottes et soutanes*, 148–9; see also *Observateur catholique*, 10: 193.

new about the commercial theme in anti-jesuit polemic. Nor did
nineteenth-century writers usually do much to distinguish the
methods of the Jesuit entrepreneur from the hunter-gatherer ways
of the Jesuit mendicant: the primitive accumulation, rather than the
sophisticated manipulation, of the order's wealth seemed to be the
chief concern of both. Finally, and most importantly, capitalistic
Jesuitism never displaced the *captation des héritages* as the dominant
anti-jesuit image of Jesuit acquisitiveness.

That intrigues spun to capture family fortunes kept this place
in the anti-jesuit imagination testifies above all to the continuing
influence of one text, the *Monita secreta Societatis Iesu* (in French,
the Jesuits' *Instructions secrètes*). This purported to be a set of secret
rules governing the Jesuits' pursuit of power, influence, and especially wealth. In reality, it originated as a satirical fabrication by a
renegade Polish Jesuit of the early seventeenth century, Zaharowski. Since its first appearance in 1613 or 1614, the text had been
rearranged, expanded, and finally standardized, by seventeenth-
and eighteenth-century editors.[31] The version on which nineteenth-
century French editions were generally based was that published
in Paris in 1761, bearing the false imprint of Paderborn, 1661. In
this standard form, the *Monita secreta* consisted of a preface and
seventeen chapters. The latter could be divided roughly into four
sections: chapters 2–5 dealt with Jesuit influence on high politics;
chapters 6–9 dictated ways of increasing revenue, especially by
exerting influence on rich widows, and by luring the heirs to
fortunes into the order; chapters 10–13 regulated Jesuit discipline
and recruitment; and chapters 14–17, together with most of the
introductory chapter 1, laid down a number of other ways of
advancing the Jesuit cause.

The first nineteenth-century French printing of the *Monita secreta*
appears to have been in 1820, in the first issue of the historical
periodical *Le Citateur politique, morale et littéraire*.[32] The text made
frequent appearances in the 1820s (especially in popular *in-32°*

---

[31] For more on the *Monita secreta* and their early publishing history, see C. Van
Aken, *La Fable des Monita secreta ou instructions secrètes des jésuites: Histoire et
bibliographie* (Brussels, n.d.); Brou, *Les Jésuites de la légende*, i. 275–301; G. Monod,
'La Politique secrète des jésuites et les Monita secreta', *Séances et travaux de
l'Académie des Sciences Morales et Politiques (Institut de France)*, 173 (1910), 210–29; H.
Rollin, *L'Apocalypse de notre temps: Les Dessous de la propagande allemande d'après des
documents inédits*, 7th edn. (Paris, 1939), 29–32.

[32] *Le Citateur politique, morale et littéraire*, 1: 144–257.

editions)[33] and was republished in the 1840s,[34] but it was in the new translation published by Charles Sauvestre, first issued in 1861, that it reached the peak of its nineteenth-century popularity. Sauvestre's version sold 20,000 copies in eighteen months, and ran to an eighteenth impression by 1879. It was reproduced in works by other anti-jesuit authors, was serialized in the Sunday supplement of the *Petite République française* in 1879, and found its way, in full, into the respectable pages of Larousse's *Grand Dictionnaire universel*.[35] Numerous anti-jesuit publicists, besides those who printed them, referred directly or obliquely to the *Monita*, and some relied heavily on them.[36] Less was said, however, about the text's origins, or to justify its authenticity.

Those anti-jesuits who said anything about how the *Monita secreta* had come to light usually repeated, as probable or certain, the claim that they had been found in the rector's library of the Jesuit college at Paderborn (or perhaps Prague), when the town had been pillaged by the Duke of Brunswick. This already garbled version of a seventeenth-century story was sometimes lifted verbatim (but unacknowledged) from the mock-1661 edition, which stated that the events in question had taken place 'a few years ago'; nineteenth-century readers might reasonably have concluded that the sack of Paderborn (actually in 1622) was some little-known episode of the Napoleonic wars.[37] The question of authorship was seldom

---

[33] The extensive (but not exhaustive) list of 19th-century French editions in C. Sommervogel (ed.), *Bibliothèque de la Compagnie de Jésus*, 12 vols. (Paris, 1890–1960), xi. 349–56, cites six different presentations of the text (the majority published by Ponthieu under the title *Instructions secrètes des jésuites*) between 1824 and 1828, to which that in A. Scheffer, *Précis de l'histoire générale de la Compagnie de Jésus, suivi des Monita secreta* (Paris, 1824) should be added. Two editions *in-32°* were issued, in 1825 and 1826, running to a 7th and an 8th impression respectively, with around 20,000 copies eventually printed in the latter case, according to figures in O. A. Rachman, *Un périodique libéral sous la Restauration: Le Mercure du XIXe siècle, avril 1823–mars 1826* (Geneva, 1984), 116, 119, 121.

[34] *Instructions secrètes des jésuites* (1845); *Almanach des jésuites*, 135–75.

[35] Salverte (ed.), *Monita secreta* (sales figs. on p. 5 of 3rd edn.); *Petite République française* (Sunday supplements 25 May–6 July 1879); Larousse (ed.), *Grand Dictionnaire universel*, ix. 961–4; also J. Lemer, *Dossier des jésuites et des libertés de l'Église gallicane* (Paris, 1877), 114–56; Michel, *Les Jésuites*, 91–136; Taxil, *Les Amours secrètes*, 2082–102.

[36] e.g. Bouis, *Calottes et soutanes*; also J. P. Ferrer, 'Premier siècle du jésuitisme', sent in manuscript to Freycinet in Mar. 1880 (contained in *AN* F[19] 6287).

[37] *Le Citateur*, 1: 141, *Instructions secrètes des jésuites; ou Monita secreta Societatis Jesu* (Paris, 1824), 1, and *Almanach des jésuites*, 135, reproduced the Paderborn story verbatim; others, including Scheffer, Sauvestre, and Lemer, referred to it more cautiously.

broached: Zaharowski (miscalled 'Zarowitch') was occasionally mentioned, as composer or divulger of the secret instructions, but this was not done in a way which cast doubt on their status as a genuine Jesuit document.[38] Positive proofs of their authenticity, in the sense of proofs grounded in textual or bibliographical scholarship, were equally lacking. Jesuit denials, predictably, were dismissed on the grounds either that Jesuits believed lying permissible,[39] or that those who issued them were simply not in the know: was it not written into the *Monita*'s own preface that, if the secret instructions became public, 'those whom one knows with certainty to be ignorant of it' should be put up to deny that the sentiments which they expressed were those of the Society?[40] As for the text's inherent plausibility, the simplest argument was that of *Le Citateur*: 'it is impossible to invent such things.'[41] The most common argument, however, stressed the alleged coincidence between actual Jesuit practice and that which the *Monita* prescribed. As Sauvestre remarked, 'it is enough to compare this document with the doctrines contained in the books of the principal doctors of the Society, and above all with the line of conduct which the Jesuits have followed for as long as they have existed, to have no doubt about its authenticity'.[42] When pressed, Sauvestre remarked that at the very least this conformity between text and practice guaranteed the former's 'reality': 'either it is the Jesuits who model themselves on it, or it is the book which is copied from them'; either way, it was clearly imbued with 'the Jesuitical spirit'.[43] Some anti-jesuits questioned whether the Jesuits would really have written down such instructions,[44] but others found Sauvestre's initial argument perfectly persuasive. For them, the *Monita* were not merely a telling portrait of Jesuit activity; they were a text of genuine explanatory usefulness. 'How have the Jesuits re-established themselves, how

[38] A. Brot and L. Lurine, *Les Couvents* (Paris, 1846), 54; Taxil, *Les Amours secrètes*, 2082.

[39] Sauvestre, *Monita secreta* (2nd edn.), 8–9; Michel, *Les Jésuites*, 90; Larousse (ed.), *Grand Dictionnaire universel*, ix. 961.   [40] *Monita secreta*, preface.

[41] *Le Citateur*, 1: 140. The editor added that the authenticity of the texts was anyway 'well recognized in Germany'.

[42] Sauvestre, *Monita secreta* (1st edn.), 2.

[43] Sauvestre, *Monita secreta* (2nd edn.), 11. Similarly, Michon, *Le Maudit*, i. 63, argued that the coincidence between the *Monita* and actual Jesuit behaviour rendered the question of authenticity simply irrelevant.

[44] De Pressensé, *La Liberté religieuse*, 27; Wallon, *Un collège de jésuites*, 353.

have they so quickly prospered?' asked *Le Constitutionnel* in 1824: 'This new secret is revealed to you by the old *Advis* [*Monita secreta*].'[45]

Nowhere more than in this readiness to believe in the relevance of the *Monita* to the description and explanation of modern Jesuit successes was the tension between the themes of continuity and of flexibility in the anti-jesuit vision apparent. To sceptical eyes, the absurdity of such a belief might be obvious: if Jesuit conduct in an age of capitalism and post-Revolutionary politics continued to be based on instructions whose early modern drafter could think of no better way of acquiring vast wealth than by systematically seducing rich widows, and supposed that political influence was a matter of whispering the right things in the ears of a small class of monarchs and great men, what became of the Jesuits' reputation for fiendish and adaptable cunning? In practice, however, anti-jesuits seldom allowed belief in the *Monita secreta* to prevent them from attributing to the Jesuits a wider range of methods. The need which the text fulfilled for them was one not so much for a definitive description of Jesuit behaviour (which they believed they could find in history) as for an affirmation of its ultimate transparency. If the authenticity (or even, at a pinch, the 'reality', providing it was assumed to be constant) of the *Monita* was accepted, Jesuit tactics, at least in certain areas of activity, were revealed as grounded not in evolving responses to circumstances, but in a fixed and detailed conspiratorial plan. The very proof of the meticulousness of Jesuit plotting made it easier to spot and to expose.

The sections of the *Monita* which dealt with court intrigue and diplomacy, and with internal discipline, contributed to the Jesuits' reputation for unscrupulous calculation and for cold inhumanity, but not, by the nineteenth century, in any particularly distinctive way. It was the sections on the pursuit of wealth ('Of the manner of winning over rich widows'; 'How to converse with widows and dispose of the property they have'; 'What must be done in order that the children of widows embrace the religious condition or that of devotion'; 'Of the augmentation of the revenues of colleges'[46]) that attracted most attention. It was thanks especially to these that *captation des héritages* was regarded as an area of peculiar Jesuit expertise.

---

[45] *Constitutionnel*, 24 June 1824 (see also 17 Mar. 1824).
[46] *Monita secreta*, chs. 6–9.

As the supposed manual of a sect of legacy-pirates, the *Monita secreta* provided a serviceable blueprint for pulp fiction. Armand Durantin, in *Un élève des jésuites*, made them the explicit basis for the instructions issued to the Jesuit Daniel Dufresne on how to secure the fortune of Mme Sorel.[47] Michon referred to them in passing in *Le Maudit*, and may well have drawn from them such details as the Jesuits' care to lure heirs into their order, their employment of servants as spies, and their use of 'jésuites galantins' to charm rich widows.[48] Most other anti-jesuit novels and plays, though not necessarily directly influenced by the *Monita*, contained Jesuit intrigues around family fortunes, often as their main plot. Nor was the theme of *captation des héritages* confined to fiction; there were frequent references in pamphlets and *brochures* to the ways in which the Jesuits besieged the death-beds of the rich, kindled illusory religious vocations in wealthy children, and induced credulous women to part with their jewellery. If Casimir Bouis was to be believed, romantic seduction was an integral part of the technique. Jesuit agents ('thoroughbred bloodhounds, elegant and supple') snuffled out fortunes in the salons and antechambers of the aristocracy: '*Mme la marquise*, absorbed in her simpers and meaningful glances, scarcely suspects that with the half-confidences let slip in the abandon of the *tête-à-tête*, she has given away the information so ardently desired, so skilfully worked round to. . . . *M. le vicomte* has his scapular under his shirt, but can she see it before the moment of defeat?' At the climax of the intrigue, 'Madame, subjugated, her eyes turned up to heaven, does not see, in the garden, Loyola holding the ladder up which the gallant Romeo has flown to his Juliet.'[49]

For concrete examples of *captation*, anti-jesuits could turn to history (the early eighteenth-century case of Ambroise Guys, for example[50]), but they relied less on it here than in the case of regicide. *Le Constitutionnel*, under the Restoration, kept a watchful eye on the columns of the *Gazette des tribunaux*, picking out such

---

[47] Durantin, *Un élève des jésuites*, 32–40.
[48] Michon, *Le Maudit*, *passim*, esp. ii. 169, 171 (possibly influenced by *Monita secreta*, ch. 6, clause 1). [49] Bouis, *Calottes et soutanes*, 151–2.
[50] See e.g. *Instructions secrètes des jésuites* (1845), pp. xxv–xxvi; Sauvestre, *Monita secreta* (1st edn.), 17–18; Michel, *Les Jésuites*, 18–20; Larousse (ed.), *Grand Dictionnaire universel*, ix. 965, for references to the Guys case, and *Almanach des jésuites*, 229–34, for another early 18th-century case, that of the dame de Clugny.

material as the Lépine case in 1826, in which the will of a one-time
Jesuit novice, leaving money to pass via an executor to the Jesuits
of Saint-Acheul, was annulled by the Cour Royale of Douai, or the
Beck case at Colmar in 1828, in which the court considered a letter
by the Jesuit Père Grivel, which had attempted to persuade Beck
to leave his fortune (again through a third party) to the Society
of Jesus rather than to the diocesan seminary.[51] Both cases were
presented as typical instances of Jesuit *captation*. That of Lépine, it
was claimed, revealed the secret of the prosperity of Saint-Acheul,
and showed the Jesuits, 'ever faithful to the *Monita secreta*', engaged
once again in 'the spoliation of families'.[52] Grivel's letter, according to *Le Constitutionnel*, reproduced 'the impious and seditious
sophisms with which, for the last fourteen years in France, the
Jesuits have tormented feeble minds, dominated timid consciences,
seized upon riches, founded establishments and despoiled legitimate heirs'.[53] Denunciations and suspicions of this sort remained a
feature of anti-jesuitism later in the century. In 1862, for example,
following a confused incident at Laon railway station, the Jesuit
Père Gruel found himself suspected of trying to abduct a female
minor, Clémence Huteaux. Public rumour, the Prefect reported,
held that his purpose had been to secure the young lady's fortune
(supposedly estimated at 60,000 francs) for his order. Further in-
vestigations, however, revealed the distortions in the testimony
of the station's over-zealous *commissaire de surveillance administrative*;
it transpired that Gruel had not known Mlle Huteaux before the
incident, that he had then met her accidentally, and that she was not
a minor after all. Nor did there seem to be any reason to implicate
Gruel's Jesuit colleagues in the episode. Nevertheless, reported the
Prefect (who himself suspected Gruel of libidinous intentions), had
the suspicion of abduction proved founded, 'people [*on*] would not
have failed to see in it the co-operation of all the Fathers, though
one alone would have undertaken to carry out the enterprise, and
then I would have demanded their expulsion'.[54]

---

[51] *Gazette des tribunaux*, 7 Apr. 1826 (Lépine case); 2, 3, 4, 5 July 1828 (Beck
case).
[52] *Constitutionnel*, 8 Apr., 28 May 1826.   [53] Ibid. 5 July 1828.
[54] AN F[19] 6188 (Dossier Gruel): Prefect of Aisne to *Ministre des Cultes*, 24 June
1862 (identical letter to *Ministre de l'Intérieur*); *procureur-général* of Amiens to *Garde
des Sceaux*, 20 June and 3 July 1862; Prefect of Aisne to *Ministre de l'Intérieur*, 3 July
1862.

The fixation with *captation* illustrates some of the general characteristics of anti-jesuit polemic about Jesuit riches. Anti-jesuits might
imagine Jesuits proclaiming (as the Jesuit General did, in Michon's
novel *Le Jésuite*) that money was 'the great lever of human affairs',[55]
but their analysis of this leverage was perfunctory. Far more attention was paid to how Jesuit wealth was amassed than to how it was
used. When possible uses were mentioned, they tended to involve
the straightforward conversion of money into something else: military might, political power (by bribery), or educational influence
(by financing Jesuit schools). Anti-jesuits might express horror at
the Affenäer affair's revelations of Jesuit financial dealings, but
specifically financial power—power exercised through the medium
of financial manipulation—had little place in their usual conceptions of their enemy's methods.[56] The belief that the creation of
Jesuit wealth was a process of spoliation, and thus subversive in
itself, on the other hand, was highly pronounced. Thanks to the
depredations of their missionaries, wrote Marcet, the Jesuits 'will
not be long in impoverishing France and in making themselves her
masters by the treasures which they have amassed'[57]—this despite
the fact that Marcet's Jesuits (more luxurious in their habits than
most in anti-jesuit literature) seemed content merely to hoard their
treasure[58] or to spend it on gluttony and libertinage. Other anti-
jesuits saw the same basic opposition of interest in commerce and
industry; one, for example, opposed the Jesuits' revival in the 1820s
on the ground that French commerce had enough competition
from overseas without having also to cope with rivals within.[59] The
assumption in either case, and even more obviously in the literature
on *captation*, was that the Jesuits' wealth was alien and parasitic. Its
increase meant the impoverishment of others—of legitimate heirs,

[55] J.-H. Michon, *Le Jésuite*, 2 vols. (Paris, 1865), ii. 109.

[56] *Les Jésuites et l'Inquisition*, 139, was relatively unusual in describing how the
Society of Jesus was able, through its various collections, to build up 'an enormous
capital, which permitted it, whether in the field of French loans or of operations
abroad, to keep watch on the coffers of the State and to draw on them, by remaining the holder [*entrepositaire*] of numerous shares taken out in the names of some of
its affiliates'.   [57] Marcet, *Nouveau Mémoire*, 204.

[58] On the Jesuit treasure-hoard, see Marcet, *Mémoires d'un jeune jésuite*, 283, and
his *Les Sept Bêtes de Montrouge: Prophétie et apocalypse: Manuscrit trouvé dans le noviciat
des jésuites de Paris* (Paris, 1829), 63.

[59] A. Grassi, *La Sainte-Alliance, les Anglais et les jésuites: Leur système politique à
l'égard de la Grèce, des gouvernements constitutionnels et des événemens actuels* (Paris, 1827),
457.

of French families, of French industry, ultimately of France herself. Where money was concerned, it was still the ancient sin of greed that best served the cause of Jesuit domination.

ESPIONAGE

For many anti-jesuits, though the *captation d'un héritage* remained the classic set-piece of Jesuitical intrigue, money itself was not the most telling of Jesuit resources. Equally hoardable, equally flexible, but more imperceptible (both in its accumulation and in its use), and perhaps more actively and insidiously deployed—not least in the *captation des héritages* itself—was the information gathered through the Jesuit intelligence network. Thanks to this, a Jesuit General of an earlier age had been able to claim (according to a story much repeated in the nineteenth century) that he ruled the whole world from a single room, 'without anyone knowing how it is done'.[60] Michon's fictionalized version of the present General, Roothaan, echoed the claim, drawing the same connection between knowledge and power, omniscience and omnipotence: 'So far as man can be God and like him see all things, I know everything that is happening, at this moment, in Europe and in all the regions of the world. It is the greatest concentration of power which can be comprehended here on earth.'[61] Other nineteenth-century anti-jesuits reinforced the picture. 'Imagine a gigantic telegraphic network encompassing the universe and converging on a single centre,' wrote Bouis; 'each member of the Society of Jesus is a wire; the General is the centre'.[62] Merely the regular official correspondence between the Jesuit Provinces and the Roman centre seemed enough, to Wallon, to make the General 'the man best informed on everything important that happens in the world',[63] and this, anti-jesuits were convinced, was merely the official tip of a largely unofficial iceberg.

All this presupposed an impressive filing system. Here the nineteenth century added a new (though not totally unprecedented) element to the mythology of Jesuit espionage. In 1843, citing the anonymous authority of 'someone who *has seen it* and who knows

---

[60] The anecdote is reported, for example, in the 1843 anti-jesuit edition of *Les Constitutions des jésuites*, 477–8; the words are said to have been addressed to the duc de Brissac.   [61] Michon, *Le Jésuite*, ii. 109.
[62] Bouis, *Calottes et soutanes*, 112–13.   [63] Wallon, *Jésus et les jésuites*, 182.

the Jesuits perfectly', Libri revealed that the Jesuit headquarters at Rome contained 'immense registers in which are inscribed the names of all the Jesuits, of all their affiliates and of all the people, friends or enemies, with whom they have dealings'. He continued:

In these registers are reported, without misrepresentations, without hatred, without passion, the facts relating to the life of each individual. It is the most gigantic biographical compilation that has ever been assembled since the world began. The conduct of a fast woman, the hidden faults of a statesman are related in this book with a cold impartiality. These biographies are truthful, because they must be useful. When they [*on*] need to act on an individual, they open the book, and they know immediately his life, his character, his qualities, his defects, his projects, his family, his friends, his most secret liaisons.[64]

The *Journal de la liberté religieuse*, in the same year, offered similar information, alleging that when the Vatican Archives had been deposited in Paris in 1810, Daunou, their keeper, had found among them 'a series of boxes containing the record [*journal*] of all revelations made to the court of Rome, by the Jesuits of all countries, revelations of confessions and of confidences obtained in the frequentation of persons of the highest dignity'.[65] In 1848 abbé Leone surpassed these indirect reports by claiming that he personally, while a Jesuit novice at Chieri in the 1820s, had entered the rector's study in his absence and there come across two volumes, entitled 'Confessions of the novices' and 'Confessions of the foreigners'. These proved to contain accurate and detailed descriptions of the mental and emotional characteristics of penitents, information of a sort which Leone judged would not only allow the Jesuits to gain an instant reputation for prescience, but would also give them 'almost infallible means' of securing their aim of theocratic world domination. Only the sudden arrival of Jesuit conspirators, who proceeded to discuss this very project, had prevented Leone, according to his account, from perusing a third volume, entitled 'Enemies of the Society'.[66] The whole scene, with

---

[64] Libri, 'Lettres sur le clergé français, II', 978–9. For an earlier mention of similar registers, said to have been found in Jesuit establishments in Bergamo and Padua, see the report to Henri IV on the Venetian Senate's reasons for expelling the Jesuits in 1606, in P. Canaye, *Lettres et ambassade de messire P. Canaye, sieur de Fresne*, 3 vols. (Paris, 1635–6), iii. 85–6.

[65] *Journal de la liberté religieuse*, i. 38.

[66] Leone, *Conjuration des jésuites*, 14–17 (similar registers are referred to on 29).

alterations of detail, and without acknowledgement to Leone, was brought to a wider audience in Michon's *Le Maudit* fifteen years later.[67]

The confessional, as several of the passages already cited make clear, was widely regarded as the principal listening-post in this intelligence network. Confession was 'a probe [*sonde*] which nothing escapes',[68] 'a precious and inexhaustible source of information, which the police of governments lacks';[69] it was also a channel of persuasion and of influence. It was the key, in Monglave and Chalas's view, to the Jesuits' ability to make the rulers of the world tremble. When the General decided to wreak vengeance on a sovereign,

He immediately gives orders to render him suspect in the eyes of the other kings, to raise up enemies against him everywhere, to rouse his own states against him. Those whom he charges with this commission glory in carrying it out with blind obedience, and since, by means of confessions, they are aware of the devoted subjects and of those who are not so, it is easy for them, by using this knowledge, to stir up troubles, seditions, and revolts.[70]

The Jesuit royal confessors of the past (as portrayed in anti-jesuit historiography[71]) still haunted such passages, but most anti-jesuits of the nineteenth century were more likely, in thinking of the confessor, to focus on a different level of Jesuit operations. Michon wrote:

It is well known that the Jesuits only undertake the [spiritual] direction of a woman of society on condition of knowing her name, the state of her fortune, her husband's political opinion, the newspapers which enter the house, the *collège* where the children are brought up. Here, clearly, is a sure means of knowing, within a short time, what goes on in the inner lives of families, better than police can ever do.[72]

[67] Michon, *Le Maudit*, iii. 54–69. Another fictional reference to Jesuit registers of this kind is in Sue, *Les Mystères du peuple; ou Histoire d'une famille de prolétaires à travers les âges*, Librairie du progrès edn., 10 vols. (Paris, 1881), vii. 82.
[68] Leone, *Conjuration des jésuites*, 172–3.   [69] Michon, *Le Maudit*, i. 168–9.
[70] Monglave and Chalas, *Histoire des conspirations*, 16.
[71] See notably abbé Grégoire's *Histoire des confesseurs des empereurs, des rois et d'autres princes* (Paris, 1824), *passim*; and A. Douarche's masonic lecture on *Les Jésuites confesseurs des rois de France* (Carcassonne, 1880).
[72] Michon, *Le Maudit*, i. 169.

Subtle and insinuating, and no respecter of confidentiality, the Jesuit confessor violated both privacy and trust. In his smaller circle, he could become as omniscient and as omnipotent as the General in the world at large. The pamphleteer Casimir Guillaume set such a scene:

> The wife passes to her confessor her husband's letters, in which there are state secrets. The chamber-maid passes the correspondence of her mistress; the mistress that of her lady's maid; the confessor holds everything, knows everything, and no one suspects it; he controls his penitents, while betraying them all; he holds the proofs of their guilty intrigues, they are devoted to him through fear after having been devoted to him through trust.[73]

Such images of Jesuit power appealed powerfully to the imagination, and helped keep the confessor prominent in the nineteenth-century anti-jesuit vision. It might be questioned, however, whether the confessor alone could bear the burden of supplying the Jesuit machine with vital intelligence in an age when fewer persons of influence than before had a Jesuit (or any other) confessor, and when (for the same reasons that made regicide look outmoded) the number of those about whom Jesuit conspirators would require information was dramatically increasing. Two other distinctive features of nineteenth-century anti-jesuitism, however, helped to sustain the plausibility of the claims made about Jesuit espionage, the one by strengthening the focus on the confessor, the other by dissipating it. The first (implicit in Guillaume's picture of the household under Jesuit control) was the emphasis placed on the special vulnerability of women to the wiles of confessors. The second was the extension of mythology concerning other Jesuit agents. The Jesuit of Bouis's imagination—'this man in black [*homme noir*] who distances himself, hidden in his cloak, whom one has never seen', but who could whisper as he passed, '"I am at your table and at your hearth, whenever I wish"'[74]—could do so because servants, tutors, doctors, lawyers, and employees all helped him keep a household under surveillance. Nor was it chiefly the action of confessors that Leone had in mind when, rejecting the Catholic writer Crétineau-Joly's claim that the Jesuits had not

---

[73] C. Guillaume, *2e pamphlet: Les Ultramontains ou jésuites* (Dôle, 1844), 4.
[74] Bouis, *Calottes et soutanes*, 140.

supplied the sources for his adulatory history of their order, he asked: 'Who, then, better than the Jesuits, could possess the art of penetrating everywhere, of seducing, of employing a thousand different agents in every corner of Europe to get hold of secret papers hidden away and carefully guarded in every chancellery, of the most mysterious diplomatic correspondences?'[75] A numerous and socially diverse class of *jésuites de robe courte* and Jesuit affiliates, it seemed, reinforced and extended the efforts of Jesuit confessors.

To pass from the themes of murder and *captation*, through that of espionage, to these further themes of Jesuit affiliation and the Jesuit conquest of the family through the woman, and finally to that of Jesuit education, is to follow a shift in anti-jesuit emphasis towards a more 'social' conception of Jesuit subversion and power. The regicide, the fortune-hunter, and the confessor as spy were moral and symbolic outrages (violators of legitimate authority, of legitimate property, of legitimate trust) and dangers to society, but the first two at least were raiders, come to destroy or to plunder, and the third, though a manipulator, was still a definable outsider. But the Jesuit affiliate, the Jesuitized woman, and the victim of Jesuit education were, in their varying degrees, the symbols of a social take-over—of a colonization, a marshalling, a perversion of society in the Jesuit interest. Their prominence in the nineteenth-century anti-jesuit vision marked a tacit recognition that, in the modern world, any effective world conspiracy would have to be as social in approach as it was antisocial in intent. Spiritually, if not physically, it was the people that must be killed.

[75] Leone, *Conjuration des jésuites*, 330–1.

7

Jesuits in Plain Clothes

THE Jesuits the most to be feared, according to the author of the pamphlet *Physiologie du jésuite* (1844), were those 'who arouse no mistrust, whom nothing draws to the attention'.[1] Secret Jesuits or Jesuit affiliates—men or women whose membership of, or intimate connection with, the Society of Jesus was concealed beneath the external appearance of ordinary members of the laity—had an important place in anti-jesuit speculations. A great deal of mystery surrounded them, some of which stemmed from the secrecy in which their activities were deemed to be cloaked, and some from anti-jesuits' uncertainty, and sometimes disagreement, over what exactly affiliation to the Jesuit order consisted of. The variety and occasional confusion of anti-jesuit views arose from the entanglement and overlapping of two mythologies, the first relating to lay organizations (*sodalités* or *congrégations*), the second to the so-called *jésuites de robe courte.*

CONGRÉGATIONS

To the reasonable question of whether twenty or thirty Jesuits (a rare anti-jesuit underestimate) existing in France in 1827 could really be considered 'a power', Salgues answered:

Not if they were alone: but Saint Ignatius has foreseen everything; ignorant as he was, he understood that he needed a light infantry, an infantry *de robe courte* to support his soldiers *de robe longue*, and he founded the *sodalités*; he has made his disciples into a political and religious society, he has said to the turbulent, the ambitious, the fanatical: join yourselves to me, and by means of his affiliations, without show [*éclat*] and without noise, he has created for himself numberless legions which have spread themselves over

[1] *Physiologie du jésuite* (Paris, 1844), 58.

all the earth, and have bound themselves by a solemn vow to the interests, to the defence, to the triumph of the Society.[2]

For Salgues, and for many other anti-jesuits, it was chiefly by being marshalled in *sodalités* or *congrégations*, ostensibly existing for the purposes of piety, charity, or Christian propaganda, that people entered the lay division of the Jesuit army. A 'redoubtable escort' of such lay *congrégations* always accompanied the Jesuits on their march, wrote the Port-Royalist Jacquemont.[3] Well before Dumesnil and Montlosier took to denouncing the Congrégation, Silvy had known what to expect: if the Jesuits were allowed to go on enrolling men and women into organizations 'under the specious pretext of association, of prayers and of other good works', he wrote in 1818, their affiliates would soon invade the Court, the Conseil d'État, the civil service, and the law-courts, forcing the government to submit either to them or to perpetual crisis.[4]

Many elements in the myth of the Restoration Congrégation, then, merely conformed to and renewed standard anti-jesuit suspicions. Where Montlosier and others were original was in their use of the term Congrégation (usually with a capital 'C') to bind different groupings together into one supposed web of affiliation. In reality, it is true that the ranks of the Congrégation directed by Père Ronsin contained a significant proportion of the members of other Catholic organizations like the Société des Bonnes Études and the Société de Saint-Joseph; a modern historian has concluded that 'without there being a direct filiation, the *congréganiste* influence on these societies remains strong up to 1826'.[5] Restoration antijesuits, however, detected a more formal connection. The Société des Bonnes Études, according to an ex-member, was a 'Jesuitical affiliation' and a 'direct affiliation of the Congrégation'.[6] The

---

[2] Salgues, *L'Antidote de Mont-Rouge; ou Six questions adressées à Mgr. l'évêque d'Hermopolis sur le projet de rétablir ou de tolérer les jésuites, et suivies de l'examen de leurs modernes apologistes, MM. Tharin, de Bonald, etc., etc.* (Paris, 1827), 210–11.

[3] Jacquemont, *Examen impartial*, 113.

[4] [L. Silvy], 'Dissertation sur la foi qui est due au témoignage de Pascal dans ses Lettres provinciales', 87–8, adjoined to his *Henri IV et les jésuites* (Paris, 1818).

[5] J.-B. Duroselle, 'Les "Filiales" de la Congrégation', *Revue d'histoire ecclésiastique*, 50 (1955), 884. Duroselle also, however, notes that the Jesuits were less closely involved with these 'filiales' than with the Congrégation itself (p. 890).

[6] S. Duchateau, *Dénonciation contre la Société des Bonnes Études, comme affiliation jésuitique, pour servir d'appendice à la dénonciation de M. le Cte de Montlosier* (Paris, 1826), 11.

Journal des débats wrote of the Association de la Propagation de la Foi: 'The soul of this great body is the Society of Jesus, from which all the branches of the *congrégation* emanate.'[7] Some definitions of the Congrégation were inclusive indeed:

By Congrégation, one means the general association of all the men imbued with Jesuitical doctrines, who, though spread among the various classes of society (from the highest to the lowest), receive, *in roundabout ways*, a single direction, have signs of recognition and passwords, and contribute, either communally or separately, by every means they have received from nature or from their social position, to the accomplishment of the projects of those who direct them *in the name of the interests of heaven*, and for the greater glory of God.[8]

Not surprisingly, the question of the Congrégation's actual structure was shrouded in obscurity. Montlosier himself did not pretend to grasp it:

The mysterious power which, under the name of CONGRÉGATION, appears today on the world's stage, seems to me as confused in its composition as in its object, and in its object as in its origin. It is as impossible for me to say with precision what it is, as to show how, in the past, it has successively formed, extended, organized itself. I say *organized*, with the reservation that sometimes its body is whole; and then one sees a trunk and limbs; at other times some of these limbs withdraw from it, it appears mutilated. The body itself is composed in such a way as to be able, when convenient, to dispel itself like a shadow; and then one wonders whether it is true that a *congrégation* exists.

In Montlosier's view, however, this structural elusiveness merely confirmed the organization's roots in Jesuit cunning.[9]

Later anti-jesuit literature, while not quite matching the grandiosity of the Congrégation myth of the 1820s, reiterated the fears which it had articulated. In 1844, for example, Génin listed a number of allegedly Jesuitical lay associations, and denounced the nocturnal meetings, disguised as workers' educational classes, which he claimed the Jesuits were holding in the crypts of Parisian

---

[7] *Débats*, 5 May 1826. The denunciation of the Association as an offshoot of the Jesuit trunk was developed at length in this and two previous articles (ibid. 1, 3 May 1826).

[8] P. Colau, *Derniers Efforts du jésuitisme expirant, ses infamies, ses crimes et ses complots, définition de ce qu'on appelle la Congrégation, du danger qu'il y aurait si une liberté mal entendue empêchait qu'on réprimât ses nouvelles tentatives* (Paris, 1830), 6.

[9] Montlosier, *Mémoire*, 17–19.

churches.[10] Under the July Monarchy such denunciations were sporadic, and did not add up either to a sustained campaign against any particular organization or to a widespread concern with lay *congrégations* in general. It was in response to the lay Catholic activity of the Second Empire and early Third Republic—especially the remarkable expansion of the Société de Saint Vincent-de-Paul in the 1850s and the spread of the *comités catholiques* and the *cercles catholiques d'ouvriers* in the 1870s—that the vision of a society held in a stranglehold by Jesuit *congrégations* once more became a commonplace feature of anti-jesuit statements. Strikingly, what anti-jesuits now detected was not so much a frightening new movement as an alarming reproduction of an old one. 'It is the same organization as under the Restoration', declared the *député* Louis Janvier de la Motte during the debate on the Ferry bill; 'one finds again all the same societies, from the Sociétés des Bons Livres to the Sociétés des Missions Étrangères. It is copied identically from the movement of 1815 to 1830.'[11]

Some anti-jesuits in the 1860s and 1870s even revived the use of the term 'Congrégation' (in the singular, usually with a capital) to denote the Jesuits' organized lay forces. Sauvestre, for example, used the term to refer vaguely to a force of incomparable discipline and unity, which he claimed was 'none other than the Company of Jesus ramified and, like the chameleon, changing its aspect according to the surroundings'.[12] Wallon saw in the old-boy associations of Jesuit schools 'a veritable political affiliation, forming the various sections of what has been called, in a single word, the CONGRÉGATION'.[13] It was in some of the literature denouncing the Société de Saint Vincent-de-Paul under the Second Empire, however, that the terms and tone of Restoration polemic, and the sense of continuity with Restoration conditions, were most apparent. One writer suggested that the Society had been created in order to enable the Jesuits to switch their alliance from the aristocracy to the bourgeoisie,[14] but most saw merely a resurgence of a familiar foe—the old Congrégation in disguise. When a character in *Le Maudit* decided to place his legal career under Jesuit auspices, he joined the Société de Saint Vincent-de-Paul 'at the same time and as a

[10] Génin, *Les Jésuites et l'Université*, 44–5, 109–15, 318–20.
[11] *ASCD*, CD 28 June 1879: 223.
[12] C. Sauvestre, *Lettres de province* (Paris, 1862), 35.
[13] Wallon, *Un collège de jésuites*, 78–9.   [14] *Les Jésuites et l'Inquisition*, 155.

corollary',[15] exactly as a careerist in a Restoration novel would have joined the Congrégation.

The fullest and most revealing exposition of the arguments involved in this extension of the mythology concerning Jesuit lay organization was supplied by Cayla in his *Ces bons messieurs de Saint Vincent-de-Paul*, published in 1863. Despite major differences in their political and religious beliefs, Cayla posed explicitly as a continuer of Montlosier;[16] his basic argument was that '*Congrégation*, Jesuitism, and Société de Saint Vincent-de-Paul are one and the same thing; the name has changed, the traditions and the statutes have remained the same.'[17] His argument to this effect involved no attempt to show that known Jesuits were involved in the Society's activities or organization. Instead, two overlapping lines of reasoning were developed at length. The first was an argument from analogy with earlier supposedly Jesuit organizations. This was stated in the most forthright terms: 'all affiliations, be they purely religious or simply charitable, derive from Jesuitism, and in the seventeenth century Jesuitical proceedings were, with few exceptions, the same as those of the Société de Saint Vincent-de-Paul.'[18] The term 'Congrégation', in Cayla's usage, denoted a mysterious Jesuitical organization, already in place by the time of the Ligue. Its successive manifestations had included the Jesuit *sodalités* of the sixteenth and seventeenth centuries, the Messieurs of the reign of Louis XV, the various crypto-Jesuit groupings of the Empire (Pères de la Foi, Paccanarists, and others), and the famous Restoration organization, which Cayla called the 'Grande-Congrégation'.[19] Cayla frequently interrupted his historical review of these organizations to indicate their supposed points of similarity with the Société de Saint Vincent-de-Paul: the structure of an international secret society, the occult leadership, the obedience to Roman command, the charitable façade. These, he maintained, were 'connections [*rapports*] so evident that it would be bad faith to deny them'; they left no doubt that the Society was 'a Jesuitical affiliation'.[20]

The second argument was similar, but more far-reaching; it proceeded from alleged resemblances between the Société de Saint Vincent-de-Paul and the Society of Jesus itself. Some of these

[15] Michon, *Le Maudit*, ii. 241.   [16] Cayla, *Ces bons messieurs*, 109–10.
[17] Ibid. 111.   [18] Ibid. 62.
[19] Ibid. 62–130, for the history of these organizations.   [20] Ibid. 90–1.

related to attitudes (religious exclusivism, hatred of Protestantism), but most were constitutional or structural: the possession of a hierarchical and dictatorial framework, an Ultramontane obedience to Rome, 'cosmopolitanism', and 'pretensions to universality'.[21] The mere fact of being a large, complex, and centralized organization seemed to condemn the Society: 'This concentration of information, of correspondence, of opinions and counsels, is it not a Jesuitical tradition?'[22] The sheer variety of the Society's works, touching human beings at all stages and in all conditions of life, suggested to Cayla that its real purpose was the Jesuitical one of comprehensive social control; this was no mere charitable organization, but 'almost a government, a state within the State'.[23] Everything, then, seemed to suggest that the Society was 'based, modelled on Jesuitism'.[24]

If criteria like those invoked by Cayla were accepted (and his arguments were a developed and explicit rendition of reasoning implicit in many other anti-jesuit statements), any number of Catholic *œuvres* and associations became automatically suspect; in fact, it was hard to see how, once anti-jesuit passions were aroused, lay Catholics could organize themselves—politically, socially, or religiously—on any significant scale without falling into this capacious stereotypical mould. The shadowy myth of the Congrégation could give a sinister coherence to the disparate and uncoordinated efforts of a mass of organizations, and an occult identity to their members' loyalties.

JÉSUITES DE ROBE COURTE

In the literature on lay *congrégations*, it was the organized, collective face of Jesuit affiliation that appeared. References to *jésuites de robe courte* (or to *jésuitesses*, their female equivalent) usually seemed to envisage a more isolated type of agent. The relationship between *congréganistes* and *jésuites de robe courte* was often unclear, however, because *jésuites de robe courte* themselves were often ill defined. Almost nothing was known about them, Adolphe Boucher admitted, except that they existed and were perhaps the most dangerous

---

[21] Ibid. 32, 136, 237, 276, 284, 300–2.   [22] Ibid. 30.
[23] Ibid. 239–40.   [24] Ibid. 32.

class of Jesuit.[25] The sister of the Jesuitical character Sainte-Agathe, in Émile Augier's comedy *Lions et renards*, was scarcely more helpful; when he asked her what she meant by *robe courte*, she replied: 'What the world means! laymen like you, affiliated like you—to *ces messieurs.*'[26] To insist on clarity here would be to misrepresent the vagueness and confusion in anti-jesuit minds. Nevertheless, four loose-knit schools of thought on the nature of *jésuites de robe courte* can be detected.

According to the first, *jésuites de robe courte* were simply the members of Jesuitical *congrégations*. The following definition was reproduced (with minor differences of wording) in several anti-jesuit tracts:

The *jésuites de robe courte* are the bounden spies [*espions obligés*] of the society of Loyola; they are secular Jesuits spread throughout all societies, and whose number increases from day to day in an extraordinary manner. They multiply like insects in summer. The reproduction takes place by means of certain *congrégations* for men and of *confréries* for women, such as the sacred *confrérie* of the Sacred Heart of Jesus; these *congrégations* form a Jesuitical Freemasonry.[27]

There was no suggestion here (though the possibility was not formally excluded) that *jésuites de robe courte* might exist outside the *congrégations*. Similarly, Bouis's chapter entitled 'Les Jésuites de robe courte' was in fact a survey of *sodalités*, and those whom Stendhal identified as the leaders of the 'short-robed Jesuits' were Mathieu de Montmorency and Ferdinand de Bertier, the actual leaders of the Chevaliers de la Foi, widely confused with the Congrégation.[28]

Other anti-jesuits, however, drew a distinction between *congréganistes* and *jésuites de robe courte*. Thus the Restoration *député* Eusèbe

---

[25] Boucher, *Histoire dramatique et pittoresque*, i. 126.

[26] E. Augier, *Lions et renards: Comédie en 5 actes, en prose* (Paris, 1870), 23.

[27] The precise version quoted here is from the *Almanach des jésuites*, 247; Dairnvaell, *Code des jésuites*, 15, is virtually identical. The earliest version of the passage I have found is in Hénin de Cuvillers, *La Monarchie des solipses*, 104–5; here the functions of *jésuites espions* and *jésuites de robe courte* were kept separate, though it was stated that the latter 'often are equally the bounden spies of the Society of Loyola'. The reference to a 'Jesuitical Freemasonry' is typical of Hénin de Cuvillers, and creates a possible case for regarding him as the originator of the passage.

[28] Bouis, *Calottes et soutanes*, ch. 3; Stendhal in *New Monthly Magazine*, 17: 303 (Oct. 1826).

Salverte distinguished between the 'affiliated Jesuits' who made up 'what today is called the *congrégation*', and 'Jesuits *in voto*' (generally an equivalent term to *jésuites de robe courte*), 'who, bound to enter the order as soon as the General requires it of them, remain meanwhile in the bosom of secular society, where their whole conduct is submissive to the direction which they receive from the General or from his subordinates'.[29] In this case, the ties binding the *jésuite de robe courte* to the Society of Jesus were both tighter and less visible than those binding the *congréganiste*. The second common conception of the *jésuite de robe courte* based this difference on social distinction. An article in *Le Constitutionnel* in 1825 explained that *jésuites de robe courte* were generally men of power and influence, drawn from the upper classes; *confréries* and *congrégations* were for lowlier social groups, 'more fit to be fanaticized'.[30] No doubt both the affiliate's vanity and the Jesuits' purposes were well served by keeping a more personal and discreet form of affiliation for persons of distinction.

This view of the *jésuite de robe courte* was not necessarily incompatible with the third view, which distinguished him by his level of commitment or degree of initiation to the Jesuit cause. A later article in *Le Constitutionnel*, for example, claimed that a minority of *congréganistes* became *jésuites de robe courte* by taking a vow of blind obedience to the General; this élite then concentrated on subverting public administration, while their humbler colleagues helped out with the disruption of families and the *captation des héritages*.[31] Without using the term *jésuites de robe courte*, Marcet described a similar two-tier Congrégation: the rank and file swore to commit their fortune to the Jesuit cause, to use their influence to secure posts for the Congrégation's protégés, and to spread the cult of the Sacred Heart of Mary; the élite underwent a more thorough initiation, involving the reading and meditation of secrets, renunciation of family and background, the donning of a scapular, and vows of secrecy, obedience, poverty, and chastity.[32] Michon, in *Le Jésuite*, drew a distinction between the members of *congrégations* and a

---

[29] *AP*, CD 21 June 1828 (annexe), 238.

[30] *Constitutionnel*, 12 June 1825.

[31] Ibid. 11 Sept. 1826. This article also used the terms 'de la petite observance' and 'du tiers ordre' as synonyms for 'de robe courte'.

[32] Marcet, *Mémoires d'un jeune jésuite*, 273–7.

higher grade of 'affiliates', to whom he claimed the term *jésuites de robe courte* was most properly applied.[33]

The fourth (and least widespread) theory about Jesuits in plain clothes (the term *jésuites de robe courte* was in this case seldom used) dealt not, as the first three did, with persons drawn into Jesuit service along a separate and secret path of lay affiliation, but with conventionally recruited Jesuits fraudulently reintroduced to lay society. The Society of Jesus might not have external members in the strict sense of the term, one hostile commentator on its Constitutions observed, but, thanks to a papal bull of 1549 which enabled it to enforce the return to its ranks of those who had left them, it was able, 'either by the chance of an unjust dismissal', or by the premeditated plan of a simulated or limited dismissal', to place in the world agents devoted to its cause and obliged to come under full Jesuit discipline when required.[34]

A *jésuite de robe courte*, then, might be anything from a humble *congréganiste* to a fully trained Jesuit in mufti. On the whole, however, whereas the typical *congréganiste* was usually thought of by anti-jesuits as a servant (sometimes even an unwitting one) rather than an actual member of the Society of Jesus, it was usual to imagine the *jésuite de robe courte* as a true Jesuit, distinguished from other members of the order only by his outward appearance and his clandestine role in the Jesuit design. Some anti-jesuits saw the *robe courte* as a sixth category of Jesuit, additional to the recognized ones of professed member, spiritual coadjutor, temporal coadjutor, scholastic, and novice.[35] When *jésuites de robe courte* were seen as men of high social rank, they were occasionally seen as honorary novices.[36] A more usual identification was with the temporal coadjutors (who were indeed Jesuit personnel neither in nor destined for holy orders, but whose domestic functions in Jesuit houses were more prosaic than those attributed to the *jésuites de robe courte*); readers of Léo Taxil's scurrilous fictions, on the other hand, would find the *robe courte* reserved for affiliates of social standing,

---

[33] Michon, *Le Jésuite*, i. 273–4. A Jesuit character in the novel remarks of one such 'affiliate': 'Many of his fellow diplomats were members of our *congrégations*, but only the *comte* was attached to our Order by the bonds of affiliation' (ibid. 362).

[34] *Les Constitutions des jésuites*, 489–92. It was on such grounds that Guettée mistrusted the liberal stance of the Italian ex-Jesuit Passaglia (*Observateur catholique*), 15: 250, 672; 17: 239–40).

[35] See e.g. Boucher, *Histoire dramatique et pittoresque*, i. 126.

[36] See e.g. Larousse (ed.), *Grand Dictionnaire universel*, ix. 958.

and temporal coadjutors depicted as a bunch of lower-class spies and thugs.[37]

JESUIT AFFILIATION AND SOCIETY

Whatever the supposed relationship between *congréganistes* and *jésuites de robe courte*, the mythology and speculation surrounding them powerfully articulated a sense of social unease, a trembling at the thought of a society either paralysed or destabilized by the proliferation in its midst of alien agents disguised as ordinary citizens. Such agents, it was feared, might be found anywhere, 'in the *bagne* of Toulon and the band of Vidocq, as in the council of ministers'.[38] Estimates of their numbers on French soil varied. 'There are in reality millions of Jesuits', declared Bouis in 1870; including all the clergy and all who went to confession or to clerical schools, he found 'a people of six million souls' sheltering under the robe of Jesuitism.[39] This, and the twenty-five million whom a writer a few years previously had considered to be 'placed under the passive obedience of the sectaries of Loyola',[40] were obviously not intended as estimates of the number bound to the Jesuits by formal ties of initiation or affiliation. Figures for this group, however, still sometimes ran to tens or hundreds of thousands. Silvy, in 1828, believed the Jesuits could count on '500,000 arms'. Half a century later Taxil estimated the number of 'coadjutors and

---

[37] The identification with temporal coadjutors (sometimes called *coadjuteurs laïques*) is clearly stated in Scheffer, *Précis de l'histoire générale*, 11–12 (though the term *jésuites de robe courte* is not used); see also e.g. *Instructions secrètes des jésuites*, (1845), pp. xxii, xxix. Taxil's use of the terms is explained on pp. 342–3 of his *Les Amours secrètes*. His temporal coadjutors make their most memorable appearance on p. 1162: 'The man came closer. He was wearing the Jesuit soutane. "You did well to accept, Giovanni", continued this personage, with an ironic intonation; "if you had definitely refused, my assistants would have taken charge of you; a stone would have been tied to your neck, and the waters of Lake Albano would have closed for ever over your body." Nicolo looked up. "You don't believe me?" the individual went on. He put a whistle to his lips, on which he blew two short and piercing notes. At the same moment, numerous shapes emerged from the shadows and approached. "They are our temporal coadjutors", said the Jesuit; "there are fifteen of them there, strong, skilful and loyal. You are being treated as a dangerous man, Giovanni; you should be flattered." '
[38] Guillaume, *1er pamphlet*, 3–4. (It was in the Toulon *bagne* that the fictional Innocent Visatout recruited Jesuit affiliates in Santo-Domingo, *Les Jésuites en action*, 114–16.)
[39] Bouis, *Calottes et soutanes*, 10, 286–8.
[40] *La Voix du peuple est la voix de Dieu*, 83.

other affiliates through the Third Order' at 50,000 and Aurélien Scholl wrote of '8,000 magistrates and 500,000 Jesuits of the civil order' ready to obey the General's commands. In the end, though, most anti-jesuits would have agreed with abbé Michaud that the number of Jesuit agents was 'absolutely incalculable'.[41]

The fear of a proliferation of Jesuit affiliates can be examined from two angles. On the one hand, the affiliate was a person lost by society through his recruitment; on the other, he was a threat to society through his action. The fear of social take-over went hand in hand, or back to back, with that of betrayal. In the first case, the emphasis was mainly, though not entirely, on the *congrégations*. The key to Jesuit recruitment was the ability to dispense, and progressively to monopolize, patronage in all its forms: careers, lucrative contracts, inside information, good marriages.[42] The polemics of the 1820s established the image of a society in which employment and promotion at all levels were determined by membership of Jesuitical associations. The negative side of the monopoly was equally important. If the Congrégation was, in Santo-Domingo's phrase, 'an insurance company against dismissal',[43] the plight of those who failed to join was pitiable: 'The poor *père de famille* is placed between shame and hunger; he must live on the one or die of the other.'[44] Forty years later, to judge by an anonymous pamphlet, the choice facing the ordinary Frenchmen was as simple: if he frequented 'the anti-religious establishments and *congrégations* of the disciples of *Loyola*', whatever his profession, his business would flourish; if he scorned them, his work, his clientele, his prospects, and his place in public esteem would fall away.[45] The long arm of the Société de Saint Vincent-de-Paul, in Cayla's view, could guarantee advancement in the civil service, the judiciary, or the military.[46]

Anti-jesuits professed themselves terrified not just by the monopolistic force with which the Jesuits allegedly bullied human

---

[41] [L. Silvy], *Les Jésuites ennemis de l'ordre social, de la morale et de la religion, par leur probabilisme, leur doctrine régicide et leur conduite dans les missions et leur système de calomnie* (Paris, 1828), 61; L. Taxil, *C'est nous qui fouettons ces vieux polissons!* (Paris, 1879), 237; Scholl in *L'Événement*, 21 Mar. 1879; Michaud, *Le Mouvement contemporain*, 135.

[42] On Jesuit marriage-broking, see e.g. Génin, *Les Jésuites et l'Université*, 45; Wallon, *Jésus et les jésuites*, 143.   [43] Santo-Domingo, *Les Jésuites en action*, 2.

[44] Santo-Domingo, *Plaidoirie*, 27.

[45] *La Voix du peuple est la voix de Dieu*, 92.

[46] Cayla, *Ces bons messieurs*, 245.

self-interest, but by the social breadth of their designs; their network of *congrégations* threatened to enrol the whole of society, class by class. It was Cayla who best conveyed this vision of a society pre-packaged for Jesuit consumption:

The Society of Saint Vincent-de-Paul, through its affiliations, its auxiliaries, its vassals, reigns and governs from the palace to the garret, from the château to the poor and humble cottage! The founders and the continuers of the *œuvre* hold everything in their nets.

They hold the aristocracy by the allurement of honours, of fortunes, and of marriages in prospect.

They hold the bourgeoisie by the same tactic, which the Jesuits employed formerly.

They hold the people by promises of well-being which they know are unfulfillable. They enrol the workers and their families.[47]

Wallon concluded his extensive catalogue of allegedly Jesuitical organizations with a study of an obscure (and unsuccessful) Académie Unitaire, because it seemed to him to embody the essence of the Jesuit spirit of domination which had inspired the spread of the *cercles catholiques d'ouvriers*. Its aims, he maintained, revealed 'the scheme of corrupting or captivating every class', and amounted to a 'vast plan for the enrolling of European society'.[48]

To envisage the Jesuit affiliate from the second angle—no longer as a Jesuit victim, but as a Jesuit agent—is to connect once again with the themes of espionage and of betrayal of trust already raised in connection with the Jesuit confessor. An occult network of Jesuit obedience, anti-jesuits believed, threatened to subvert the system of legitimate loyalties, both political and social, on which State and society depended. The threat to the State was summarized by the ex-*député* Duvergier de Hauranne in 1826. By means of a double organization of influential 'affiliates' and *congréganiste* 'demi-affiliates', he claimed,

an innumerable quantity of subjects may be removed from the obedience due to the prince and pass under the absolute domination of a foreign monk . . . The councils of the prince, the court, the law courts, the clergy, the *corps constitués*, and the ranks of all the citizens may be filled with affiliates unknown both to the prince and to the public, all acting in accord

---

[47] Ibid. 311.   [48] Wallon, *Un collège de jésuites*, 216, 228.

with secret orders, and exerting themselves to secure the acceptance of maxims contrary to the interests of the monarch and of the State.[49]

The threat to the private citizen could seem equally alarming. The *jésuite de robe courte*, as Auguste Arnould pointed out, could be anyone: 'He is your friend, he is your brother, he is your servant.'[50]

The generalized apprehension engendered by a sense of the invisibility (and a presumption of the ubiquity) of Jesuit agents sometimes crystallized around specific points: the possibility and the dangerousness of Jesuit affiliates in certain social or professional positions seemed to arouse particular anxiety. The selection of these points of concern might on occasion reflect the real activity of Catholic *œuvres* in specific areas of society (among soldiers for example). It could also, however, reflect anti-jesuits' own sensitivities, both to possible chinks in the armour of State, society, and the individual (where would a cunning enemy, bent on undoing or conquering all three, take care to have its agents?), and to the social geography of trust (in what areas were the State, society, and the individual most dependent on personal or professional fidelity, and hence most vulnerable to betrayal?). Soldiers, writers, doctors, and servants were four groups on which attention sometimes focused.

The Jesuitical soldier underwent an evolution. Under the Restoration, when the army was widely associated with Napoleonic triumphs and with sentiments antipathetic to the ruling (supposedly 'Jesuitical') power, what was feared was not an unholy alliance between Jesuitism and militarism, but a sapping of martial vigour through Jesuit *congrégations*. Marcet mocked the effeminacy of the *congréganiste* military, whose 'softened skulls' and 'perfumed hair' could scarcely tolerate the weight of their gilded helmets, and whose 'pale and delicate hands' were too weak to hold their shining swords, but who found no difficulty in bearing 'the yoke of servitude'.[51] Later in the century, though the inefficiency of Jesuitical soldiers remained an occasional theme (recurring in 1870, for example), the political co-ordinates were different. The influx of Jesuit pupils into the military *grandes écoles* and the legitimism (both real and imagined) of Jesuit-educated officers led anti-jesuits in the 1860s and 1870s to focus primarily on the dangers of military

---

[49] J.-M. Duvergier de Hauranne, *De l'ordre légal en France, et des abus d'autorité*, 2 vols. (Paris, 1826–8), i. 199.

[50] Arnould, *Les Jésuites*, vol. i, p. xi.   [51] Marcet, *Nouveau Mémoire*, 112.

disunity and disloyalty.[52] The chapter on this subject in Wallon's
Un collège de jésuites (published in 1880) already gives an outline of
the thesis of Jesuitico-military conspiracy that would become so
pronounced a feature of Dreyfusard polemics at the end of the
century. The Jesuits' efforts to control the army (through *congrégations*, education, and military chaplains) were undermining military discipline and causing 'disaggregation' and 'denationalization'
in military circles, Wallon argued. The order sought to use the
army for ultra-clerical and ultra-monarchist purposes, and even to
engineer a civil war; so long as it was allowed to train the majority
(according to Wallon) of French officers, there would be 'neither
liberty nor security for anyone'.[53]

If Jesuitical soldiers betrayed the nation, Jesuitical writers betrayed a public which trusted in freedom of the press and the
status of the author as a free and independent agent. The readiness
of many anti-jesuits to see the polemics of their opponents as those
of puppets parroting inspirations from a Jesuit source suggests the
limits of their own ability to accept the expression of discordant
opinions as a necessary effect of freedom. Leone was one who
developed this theme on a European scale, citing de Maistre,
Goerres, and Pusey among the more prominent Jesuitical writers;
Génin and others perfected its application to France.[54] Wallon, in
his survey of Jesuitical *congrégations*, conceded that no proper *congrégation* of men of letters had yet been established, but denounced Le
Play's Union de la Paix Sociale as an attempt to found one.[55]

Through the doctor (and his frequent partner, the lawyer), the
Jesuits could close in on families and individuals. Michelet warned
of the dangers posed by Jesuit seduction of medical and legal
students: 'Won over today, tomorrow they will deliver the whole
of society, as doctors the secret of families, as notaries that of
fortunes, as prosecutors [*parquet*] impunity.'[56] Because of their
intimate knowledge of and access to their clients, doctors were
precious and flexible auxiliaries. They could ensure that the Jesuits
were called to the sick-beds and death-beds of the rich, as the
Monita secreta (chapter 9, clause 14) prescribed. Their well-timed

[52] See e.g. Sauvestre, *Les Congrégations religieuses*, 118–19.
[53] Wallon, *Un collège de jésuites*, 121–36.
[54] Leone, *Conjuration des jésuites*, 187–297; Génin, *Les Jésuites et l'Université*, *passim*.
[55] Wallon, *Un collège de jésuites*, 207–15.   [56] Michelet, *Des jésuites*, 29.

cures could provide 'a sure means of controlling and seducing women and feeble minds' (a fact which Marcet claimed was appreciated by 'the two pious doctors of Montrouge', Fiseau and Récamier[57]). Wicked doctors made frequent appearances in anti-jesuit fiction. Some of them—Taxil's Dr Testasetta, for instance —were little more than professional poisoners.[58] Others, however, had subtler tricks up their sleeves; the serviceable Dr Baleinier, in *Le Juif errant*, for example, made his patients better when they were docile to Jesuit wishes, and gently sickened them when they were not; he also obliged his masters by getting a young heiress committed to a madhouse.[59] At least one real doctor in 1844 found Sue's fictions interfering with his practice; his patients (according to a letter from a colleague to the *Gazette des hôpitaux*) had taken to calling him Rodin and Baleinier, and one of them had written to him as follows:

Monsieur, to be a Jesuit is not everything. One must also be adroit. The clumsiness with which you tried to surround me with people of your own kind quickly showed me with whom I was dealing. I detest Rodins *en robe courte* and with diplomas [*en diplôme*]. Eugène Sue teaches us the ways to know them and to unmask them.[60]

Their power as healers and diagnosers, and their intimate involvement with clients, may possibly, in the nineteenth century, have enabled doctors to inherit some of the prestige and moral authority traditionally enjoyed by the priest; anti-jesuit literature provides reminders that, if so, they inherited with it some of the priest's vulnerability to charges of abusing confidence, exploiting ignorance, and infringing privacy.[61]

A more transparent form of social uneasiness was involved in anxieties about Jesuit corruption of servants. Like Jesuitical doctors, servant-spies were mentioned in the *Monita secreta* (chapter 1, clause 5, and chapter 6, clause 4) and appeared frequently in anti-jesuit novels, where they were divided into rascals, dupes, and

[57] Marcet, *Mémoires d'un jeune jésuite*, 254–5.
[58] Taxil, *Les Amours secrètes*, esp. 158, 1847. Other Jesuitical doctors included Grisart in A. Dumas, *Le Vicomte de Bragelonne*, 6 vols. (Paris, 1851) and Déteilh in Michon, *Le Maudit*.   [59] Sue, *Le Juif errant*, ii. 28–32 and *passim*.
[60] *Gazette des hôpitaux*, 19 Nov. 1844 (quoted in Burnichon, *La Compagnie de Jésus en France*, ii. 521).
[61] For a similar argument, see T. Zeldin, *France 1848–1945*, 2 vols. (Oxford, 1973–7), vol. i, ch. 2, esp. 30, 42.

victims of Jesuit blackmail.[62] Outside fiction, Stendhal claimed in 1826 that scarcely a respectable man in France had not detected attempts to suborn his servants for purposes of Jesuitical espionage; other writers also referred to this aspect of the servant problem.[63] Under the July Monarchy, suspicion was fuelled by the creation, at Lyons, of a *congrégation* for servants, the *Blandines*.[64] The Jesuits, wrote Casimir Guillaume, had a use for every servant, from the humblest scullion to the craftiest lady's maid, 'who betrays her mistress, opens her letters, and makes assignations with her master to divide him from his wife'.[65]

These were some of the variations on the theme of betrayal that anti-jesuit literature produced. Belief in a secret network of Jesuit agents dramatized the riskiness of trust, and magnified the possibilities of hidden danger in the social world. It blended the insecurities of the private citizen with the supposed vulnerability of State and society to hostile conspiracy, making a vigilant suspiciousness of others seem a public as well as a private duty. It is when dealing with the theme of lay affiliation that the term 'paranoia' seems most applicable to the anti-jesuit mentality. Yet a reservation is in order. In practice, few anti-jesuits seem to have allowed the fear of encountering *jésuites de robe courte* to spoil their social lives. Alertness to the probable role of Jesuit affiliates showed itself more usually in heightened intransigence and dismissive contempt for opponents than in mistrust of friends. It might be proclaimed that the Jesuits had affiliates among Jews, Protestants, and atheists,[66] but in practice it was generally Catholics and reactionaries who were denounced.

---

[62] Representative examples include Florine and Jocrisse in Sue, *Le Juif errant*, and Madelette in Michon, *Le Maudit*; see also the Jesuit use of servants in Michon, *Le Jésuite*, ii. 464, and Durantin, *Un élève des jésuites*, 285.

[63] Stendhal, *New Monthly Magazine*, 17: 303 (Oct. 1826); also e.g. Duvergier de Hauranne, *De l'ordre légal*, i. 206.

[64] *Journal de la liberté religieuse*, 1: 375; Michelet, *Du prêtre*, 264–5.

[65] Guillaume, *1er pamphlet*, 4.

[66] On Jesuit affiliates outwardly professing the Jewish or Protestant faith (the latter including Guizot), see Raspail, *Nouvelles Études*, 212–13; also, on Protestants, Dairnvaell, *Code des jésuites*, 16. [L.-J. Gohier], *Un mot sur le procès intenté par la famille La Chalotais, contre le journal l'Étoile* (Paris, 1826), 22–3 n., claimed that the astronomer Lalande had revealed in conversation that he was a 'jésuite de robe courte': ' "What!" I said, "*An atheist and a Jesuit!*" Lalande smiled. He told me that *all the big cheeses* [*grands colliers*] *of the order* (this was his expression), who alone knew the aim which the society set itself, were atheists like himself.'

Belief in secret Jesuit affiliates helped, in fact, to plug the gaps between visible Jesuit actions in anti-jesuit accounts both of history and of current affairs. 'In all the crimes which we have indicated,' observed Bouis, after attributing a string of past misdeeds to the Jesuits, 'we have never been able to perceive the actual arm of the Society.'[67] Far from weakening his case, he implied, this circumstance merely showed how successfully the Jesuits had delegated compromising actions to their accomplices. A writer in the *Observateur catholique* (probably Guettée) made the point, when dealing with the Ligue's resistance to Henri IV: 'The Jesuits showed themselves much less than several monks, *curés* of Paris; their plan is always to hide themselves behind their affiliates, whom they thrust forward and whom they compromise. They had, in their own persons, no influence on the people of Paris; but they made use of a few affiliates to fanaticize the vilest populace.'[68]

Certainly, as far as anti-jesuits were concerned, anyone benighted enough to approve of the Society of Jesus was likely to be one of its affiliates. In 1826, when *conseils généraux* in the *départements* voted motions favouring the Jesuits, *Le Constitutionnel* scoffed knowingly: 'What a great surprise that twenty people, among whom are perhaps fifteen *jésuites de robe courte*, make vows for the triumph of the Company of Jesus!'[69] When Guettée wrote that, in composing his *Histoire des jésuites*, he had 'thought it a duty to reject as apocryphal all the good that the Jesuits have attributed to themselves or that they have had their affiliates attribute to them',[70] he meant that he had rejected or ignored just about every favourable comment on the Jesuits ever made. In the vilification which he and his book predictably encountered in Ultramontane circles, he saw a display of the effectiveness of the network of Jesuitical *congrégations* as a vehicle for organized denigration:

From a central establishment the watchword goes out; from the secondary establishments, the word is given to the *congrégations*, which almost all take their orders from [*dépendent de*] the Company; from the *congrégations* the watchword passes to the associations, and, through them, to all the affiliates, to all the *dévots* and *dévotes*. Calumny thus established defies all refutations.[71]

---

[67] Bouis, *Calottes et soutanes*, 125–8.

[68] *Observateur catholique*, 9: 206 n. Much material probably by Guettée, including this, was attributed in the journal to Martial Parent-Duchâtelet.

[69] *Constitutionnel*, 1 Oct. 1826.   [70] Guettée, *Histoire des jésuites*, iii. 460.

[71] Guettée, *Souvenirs*, 276.

The mythology of affiliation greatly extended the scope of anti-jesuit conspiracy theory. It also encouraged scepticism about the efficacy of anti-jesuit measures. The sternest repression of the *robe longue* might leave the *robe courte* untouched. 'No one is deceived by this departure,' Arnould told the dispersing Jesuits in 1845. 'The least clear-sighted and the most credulous are beginning to recognize your allies under their ministerial livery, under their lawyer's gowns, under their cloaks of *pairs de France!*' In the elusiveness of *jésuites de robe courte* lay 'the secret of the endurance of the order, raising itself continually from its ruins'.[72]

[72] Arnould, *Les Jésuites*, ii. 360; p. xi.

8

The Confessor and the School

THE two faces of Jesuitical affiliation—the *congrégation* and the *robe courte*—stood for two different subversive strategies: on the one hand, the creation of an alternative framework of social organiza-tion, into which individuals were removed (though not always ostensibly) from their place in the conventional framework of social relations; on the other, a subtle and imperceptible penetration and perversion of the conventional system itself. This duality in alleged Jesuit strategy can be developed further, taking the family as an initial focus.

The family, as far as the great majority of anti-jesuits were concerned, was the basic and universal unit of legitimate social organization. Its claims to the solidarity and affections of its mem-bers were natural, and (when properly understood) harmonious with those of the State, and its role in the rearing of children was a crucial, though unofficial, part of society's educational system. The State had an interest in the welfare and stability of families, so long as families recognized the legitimate claims of the State, and their own partnership with it in the production of sturdy citizens, well adapted to the needs of the modern world. It followed that any group determined to dominate society would have either to control the family or to undermine it; perhaps both, since families could often not be controlled unless their cohesion was first undermined.

The Jesuits, therefore, were taken to be interested in the family not simply as a unit to be despoiled of its wealth, but as an obstacle to, and potential vehicle for, their power over society. Their sup-posed assault on it took two co-ordinated forms. On the one hand, the confessor worked by penetration, engaging in an intimate con-test for influence within the family itself. On the other, the Jesuit school proceeded by circumvention or sequestration, removing children from the family for lengthy periods, during which, far from preparing them for responsible citizenship, it worked either to alienate them from their families, or to imbue them with poisonous doctrines and attitudes to carry back to the domestic hearth, and out into the wider world.

THE CONFESSOR AND THE FAMILY

To many a Jesuit of fact as well as of fiction, if anti-jesuits were to be believed, might the charge directed at the Jesuit villain of *Le Tartufe moderne* have been addressed: 'Behold a family so tenderly united before it knew you, and whose ties you alone have broken, whose happiness in no longer possible.'[1] Many a family, it seemed, would have done well to heed the advice offered it by the abbé de Pradt: 'close your doors to the Jesuits, or renounce the hope of *peace*.'[2] For the Jesuits knew, in a double sense, how to undo a family; if given the chance, Salverte implied, they 'might secretly deprive the wife of the first affection of the husband, and the husband of the affectionate subordination of the wife; might separate—in their sentiments of obedience, of love, of condescension, of mutual defence—children, parents, friends, fellow-citizens'.[3] Their ways of doing this were known, and revolved around the institution of confession.

In this dimension of its attack on the confessor, anti-jesuit literature merges into a broader anticlerical tradition. Though the Jesuits were the presumed originators of the methods of *direction de conscience* (confession in its most developed and active form), which inspired much of the criticism, and though they were assumed, characteristically, to employ these methods with especial cunning and peculiarly vicious intent, little was said about Jesuit confessors (in this respect, though not in all others) that was not also said, with roughly equal vehemence, about confessors in general. Indeed no discussion of this theme, from the 1840s onwards, can escape the spell of Michelet's *Du prêtre, de la femme, de la famille*, a work whose title reveals its general anticlerical concerns. Even before that, a work like Paul-Louis Courier's second *Réponse aux anonymes* (a sensationalistic attack on confession and clerical celibacy inspired by the case of the clerical sex-murderer Mingrat) may have done more to shape the more salacious strand of anti-jesuit comment

[1] Mortonval, *Le Tartufe moderne*, iii. 215.
[2] De Pradt, *Du jésuitisme ancien et moderne*, 293.
[3] *AP*, CD 21 June 1828 (annexe), 239.

about confessors and their female penitents than any specifically anti-jesuit text.

For Michelet and others, half the key to the confessor's purchase on the family lay in the access his confidential position gave him to its innermost secrets. It could do so, however, only because the family was so arranged as to allow it. Few anti-jesuits, in the nineteenth century, had much difficulty in pinpointing the point of leverage at which Jesuit efforts were directed, and through which the family might be prised first open, and then apart. The Jesuits' recent successes, declared Michelet in 1843, owed much to 'a mysterious hand': 'That which, well directed, from the first day of the world, has submissively performed the miracles of cunning. A feeble hand, which nothing resists, the hand of woman. The Jesuits have employed the instrument of which Saint Jerome speaks: "Poor little women, all covered in sins!" '[4] Like Satan, as an anonymous writer later remarked, the Jesuits sought to conquer the world 'through woman seduced and led astray [*détournée*]'.[5]

Social reasons might be adduced in partial explanation of women's vulnerability to Jesuit seduction. The modern separation of masculine work from family life might be part of the problem: too often, Michelet argued, wives were left in domestic boredom, isolated from the great world of ideas and progress in which their husbands moved, and open to the excitement of priestly influence.[6] Education was also to blame. Women were raised 'by our enemies, by the enemies of the Revolution and the future'.[7] About this, of course, something could be done. The Restoration writer Isidore Lebrun had urged men to fight Jesuitism by providing 'solid and extensive instruction' for 'this sex whose influence is deadly if it is given up to error'.[8] Many later anti-jesuits would no doubt have shared Jules Ferry's view, expressed in a famous speech in 1870, that 'equality of education' between the sexes would mean 'unity reconstituted in the family'.[9]

A more basic contempt for the female sex, however, sometimes shone through. The shameless wife in Raban's *La Femme jésuite*,

[4] Michelet, *Des jésuites*, 25.
[5] *Les Jésuites et la propriété: Lettre grenobloise aux conservateurs* (Grenoble, 1880), 6.
[6] Michelet, *Du prêtre*, 32–3 (preface to 3rd edn.), 339.
[7] Ibid. 320.   [8] I. Lebrun, *Du sacrilège et des jésuites* (Paris, 1825), 51.
[9] J. Ferry, *Discours et opinions*, ed. J. Robiquet, 7 vols. (Paris, 1893–8), i. 304–5 (speech at Salle Molière, 10 Apr. 1870).

having consorted endlessly with her Jesuit confessor, neglected her child, and dishonoured her husband—acted, in fact, for all the world 'as if she had been the sole mistress of her actions'—finally expires in convulsive rage after being forcibly and publicly restrained by her justly outraged spouse.[10] The ill-controlled misogyny of such a text, however, was less typical and less influential than Michelet's belittling condescension:

One shows a child an apple to make it come to one. Well, women have been shown pretty little feminine devotions, toy saints invented yesterday; a little idolatrous world has been arranged for them ... These new fashions were necessary to win women over. Whoever wishes to catch them, must be indulgent of little weaknesses, of little tricks [*petit manège*], often also of the taste for falsehood.[11]

The Jesuits played, anti-jesuits believed, on women's helpless subjection to the senses, their unstable imagination, their liability to superstitious terror. The very circumstances of the confessional —the shadowy and deserted church, the physical closeness, the breathless whispering of intimate secrets—seemed, to readers of Courier and Michelet, to breathe a latent sexuality fit to unbalance the feminine imagination.[12] It was scarcely surprising, then, that women allowed themselves to be mesmerized by their confessors. For Michelet, who gave the most influential account of 'this shadowy art ... of surprising the will, of fascinating it, of sending it to sleep, of annihilating it'[13] (and who found this technique most highly developed in Jesuitical methods of *direction de conscience*), the unfolding sequence by which the priest took possession of a woman's thoughts, her spirit, her soul, even perhaps her body, was implicit in her first acceptance of his authority to hear and judge her thoughts: 'The master of the thoughts is the one to whom the person belongs. The priest holds the soul, from the moment he has the dangerous pledge of the first secrets, and he will hold it more and more.'[14]

In accounts like Michelet's, once the priest held the wife (and perhaps the daughter and female servants), the family itself would

---

[10] L.-F. Raban, *La Femme jésuite: Histoire véritable, écrite par une victime du jésuitisme* (Paris, 1826), quotation on p. 27.

[11] Michelet, *Des jésuites*, 25–6 (preface to 3rd edn.).

[12] For the classic evocation, see P.-L. Courier, *Œuvres complètes*, Pléiade edn. (Paris, 1851), 160–1 (from his second *Réponse aux anonymes*).

[13] Michelet, *Du prêtre*, 51.   [14] Ibid. 259.

begin to crumble into his hands. As confessor, then maybe as *directeur*, he would extend his knowledge and control into each area of domestic life, as Génin (in a passage published the year before Michelet's book) made clear:

The *directeur* follows the wife and mother incessantly; he sits at her hearth, presides over everything, dominates and regulates everything, domestic economy and the education of the children. The husband imagines himself in private with his wife: he is wrong: the *directeur* is present as a third party. The *directeur*'s thoughts reach into the bedroom, into the alcove, slide into the bed between husband and wife and there watch and supervise the most secret privileges of wedlock.[15]

Michelet eloquently evoked the plight of the *père de famille*, who found his home no longer a haven of peace and privacy, whose every word (even in his sleep) was reported by his wife or servants, and who sat at his own table isolated and confronted by the sullen opposition of his womenfolk. Domestic tranquillity was replaced by the sulking and nagging of a wife urged on by her *directeur* to secure a clerical education for her children: 'Murmuring by the fireside, gloom at the table, often neither opening her mouth to speak, nor to eat; then at bedtime, the inevitable repetition of the lesson she has learnt, and even on the pillow—The same sound of the same bell, over and over again—who could stand it? What can he do? Yield or go mad!'[16]

Michelet depicted the conflict between priest and *père de famille* as, for the latter, a crisis both of property and of virility. His patriarchalism was intensely proprietorial in tone:

It is necessary that this hearth be truly our hearth, and this table our table, and that we do not find, in place of repose at home [*chez nous*], the old dispute which is finished both in science and in society [*le monde*], that our wife or our child do not tell us on the pillow a lesson they have learnt and the words of another man.[17]

To be the legitimate proprietor of the social world of one's own family was to be its rightful mentor; the rearing of children was mother's work, but to be performed 'under the direction of the father', thus realizing 'the true idea of the family': 'to be an initiation of the child by the woman, and of the woman by the man.'[18]

[15] Génin, *Les Jésuites et l'Université*, 457. [16] Michelet, *Du prêtre*, 320–2.
[17] Ibid. 51. [18] Ibid. 340–1.

The priest who set himself up as mentor of another man's wife was thus a spiritual adulterer, a usurper, a thief. His tug-of-war with the *père de famille* produced a division of the contested property between 'the two husbands, for henceforward there will be two of them, the soul to one, to the other the body'. As the original husband quickly discovered, however, the division was illusory, for to hold the body without the soul was to hold it only on sufferance. His humiliation, as Michelet described it, derived from continuing contact with his lost property, from a sense of living on the disdainful charity of the man who had cheated him: 'A humiliating thing, to obtain nothing of what was once yours except under authorization and by indulgence, to be observed, followed in the most intimate of intimacies by an invisible witness who regulates you and allots you your share.'[19] The crisis of virility was equally acute. In Michelet's somewhat schematic view of gender relations, men were by nature strong and women ('the feeble hand') were weak creatures who 'willingly follow the strong'. The priest was a hermaphroditic figure, 'born man and strong, but who is willing to make himself weak, to resemble woman'. The natural advantage which the husband ought to have enjoyed over him was nullified, however, because the priest had found, in the technique of *direction de conscience*, 'an art for lending strength to the weak'.[20]

The solution of the crisis, both of property and of virility, was for men to realize the necessity of making the family a place of initiation into the modern world. Providing he was patient, the husband had the opportunity, especially at the outset of marriage, 'truly to acquire the woman, to remove her from alien influence, and to assure himself of her for ever', by introducing her to his own ideas and endeavours.[21] 'The day your people [*les vôtres*] perceive in you the man of the future and of noble will, the family will be rallied. The woman will follow you everywhere if she can say to herself: "I am the wife of the strong man".'[22] A true marriage, based on the exchange of masculine intellectual leadership for feminine spiritual solace, would stand immune to priestly meddling. Few anti-jesuits were as determined as Michelet to spell out this remedy (or any other one, short of the Jesuits' expulsion) for the domestic crisis, but many made his account of family

---

[19] Ibid. 259–60. [20] Ibid. 12 (preface to 3rd edn.), 51.
[21] Ibid. 328. [22] Ibid. 32 (preface to 3rd edn.).

breakdown their own.[23] The tension between Michelet's ideal
vision of the domestic hearth as a haven of peace and refuge for the
male from the strain of the public world,[24] and his nightmare of it
as a place of danger and betrayal, where the warrior of modernity
was caught, isolated, unmanned, and delivered by his womenfolk
to the enemy who could never vanquish him in open fight, was a
powerful one. Few anti-jesuits had Michelet's powers of feverish
expression, or experienced their insecurities with such vividness,
but many projected a similar sense of maleness under threat. Rue-
ful admissions of the instrumental power of feminine weakness
abound: 'Whoever has the women is sure to have the men in the
end'; 'the good Fathers know too well that it is through the women
that one enslaves the men'; 'the master of the woman is the master
of the man'.[25] *Le Siècle*, in 1847, made the striking claim that
women were being used to hold 'the whole masculine part of the
population' in 'a state of siege and blockade'.[26] In each of these
cases, of course, the syntax is revelatory: all men (or men in
general) were threatened, but the enemies were not women themselves, but their Jesuit controllers. In accounts of the Jesuits'
manœuvres against the family, tensions between the sexes were
both dramatized and (since the insecurities of patriarchy were
converted into those of modernity) defused. The Jesuits, in the
process, became all the more frightening.

THE JESUIT SCHOOL

In Michelet's account, a crucial moment in the priestly conquest of
the family arrived when the *père de famille* gave way on the question
of education. Once his son was at the *petit séminaire* and his daughter at the convent school, where the nuns would teach her to
contradict her father, further resistance would be in vain.[27] In the

---

[23] Dionys Ordinaire is a good example; see nos. 12 and 13 of his *Lettres aux
jésuites* (Tours, 1883). Ordinaire shared Michelet's proprietorial attitude: the young
woman could be saved only if her husband 'envelops his wife in a jealous and
exclusive protection, if he desires her whole, body and spirit, if he allows no
division' (p. 87).　　　　　　　　　　　　　　　[24] Michelet, *Du prêtre*, 332.
[25] Michelet, *Des jésuites*, 27; Mortonval, *Le Tartufe moderne*, i. 33; Bert, *La Morale
des jésuites*, p. xxxii.
[26] *Siècle*, 17 Dec. 1847 (quoted in Leone, *Conjuration des jésuites*, p. xiii).
[27] Michelet, *Du prêtre*, 321–3.

eyes of anti-jesuits, the work of the Jesuit school complemented
that of the confessor and decisively extended it, from generation to
generation, and from the female to the male sex. Once the Jesuits
had the child, they would not let him go. The more lurid sort of
anti-jesuit literature meant this literally. Sauvestre printed extensive
details of the Anna-Bella Kohrsch affair (1857–60), in which a
Jesuit was among those accused of converting a Belgian Lutheran
girl against her family's wishes, persuading her to leave her guardian, and then hiding her away from him in a succession of Belgian
and French convents.[28] Neither the Kohrsch case nor the similar
one of Madeleine Garay (1844–5)[29] involved Jesuit schools, but
Casimir Bouis drew on the fund of alarmism to which they contributed, suggesting that parents trying to get their child back from
a Jesuit school might perhaps recover him only as a skeleton
eventually retrieved by the police.[30] Most attacks on Jesuit schools
stopped short of this sort of sensationalistic fantasy, but told how
Jesuit pupils were encouraged to distance themselves from their
families, to avoid going home during holidays, to transfer affection
from parents to teachers. Sauvestre, in an imagined row with his
wife over whether to send their son to a Jesuit school, demanded to
know: 'Have the Jesuits replaced the family then?'[31]

In separating the child from the family, the first legitimate focus
for his affections, the Jesuits, it was argued, did nothing to prepare
him for the service of the second, the nation. For one thing, the
purpose of their schools was the sectarian one of recruitment: 'they
do not teach in order to instruct, to develop the judgement, to
make citizens and men; they teach in order to create adherents
[*adeptes*], and, through these adherents, to slide into the direction
of public affairs', wrote Castagnary.[32] Jesuit *collèges*, according to an
earlier writer, were merely 'nurseries of Jesuits'; one could never be
sure that the child who entered one would not emerge as a member
of the Society of Jesus.[33] Attention and favour were lavished on
pupils thought likely to be an asset to the order, either as regular
members or as *jésuites de robe courte*; the production of good citizens

---

[28] Sauvestre, *Les Congrégations religieuses*, 157–8, 220–36. Sauvestre harped
repeatedly on these themes of sequestration and denial of parental rights: see e.g.
his *Lettres de province* (letters 11 and 12) and an article in *L'Opinion nationale*, 24 Dec.
1868.
[29] See *Débats*, 5 July 1845.   [30] Bouis, *Calottes et soutanes*, 157–8.
[31] C. Sauvestre, *Les Jésuites peints par eux-mêmes* (Paris, 1878), 15–16.
[32] Castagnary, *Les Jésuites*, 90–1.   [33] *Les Constitutions des jésuites*, 434.

was beside, or against, the point. But even if the Jesuits had had a
more public-spirited purpose in mind, anti-jesuits felt, they could
not have achieved it. They could contribute nothing to national
education, the *sénateur* Foucher de Careil argued during the debate
on the Ferry bill, because they were fundamentally at odds with the
three developments on which such education must be based: the
scientific renovation based on the experimental method, the movement for practical liberty and equality derived from 1789, and the
philosophes' call for an 'aesthetic education of humanity' in which
arts, sciences, and humanity would be harmoniously intertwined.[34]
Not all nineteenth-century anti-jesuits would have accepted in full
Foucher's Republican view of the bases of national education, but
(under Restoration, July Monarchy, Empire, and Republic alike)
there was agreement among them that once the Jesuits were
allowed to teach, national disunity could only follow. As one
wrote in 1827, 'two generations are raised side by side, the one
in truth, the other in falsehood, the one in the love of reason,
the other in the zeal of fanaticism, and the seeds of civil discords
are cast upon the soil of France'.[35] Bonjean, in 1865, warned of
the division of France into 'two nations, at least in the upper
classes: the one raised in the State's establishments in the great
national traditions; the other raised in different establishments, with
doctrines which I have the right not to recognize as the national
doctrines.'[36]

Anti-jesuit criticisms of Jesuit education embraced not only its
doctrinal content (attacks on which will be considered in the next
chapter), but its whole pedagogical spirit and method. Essentially,
two suggestions were made: first, that, like other branches of the
order's activity, Jesuit education was designed solely to promote
the political and social domination of the Society of Jesus; second,
that, in accord with this aim, its methods were systematically
opposed to the development of those faculties on which the meta-
morphosis of the child into a free and responsible modern citizen
depended. The Jesuits' long-standing reputation as educators was
disparaged as the product of propaganda, charlatanism, or intrigue,
sustained only by slandering superior rivals (Port-Royal, the

[34] *ASCD*, Sénat 4 Mar. 1880: 170.
[35] [P.-F.-X. Bourguignon d'Herbigny], *Revue politique de la France en 1826* (Paris,
1827), 123–4.   [36] *ASCL*, Sénat 15 Mar. 1865: 123.

Oratorians, the Université).[37] According to Michelet and others, they failed a simple and decisive test: in three centuries, their schooling had not produced a single great man.[38] This sweeping assertion had to be sustained partly by disqualification (Bourdaloue, though possibly a great man, was a Jesuit 'in name only',[39] and men like Voltaire were great despite rather than because of their Jesuit education); nevertheless, it became a minor anti-jesuit dogma. In Jesuit pedagogy, as in everything the order undertook, it was implied, the arts of trickery, of illusion, of manipulation were paramount; no great men, and no sound citizens, could develop where the cultivation of reason and of conscience were so cynically neglected.

If Quinet (probably its most influential nineteenth-century French critic) was to be believed, the whole enterprise of Jesuit education was a fraud; everything about it bore the mark of its original purpose, which had been to stifle by stealth the turbulent and dangerously creative intellectual movement of the sixteenth century.

There was only one way of doing that; it was that which the heads of the order of Jesus tried: to make themselves the representatives of this tendency, to obey it in order the better to arrest it, to build mansions for science throughout the world in order to imprison its soaring, to give an apparent movement to the mind which would make all real movement impossible for it, to wear it out by incessant gymnastics, and under the pretence of activity, to sooth [*caresser*] curiosity, to extinguish the spirit of discovery at its source, to stifle knowledge beneath the dust of books, in short to make the restless thinking of the sixteenth century revolve in a wheel of Ixion—this was, from its beginning, the great educational plan followed with so much prudence and so consummate an art. Never was so much reason put into conspiring against reason.[40]

The more the Jesuits petrified the spirit of intellectual enquiry, the more they elaborated its ceremonies; a proliferation of literary and rhetorical competitions and spectacles concealed the essential nullity of debate confined to a tight circle of old and harmless questions. 'This was the miracle of the Society of Jesus' teaching methods

---

[37] See e.g. Wallon, *Un collège de jésuites*, 47. For adverse comparisons with other pedagogical traditions, see e.g. Cousin in *Moniteur*, CP 22 Apr. 1844: 1044 (on the Oratorians) and de Pressensé, *La Liberté religieuse*, 86–7 (on Port-Royal).
[38] Michelet, *Des jésuites*, 46 (the same point was made by Quinet, Guettée, and others).
[39] Guettée, *Histoire des jésuites*, i. 298.   [40] Quinet, *Des jésuites*, 272.

[*enseignement*]: to bind man to vast labours which could produce nothing, to amuse him with smoke, so as to keep him away from glory, to render him immobile at the very moment that he was deceived by the illusion of a literary and philosophical movement.'[41]

Camouflaged anti-intellectualism remained the essential character of Jesuit education in the nineteenth century, according to anti-jesuits. It showed itself, for example, in a love of rote-learning, designed to develop the child's memory, 'at the expense of other faculties which would help him to emancipate himself'.[42] Most notably, however, it could be seen in the way Jesuit education circumvented the child's reason by playing systematically on the senses and the imagination.

Here the attack on Jesuit education supplied one strand (Michelet's remarks on the Jesuits' appeal to the feminine psyche were another) in a wider anti-jesuit argument, which considered a deeply exploitative sensualism to be a distinguishing feature of Jesuitism in all its cultural manifestations. The Jesuit style of piety was reproached for its emphasis on external religiosity (devotional ritual, the cult of the Sacred Heart, miraculous images, and so on). Jesuit art was also scathingly attacked. Michelet, the most scornful of aesthetic anti-jesuits, regarded 'that decrepit coquetry which believes that it smiles, but grimaces, those ridiculous glances [*œillades*], those languishing eyes, and all the rest', as irrefutable signs of spiritual disease: 'it is hard, I must say, to be optimistic about their soul. Such taste is a grave symptom.'[43] Taine, whose remarks were prompted by a visit to the Church of the Gesù at Venice, was less dismissive: in the boudoir-like alcoves and gracile madonnas, the balustrades and lapis lazuli of Jesuit churches, and in the mannered and sickly sweet style of Jesuit writings like the *Imago primi saeculi*, he detected a profound exercise in the technique of domination. Where Protestants sought to curb human instincts through the conscience, he argued, the Jesuits sought to do so through 'the methodical and mechanical direction of the imagination'. Taine here affirmed of humanity in general something which

---

[41] Ibid. 277.

[42] *Les Nihilistes de robe noire*, 87. See also the remarks of A. Aulard, *Polémique et histoire* (Paris, 1904), 273–87 ('Les Jésuites et le baccalauréat'), predicting a stream of failures by Jesuit pupils once the intelligence-orientated French composition replaced the memory-orientated Latin speech exercise in the *baccalauréat* in 1880.

[43] Michelet, *Du prêtre*, 227–9.

many anti-jesuits preferred to believe was true only of women, children, and superstitious peasantry: 'Our inner foundation [*fond intime*] is neither reason nor reasoning, but images. The sensible figures of things, once transported into our brain, arrange themselves there, repeat themselves there, sink in there, with involuntary affinities and adhesions; when later we act, it is in the direction and by the impulsion of the forces thus produced.' The Jesuits' appreciation of the importance of controlling the implantation of images was, according to Taine, most evident in their *Spiritual Exercises*. Practitioners of these were required to exercise their imagination on the different material aspects of each scene envisaged: 'Each tooth of the gear-wheel bites in its turn: first the images of sight, then those of hearing, then those of smell, of taste, of touch; the repetition and the persistence of the impact deepen the imprint.'[44] Other anti-jesuits shared this view of the *Spiritual Exercises* as the ultimate vehicle of the Jesuits' sensual manipulation. Quinet ridiculed the *Exercises* for focusing attention on the height, shape, and vegetation of Mount Tabor, rather than on the spiritual meaning of the Transfiguration; where true Christianity relied on the Word to illuminate the material world, Loyola did the opposite: 'He uses the sensations like an ambush to entice souls.'[45]

Attacks on Jesuit schools echoed these judgements on Jesuit art and on the *Spiritual Exercises*. The studies conducted in these schools had never been 'virile', declared Victor Cousin; 'solidity was sacrificed to agreeableness: the mind was spared the very efforts which cultivate it; families were deceived by brilliant and futile exercises.'[46] Wallon re-emphasized the point: 'So as to extinguish in their pupils the mind's curiosity, they cultivate in them the love of rhetoric, the taste for literary and theoretical composition, oratorical pomp, that of ceremonies and of worship, in short everything that occupies the senses, everything that speaks to the imagination and to the eye.'[47] Everything in a Jesuit schooling, according to the Protestant pastor Edmond de Pressensé, was geared to polish, to facile elegance, to the reproduction of good manners—in short, to appearances. The point was 'to assure the captivity of the human spirit by gilding its chains'.[48] Viewed in

[44] H. Taine, *Voyage en Italie*, 9th edn., 2 vols. (Paris, 1898), i. 283–9.
[45] Quinet, *Des jésuites*, 189–90. See also Wallon, *Jésus et les jésuites*, 86, 101.
[46] *Moniteur*, CP 22 Apr. 1844: 1044.   [47] Wallon, *Jésus et les jésuites*, 144.
[48] De Pressensé, *La Liberté religieuse*, 82–5.

such a light, the social glamour and superior comforts and facilities of Jesuit schools became suspect, and the Spartan dreariness of the *lycée* a guarantee of pedagogical responsibility. The novelist Gustave Graux observed, with fine inverted snobbery, that a Jesuit school could never be like a *lycée*, 'since in the one men are to be formed, and in the other gentlemen, two things which must not be confused'.[49] It was by churning out soft-brained paragons of social deportment and rhetorical proficiency that the Jesuits (in their enemies' view) were able to keep their ill-gotten reputation for educational excellence, while fulfilling their fundamentally obscurantist purpose.

The circumvention of the child's reason through his imagination was, however, only half of the task which anti-jesuits suggested the Jesuits had set themselves; the circumvention of his conscience through his selfish instincts was the other half. Here the criticism was primarily directed at the Jesuit schools' disciplinary system. This, it was suggested, was a system of rewards, punishments, and mutual surveillance, designed to bribe, humiliate, or frighten the child into a semblance of moral conduct, but doing nothing to stimulate a true sense of moral responsibility. Insinuations of sadism or perversion were also involved in the suggestion that the Jesuits had a special predilection for corporal punishment. In the refrain to Béranger's 'Les Révérends Pères', they announced the interest:

> C'est nous qui fessons,
> Et qui refessons
> Les jolis petits, les jolis garçons.[50]

A pamphlet of 1764, *Mémoire historique sur l'orbilianisme et les correcteurs des jésuites*, supplied the material for extended discussions of this theme by Salgues in 1827 and by Compayré in 1878.[51] Though Compayré believed that the modern Jesuits had reluctantly abandoned the practices he described, other anti-jesuits had been quick to raise an outcry over the revelations of beatings at the Collège Saint-Joseph at Tivoli (Bordeaux) which came to light

[49] G. Graux, *Les Amours d'un jésuite: Histoire vraie*, 9th edn. (Bordeaux, 1872), 160.   [50] Béranger, *Œuvres complètes*, 236–8.
[51] Salgues, *L'Antidote de Mont-Rouge*, 100–11; G. Compayré, *Curiosités pédagogiques: L'Orbilianisme; ou L'Usage du fouet dans les collèges des jésuites au dix-huitième siècle* (Toulouse, 1878).

through the trial of two of its Jesuit staff in 1868–9.[52] Wallon, who commented on the case, declared that 'manual correction' was as basic to the Ignatian system as was the executioner to that of Joseph de Maistre. Corporal punishments, in his view, were an integral part of a Jesuit programme of corruption: 'They break the will, they humiliate the character. They prepare it for still greater sacrifices of dignity, of honour. After having obeyed out of fear, one believes out of prudence, and one comes to think, with the doctors of the Company, that it is better to practise without believing than to believe without practising.'[53]

It was against the system of mutual surveillance in Jesuit schools, however, that the loudest indignation was expressed. Jesuit schools were portrayed as miniature police states in which the pupils themselves were made to act as spies and informers. A pamphlet by Hyacinthe, published in 1826 and purporting to describe life at Saint-Acheul, gave details of the system. Besides attacking the Jesuits for punishing a single pupil for the crimes of numerous supposedly lesser miscreants, and conversely for dispensing collective punishment for the misdeeds of an individual, Hyacinthe took particular exception to the institution of the *signum*. This was a medal or token given to a miscreant, which he could pass on to another by catching him in the act of misbehaviour. At Saint-Acheul, according to Hyacinthe, the pupil left with the *signum* at meal-time was forced to stand without food in a cold courtyard. If he had not passed it on by the third meal-time, he was condemned 'to have his hands lacerated beneath the blows of a perfidious instrument', a scene which Hyacinthe evoked with graphic violence.[54]

Such a system, anti-jesuits claimed, forced pupils to develop the arts of espionage, of betrayal, and of dissimulation. As a training for police spies it was incomparable (a point which some anti-jesuits made with at least a hint that this was its intended purpose[55]) but as an education for honest citizens it could hardly be worse. A letter in the *Mercure du XIXe siècle* under the Restoration, purporting to be addressed by an ex-pupil of the Jesuits to a lady

[52] For anti-jesuit comment, see C. Sauvestre, *La Sonnette du sacristain* (Paris, 1869), 35–7; J.-M. Cayla, *Les Jésuites hors la loi* (Paris, 1869), 149–53; Wallon, *Un collège de jésuites*, 65–75 (reproducing his comments of 1868).

[53] Wallon, *Un collège de jésuites*, 58, 60.

[54] N. Hyacinthe, *Coup d'œil dans l'intérieur de Saint-Acheul; ou De l'éducation que donnent les jésuites modernes à la jeunesse française* (Paris, 1826), 3–5.

[55] Ibid. 8; Michon, *Le Jésuite*, i. 418.

proposing to entrust her son to them, described its effect on the character:

The heart debases itself, becomes depraved; a cold egoism, a sombre mistrust takes over the most trusting and most generous souls; the hand learns to caress him whom the mouth must betray, and the eye searches avidly for evil in the actions of others, since it turns to the profit of him who discovers and denounces it. From the baseness which abuses a secret to the wickedness that today supposes faults and tomorrow will invent plots in order to receive the reward promised to the informer, there is no distance but that from the door of the *collège* to the door of a lieutenant of police.[56]

To imagine, as Michelet did, the permeation of an entire society by 'Jesuitism, the spirit of police and of denunciation, the base habits of the schoolboy sneak', hatched in the interior of the Jesuit school, was indeed to imagine a 'hideous spectacle': 'A whole people living like a house of Jesuits, in other words, from top to bottom, occupied with denouncing each other.'[57]

The teaching methods and disciplinary system of Jesuit schools, as anti-jesuits described them, combined to corrupt the child, and thus to betray both the trust of parents and the civic purpose of education. 'The children of Loyola will pervert the heart of your Henri in its youth, without embellishing his spirit, without enlightening his intelligence,' the writer in *La Mercure* warned the misguided mother.[58] 'It is impossible, on emerging from the hands of these teachers, for a young man to live in society without being either a knave or a fool,' Marcet echoed.[59] The anti-jesuit tune, as played by Gustave Graux, remained the same nearly half a century later:

What is to be expected from these impressionable imaginations, troubled from the earliest age by the most obscene images? What is to be expected of these hearts habituated to hypocrisy? Ask the generation of young men whom the Jesuits' establishments have formed in the last ten years: a generation ignorant of the great passions, incapable of enthusiasm and of love, which goes to seek its pleasures in the arms of licensed prostitutes,

---

[56] *Mercure du XIXe siècle*, 14: 349 ('Lettre d'un ex-élève des jésuites').

[57] Michelet, *Des jésuites*, 14–15. For a similar vision see the dream of abbé des Martyrs in Mouls, *Les Mystères d'un évêché*, ii. 217–24.

[58] *Mercure du XIXe siècle*, 14: 341.   [59] Marcet, *Mémoires d'un jeune jésuite*, 257.

and which passes with equal tranquillity from the brothel to the church and from the church to the brothel.[60]

To anti-jesuit eyes, Jesuit schools were both the showcases and the hothouses of a special kind of hypocrisy. Everything in them undercut the advertised purpose of schooling. Whatever might give man freedom and dignity—his reason, his conscience, his soul— was surreptitiously suffocated in infancy, and whatever might keep him mired in dependence and sterility was cultivated. The schoolboy went into the world a superficial, irresponsible, and deceitful puppet, fit for the labours of the *jésuite de robe courte*, but incapable of the feats of moral grandeur and intellectual endeavour to which modern man seemed called. The system which shaped him in this form was at once the most elaborate embodiment of the Jesuits' moral, spiritual, and intellectual bankruptcy, and the greatest, vilest triumph of their corrupting art.

[60] Graux, *Les Amours d'un jésuite*, 161–2.

9

History and Morality

INTERTWINED with anti-jesuit attacks on each of the three main prongs in the Jesuit war-machine—affiliation, confession, and schooling—was a denunciation of Jesuit doctrine. The theories and teachings of the Jesuits were seen both as an instrument and as an index of corruption—both as an influence on the actions of the Jesuits themselves and of their affiliates, and as a poison injected into society through the confessional and the Jesuit school. More invisible and more dangerous even than the pullulation of *jésuites de robe courte*, the spread of Jesuitical notions was Jesuit subversion in its most abstract, but therefore potentially most socially pervasive, form.

Two aspects of this Jesuit contamination of the intellect received particular attention from nineteenth-century anti-jesuits: the falsification of history (chiefly in schoolbooks), and the propagation (primarily through the confessional) of a corrupt and corrupting body of moral doctrine. Here again, the blend of old and new in anti-jesuit polemic is apparent: the concern with history reflected a distinctively nineteenth-century conviction of its political importance, and the material cited against the Jesuits in this connection was almost entirely modern; the denunciation of the order's *morale relâchée*, by contrast, strayed little from the traditional lines and long-established materials of an old attack on Jesuit casuistry.

HISTORICAL FALSIFICATION

The stress on the pedagogic function of history, and on its intimate connection with political education, was probably strongest, among anti-jesuits, during the early years of the Third Republic. The purpose of history-teaching, according to Sauvestre in 1878, was to provide examples to stimulate patriotism and good citizenship in children. History should serve as an *aide-mémoire* to civic values:

'one will find . . . a striking tableau for each freedom; the fires of
the Inquisition, the horrors of our wars of religion, the massacre of
St Bartholomew's Eve, the Revocation of the Edict of Nantes and
the *Dragonnades*, will assist in making understood the full price of
freedom of conscience.'[1] Such a view required history to be taught
as an orthodoxy: the child must know for sure what were the
important episodes, what each one signified, and what they signified when strung together. Above all, for Republicans, it was
essential that children be imbued with the right views on that most
significant and instructive of all historical episodes, the French
Revolution. Taught as prescribed by Bert in 1880, Revolutionary
history could impress on children not just the right political theory,
but the political demeanour appropriate to citizens of the Third
Republic, namely contented passivity. In teaching the child to
admire the great national revolt against royal despotism, the teacher
should draw attention to 'the superiority of the democratic regime
over the monarchical regime', which lay in the fact that 'today we
have no need of revolution, we have no need of insurrection . . . !
What we need in a democracy is a little patience; for, every three
or four years, if we have any complaint, it is sufficient for us to
deposit a little square of paper in a pinewood box. Yes, that is
enough!'[2] In Ferry's view, the very stability of contemporary
society depended on raising children in a properly balanced attitude
to the Revolution—neither in admiration for 'certain contested
and contestable moments' which had marred it, nor in systematic
hostility to its achievements. National unity and social cohesion
would simply disappear if a portion of the nation were trained to
despise the work of the Constituante, the Tennis Court oath, and
the decrees of 4 August 1789. Privately, perhaps, the individual
might judge the Revolution as he pleased, but the State had the
right and duty to control the way its history was taught.[3]

These were the views of Republican politicians and polemicists;
not all nineteenth-century French anti-jesuits would have agreed
with them over the details of historical orthodoxy, nor would all
have insisted like Ferry on a state monopoly over the definition of
historical truth for educational purposes. It does, however, seem

[1] Sauvestre, *Les Jésuites peints par eux-mêmes*, 129–31.
[2] P. Bert, *Le Cléricalisme: Questions d'éducation nationale* (Paris, 1900), 123 (speech
to the Cercle Franklin at Le Havre, 21 Mar. 1880).
[3] *ASCD*, Sénat 6 Mar. 1880: 227–30.

to have been widely assumed both that a serviceable version of historical truth could be laid down and that a close connection existed between correct and uniform history-teaching and the political health of society. It followed naturally that the Jesuits, believed to be trying systematically to weaken society so as to control it, would be suspected of teaching radically perverted history. Excepting only their writings on China, Alphonse Peyrat remarked that they had dealt with history only 'in order to falsify it, to spread errors, to propagate lies, or dissimulate the most important truths'.[4] Anti-jesuits (with few exceptions) were broadly agreed on what was wrong with the version of history taught by Jesuit or 'Jesuitical' historians. It denigrated the French nation, both collectively (by defaming the glories of the Revolutionary and Imperial past) and in the persons of its national heroes. It preferred the interests and viewpoint of the Church or of a particular party to those of France, and tended to provoke civil war. It was anti-liberal and anti-progressive, casting aspersions on Revolutionary achievements while glorifying feudalism and divine right monarchy. It was fond of detecting divine intervention in history on behalf of a sectarian cause. As an inspector commissioned by Ferry to examine the *cahiers d'histoire* in use at the École Sainte-Geneviève reported: 'To sum up, the Company of Jesus, in the exposition of modern history, vilifies and stigmatizes that which we respect, curses that which we bless, detests that which we love, loves that which we detest. Its desire, unavowed, but obvious, is for the overthrow of modern society.'[5]

One Jesuit in particular was so repeatedly attacked or ridiculed for his supposed distortions that his name became a byword for the systematic falsification of history. This was Père Loriquet, rector of Saint-Acheul under the Restoration and of Brugelette during the July Monarchy.[6] Though Loriquet was a prolific author of textbooks on various subjects, his evil reputation among anti-jesuits

[4] A Peyrat, *Histoire et religion* (Paris, 1858), 99 ('La Compagnie de Jésus').

[5] Quoted by Ferry, *ASCD*, Sénat 6 Mar. 1880: 234.

[6] On Loriquet, see Bliard, *Le Père Loriquet*. Athanase Cucheval-Clarigny wrote in 1847 that Loriquet's name 'was the occasion of a bitter struggle under the Restoration; ceaselessly cast into the midst of the most ardent and impassioned polemic, it had become a rallying-cry for the parties. Even now, it is often evoked as an argument in itself; it is, as it were, in accepted use to refer to the systematic falsification of history' (A. Cucheval-Clarigny, 'Le Révérend Père Loriquet: Sa vie et ses écrits', *La Liberté de penser*, 1 (1847), 165).

concentrated almost entirely on his *Histoire de France à l'usage de la jeunesse*. Originally written under the Empire, the *Histoire de France* was rejected by Lacretelle, then Imperial censor, as the work of a corrupter of youth, containing an apology of the St Bartholomew's Eve massacre.[7] It was finally published in July 1814, bearing a false date (1810) and disguising its authorship under a pseudonym ('A.M.D.G***') blatantly concocted from the Jesuit motto (*Ad maiorem Dei gloriam*). Official hostility again overtook it in 1818, when the Prefect of the Rhône instructed both civil and ecclesiastical educational authorities to prevent its use in schools, a step approved by Lainé as Minister of the Interior.[8] The book was attacked in the press,[9] but so far its author had neither been named nor identified as a Jesuit. Both these omissions were remedied, however, in a work by Kératry in 1821,[10] and thereafter Loriquet's alleged atrocities against historical veracity became an increasingly established part of anti-jesuit mythology.[11] Other historians or teachers were also singled out for attack later in the century, some of them Jesuits (Gazeau, Terret), others supposedly 'Jesuitical' (Lefranc, Delandine de Saint Esprit, abbé Courval, Charles Barthélemy, Chantrel). But Ferry, in a major onslaught on Jesuit history-teaching during the debates on Article 7, was at pains to point out that the works of Gazeau and Courval were merely updated versions of Loriquet. The latter remained 'the Jesuitical historian *par excellence*'.[12]

---

[7] Cucheval-Clarigny, 'Le Révérend Père Loriquet', 174, and Charles Loriquet in *Intermédiaire*, 1: 230 (both citing a letter by Loriquet himself).

[8] AN F[18] 20. Prefect of the Rhône to *Ministre de Police*, 9 Feb. 1818, and enclosed copy of Prefect to *recteur de l'Académie* (Lyons) and diocesan vicars-general (same date); A . H. de Kératry, *La France telle qu'on l'a faite; ou Suite aux Documents pour servir à l'intelligence de l'histoire de France en 1820 et 1821*, 2nd edn. (Paris, 1821), 252–5. For further official bans under the July Monarchy and Second Empire, see Bliard, *Le Père Loriquet*, 160–1; *Observateur catholique*, 8: 31.

[9] *Chronique religieuse*, ii. 478–80 (letter 1 June 1819); A. H. de Kératry, *Documents pour servir à l'histoire de France en 1820*, 4th edn. (Paris, 1820), 58–9. According to Kératry, every page of the book proclaimed 'contempt for the French nation and its institutions, for its armies and its citizens'; its author was accused, *inter alia*, of fomenting strife between the two branches of the royal family, and of giving indecent details of Louis XV's final illness.

[10] Kératry, *La France telle qu'on l'a faite*, 139.

[11] See *inter alia* Michelet, *Des jésuites*, 73–6; Génin, *Les Jésuites et l'Université*, 345–7; Guettée in *Observateur catholique*, 3: 29–31; Ferry in *ASCD*, CD 26 June 1879: 172.

[12] Ferry in *ASCD*, Sénat 6 Mar. 1880: 226–7 (see also his speech in CD 26 June 1879). Other attacks on Jesuit or 'Jesuitical' historians include Génin, *Les Jésuites et l'Université*, 345–63; *Les Nihilistes de robe noire*.

The differences in historical judgement between anti-jesuits and the historians they denounced were neither imaginary nor unimportant. Loriquet was as convinced as Bert and Ferry were later to be that history should deliver an unambiguous political message to the child, and his legitimist and clerical preferences were explicit. Liberals or republicans could scarcely be expected to approve a historian who described the decrees of 4 August 1789 as 'a host of injustices' enacted by an Assembly 'inspired solely by the vapours of wine'.[13] Nor did one have to be a Bonapartist to consider that Loriquet's interpretation of the decimation of the Grande Armée in 1812, as God's way of preparing the restoration of the Bourbons by purging France of 'an impious and sanguinary generation',[14] was a blindly fanatical judgement, insulting to the countless French families whose men had served and fallen in the Revolutionary and Imperial armies. Nevertheless, the assumption that the writings of Jesuit historians were informed not just by honest (or even dishonest) bias, but by a fundamentally perverted intellectual purpose, did lead anti-jesuits to exaggerate the real offences of the incriminated texts. Loriquet's account of the St Bartholomew's Eve massacre,[15] though it dwelt on attenuating circumstances, was scarcely the full-blown apology anti-jesuits claimed, and his version of Waterloo, while strongly anti-Napoleonic, did not, as Michelet maintained, display 'everywhere an English heart, everywhere the glory of Wellington'.[16] Not content with rebuking the Jesuits as theocrats and legitimists in general tendency, anti-jesuits strained to find a falsehood in every detail, to show that history as the Jesuits taught it was not a would-be history, led astray by the historian's passions, but a pseudo-history, cold-bloodedly constructed to mislead.

Deliberate omission of inconvenient facts was sometimes said to be the basic feature of Jesuit historical method.[17] However, it was the rumour of one positive lie allegedly perpetrated by Loriquet

[13] [J.-N. Loriquet], *Histoire de France à l'usage de la jeunesse: Par A.M.D.G.****, 2nd edn., 2 vols. (Lyons, 1816), ii. 131.

[14] Ibid. 322 (this passage was singled out for attack by the Prefect of the Rhône in 1818 and by Passy in *Moniteur*, CP 8 May 1844: 1277).

[15] [Loriquet], *Histoire de France*, i. 299–302.

[16] Loriquet's critics were particularly outraged by his description (ibid. ii. 356) of the Imperial Guard as 'madmen [*forcenés*]' despairingly massacring each other under the horrified eyes of the English soldiery. Michelet's comments are in *Des jésuites*, 74; see Bliard, *Le Père Loriquet*, 189–203, for discussion.

[17] See Aulard, *Polémique et histoire*, 278.

that simultaneously assured that historian of his peculiar place in the anti-jesuit rogues' gallery and crystallized the general reputation of Jesuit historians for systematic mendacity. The origin of the tale that Loriquet, in his *Histoire de France*, had referred to Napoleon as the 'marquis de Bonaparte' (or Buonaparte), a general in the armies of Louis XVIII, is obscure. Recanting his earlier anti-jesuitism in 1845, Marcet stated that it had been invented in the offices of *Le Constitutionnel* by one of the Jesuits' ex-pupils (a possible reference to himself).[18] Others claimed that it had been concocted in 1825 by three young *littérateurs*, who later became members of the Académie Française,[19] though there is possible evidence that it was current in student circles several years earlier.[20] Two later suggestions, locating the origin of the rumour on the one hand in a misattribution to Loriquet of a different work published in 1819,[21] and on the other in a mischievously exaggerated adaptation of some of his comments on Napoleon's consulate,[22] may conceivably throw some light on that part of the alleged falsification that described Napoleon as Louis XVIII's subordinate; neither, however, explains the *marquis de Bonaparte*.

[18] M. Marcet, *Mémoire à consulter sur le rétablissement légal des jésuites en France* (Paris, 1845), 42–3. The apparently confident claim by a correspondent in the *Intermédiaire*, i. 126, that Marcet invented the story in a newspaper office in 1824, seems to have been based on an inaccurate reading of a passage in L.-G. Michaud's *Biographie universelle ancienne et moderne*, 2nd edn., 45 vols, (Paris, 1843–65), xxv. 113. The attribution to Marcet (who certainly invented equally outlandish stories) is not implausible (though 1824 is too early for him to have been involved); positive evidence, however, is lacking.

[19] This account, mentioned by two correspondents in the *Intermédiaire*, 1: 230, 297, seems to have been first advanced in the *Petite Revue* (no. 42). Loriquet himself (quoted in Michaud, *Biographie universelle*, xxv. 114) considered the possibility that a *carton* bearing the notorious words might have been maliciously inserted into a few copies of his book.

[20] Charles Loriquet, in *Intermédiaire*, 1: 231, quotes an 1857 letter of N.-E. Geruzez, in which the writer, recalling 'the hospitality which I received at the rue Notre-Dame-des-Champs, on leaving [*au sortir de*] the École Normale' (which he attended from 1819 to 1822), remarks: 'As for Père Loriquet, I have completely forgotten that we talked about him together. It is indeed true that the phrase in dispute was then in circulation, and that it was quite agreed that Père Loriquet had written it.' This probably indicates that the phrase was current significantly before 1825, but the apparent vagueness of Geruzez's recollections, and our own ignorance of the letter to which he was responding, make it impossible to be certain.

[21] See *Intermédiaire*, 15: 321–2; 16: 619: the reference is to the *Historiae franciae* (attrib. to abbé Gley), containing the passage: 'Francia Ludovico XVIII regnante, rempublicam administrante Buonaparte, sub imperatoris nomine.'

[22] *Intermédiaire*, 1: 155–6.

Whatever or whenever his oral or written origins, the bogus marquis figured neither in the early criticisms of the *Histoire de France* by Kératry and others nor in the two savage attacks on Loriquet made by Marcet in 1826 and 1828.[23] By early 1830, however, *Le Constitutionnel* was accusing *La Gazette* of falsifying history 'in the manner of Père Loriquet who makes the marquis de Bonaparte, lieutenant-general in the armies of the king, enter Vienna, in 1805, at the head of 200,000 Frenchmen'.[24] The preposterous phrase re-emerged in the 1840s, first invoked by Lacretelle at the Sorbonne and then, in 1844, by Hippolyte Passy in the Chambre des Pairs. Challenged by Montalembert to produce his source, Passy remarked that the first edition of Loriquet's history was not in the Bibliothèque Royale: 'Could this be the proof that care has been taken to make it disappear? I cannot tell.'[25]

With minor variations of detail,[26] the reference remained popular with anti-jesuits under subsequent regimes. Nevertheless, despite an offer of 30,000 francs from Loriquet's publisher to anyone who presented a copy of the *Histoire de France* actually containing the *marquis de Bonaparte* phrase, and despite extensive correspondence in the *Intermédiaire des chercheurs et curieux*, nobody ever succeeded in indicating the offending passage *in situ*.[27] Instead (no doubt encouraged by Michelet's claim that the Jesuits modified the *Histoire de France* not just annually, but even monthly) believers in the passage followed Passy's example, dwelling portentously on missing editions. A curious bibliographical chase developed, with anti-jesuits striving always to show that further editions existed, or had once existed, which might contain the passage, and Loriquet's

---

[23] Marcet, *Les Jésuites modernes*, 107–12; Marcet, *Mémoires d'un jeune jésuite*, 169–71. The absence is particularly striking in the latter case since Marcet was especially severe on Loriquet for his treatment of Napoleon.

[24] *Constitutionnel*, 15 Feb. 1830 (see also 10 Mar. 1830).

[25] Lacretelle, *Discours prononcé . . . le 29 novembre 1843*, 27 (see also Lacretelle, *Histoire de France depuis la Restauration*, iv. 230); *Moniteur*, CP 29 Apr. 1844: 1145, and 8 May 1844: 1277).

[26] To my knowledge, only Sauvestre, *Lettres de province*, 36, offered a purported verbatim quotation of the whole sentence containing the phrase: 'During the absence of the king, M. le marquis de Buonaparte, lieutenant-general of the armies of His Majesty, governed the kingdom and won several battles.'

[27] The offer is mentioned in *Intermédiaire*, 1: 155, 229. For further correspondence on the issue see ibid. 1: 100, 126, 154–6, 183–4, 229–32, 297; 2: 145–8, 202–4, 267, 299; 3: 638; 4: 328–9, 396; 5: 75, 249; 7: 530–1; 8: 414; 15: 331–2; 16: 619.

defenders on their heels with efforts to prove either that these editions were imaginary or that they could be found and did not contain it. The 1816 edition, for example, which Cucheval-Clarigny claimed was 'absolutely unfindable', was found (together with a separately printed supplement of the same year) and revealed nothing.[28] Baron de Ponnat attempted to prove the existence of a phantom second edition by demonstrating that the page-references given by Kératry in 1820, which could not refer to the 1814 edition since some of them related to events in 1815, did not correspond either to the 1816 or the 1817 edition (which he wrongly supposed to be the only official ones between 1814 and 1820).[29] It was soon pointed out, however, that if Kératry's copy of the *Histoire de France* had contained a distortion as gross as the *marquis de Bonaparte*, he would hardly have refrained from mentioning it in his own attack on the author.[30]

Anti-jesuits were aided in their bibliographical speculations by a highly developed belief in the Jesuits' ability, through their agents, to buy up and remove from circulation those books which they found hostile or compromising.[31] It followed that failure to find the *marquis de Bonaparte* in Loriquet's pages could never be regarded as conclusive. By an inversion characteristic of conspiracy theories, the very lack of evidence which condemned the reference in the eyes of unbelievers bolstered it for believers; it became the ultimate evidence of the Jesuits' cunning in concealing their outrages against historical truth. This was probably one reason for the absurd phrase's durable place in anti-jesuit mythology. As anti-jesuits who doubted its existence remarked, it was scarcely indispensable to the case against Loriquet.[32] Had its existence been uncontested, the *marquis de Bonaparte* passage would have been one

[28] Cucheval-Clarigny, 'Le Révérend Père Loriquet', 191; *Intermédiaire*, 1: 155. (See also A. Jacques, 'Bulletin: Supplément à l'histoire de France depuis la mort de Louis XVI jusqu'à l'an 1816, par A.M.D.G.***', *La Liberté de penser*, 1 (1848), 398–400.) For details of other bibliographical speculations, see Cubitt, 'The Myth of a Jesuit Conspiracy', 582 n.

[29] *Intermédiaire*, 2: 148, 202–4 (citing de Ponnat in *Phare de la Loire*, 4 Dec. 1864).

[30] *Intermédiaire*, 4: 328–9.

[31] See e.g. *Constitutionnel*, 6 Mar. 1826; Cucheval-Clarigny, 'Le Révérend Père Loriquet', 193; Wallon, *Jésus et les jésuites*, 223–4 n.

[32] See Cucheval-Clarigny, 'Le Révérend Père Loriquet', 192. Even Loriquet's defender Montalembert admitted that the *Histoire de France* contained 'a host of judgements contrary to the Imperial glory and to historical impartiality' (*Moniteur*, CP 8 May 1844: 1145).

further example among many suggesting that Loriquet played fast-and-loose with history; its mythical disappearance, however, had a wider significance as a vivid reminder of the Jesuits' collective powers of surreptitious influence. The care allegedly taken to suppress it enhanced its special status among examples of Jesuit untruthfulness. On occasion, of course, this was the status of an anti-jesuit standing joke. But humour, when present, was seldom divorced from serious anxiety, and Passy specifically warned his listeners not to be diverted by 'the burlesque side of things'. Truthfulness, he declared, was the most important and serious lesson for children to learn.[33] Preposterous and unprovable as he was, the *marquis de Bonaparte* served anti-jesuits as an emblem of the Jesuits' sheer contempt for the sovereign principle of veracity. He highlighted the alleged link between the Jesuits' perversion of history and their broader moral doctrines.

LA MORALE RELÂCHÉE DES JÉSUITES

The preoccupation with a certain sort of moral corruption was one of anti-jesuitism's most distinctive features. Many conspiracy theories have accused their chosen scapegoats of perverting public morals, but few have stressed the theme so incessantly, and none, in doing so, has attached such vital importance to doctrine. Few anti-jesuit writers failed to make at least passing reference to *la morale relâchée des jésuites*, and many dwelt on it at considerable length. The term was not meant to be a vague one; it referred specifically to moral theology, and in practice principally to the teachings of Jesuit casuists from the late sixteenth to the early eighteenth centuries. In denouncing these teachings, anti-jesuits paid little heed to the specialist purpose of casuistical literature, which was to guide confessors and *directeurs de conscience* in dealing with sins already committed; they saw instead a set of maxims and principles determining and excusing the Jesuits' own actions and those of their penitents, and spread not just through confession but through the teaching of Jesuit schools.

The obsession with ancient casuists is a striking instance of the reliance of nineteenth-century anti-jesuitism on evidence from

---

[33] *Moniteur*, CP 29 Apr. 1844: 1145.

earlier centuries. The theologians denounced were, for the most part, still those so memorably mauled by Pascal in his *Lettres provinciales*, a text which itself went through over thirty nineteenth-century editions in France. It was not, however, directly from Pascal that nineteenth-century anti-jesuits drew their material; directly or indirectly, their source was the compendium of extracts from Jesuit writings compiled on the orders of the Parlement of Paris and appended to its ruling against the Jesuits in 1762, under the title *Extraits des assertions en tout genre que les soi-disans Jésuites ont, dans tous les temps et persévéramment soutenues, enseignées et publiées dans leurs livres avec l'approbation de leurs supérieurs et généraux*. Several abridgements of this compendium, or similar compilations based on it, appeared in the course of the century, and virtually all of the numerous shorter collections of extracts published in anti-jesuit tracts seem ultimately to derive from the same source. Such literature made names like Sanchez, Henriquez, Busenbaum, Fagundez, Sa, Casnedi, Lessius, and Vasquez part of the common currency of nineteenth-century anti-jesuitism. Most famous of all (thanks chiefly to Pascal) was Escobar, whose name was to morality what that of Loriquet was to history: the symbol of its deceitful subversion.[34] The difference was that Loriquet had lived till 1845, and Escobar been dead since 1669.

Suggestions that the Jesuits of modern times ought not to be condemned on the basis of such ancient evidence were ignored by anti-jesuits, or else countered either with reminders of the supposed Jesuit maxim *Sint ut sunt aut non sint* (taken to imply that the Jesuits never changed), or with claims that, since modern Jesuits had not publicly disavowed the teachings of their predecessors, they must be presumed to abide by them. Discoveries of more recent material were rare, and the attribution of it to the Society of Jesus tended to depend on comparison with the notorious casuists of old. Thus, in 1843, a Strasbourg Protestant, Frédéric Busch, triggered a chorus of indignation among anti-jesuits by denouncing J. P. Moullet's *Compendium theologiae moralis* and P. J. Rousselot's expanded edition of Saettler's comments on the sixth commandment. Neither of

---

[34] According to Littré, *Dictionnaire*, 1488, 'Escobar' was used to mean 'Cunning hypocrite, who knows how to resolve, in the way most convenient to his interests, the subtlest cases of conscience'. From it were derived 'escobarder' ('To use non-disclosure, or words with double meaning, with intent to deceive'), 'escobarderie', and 'escobartin'.

these works was by a Jesuit (though Moullet's carried an imprimatur which stated that Jesuit moral theology teachers already used it); for the benefit of those who failed to recognize the Jesuitical maxims they contained, however, Busch added a note enumerating the Jesuit casuists whose comparable teachings could be found in the *Extraits des assertions*.[35] Génin illustrated the turpitude of Jesuit confessors by citing the non-Jesuit Bishop Bouvier's teachings on sexual matters, and Sauvestre quoted the non-Jesuit abbé Marotte (again with the ancient casuists alongside for comparison) to show how the Jesuits' pernicious doctrines had infected the whole Church.[36] It was left to Paul Bert, in the debate on Article 7, to expose to view a real nineteenth-century Jesuit theologian, Père Gury; even then, he only did so after his initial attempts to damn the Jesuits by quoting non-Jesuit authors had been objected to. In his *La Morale des jésuites* he published lengthy portions of Gury's *Casus conscientiae* and *Compendium theologiae moralis*, but also of Rousselot's book, and gave the obligatory citations drawn from the *Extraits des assertions* in the footnotes.[37] In all these cases, then, the real burden of proving that the Jesuits were responsible for the currency of certain doctrines fell back on the Parlement's collection. New revelations were welcomed, and revivified the long-standing critique of *morale relâchée*, not because they enabled anti-jesuits to replace outdated quotations with fresh ones, but because they reassured them that the old ones were still valid. The agenda for attacks on Jesuit morality remained a traditional one.

A rough idea of that agenda can be gained from Table 1, which sets out the number of Jesuit authors quoted under different thematic headings both in the *Extraits des assertions* and in three of the nineteenth-century compilations (dating from 1824, 1826, and 1844) based on it. Since some authors were quoted at greater length than others, these figures give only an approximate indication of the amount of space devoted to each issue, but they do give some idea of the compendia's standard concerns, and of continuities and differences of emphasis between them.

[35] [F. Busch], *Découvertes d'un bibliophile; ou Lettres sur différents points de morale enseignés dans quelques séminaires de France*, 2nd edn. (Strasbourg, 1843), note at end. On the controversy provoked by Busch's work, see F. Ponteil, *L'Opposition politique à Strasbourg sous la Monarchie de Juillet (1830–1848)* (Paris, 1932), 723–6, 729–32.

[36] Génin, *Les Jésuites et l'Université* part III, ch. 5; Sauvestre, *Sur les genoux de l'Église*; Sauvestre, *Les Jésuites peints par eux-mêmes*, 10–12, and part II (*passim*).

[37] *ASCD*, CD 5, 7 July 1879; Bert, *La Morale des jésuites*.

TABLE 1. *Treatment of casuistical themes in four anti-jesuit compendia*

	Number of authors quoted			
	1762	1824	1826	1844
Unity of sentiments	5	0	5	4
Probabilism	57	22	32	20
'Philosophical sin'	40	11	21	9
Simony and 'confidence'	14	0	12	4
Blasphemy	5	1	4	3
Sacrilege	2	3	0	0
Irreligion	7	3	0	2
Magic and astrology	37	9	5	22
Idolatry	2	1	0	3
Chinese and Malabar idolatry	30	0	0	12
Indecency	17	3	17	17
Perjury, falsehood, etc.	29	17	16	20
Judicial corruption	5	2	5	4
Theft, occult compensation	34	13	16	18
Homicide	36	11	24	31
Parricide	5	4	5	4
Suicide	2	2	0	1
Lèse-majesté and regicide	76	26	41	58
Others	0	1	0	0

Note: Table 1 is based on the table printed by the editor of *Résumé de la doctrine des jésuites; ou Extraits des assertions dangereuses et pernicieuses soutenues par les jésuites dans leurs ouvrages dogmatiques, recueillies et imprimées par ordre du Parlement en 1762* (Paris, 1826), p. xvi, comparing the contents of his abridgement with those of the 1762 *Extraits des assertions*. Comparable figures have been added for Flocon and Beck-haus, *Dictionnaire de la morale jésuitique* (1824) and for *Doctrines morales et politiques, cas de conscience et aphorismes des jésuites, textuellement extraits et traduits des écrivains de la Compagnie de Jésus* (Paris, 1844). The figures are for the number of different *authors* quoted by each compilation under each heading, counting joint authors as one (and correcting the 1826 table where it actually gave the number of *books*). The 1844 compilation listed only eight authors under the heading 'Irréligion' in its table of contents; I have added another fourteen that were listed under other headings of a religious or theological nature.

Certain areas of subject-matter revealed in Table 1 relate only tangentially or coincidentally to the theme of *morale relâchée* as expounded in the nineteenth century, the essence of which was the scandalous permissiveness of Jesuit doctrine. The Jesuits' teachings on regicide and *lèse-majesté* (on which all four compendia quoted

most authors) are the most obvious case: it was the political dangerousness, not the moral laxity, of these teachings that nineteenth-
century critics denounced. Some of the matters dealt with under
religious headings (blasphemy, sacrilege, magic and astrology,
irreligion, idolatry[38]) were either more theological than moral in
character, or else marginal to nineteenth-century concerns (a fact
reflected in their reduced place in the compendia of 1824 and 1826).
The 1826 editor pointed out that the Jesuits' once-scandalous tolerance of magicians and astrologers now seemed preferable to the
Parlement's intolerance.[39] The 1844 compendium, more attentive
to religious questions, cited various Jesuit propositions dealing
with essentially abstract issues (such as whether the Christian religion was 'evidently true' or merely 'evidently believable'[40]) whose
relevance to the question of moral corruption most nineteenth-
century anti-jesuits would have been prepared to overlook. Once
the extracts dealing with these political and religious matters (and
the small group asserting the Jesuits' 'unity of sentiments', used
by anti-jesuits to justify blaming the Jesuits collectively for the
opinions of individual theologians) are discarded, the material on
which the polemic against *morale relâchée* was conventionally based
remains.

Within that polemic, however, one realm of moral corruption
stood somewhat apart from the rest. Jesuit teachings on indecency
(*impudicité*) were certainly considered permissive, but this was
seldom the main charge against them. The theologian who separated swearing equivocally from swearing falsely would be accused
of etching a false distinction on to the moral map of human behaviour; the one who distinguished 'perfect' from 'imperfect' sodomy,
however, was more likely to be charged with using moral cartogra-
phy as a cover for pornography. Casuistical theorizing about sexual
relations between fiancés or within the family was regarded as a
lewd infringement of privacy; to envisage the possibility of mothers
being sexually attracted to their children (to take an example some
writers found especially offensive[41]) was to perpetrate a smutty

---

[38] In general, the quotations on Chinese and Malabar idolatry were from historical documents relating to the Jesuit missions, rather than from Jesuit casuistry.

[39] *Résumé de la doctrine des jésuites*, pp. xiv–xv.

[40] *Doctrines morales et politiques*, 41–2.

[41] Thus Génin, *Les Jésuites et l'Université*, 440–1: 'No, a mother's heart and that
of a son will never conceive that which the brain of a casuist of the Society of Jesus
gives birth to without difficulty.'

outrage against the purity of maternal affection. The most general objection to the casuists' relentless subdivision and categorization of sexual misdemeanours, however, was that it drew the attention of young minds to sins which they would otherwise never have contemplated, and many of which, it was claimed, could have been conceived only by the diseased mind of a Jesuit casuist. Anti-jesuits loudly proclaimed their own inability to quote such disgusting literature[42] (except sometimes in Latin), but did not mind titillating their readers' imaginations with lurid generalities: 'the cases of conscience of erotomaniacs, indicating a dilletantist lubricity'; 'unheard-of inventions of unimaginable crimes, sacrilegious fornications, unnatural debauchery, such as only enforced celibacy can cause to hatch in a troubled mind'; 'pornography [which] surpasses in turpitude anything ignoble that can be said or done, even in houses of prostitution'.[43] Far from knowledge of such obscenities being necessary to the confessor, anti-jesuits argued, it could only endanger the spiritual, and even the physical, well-being of young priests and of penitents alike. Confession risked becoming 'a sort of school of debauchery'.[44] Sue had his hero Gabriel Rennepont suffer hallucination and fainting while attempting to read a confession manual as part of his Jesuit training.[45] The effect of such a book on a young boy in Charles Laumier's novel *L'Enfant du jésuite* was even more alarming: 'He read it, and six months later he was in the final stages of consumption.'[46]

Expressions of outrage at the perverted imaginings of Jesuit casuists were a common and a sensational feature of anti-jesuit polemic, but the bedrock of complaint about the Jesuits' *morale relâchée* was of a different order. The remaining extracts in the compendia were grouped, as Table 1 shows, under two types of heading, relating respectively to specific categories of sin (simony, perjury, judicial corruption, theft, homicide, parricide, suicide) and to general casuistical concepts or principles (probabilism, philosophic sin). This makes clear the double nature of the anti-jesuit attack on Jesuit moral doctrine, in which aversion to the casuists'

---

[42] See Isambert in *Moniteur*, CD 15 Jan. 1844: 160; Bert, *ASCD*, CD 5 July 1879: 68–9.

[43] Larousse (ed.), *Grand Dictionnaire universel*, xvii. 1458; Sauvestre, *Monita secreta*, 14; Durantin, *Un élève des jésuites*, 69.

[44] *Journal de la liberté religieuse*, 186.   [45] Sue, *Le Juif errant*, ii. 455–7.

[46] C. Laumier, *L'Enfant du jésuite*, 2 vols. (Paris, 1822), i. 23.

conclusions on specific questions was consistently coupled to a
general moral recoil from their modes of reasoning. Here attention
was focused above all on two concepts that were considered characteristic of Jesuit moral doctrine. The first—the 'fecund mother' of
all the Jesuits' other errors, according to the *Revue ecclésiastique*[47]—
was probabilism, the doctrine that, given conflicting opinions on a
particular moral question, it was permissible to follow any probable
opinion (generally meaning one having the authority of learned
doctors behind it), even if an opposing opinion was more probable.
The second (illustrated by numerous extracts in the compendia,
though not given a separate place in their tables of contents) was
the notion of 'direction of intention', according to which the intention with which an action was performed was a crucial factor in
determining its degree of sinfulness. As far as anti-jesuits were
concerned, probabilism enabled one to jettison one's conscience
whenever one could' shelter behind the authority of a Jesuit casuist,
and direction of intention was a device for whitewashing wicked
actions. Essentially, it was argued, the Jesuits had developed 'the
art of sinning innocently'.[48] Where Christ pardoned the sins of the
past, remarked the Protestant propagandist Napoléon Roussel,
the Jesuits excused those of the future.[49]

The attack on *morale relâchée* enriched the fund of anti-jesuit
humour. Probabilism and direction of intention, and the apparatus
of fine distinctions and subtle reasonings built around them, invited
satire and ridicule. The vein so brilliantly exploited by Pascal was
now more crudely dug by men like Laumier, whose *L'Enfant du
jésuite* charted the Rake's Progress of a young man living his life
in accord with the principles of Jesuit morality, with predictably
disastrous consequences for himself and others. In the person of
Père Jobardini, the anti-hero's Jesuit mentor, Laumier offered a
caricature of the casuistical virtuoso:

He knew the precise point at which, in order not to incur eternal
damnation, it was necessary to halt yourself in an action believed by the
ignorant to be criminal. He cut a mortal sin in half for you, and made it
into two very insignificant little venial sins, for which he did not even
command penitence. When he could not carry out this dissection, he

---

[47] *Revue ecclésiastique*, 2: 56.   [48] Jacquemont, *Examen impartial*, 35.
[49] N. Roussel, *Jésus et jésuite* (Paris, 1845), 14.

taught you to get yourself out of trouble by directing your thoughts to a different object, and showed you how to lie in security of conscience.[50]

The comical Jesuit Serinet, in the play *La Contre-lettre*, hung a lewd female portrait in his oratory, remarking: 'I will suppose she is a saint. The intention sanctifies everything.'[51] When his paper was sued by Père du Lac in 1876, Dionys Ordinaire composed a mock-Jesuitical dialogue in which, when summoned to say whether he was the author of an incriminated article, the defendant replied: 'Let us distinguish. I am its author and I am not its author. It is probable that I wrote it, but it is equally probable that I did not write it: I defer to the judgement of Père Escobar.'[52]

Skittish jocularity, however, was by no means the only tone in which the tricks of Jesuit casuistry were discussed. Men as separate in time and as dissimilar in religious outlook as Silvy and Bert could agree that probabilism was the practical negation of any notion of moral law (whether divine or human), and they were not amused by the prospect. Bert pictured the casuists perorating over the debris of moral principles, each touting his 'probable' opinion to the self-interested passer-by.[53] 'But where does such a system lead us?' Silvy demanded. 'When the divine law is no longer our rule, when conscience is set aside, the fence is broken down, and once the field is opened to the licence of human opinions, there is nothing that cannot be excused, permitted, and executed.'[54] At a more general level, the same mental habits that Laumier had lampooned in the person of Jobardini can be found condemned, with the deep moral seriousness of a Protestant pastor, by Edmond de Pressensé. According to him, the casuists' emphasis on a practical distinction between mortal and venial sins led them into a ceaseless 'frontier diplomacy', designed to expand the realm of the venial at the expense of that of the mortal. The true moral law was indivisible. Casuistry, however, treated it 'as a body of regulations composed of innumerable articles between which one must seek to pass as if through the bent bars of a prison. One must observe the most important, neglect the lesser ones; a ratio is to be established

---

[50] Laumier, *L'Enfant du jésuite*, i. 11.

[51] P. Duport and E. Monnais, *La Contre-lettre; ou Le Jésuite: Drame en deux actes, mêlé de chant* (Paris, 1830), 23.

[52] Ordinaire, *Seize lettres*, 48.   [53] Bert, *La Morale des jésuites*, p. xxi.

[54] [Silvy], *Les Jésuites ennemis de l'ordre social*, 5–6.

between the risk to be run and the advantage to be gained.' When morality was thus shattered into an incoherent collection of procedural rules, personal interest became the only moral touchstone, and the advice of the *directeur de conscience* the only practical guide.[55]

The casuists, then, seemed to their nineteenth-century critics to be engaged not in the legitimate business of applying general moral principles to particular cases, but in the pernicious one of sacrificing principles to an obsession with the particularity of cases. By a ceaseless multiplication of distinctions and mitigations, they reduced morality to a series of precise instructions on how to behave in carefully defined instances, ungoverned by any general law. Anti-jesuits professed themselves equally horrified by the practical detail of Jesuit permissiveness. One critic, applying his findings about casuistry also to Jesuit schools, spoke of 'an education based on principles which permit or excuse assassination, parricide, rape, and adultery'.[56] Others condemned the casuists' notion of occult compensation as the perfect excuse for thieving servants, that of mental reservation as a similar assistance to liars and perjurers, and that of direction of intention as a general purpose sinner's licence.[57] A host of casuistical rulings (on anything from calumny to self-abuse, from the compensation of seduced maidens to the accidental slaughter of one's neighbour's livestock) seemed to lie at the service of any knave who cared to learn the necessary mental tricks. *Le Constitutionnel*, in 1825, reacted in horror to a proposal to entrust prison administration to a religious corporation: 'If the doctrines of Jesuitism are often fatal to virtuous souls, what dreadful fermentation will they not produce in perverted ones? What a supplement to a mind already warped by the habit of contemplating crime, will be the theory of mental reservations and of compromises of conscience!'[58] To anti-jesuit minds, the social ill-effects to be expected from the casuists' teachings were obvious. Bourzat saw them as a threat to family, to property, and to morality; Bouis claimed that rulings which (for example) permitted mothers to hope for the death of unmarriageable daughters, or children to refuse food to heretic parents,

---

[55] De Pressensé, *La Liberté religieuse*, 60–3.

[56] E. Albert, in the introd. to the 18th edn. (Paris, 1879) of Dairnvaell, *Code des jésuites*, 8.

[57] e.g. Bouis, *Calottes et soutanes*, 205–6.   [58] *Constitutionnel*, 30 June 1825.

would leave no room in the family for true love, but only for the disgusting erotic activities described in Sanchez's *De matrimonio*.[59] Jacquemont suggested that Jesuit teachings on homicide, if ever put into general effect, would reduce society to 'hordes of cannibals always ready to slit each other's throats'. In short, Jesuit morality 'saps all the foundations of human societies, and makes them into a monstrous chaos, a brigands' den'.[60]

A frequent tendency to detect a sinister Jesuit influence behind the occurrence of certain forms of immoral or antisocial behaviour was a corollary of these beliefs about the order's *morale relâchée*. The case for associating governments like that of Villèle with the Jesuits, for example, often relied heavily on the supposed conformity of their behaviour to casuistical standards; *Le Constitutionnel* in 1827, for example, denounced 'Jesuitical morality applied to government and accommodated to ministerial needs', and Hénin de Cuvillers argued that, since 'la morale des intérêts' was a Jesuitical invention, any government whose actions conformed to it must be under Jesuit influence.[61] Anti-jesuits also registered the apparent progress of Jesuitical dishonesty in society. Étienne wrote in 1819 that 'already the Jesuits' return makes itself felt, and people are learning at their school the art of compromising with consciences, and with oaths'.[62] The *député* Méchin denounced the influence of theories of direction of intention and mental reservation, especially in the civil service, and *Le Constitutionnel*, throughout the 1820s, was alert to pick out the possible mental reservations of its political opponents.[63] Anti-jesuits under the July Monarchy took up the theme. Kératry, in 1844, detected 'pernicious mental reservations, transmitted by this society' in insincere oaths of loyalty to the regime.[64] A confidential report on Jesuit progress in Brittany submitted to the government two years later confirmed that 'Their political theory on the non-binding character [*non-valeur obligatoire*] of the political oath has made numerous proselytes.'[65] Though perjury and equivocation were the misdeeds most commonly

---

[59] *Moniteur*, Ass. N. 18 Feb. 1850: 660; Bouis, *Calottes et soutanes*, 207–14.

[60] Jacquemont, *Examen impartial*, 144, 115–16.

[61] *Constitutionnel*, 9 July 1825; Hénin de Cuvillers, *La Monarchie des solipses*, 107, 110–11.   [62] *Minerve*, 8: 22 (Nov. 1819).

[63] *AP*, CD 6 Apr. 1825: 455; *Constitutionnel*, 11 Feb. 1820, 24 Jan. 1826, 13 Mar., 4 Apr., 6 May 1828.   [64] *Moniteur*, CP 17 Apr. 1844: 1124–5.

[65] AN F¹⁹ 6287 [confidential circulars relating to the Jesuits] Note confidentielle (Mar. 1846).

attributed to Jesuit influence, they were not the only ones. In 1826, for example, *Le Constitutionnel* speculated about the connection between the teachings of casuists like Molina and Bauny and the recent increase in robbery with violence: 'Who knows whether the people who, every night, put Jesuitical morality into practice, have not received lessons in this morality in some association, instituted by the good Fathers, and specially placed under their direction!'[66]

No doubt the belief that Jesuit moral teachings were a threat to family, to property, to sexual propriety, and to fair dealing in politics led anti-jesuits to expect signs of corruption in these fields wherever they believed the Jesuits to be active. It also, however, transformed or modified anxieties which they might have had anyway. In effect, the literature on *morale relâchée* (like that on *jésuites de robe courte*) expanded the explanatory power of the anti-jesuit conspiracy theory so that it covered not only large political or social developments like reactionary legislation or the growth of Catholic organizations, but a whole range of mundane hazards affecting the lives of ordinary citizens (perhaps especially in the middle classes): domestic betrayal and marital infidelity, corruption and dishonesty among public officials, lechery, violence, and petty crime. As in other cases, the effect of the conspiracy theory was simultaneously to alarm and to reassure. On the one hand, everyday dishonesties, often insignificant in isolation, were seen as manifestations of a methodical and sustained attack on moral values, serving the interest of a malevolent power. On the other, blaming the Jesuits made it possible to play down the extent to which delinquency and infringements of the moral code were produced by genuine differences of interest or inequalities of condition within society, or indeed by deep-rooted human perversity. War on the Jesuits could be presented as a cure for immorality.

That Jesuit moral doctrine was a species of mental trickery, which obscured the crucial distinction between vice and virtue, and thus removed the vital obstacles to immoral behaviour, was a standard anti-jesuit view. But why should the Jesuits promote such a corrupting doctrine? The simplest answer, and the initial impression often given by anti-jesuit writing, was that they sought to corrupt morality out of sheer perversity. 'The Jesuits have as it were an instinctive hatred of truth,' affirmed Sauvestre. 'All their teaching

---

[66] *Constitutionnel*, 9 Nov. 1826.

seems to have the aim of cultivating falsehood.'[67] Those anti-jesuits who discussed the matter, however, rarely sustained for long an image of the Jesuits either as dedicated libertines or as principled nihilists;[68] simple perversity seemed a partial or a superficial explanation. Some writers saw the casuists' pernicious moral doctrines as stemming inevitably from some fundamental feature of Jesuitism: self-abnegation and absolute obedience (Wallon); mistrust of the human soul (Quinet); the belief that the end justifies the means (Tabaraud, Génin).[69] Others, however, emphasized the tactical quality of *morale relâchée*, its place in the Jesuit system of world domination.

There were two main versions of this view. The first could claim the authority of Pascal. The Jesuits, he had claimed, did not deliberately set out to corrupt morals; nor, however, did they set out to reform them. Instead, believing that the good of religion depended on their own influence, they used moral doctrine simply as a way of maximizing that influence. This meant tailoring morality to fit the dispositions of penitents. Persons of an austere disposition were most effectively governed with severity, and the Jesuits were prepared to be strict in such cases, but the worldly and sinful majority of men were more amenable to moral laxism, and this was therefore the more usual Jesuit approach.[70] Though nineteenth-century anti-jesuits were seldom as charitable as Pascal in their assessment of the Jesuits' basic motives, many of them shared this interpretation of *morale relâchée* as an instrument of seduction, designed to establish a bond of complicity between penitent and confessor, and to win support for the Jesuits in exchange for permission to sin in security of conscience. As Collin de Plancy put it:

> Le vol, l'usure
> Et la luxure
> Vous sont permis;
> Mais soyez nos amis.[71]

---

[67] Sauvestre, *Les Jésuites peints par eux-mêmes*, 34–5.

[68] The attempt by the author of *Les Nihilistes de robe noire* to sustain a comparison between the Jesuits and Russian nihilists was soon abandoned.

[69] Wallon, *Jésus et les jésuites*, 113; Quinet, *Des jésuites*, 211–12; [M.-M. Tabaraud], *Du pape et des jésuites* (Paris, 1844), 61; Génin, *Les Jésuites et l'Université*, 430.

[70] B. Pascal, *Les Provinciales; ou Les Lettres écrites par Louis de Montalte à un provincial de ses amis et aux RR.PP. jésuites*, Classiques Garnier edn. (Paris, 1965), 75.

[71] J.-A.-S. Collin de Plancy, *Histoire des jésuites, en 82 couplets, sur de beaux airs de complaintes, avec des notes instructives, depuis la naissance de saint Ignace, en 1492, jusqu'à cet an de grâce 1826* (Paris, 1826), 20.

The Jesuits' aim, according to another Restoration writer, was to establish an alliance with 'that horde of bigoted scoundrels of all classes, whose constricted souls, as wicked as they are superstitious, see an enemy in whoever censures them, a God in whoever obligingly finds an excuse for their vices'.[72]

In its extreme forms, this view of the purpose of *morale relâchée* implied an unflattering image of a humanity most of whose members awaited only the excuse to plunge into vice. It accorded well with a rigorist emphasis on the arduousness of virtue and the need to avoid all concessions to worldly weaknesses. For this reason, it was highly developed among Port-Royalists, who retained Pascal's own theological emphasis. Pascal had argued that the Jesuits could reject the theological truth of efficacious grace only because they were satisfied with so minimal a standard of morality that unaided human nature could achieve it; since, however, true virtue was infinitely more taxing, it must be recognized that only the direct involvement of an omnipotent deity could be responsible for its occurrence.[73] Nineteenth-century Port-Royalists like Silvy echoed these arguments, accusing the Jesuits of falsely offering to reconcile pleasure on earth with future salvation. For them, *morale relâchée* was part of a more general 'system of accommodation', undermining all the truths of religion.[74]

Though by no means all those who accused the Jesuits of making a pact with sinners were Port-Royalist in their rigorism, some anti-jesuits seem to have preferred a second interpretation of the purpose of *morale relâchée* — one which, while retaining the emphasis on the unity and clarity of moral imperatives, was less implicitly scornful of human corruptibility, and therefore arguably more congenial to those whose concern was merely to preserve a simple code of day-to-day worldly rectitude. This second view stressed the ideas of confusion and arbitration, rather than those of seduction and complicity. What could the Jesuits' aim have been, Ferdinand Flocon demanded, 'if not to demoralize the nation, to throw consciences into an appalling labyrinth of errors and doubts, to which they alone claimed to hold the clue, and finally to render themselves, by means of the confessional and of the pulpit, the sole arbiters of good and evil, the judges of thoughts, and the directors

---

[72] Dinocourt, *L'Ombre d'Escobar*, 21.   [73] Pascal, *Les Provinciales*, 78–9.

[74] [L. Silvy], *Les Jésuites tels qu'ils ont été dans l'ordre politique, religieux et moral* (Paris, 1816), 89–90; *Revue ecclésiastique*, 4: 7; 7: 306; 10: 40.

of actions?'[75] According to Sauvestre, the Jesuits realized that the human conscience, if left free, would lead men to liberty. 'It was necessary therefore to accustom it to fear, to uncertainty; it was necessary to humble the conscience forever in such a way that it would no longer dare to judge by itself and that it would surrender itself entirely to the *directeur*'s decision.'[76] What these anti-jesuits feared was not so much that people might, under the influence of Jesuit casuistry, cease to care about the distinction between good and evil, but rather that they might continue to care about it while being unable to discern it without Jesuit assistance. The Jesuits, in short, were accused of deliberately making morality incomprehensible, with a view to extending their own power.

Attacks on Jesuit *morale relâchée* seldom involved strong positive statements about the origins and content of true moral imperatives. Had they often done so, the extensive agreement on the surface between anti-jesuits of diverse religious opinions—freethinkers, Protestants, Gallicans, even Port-Royalists—about the evils of Jesuit morality could scarcely have subsisted. Besides the obvious room for disagreement between theological and secular conceptions of morality, there was a major difference in tone between, for example, Hénin de Cuvillers's masonic religion, with its stress on charity, tolerance, and good works, and the apparent (but slightly bogus) ferocity of Sauvestre's claim to prefer the example of Virginius slaughtering his own daughter to save her from dishonour to the casuist Taberna's suggestion that a woman threatened with death by her rapist was not obliged to resist by all available means.[77] Equally importantly, standardized expressions of outrage at the Jesuits' falsification of morality could be harnessed to a variety of different understandings of where that falsification began; what struck one anti-jesuit as the linchpin of Jesuit chicanery might strike another as a fundament of moral order. For a freethinker, the falsification might begin with the Jesuits' exploitation of superstitious anxieties about salvation and damnation. For a Protestant, however, these questions were fundamental to moral reasoning; Jesuitical corruption entered with the inherently manipulative institution of confession, and with the associated casuistical traditions. For a Gallican or a Port-Royalist, finally, confession was an integral

[75] Flocon and Beckhaus, *Dictionnaire de morale jésuitique*, p. xvii.
[76] Sauvestre, *Les Jésuites peints par eux-mêmes*, 18–19.
[77] Ibid. 70–1; Hénin de Cuvillers, *La Monarchie des solipses*, 70–1.

part of moral discipline; the perversion of morals stemmed only from Jesuit casuistry, especially probabilism.

What bound people of such potentially conflicting views together was their agreement that, whatever its origin and contents, true morality was coherent, indivisible, and not open to negotiation, and that the Jesuitical imitation of it had none of these characteristics. Anti-jesuits did not see themselves as participants in a debate between rival moral theories; they believed that the Jesuits were interested only in exploiting moral questions, not in answering them sincerely. Something more was involved here than a conventional concern with hypocrisy. The conventional hypocrite, the Tartuffe, profited publicly from a moral code which he privately repudiated, but his own double-dealing left the code intact for others to follow in a sincerer spirit. The Jesuits, on the other hand, were accused of eroding the substance and the possibility of morality while preserving the appearance of moral discourse. Where a Loriquet falsified the map of history, the ancient and modern Escobars covered that of morality with so many fine or uncertain lines that its features became indistinguishable. By the corruption of these two maps, the Jesuits' victims were deprived of the true bearings (political in the one case, conscientious in the other) that they needed to steer a straight course in the modern world; they were left at the mercy of treacherous guides.

La morale relâchée was thus perceived to play an important part in the Jesuit system of world domination. It was also, however, invoked in judgement on the Jesuits' own character. Beliefs about it made a contribution to the almost total lack of trust with which the Jesuits and those associated with them were regarded by many of their opponents. In the preface to *La Morale des jésuites*, Bert sketched the portrait of 'a thoroughly finished product of their intellectual and moral manufacture'. With ample reference to Gury's teachings, he explained how abominably such a creature would behave towards, for example, parents, young women, friends, employers, tax-collectors; paragraph after paragraph began with 'Don't trust him' or a similar injunction.[78] Though Bert finally conceded that so perfect a Jesuit pupil did not exist, the cumulative effect of his warnings could only be to foment mistrust of anyone who had received a Jesuit education. And the ultimate specimens of

---

[78] Bert, *La Morale des jésuites*, pp. xxxv–xliv.

this Jesuitical deformity of moral character, anti-jesuits presumed, were the Jesuits themselves. Never to take a Jesuit's word for anything was, according to Raspail, 'an axiom of law'.[79] Certainly it was an axiom applied by those who refused to accept Jesuit denials of the *Monita secreta*, or to accept the *déclaration de non-appartenance* as an adequate protection against Jesuit education.

In accord with the double nature of the criticism directed at the casuists, anti-jesuit mistrust extended not just to the detail of the Jesuits' conduct, but to their general modes of thought. Jesuits did not simply lie; they were incapable of telling the truth, because frankness and straightforwardness, the prerequisites for truth-telling, were alien to them. 'It is an axiom of the logic of Escobar, that speech has been given to man to hide and not to express his thoughts,' declared *Le Constitutionnel*; another feature of Jesuit logic was its tendency to draw specious consequences from false principles, and captious arguments from true ones.[80] Raspail agreed: 'The Jesuit has learnt, ever since his earliest studies, to give what is true such a twist that a falsehood results from it.'[81]

The conviction that (to use one of de Pressensé's expressions) the Jesuits conducted all their intellectual exchanges in false coinage[82] encouraged a certain moral self-congratulation among anti-jesuits. Salgues described the difference between the Jesuits' opponents and their defenders:

The first grapple with the enemy willingly [*de bonne grâce*], their discussion is clear, frank, and precise; they do not dissimulate, they do not lie. The second bring to the struggle all the cunning of the fox, disguise themselves in a thousand forms, envelop their adversaries with so many subtleties, so many artifices and deceptions, that all the wisdom of the sphinx is needed to penetrate their sophisms, to escape their snares.[83]

Le Constitutionnel saw the convergence of forces against the Jesuits under the Restoration as 'the accordance of public probity against lies and bad faith'.[84] The contrast between Jesuitism and French-ness elaborated by Quinet, and repeated by many others, carried a similar message. Alphonse Aulard, under the Third Republic,

[79] Raspail, *Revue complémentaire*, iii. 221.
[80] *Constitutionnel*, 25 July 1830, 9 July 1825.
[81] Raspail, *Revue complémentaire*, iii. 222.
[82] De Pressensé, *La Liberté religieuse*, 66.
[83] Salgues, *L'Antidote de Mont-Rouge*, 315.
[84] *Constitutionnel*, 11 Apr. 1827.

translated this into linguistic terms: 'If the Jesuits have ever known French, they have unlearnt it and are not fit to teach it. They have ended up, I believe, by mistrusting our language, which is a school of clarity, of frankness, of straight and firm reasoning.'[85]

Directly and indirectly, the literature on *morale relâchée* made a major contribution to this view of Jesuits as creatures who, in their interior, spoke a different language from that of other people, and who, in speaking the same one externally, did so on different terms—fundamentally deceitful and manipulative creatures, from the inner logic of whose personalities the normal functioning both of conscience and of the truth-seeking intellect had been excluded. With this vision of the Jesuit personality, one passes from the anti-jesuit discussion of Jesuit tactics to the supposed inspiration of so much wickedness—the spirit of Jesuitism itself.

[85] Aulard, *Polémique et histoire*, 282.

10

Jesuits and Jesuitism

In the anti-jesuit vision, the actions of Jesuits were the product of Jesuitism. In this one of its several possible senses, 'Jesuitism' meant a spiritual property or essence which anti-jesuits deemed to be fundamentally characteristic both of the Society of Jesus as an institution and of the psychology of its members. It, and not personal motives or interests, was thought to shape the way Jesuits behaved, and because it was considered immutable, the general direction of their behaviour was believed to be reliably predictable, for all the diversions particular circumstances might impose upon it.

Most of the Jesuits' enemies would have echoed the opinion which Barante expressed in the Chambre des Pairs in 1827: 'the essence of their institute is the insatiable need for domination.'[1] Yet such a remark left it unclear how the need arose. Did it stem from the ambitions of individual Jesuits? If so, what was there about their order's organization that replaced anarchic self-interest with the disciplined assault on society described in anti-jesuit polemic? Or was the ambition somehow collective; in which case, how did it have purchase on the attitudes and behaviour of individual members? To indicate the ambiguity in remarks like Barante's is not to imply that anti-jesuits were much perturbed by it, or did much to resolve it. It is, however, to suggest that, in so far as they sought to elaborate on such statements, they were driven to consider the question of Jesuitism on two levels, that of the organization of the Society of Jesus, and that of the character and motivation of individual Jesuits. To explore what anti-jesuits meant by Jesuitism, then, the historian must examine two ostensibly very different types of anti-jesuit expression. Criticisms of the Jesuit *Constitutions* are, in a sense, the most straightforwardly understandable charges in the anti-jesuit weaponry, since they commented directly on generally

[1] *AP*, CP 19 Jan. 1827: 199.

agreed evidence; aside from occasional questions of translation or distorted quotation, nobody questioned the authenticity or relevance of the texts cited. The image of the typical Jesuit character, on the other hand, was developed most strikingly in novels and plays, on the face of it the most freely imaginative and factually irresponsible sorts of anti-jesuit literature. The difference, however, was more stylistic than substantial. The evidential basis for the assumptions that typically dominated anti-jesuit attacks on the *Constitutions* was by no means as secure as that for the constitutional texts themselves. Most notably, it was believed, largely on the basis of a sweeping view of Jesuit history, that the Society of Jesus tended by inner fatality towards the perpetual extension and maintenance of its own domination. Usually, and almost invariably as far as the less sophisticated of its critics were concerned, this urge to dominate was assumed to be the initial impulse behind the Society, and its sole *raison d'être*. It followed that the interpretation of each detail of the *Constitutions* was incomplete until one had shown how it was designed to increase the order's imperialistic strength. Anti-jesuits approached the *Constitutions* with the primary intention of stripping bare the mechanism whereby the efforts, affections, and aspirations of Jesuits were harnessed or subordinated to the Society of Jesus' unrelenting pursuit of power. At the same time, speculation about the Jesuit character in anti-jesuit fiction tended to rest on ideas about the *Constitutions*. Eugène Sue insisted that the Jesuits in *Le Juif errant* were merely embodiments of 'the detestable principles of *their classic theologians*' and 'the abominable spirit' of their *Constitutions*.[2] The intention of anti-jesuit novelists and playwrights was not usually to create Jesuits thoroughly convincing as individuals, in isolation from the theories of anti-jesuit non-fiction, but rather to translate such theories as convincingly as possible into a fictional context.

JESUITISM AND THE *CONSTITUTIONS*

Though anti-jesuits were generally agreed in seeing the central evils of Jesuitism writ large in the Jesuit *Constitutions*, their criticisms of the text varied in tone. Michelet, tending to see here, as in all things

[2] Sue, *Le Juif errant*, v. 407.

Jesuit, the signs of spiritual disease rather than of political conspiracy, displayed a sneering contempt. The *Constitutions* manifested 'the mind of a scribe, an endless mania for regulation, a governmental curiosity which never stops . . . In sum, a petty mind, artful and meticulous, a bastard mixture of bureaucracy and scholasticism—More police than politics.'[3] Most anti-jesuits, seeking the mainspring of the Jesuit conspiracy, were more awestruck. Silvy marvelled in horror at 'their astonishing constitutions, a veritable masterpiece of the genre, in which human politics joins hands with fanaticism, to attain the great end of universal domination'.[4] Abbé de Pradt scarcely bothered to keep his admiration for the Jesuit organization and its creator grudging: Loyola was 'great, and great among the greatest, great with a greatness unknown before him', and the Society of Jesus was the strongest association yet formed by human genius; 'in her are revealed the most profound contrivances for enlacing the whole world, contrivances based at once on human nature and on knowledge of the times'.[5]

It was, of course, purely for its powers of mobilization and organizational strength, and not for any quality of holiness or rectitude, that Loyola's creation gathered these accolades. Silvy described the *Constitutions* as 'less the rule of a religious order than a veritable code as much of politics as of despotism'.[6] There was a widespread refusal to accept that the Society of Jesus was a religious organization in anything but name. Some saw it as 'an army, a war machine',[7] though perhaps (as Quinet stressed) one not geared to war 'in full daylight': 'the established police of Catholicism' rather than its 'Theban legion'.[8] For others, it was the perfected form of the conspiratorial secret society: 'never was a secret society organized with a purpose more subversive of all temporal legitimacy, with a more exactly defined division of powers, with more vigorous policing.'[9] Whichever view was taken, anti-jesuits were agreed that the order's *Constitutions* were a monument not to divine inspiration but to perverse human cunning, and that they amounted

---

[3] Michelet, *Des jésuites*, 86 n.   [4] [Silvy], *Les Jésuites tels qu'ils ont été*, 78–9.
[5] Pradt, *Du jésuitisme ancien et moderne*, 121, 125.
[6] [Silvy], *Les Jésuites tels qu'ils ont été*, 62.
[7] Michel, *Les Jésuites*, 11.   [8] Quinet, *Des jésuites*, 170, 207–8.
[9] B. Hauréau, 'Jésuitisme', in *Dictionnaire politique: Encyclopédie du langage et de la science politiques, rédigés par une réunion de députés, de publicistes et de journalistes* (Paris, 1842), 495–6.

to regulations for an organization at war with civilized society. They were also sometimes seen as Loyola's blueprint for an entire society under Jesuit control, 'the Caudine forks under which he wishes to make the conquered world pass'.[10]

Anti-jesuit criticisms of the rules governing Jesuit existence may be divided into two groups. The first group related to the Society of Jesus' privileges and the rules concerning its relations with spiritual and temporal power and with outside society. Here little need be added to what has already been said about anti-jesuit apprehensions of 'a state within the State'.[11] Eugène Pelletan summarized the argument:

The Society of Jesus is thus a society independent of society, a society within society, a society above society, with no direct or indirect relationship to society beyond its own benefit or its own advantage. It has or it claims to have its own separate law, its own separate jurisdiction, its own separate territorial division, and even its own geographical map.[12]

This separateness and would-be independence of the Society of Jesus struck anti-jesuits as at best a derogation of (and at worst an open aggression against) the rights of legitimate temporal and spiritual authorities. Three features of the Society of Jesus' external character were considered especially suspicious. One was the special relationship with the Papacy implied in the Jesuits' fourth vow, of obedience to the Pope, an engagement which, in the opinion of anti-jesuits, conflicted with loyalty to the French State.[13] The second was the *Constitutions'* emphasis on the need for Jesuits to sever their connections with family and friends, and renounce all possibility of receiving dignities outside the order. Thus deliberately isolated from the interests and affections of the broader society, the Jesuit, it was felt, was likely to embrace those of his order with a blind sectarian fanaticism; the Society of Jesus became, in Casimir Bouis's words, 'the God who must be adored above all'.[14] The third feature—illustrated by the oft-repeated *tales quales* story—was the Jesuits' resistance to classification within the rather simple typology of religious species that was familiar to most anti-jesuits. This, together with the secrecy in which the order was said

[10] Brot and Lurine, *Les Couvents*, 42.
[11] See above, 48.   [12] *Siècle*, 25 Mar. 1854.
[13] For an extended anti-jesuit discussion, see *Observation sur le vœu spécial d'obéissance que font au pape les jésuites profès des quatre vœux* (Paris, n.d.).
[14] Bouis, *Calottes et soutanes*, 101.

to shroud its *Constitutions*, was regarded as amounting to a deliberate mystification. 'Equivocation placed herself in Jesuitism's cradle,' wrote Pradt, 'she accompanied it to the tomb, she returns following its resurrection; for it will be no more clearly designated today than it was during two hundred and more years of dubiously coloured existence.' The conclusion he drew was typical: 'He who hates the light wishes to be able to act for the bad.'[15]

The second group of anti-jesuit criticisms concerned the Society of Jesus' internal power structure and discipline. Here again the weight of the attack fell on three points. The first was the absolute and autocratic power of the General. Eugène Pelletan called the Society of Jesus 'the pearl of autocratism' and 'the last word in servitude'.[16] So perfect a specimen of arbitrary despotism did the order's government seem to anti-jesuits that some of them were inclined to believe it must be of Middle Eastern origin, perhaps modelled by Loyola on Islamic secret societies he had encountered in Palestine.[17] Anti-jesuits imbued with liberal or democratic ideals found the General's virtually unlimited authority an obvious target for attack. They were, if anything, even more outraged by the rules which, in their opinion, ensured the disciplined submissiveness of his subordinates. The second and third points on which the anti-jesuit attack concentrated were the two bases on which, according to Bouis, the General's power rested: obedience and delation. 'The one gives the master the body of his slaves, the other opens their thoughts to him, and, by them, he acts with the arm and sees with the eyes of several thousands of men.'[18]

'All built on one principle: mutual surveillance, mutual denunciation, perfect contempt for human nature': this was Michelet's judgement on the *Constitutions*. Though he conceded that this contempt was 'perhaps natural in the terrible times when this institute was founded', neither he nor other anti-jesuits were prepared to accept that it had any place in the modern world.[19] They took the same view of mutual surveillance among adult Jesuits as they did of its use in the disciplinary system of Jesuit schools: such a

---

[15] Pradt, *Du jésuitisme ancien et moderne*, 114–15.   [16] *Siècle*, 25 Mar. 1854.
[17] See the speculations of Hénin de Cuvillers, *La Monarchie des solipses*, 68, 81–2, 92–3; Bert in *ASCD*, CD 5 July 1879: 76; and especially the later work by V. Charbonnel, *L'Origine musulmane des jésuites* (Paris, 1900).
[18] Bouis, *Calottes et soutanes*, 113–14.   [19] Michelet, *Des jésuites*, 86–7.

method was profoundly, and perhaps deliberately, corrupting. As the *Chronique religieuse* put it:

To make *religieux*, to make men, spy on each other out of duty, is to fashion souls for dissimulation and falsehood; it is to corrupt the heart and degrade the spirit, to deprive men of all sentiments of honour, all grounds for praiseworthy emulation; it is to debase humanity; and what use cannot an ambitions and criminal superior make of such instruments?[20]

The evil effects of mutual surveillance were compounded, according to anti-jesuits, by those of the Jesuit conception of obedience. Of all features of Jesuit organization, this was the one most consistently and most vehemently attacked.[21] The comparison frequently drawn between the General and the Old Man of the Mountains, despotic chief of the sect of the Assassins,[22] hinged as much on the blindly obedient fanaticism of Jesuit underlings as on the tyrannical authority of their head. Abbé Michaud explained the centrality of obedience to the Jesuit organization:

In reality, what is Jesuitism, considered in its very essence, if not the system of *blind* and *passive* obedience of the inferior to the superior? According to the maxims of St Ignatius, everything the superior says is true, and consequently the inferior must obey him blindly; everything the superior desires is just, and consequently the inferior must obey him passively. Such are the two principles on which the whole organization of the Jesuitical militia rests, so that all this army of corpses lives in one man only, the General who is in Rome.[23]

Anti-jesuits placed great stress on the terms in which Loyola described the obedience required of Jesuits—like that of a corpse (*perinde ac cadaver*) or of a stick (*sicut baculus*) in the hands of an old man. In their view, these expressions described an objective the realization of which required more than a mere suspension of individual judgement in face of a superior's command; such obedience could rest only on complete self-annihilation. A true Jesuit, Pelletan explained, must become dead not only to the world but

---

[20] *Chronique religieuse*, iii. 72.

[21] Virtually alone among anti-jesuits, the Port-Royalists of the *Revue ecclésiastique* were prepared to defend the letter of the Jesuit rules on obedience, while deploring the way in which this religious virtue was put at the service of the Jesuits' doctrinal innovations (*Revue ecclésiastique*, 6: 279–88).

[22] e.g. by Santo-Domingo, *Plaidoirie*, 9; *Constitutionnel*, 25 Apr. 1825.

[23] Michaud, *Le Mouvement contemporain*, 9.

to himself, to every sentiment of individuality, until finally, from the old man, denatured and annihilated in him, he has drawn forth a new man, an impersonal being who thinks only with another's thought, who wills only with another's will, who acts only on another's order, and who must always obey without a word, that is to say without responsibility.[24]

The Jesuit thus became the automaton described by Michelet: 'What is the nature of the Jesuit? There is none, he is good for everything: a machine, a simple instrument of action has no personal nature.'[25] Few anti-jesuits would have contested Castagnary's judgement: 'Never has more audacious violence been done to nature, never has a graver blow been struck at human individuality.'[26]

Those anti-jesuits who sought to combine their attacks on the Society of Jesus' written rules with an account or explanation of Jesuitism as a mental condition almost invariably focused on this alleged assault on individuality and selfhood. Two different psychological interpretations emerged. The first, which most anti-jesuits seem implicitly to have accepted, assumed that the attempt at self-annihilation was successful, and saw the supposed defects of the Jesuit character as the direct product of the *Constitutions*. Much anti-jesuit commentary on the *Constitutions* reveals a tendency to treat them not as a set of prescriptions, embodying theory and wishful thinking, artificial and hence not automatically self-fulfilling, but as direct translations of Jesuit spirit, to which the reality of Jesuit life could be assumed to conform closely. Even blind, self-abnegating obedience, the most strenuous of constitutional requirements, was discussed as if it were a state which Jesuits had the power to achieve perfectly. The anti-jesuit had simply to explain how, and with what results, this was done. Eusèbe Salvert argued in 1828 that the key to this psychological transformation lay in the *Spiritual Exercises*, in the practice of which the individual's judgement and will were totally subordinated to the director's authority. This delivered senior Jesuits to 'that proud and tyrannical intoxication, inseparable companion to an excess of power', and the rank and file to a blind devotion to their order's aggrandizement, and to acceptance of the principle that the end justifies the means.[27] Though not all anti-jesuits drew Salverte's distinction between the mentalities of Jesuit leaders and followers,

[24] *ASCD*, Sénat 24 Feb. 1880: 265. [25] Michelet, *Des jésuites*, 46–7.
[26] Castagnary, *Les Jésuites*, 84. [27] *AP*, CD 21 June 1828 (annexe), 238–9.

his emphasis on the disastrous effects of a practical realization
of the Jesuit conception of authority was shared by many. De
Pressensé, for example, considered that what was normally called
'Jesuitism'—'cunning artful cleverness'—was

a natural consequence of the exaggeration of the doctrine of authority.
Ignatius makes a power of religion; it follows that morality for him and
his people will be essentially political, that everything will be subordinated
to the triumph of this power, that they will believe themselves authorized
to serve it by a skilful diplomacy which will sacrifice the moral absolute of
the conscience.[28]

The second psychological interpretation of Jesuitism took as its
starting-point the very tension between theory and reality that the
first interpretation ignored. It saw the Jesuits' exaggerated and unscrupulous *esprit de corps* not as the natural outcome of a successful abolition of individuality, but as the necessary psychological
compensation for a submergence of selfhood which could never be
properly achieved. According to the openly anti-jesuit Lamennais
of *Affaires de Rome* (1836), Loyola had demanded the impossible:

Whatever the man does, it is completely impossible for him to abdicate
himself to this extent. His efforts to do so succeed only in displacing what
he persuades himself he has annihilated. His whole being turns in on the
complex being to which it is united, with which it merges. . . . Thus the
passions, contained by a severe rule so long as they relate indirectly to
the individual, are sanctified and not destroyed. They pass over, as it were,
to the service of the corps which directs them and uses them to attain its
object. . . . No personal pride, no ambition, no desire for riches in each of
its members considered in isolation; but an immense collective cupidity,
ambition, and pride.[29]

In practice, the distinctions between such an interpretation and
that advanced by men like Salverte or de Pressensé were often
blurred. Jean Wallon, for example, echoed Lamennais's insight, but
dimmed its brightness by trying to have it both ways: 'How could
the Jesuits annihilate the human personality, if they did not offer it,
like Satan, the kingdom of the world in consequence? And how
could they dream of universal domination for their Company, if
they did not first annihilate the personality of each of its members?'

---

[28] De Pressensé, *La Liberté religieuse*, 11.
[29] F. de Lamennais, *Œuvres complètes*, 10 vols. (Paris, 1843–4), viii. 18–20.

He also advanced a modified version of Salverte's argument about
the role of the *Spiritual Exercises*: the individual Jesuit could only
abolish his sense of self by practising the *Exercises* under the
control of a superior, who must himself do so under that of his
superior, and so on up the hierarchy, till the surrender of each
Jesuit's conscience and judgement turned the order as a whole into
'a monster, a soul with a thousand heads, an intelligent force without conscience and consequently without responsibility'.[30]

Anyway, the differences between the proponents of these different interpretations of Jesuit psychology perhaps mattered less than
what they had in common. Salverte, de Pressensé, Lamennais, and
Wallon all traced the defects of the Jesuit mentality (even including
the taste for intrigue, in Lamennais's case, and for probabilistic
moral theology, in Wallon's[31]) to the order's conception of obedience and submission. They all implied that the effort to live up
to this conception brought about a radical transformation in the
Jesuit's character, replacing his own personality with a standard
Jesuit imprint. The emphasis which (with the exception of Lamennais) they placed on the *Spiritual Exercises* in this context was a common one, though some anti-jesuits preferred to stress the role of
education. The general agreement that Jesuitism was a form of
artificially induced freakishness was well captured in de Pressensé's
description of

that strange, impersonal being which one calls a Jesuit, the brilliant and
artificial product of a refined culture, which has only broken the spring of
the mind to give it that marvellous suppleness of acrobats, whose limbs
are broken in childhood. He is a man both fervent and crafty, austere and
accommodating, indomitable and evasive, the most perfect instrument of a
religious politics inflexible in its intentions beneath the deviousness of its
methods.[32]

Finally, whatever view was taken of the origins of the Jesuit
mentality, there was fairly general agreement among anti-jesuits on
its distinctive features. Wallon wrote: 'After the spirit of domination which gave birth to it and which sustains it, or is rather
its soul, these two characteristics—the fanaticism of the will and
the perversion of the conscience—are the signs by which, in

[30] Wallon, *Jésus et les jésuites*, 11, 15.
[31] Ibid. 113; Lamennais, *Œuvres complètes*, viii. 20–1.
[32] De Pressensé, *La Liberté religieuse*, 24.

history, the existence of the Society of Jesus most reliably gives itself away.'[33]

THE JESUIT CHARACTER

In the course of the nineteenth century, the three features enumerated by Wallon—'the spirit of domination', 'the fanaticism of the will', 'the perversion of the conscience'—were increasingly established as the constituent elements in a conventional stereotype of Jesuit character in fictional literature. In novels and plays, the psychological generalizations of anti-jesuits about Jesuitism in the abstract or Jesuits in the plural were transformed into imaginative depictions of individual Jesuit personalities. These often rudimentary efforts at characterization made a distinctive and important contribution to the anti-jesuit mythology. By creating and reproducing Jesuit characters in whom certain qualities—for example, passive obedience, machiavellian unscrupulousness, and the passion for domination—were combined, novelists and dramatists encouraged their readers, many of whom had little opportunity to observe real Jesuits, to see these qualities as intrinsically connected. The stereotype acquired the coherence of tradition, if not of psychology.

This happened in two ways. First, whether because they were unusually powerfully portrayed or because they appeared in unusually successful books, a few fictional characters acquired their own mythical status. Just as Tartuffe was the prototypical religious hypocrite, so the two leading villains of *Le Juif errant*, Rodin and d'Aigrigny, became the prototypical Jesuit intriguers. It was to them, for example, that a commentator on the de Buck trial in Belgium, two decades after the publication of Sue's novel, compared two of the Jesuits involved in the case.[34] But the impact of such individual figures will be misunderstood if it is isolated from the more persistent influence of constantly repeated stereotypes. Anti-jesuits could, and sometimes did, invoke the name of Rodin in support of a stereotypical view of Jesuit character to which Sue's monster, if carefully examined, conformed only very

---

[33] Wallon, *Jésus et les jésuites*, 113.
[34] *Les Jésuites et l'affaire Debuck*, 6th edn. (Brussels, 1864), 17.

imperfectly.[35] The prototype, in short, was filtered through the stereotype; the repetitious conventions of anti-jesuit characterization are at least as important as its most famous products.

Some of these conventions remained constant throughout the nineteenth century. The Jesuits of fiction combined profound untrustworthiness with dangerous seductiveness. This combination of qualities showed in their physical appearance, which was usually of one of two recurrent types. Specimens of the first were unprepossessing, sometimes even repulsive, to the eye. Few were more so than Rodin:

His grey hairs were flattened on his temples and crowned his bald forehead; his eyebrows were barely marked; his eyelid, limp and drooping like the membrane which half masks the eyes of reptiles, half hid his lively and black little eye; his thin lips, absolutely colourless, merged with the pallid tint of his thin face, with its sharp nose and sharp chin. This livid and as it were lipless mask seemed all the stranger for its sepulchral immobility; without the rapid movement of M. Rodin's fingers, which, bent over his desk, were scratching away with his pen, one would have taken him for a corpse.[36]

Yet, by some infernal magnetism in their personality, such Jesuits were all too often able to overcome the handicap of their ugliness; Rodin seduced his victims with an entirely deceptive display of affability and sincerity.[37]

The second Jesuit physical type inverted the first. Where Rodin's vile exterior was falsely redeemed by his insidious charm, his colleague d'Aigrigny's handsome surface—the 'strength of mind, strength of body, and extreme elegance of manners' of the high-society Jesuit—was undermined by a subtle whiff of corruption:

Nevertheless, despite the combination of so many advantages, and although he left you almost always under the influence of his irresistible seduction, this feeling was mixed with a vague uneasiness, as if the grace and exquisite urbanity of this personage's manners, the enchantment of his speech, his delicate flatteries, the tender charm of his smile, had concealed some insidious trap.[38]

---

[35] E. Paradis, *Les Jésuites* (Paris, 1873), 14, is an example.
[36] Sue, *Le Juif errant*, i. 167. A less extreme specimen of the type is Sainte-Agathe in Augier's *Lions et renards*.   [37] Sue, *Le Juif errant*, esp. i. 268.
[38] Ibid. i. 168–9. Other versions of this model (some of them *jésuites de robe courte*) include Judacin in V. Ducange, *Les Trois Filles de la veuve*, 6 vols. (Paris, 1826), who was only explicitly identified as a Jesuit in the later dramatizations of

These conventions of physical description made clear that the plots of anti-jesuit fiction would hinge on deceit and seduction, but they left plenty of room for manœuvre in the interpretation of Jesuit motives. It was here that major changes in the Jesuit stereotype took place during the nineteenth century.

The 1820s saw renewed interest in French literature's most famous seducing deceiver, Tartuffe. Performances and loose imitations of Molière's play were popular among those who hoped to undermine the credit of Catholic *dévots* and remind the government of its duty to curtail the exploitation of religious sentiment for non-religious ends.[39] Similar concerns informed anti-jesuit literature, and shaped the characters of its fictional villains. It was remarked at the time that the two words 'Jesuit' and 'Tartuffe' expressed the same combination of three qualities: 'guile, hypocrisy, bad faith'.[40] Jesuit characters like Laumier's Jobardini, Dinocourt's Candini, Mortonval's Royant, and most of Santo-Domingo's Visatout family were all freelance *ambitieux*, using the appearance of religion to further their purely selfish ends.[41] The same held true of the wicked Jesuit figures who flooded the Parisian stage in the aftermath of the July Revolution. 'The roles of intriguers, of swindlers, of malefactors, in comedies and melodramas are always represented by Jesuits,' observed the Austrian ambassador early in September 1830.[42] He was no doubt thinking of plays like *La Contre-lettre*, whose Jesuit villain was an engagingly unscrupulous comic-opera intriguer, with daggers and pistols falling out of his pockets; or *La Demande en mariage*, in which a *jésuite de robe courte* resorted to forgery in order to win money and a bride; or the two stage versions of Ducange's *Les Trois Filles de la veuve*, in which Judacin, earlier described in the novel as 'a contraband Tartuffe, a moral rascal, who speculated adroitly in weakness, credulity,

---

the novel (see below, n. 43); Gabriel in [F. Reybaud], *La Protestante; ou Les Cevennes au commencement du XVIIIe siècle*, 3 vols. (Paris, 1828); the Chipard brothers in J. Erckmann, *Les Disciples d'Escobar* (Paris, 1846); Pingard in A. Durantin, *Un jésuite de robe courte* (Paris, 1870).

[39] See P. Salvan, 'Le Tartuffe de Molière et l'agitation anticléricale en 1825', *Revue de la Société d'Histoire du Théâtre*, 12 (1960), 7–19.

[40] *Les Jésuites marchands*, 20.

[41] They appear respectively in *L'Enfant du jésuite*, *Le Camisard*, *Le Tartufe moderne*, and *Les Jésuites en action*. (In the original version, serialized in *Le Mercure du XIXe siècle* in 1826, the Visatout were called Bonifoux.)

[42] Apponyi, *Vingt-cinq ans*, i. 373.

hypocrisy', was now explicitly branded a Jesuit as well.[43] If all villains were Jesuits, there was unlikely to be anything very distinctive about a Jesuit villain.

Not all the Jesuit characters portrayed by anti-jesuits during the Restoration and its immediate aftermath could be assimilated to the Tartuffe-model, however. Though Marcet allowed occasional variety in the highly abusive (and supposedly non-fictional) thumbnail sketches of contemporary Jesuits which made up his *Les Jésuites modernes*, he gave the impression that most Jesuits were black-hearted fanatics rather than self-serving seducers.[44] Despite the title of Mortonval's novel, *Le Tartufe moderne*, its leading Jesuit, Laurent, was a zealous persecutor, absolved in his own eyes by his vow of obedience, and quite different from his more Tartuffe-like teacher Royant.[45] The contrast between these two types of 'Jesuit' character was deliberately highlighted by Santo-Domingo in the final chapter of *Les Jésuites en action*, when the Jesuit Innocent Visatout harangues the selfish careerist Jesuit affiliates who make up the rest of his family: 'Know, my dear father and mother, that I myself will be the executor of the wishes of my order against you; for my father is the General of the Jesuits, my mother the *congrégation*.'[46]

The Jesuit totally devoted to his order, ready to do anything to expand and fortify its power, and scornful of all other interests, was not a wholly new figure; Saint-Simon had long ago, in a passage sometimes cited by nineteenth-century anti-jesuits, described Père Letellier in similar terms.[47] In terms of the conventions of nineteenth-century anti-jesuit fiction, however, such characterization was novel, and raised new questions, since fanaticism seems to

---

[43] Duport and Monnais, *La Contre-lettre*; E. Monnais and E. Arago, *La Demande en mariage; ou Le Jésuite retourné: Comédie-vaudeville en 1 acte* (Paris, 1830); Villeneuve and Bourgeois, *Le Congréganiste*; V. Ducange and R.-C. Guilbert de Pixérécourt, *Le Jésuite: Drame en 3 actes et en 6 tableaux* (Paris, 1830); Ducange, *Les Trois Filles*, ii. 76.

[44] Thus Père Jean was 'without humanity, without love, full of that unfortunate religion which heaven in its wrath sometimes inspires in wicked hearts'; Père Dutems believed 'that friendship had caused all the evils that desolate the world'; and Père Becquet was distinguished by 'that Jesuitical goodness which would embrace you right up to the stake which it had set up itself' (Marcet, *Les Jésuites modernes*, 89, 54–5, 13).

[45] Mortonval, *Le Tartufe moderne*, esp. iii. 136.

[46] Santo-Domingo, *Les Jésuites en action*, 146.

[47] Duc de Saint-Simon, *Mémoires*, ed. A. de Boislisle, 41 vols. (Paris, 1879–1928), xxiv. 117.

call for explanation and analysis of a kind not usually felt to be required by the fact that self-interested people take advantage of
opportunities for profitable hypocrisy. Though neither Mortonval
nor Santo-Domingo offered much in the way of such analysis, their
introduction of fanatical Jesuits marked the path along which the
stereotypical Jesuit would escape from the Tartuffe-mould. Anti-
jesuit fiction began to show signs of the radical shift in emphasis
which George Sand would make explicit, in a broader anticlerical
context, when, in the preface to *Mademoiselle La Quintinie*, she
disclaimed any intention to 'pit sincerity and hypocrisy against each
other', arguing that the progress of public morality, by killing
hypocrisy, had made such an opposition anachronistic. Many a
Jesuit in the anti-jesuit fiction of later decades could best be
described, as Émile Lemontier described the meddling priest
Moréali in Sand's novel, not as an ordinary hypocrite, but as an
'hypocrite de profession', sincerely undertaking 'one of those
perfidious and mysterious campaigns that believes itself to have a
sacred aim'.[48]

As anti-jesuits switched their energies from denouncing the
insincere manipulation of religious language and values to exploring the nature of Jesuit fanaticism, the Society of Jesus, as the presumed focus and generator of Jesuit loyalties, became increasingly
central to their analyses of Jesuitical behaviour. As a result, having
figured in most Restoration anti-jesuit fiction only peripherally, as
a vehicle for ambitions conceived independently of it, the Jesuit
organization itself now became a forceful presence in the novels.
The novels of the 1820s generally described small-scale intrigues
involving isolated egotists, who would be defeated if their deceptions were exposed decisively before reaching fruition. A satirical
or comic approach was often considered appropriate, and happy
endings were usual. Once Jesuits came to be seen as fanatical and
obedient servants of their order, the power balance was over-
thrown. On the one side were the Jesuits' scattered and unorganized
victims; on the other a unified corporation, possessing continuity
of purpose from generation to generation and resources of power
not significantly diminishable by the set-backs of its individual members. Anti-jesuit novels now tended to melodrama on
a national or international scale, displaying the extent of Jesuit

---

[48] G. Sand, *Mademoiselle La Quintinie*, 2nd edn. (Paris, 1863), pp. vi, 203.

power, and their endings often towards tragedy, mitigated only by the vague hope that Evil might not triumph forever. Anti-jesuit fiction was increasingly rarely a gleeful deflation of egotistical ambitions and increasingly often a rather sadistic account of relentless victimization.

The Jesuits in Sue's *Le Juif errant*, who hounded the heirs to the Rennepont fortune across the globe, from Siberia and Java to Paris, till all but one were dead and the fortune lost forever, were meant to inspire terror, not laughter. At their first appearance in the novel the two principal Jesuits, d'Aigrigny and Rodin, are explicitly contrasted. Sue compares the former, who seemingly personifies 'the demon of pride and domination' yet who humbles himself in passive obedience to a summons to Rome rather than visit his beloved and dying mother, to an eagle, and the latter, with his 'diabolical cunning', to a reptile.[49] Later chapters add detail to the two portraits. D'Aigrigny finds difficulty in achieving the total detachment from personal relationships demanded by the Society of Jesus, but submits to its discipline because it gives him greater power and domination over his subordinates even than he once had as a military commander.[50] Yet he himself is often dominated by the cunning and ruthless determination of his secretary Rodin. When d'Aigrigny's violent methods fail to secure the Rennepont fortune, Rodin takes command, delivering a scornful attack on his predecessor:

You have been a handsome soldier, dashing and affected: you have roamed the wars, the festivities, the gay life, the women—These things have half burnt you out. . . . You will always lack that vigour, that single-mindedness which dominates men and events. I have that vigour, that single-mindedness, and I have it—Do you know why? It's because, uniquely devoted to the service of our company, I have always been ugly, dirty, and a virgin—yes, a virgin—all my virility is in this.[51]

This self-portrait had little in common with Tartuffe. Yet Sue, as if uncertain how to flesh it out, proceeded in the rest of the novel to dismantle it. Rodin's vigour, ruthlessness, and fanatical single-mindedness[52] were still stressed (as was his virginity) and were

[49] Sue, *Le Juif errant*, i. 174–5, 191.
[50] Ibid. i. 187–9; ii. 18–19. [51] Ibid. iii. 82.
[52] In one scene Rodin continues to write orders while undergoing a painful operation (ibid. iv. 265–73).

to secure him his place as the archetypal Jesuit in anti-jesuit mythology, but his total devotion to his order was revealed as an imposture. Rodin's driving passion, Sue disclosed, was a personal ambition to become Pope. He used the Society of Jesus as a stepping-stone, intent on subjugating it once it had raised him to the Papacy, and meanwhile breaking its regulations when it suited him.[53] In short, Rodin turned out to be a double hypocrite, exploiting the codes of Jesuitism as well as those of religion for self-interested purposes. Only his extreme megalomania, a trace of clericalism,[54] and Sue's decisive break with satire put him in a different class from Tartuffe. In the end, Sue had him poisoned as a traitor to his order.[55]

If all Jesuits were Rodins, the Society of Jesus would tear itself apart. Nor could they all be d'Aigrignys, who became Jesuits for the pleasure of manipulating passively obedient underlings. *Le Juif errant* maintained the same distinction as did Salverte, between the mental constitution of the Jesuit leadership and that of the rank and file. The latter appeared only briefly, and were presented as entirely devoted to the performance of the will of their superiors.[56] Significantly, while Sue revealed nothing about the education of Rodin or d'Aigrigny, he made clear that their subordinates were the artificial products of a process akin to brainwashing. D'Aigrigny rejoiced at his order's ability, through its discipline of obedience and its mysterious exercises, to drain a man of his individual intelligence, conscience, and free will:

Then, into these soulless bodies, mute, sullen, cold as corpses, we breathe the spirit of our order; instantly the corpses walk, act, perform orders, but without leaving the circle in which they are forever enclosed; it is thus that they become members of this gigantic body whose will they mechanically perform, but of whose plans they are ignorant, just as the hand performs the hardest tasks, without knowing, without understanding the thought which directs it.[57]

This process is described, from the victim's point of view, by one of the novel's heroes, Gabriel Rennepont. Having been drawn into the Jesuit net at an early age because of his connection with the

[53] Ibid. iii. 109; iv. 232; v. 310–13.   [54] Ibid. v. 311–12.
[55] Ibid. v. 389–92.   [56] Ibid. iv. 216–17.
[57] This passage is not in the 1844–5 Brussels edn. but can be found on p. 34 of vol. iii of the 1845 Paris edn.

Rennepont fortune, Gabriel reveals how, in his Jesuit education, everything was arranged to impose on him and his fellow victims 'the same pale, dreary, washed-out stamp', and to bring him to the point where he takes Jesuit vows as a sort of escape into 'the peace of the tomb'.[58] It must be said that Sue somewhat undermined the force of his character's complaint by making him do duty also as a model priest, representing a Christianity antithetical to Jesuitism; Gabriel it too palpably angelic for his claim to have been irreparably soiled by Jesuit education to be very persuasive. Indeed, in his case the process of Jesuitization breaks down; he soon comes to doubt the goodness of the Jesuit cause, and to demand release from his vows, praying God to enlighten the many of his fellow Jesuits who remain docile servants of interests of the real nature of which they are ignorant.[59] Gabriel's account of his education is nevertheless significant because in it Sue forcefully asserted, for the first time in nineteenth-century French fiction, both that rank and file Jesuits were victims, not responsible for their actions, blindly obedient believers in their order's glorious mission; and that the Society of Jesus was able, by its educational methods, to induce this state of mind more or less at will. The ordinary Jesuit, then, was no more hypocritical than the soldier who crept camouflaged upon his enemy; to question his behaviour, one must start not with the ethics of camouflage, but with habits of obedience and military training.

This was also the view of Michon, who based his view of Jesuit psychology on Lamennais's notion of the displacement of ambition.[60] In *Le Maudit*, Michon wasted little effort on the characterization of individual Jesuits; it was the social mechanism binding them together that mattered. Sue's Jesuit dictators, quivering with pride and ambition, were here replaced by business-like committees.[61] In *Le Jésuite*, his third novel, Michon repeated the trick of Gabriel Rennepont's lament. Belatedly awakening to the liberties his superiors have taken with his personality, Père de Sainte-Maure complains that Jesuit education, and indeed the whole regime of Jesuit life, promotes perpetual intellectual infancy and moral malleability. The devotional exercises required of a Jesuit novice,

---

[58] Sue, *Le Juif errant* (Brussels, 1844–5), ii. 445–54.   [59] Ibid. ii. 461.
[60] Michon, *Le Maudit*, i. 165–8, quoting Lamennais extensively.
[61] Ibid. i. 153–9; ii. 425–37; iii. 57–69.

for example, are a 'veritable machine, with a thousand gears, in which, once you have entered, you are no longer master of yourself, and which takes the human souls as do those modern mechanisms which take clay, beat it, roll it, cut it, compress it, and turn it out all moulded, ready to be baked in the potter's kiln'.[62]

Imagery of this sort, depicting the routine of Jesuit life, discipline, or education as a carefully constructed machine which imposed a uniform *empreinte* or *cachet* on the malleable, mouldable substance of human personality, was common in anti-jesuit literature. In the later years of the century, Octave Mirbeau and Édouard Estaunié (both one-time Jesuit pupils) would concentrate on this mangling, stereotyping process, producing anti-jesuit novels which belong to the genre of psychological drama rather than melodrama.[63] For the time being, however, the bitter, self-pitying résumés of Gabriel and Sainte-Maure remained nuggets of crude educational psychology stuck in the melodramatic mud-bed, and the process they described was simply glossed over or taken for granted in most anti-jesuit fiction. Though their plots were often more domestic in scale than those spun by Sue and Michon, the anti-jesuit novels and plays of the late 1860s and 1870s were still tales of intrigue, in which the Jesuit as villain overshadowed the Jesuit as victim. The figure of the Jesuit fanatic, identifying totally with the power and glory of his order, was constantly repeated. The Jesuit Sainte-Agathe, in Augier's satirical comedy *Lions et renards*, performed in 1869, spends most of the play behaving like a Restoration Tartuffe, yet when asked what passion he is obeying, he replies:

A passion you have no suspicion of, you voluptuaries, you happy ones of the world! A passion which dries up all others—that of domination. What could I achieve, puny creature that I am, with my individual will? I have abdicated it to espouse a collective will and serve it blindly. What does it matter to me to be poor and unknown! I immolate my mind and body to the omnipotence of my order, which is my satisfaction; when they put me in the ground after a life of obscurity and privation, the world will not suspect that this nameless corpse has had orgies of power, that it has felt in its bones the sharpest delights of despotism![64]

---

[62] Michon, *Le Jésuite*, i. 168; also ii. 61.

[63] O. Mirbeau, *Sébastien Roch: Roman de mœurs* (Paris, 1890); E. Estaunié, *L'Empreinte* (Paris, 1896).   [64] Augier, *Lions et renards*, 152.

The Jesuit critic Longhaye rightly protested that Sainte-Agathe was 'an impossible monster', 'the extreme of abnegation in the extreme of egotism'.[65] The idea of immolating oneself in order oneself to feel the thrill of despotism is paradoxical, and Augier unconvincingly makes the process of doing it sound the easiest matter in the world. The same objection could be raised against many a Jesuit villain of the early Third Republic. Gustave Graux's Père Bloom, for example, was allegedly motivated by 'collective egoism'; readers wishing to know how proud individuals could be turned into such de-individualized machines were referred rather surprisingly to Stendhal's *Le Rouge et le noir*.[66] Sirven and Le Verdier's Père Anselme identified with his order, to the point of sacrificing his life for it, apparently mainly out of an amoral fascination with its incomparable efficiency as a fighting organization.[67] Armand Durantin's Père Ronsin, a remarkably crudely sketched fanatic even by the standards of anti-jesuit fiction, was 'a sectarian . . . who had succeeded long ago in stifling in his heart all human affection, all worldly weakness, who had only one aim, the greatness of the order of Loyola', but whose fanaticism went otherwise unexplained.[68] His subordinate Daniel Dufresne was said to have lost his moral sense through Jesuit education[69] (only to have it reawaken embarrassingly as the misdeeds required of him by his superior became ever more preposterous, driving him to hopeless resistance and eventual suicide), but this process was merely mentioned, not analysed. The anti-jesuit novelists of the early Third Republic were reproducing a by now standard figure, and did not feel it necessary to dwell on character-formation. The flashy paradox about self-abnegation as sublimation of ambition may have made sense only because it had now become so familiar, but the frequency with which it was repeated indicates its hold over the anti-jesuit imagination. Within the envelope of the seducer, Tartuffe had given way to the corporate fanatic.

In their different ways, the seducer and the fanatic were each the antithesis of the liberal ideal: the one opposed his deceptions to the

---

[65] G. Longhaye, 'Types cléricaux dans le drame et le roman modernes: Étude morale et littéraire: Troisième article', *Études religieuses, historiques et littéraires*, 4th ser. 5 (1870), 353–4.   [66] Graux, *Les Amours d'un jésuite*, 11–12.
[67] Sirven and Le Verdier, *Le Jésuite rouge*, 95–6.
[68] Durantin, *Un élève des jésuites*, 126–7. On p. 250 Ronsin actually declares: 'Let the whole world perish rather than the Society of Jesus!'   [69] Ibid. 41.

transparency of rational debate; the other, the blind fury of his passion to the balanced harmony of individual interests and the freedom of individual consciences. When the amalgam of the two was suffused with a corporate spirit, the security of liberal society was triply threatened, through a treacherous mockery of its basic individualism. The Jesuit of myth—that perfect, poisonous automaton, the shell of human selfhood gutted and reanimated by the consuming fire of Jesuit identity—was not just a chilling villain for melodramatic fiction. He was a symbol of social and political menace whose roots sank deep into the anxious side of post-Revolutionary liberalism.

Conclusion

To account for the readiness of so many Frenchmen to explain the nation's difficulties in terms of a large-scale Jesuit conspiracy is not a simple matter, for a conspiracy theory, though it projects a simplistic vision of politics, is not an uncomplex thing. 'Conspiracy theory' is a name given to frameworks within which a variety of disparate elements are brought and held together, and the relationship between the framework and the elements is both intricate and often unclear. To put it another way, conspiracy theories seldom spring into existence fully formed. They are fashioned with argument of an often piecemeal kind, and crystallize around themes and images many of which can also exist outside them. In this sense, conspiracy theories draw some of their emotional or intellectual or cultural resonance from their constituent parts, whether thematic or rhetorical; the whole exists and commands assent partly because the ingredients are found convincing. At the same time, however, any conspiracy theory which survives for long in a developed form exerts, as a framework, an influence on its own ingredients, attracting new ones and moulding old ones. The parts, in this sense, are found appealing at least partially because the whole has an appeal of its own. In assessing what it is that gives conspiracy theories their influence and assures their survival, there seem to be no obvious grounds for assigning an automatic priority to the charms either of their overall vision of conspiracy or of their more specific components.

Any enquiry into such matters may, in fact, usefully proceed on three levels: the thematic, the rhetorical, and the structural. On the first level, to take the case that has been studied in this book, are the themes and images that found a place in the anti-jesuit conspiracy theory; on the second are the arguments and rhetorical habits through which that conspiracy theory was built up and sustained; on the third is its overarching structure, as manifested in the grand vision of Jesuit conspiracy.

Recent chapters have dealt at length with the principal contents of the first level. They have suggested a number of ways in which particular elements in the nineteenth-century mythology concerning the Jesuits may have articulated or reflected broader contemporary anxieties, whether specific (e.g. betrayal of trust by servants or professional advisers), or more general (e.g. crisis in the family, corruption of morals, perversion of historical knowledge). In particular they have revealed the widespread recurrence and central importance in the anti-jesuit mythology (especially in those parts of it which deal with affiliation and with the Jesuit character) of the themes of fake individuality and concealed corporate identity, whose relationship to the insecurities of believers in a State-sponsored liberal individualism, faced with the pluralist tendencies and particular loyalties of modern societies, was suggested earlier. In some areas, then, the mythology of anti-jesuitism had its own direct relevance to nineteenth-century concerns; in others, however —regicide, for example—its appeal seems harder to explain without referring to the broader structures in which it was lodged.

The contents of the rhetorical level—the types of argument used in detecting, defining, and denouncing Jesuit conspiracy—were discussed at some length in Chapter 5, and have been illustrated in other parts of the book. It may be useful in analysing them to distinguish between two rhetorical styles which conspiracy theorists employ.[1] In the first, the 'conspirator-centred' style, the emphasis is on the identification and labelling of those supposedly involved in the conspiracy, and the establishment of connections between them; a conspiracy theory elaborated in this style tends to depict conspiracy as a human network. In the second, the 'plan-centred' style, connections are established between events or circumstances rather than between individuals; conspiracy is perceived as a sinister pattern in what happens, supposedly reflecting the operation of a more or less formal conspiratorial plan. The elaboration of a conspiracy theory typically involves some combination of, and interaction between, these two styles—the identification of suspect individuals contributing to that of sinister events, and vice versa —but the balance between them can vary considerably.

Specimens of both styles can certainly be found in the literature and oratory of nineteenth-century French anti-jesuitism. Denunciation of the personnel of Jesuit conspiracy was a significant element

---

[1] The distinction drawn here is established in more detail in G. T. Cubitt, 'Conspiracy Myths and Conspiracy Theories', *JASO* (*Journal of the Anthropological Society of Oxford*), 20 (1989), 18–24.

in the Restoration attacks on the Jesuit–Congrégation tandem ('M. Franchet, director-general of police, is he not a Jesuit? Have we not M. Delavau, prefect of police, Jesuit? Have we not M. the director-general of the letter post? Is he not a Jesuit?', demanded *Le Constitutionnel*[2]), as it was in Raspail's castigation of his scientific and political rivals. Often, however, such denunciations, though themselves 'conspirator-centred' in style, appear to have been prem-issed on predominantly 'plan-centred' reasoning: it was the per-ceived coincidence of an individual's behaviour with the Jesuits' conspiratorial design, or his involvement in a type of organization traditionally associated with that design, rather than (or more than) any specified personal connection with other Jesuit personnel, that made him a 'Jesuit' in anti-jesuit eyes. Anti-jesuits showed, on the whole, relatively little interest in mapping the human networks of Jesuitism in concrete factual detail (they were ready enough to do so in the abstract or in fiction); it is significant, as already noted, how little attention was paid to compiling information on the activities, the personal contacts, or even the individual identities of actual living French Jesuits. Instead, it was largely by argument in the 'plan-centred' style that the conspiracy theory was built up and extended to cover new historical circumstances. Sometimes, as in the case of the *Monita secreta*, or of *Le Constitutionnel*'s revelations of the conversations on the Mont-Saint-Bernard, or of Leone's Chieri conference, anti-jesuits claimed formal textual knowledge of a Jesuit conspiratorial plan. Sometimes the argument was more straightforwardly teleological ('Cui prodest scelus, is fecit,' was Jacquemont's reason for implicating the Jesuits in the French Re-volution[3]). Typically and pervasively, however, it was myth that supplied the outline of the Jesuit design: anti-jesuits developed their awareness of Jesuit conspiracy in the present by connecting present happenings with the patterns familiar from their mythical version of the Jesuit past. This dominance of the 'plan-centred' over the 'conspirator-centred' style gives to anti-jesuit reasoning an in some ways uninquisitorial feel. This is not the operative rhetoric of witch-hunt and purge (though it could of course help prepare the way for them). In superficial appearance, it is a rhetoric of clarification, geared more to the understanding of events than to the relentless quest for guilty men. The appearance is not always to

---

[2] *Constitutionnel*, 12 Nov. 1827.   [3] Jacquemont, *Examen impartial*, 48.

be trusted; rapid shifts to a more inquisitorial style could never be ruled out. Neither, however, is it insignificant. Anti-jesuits were of course interested in establishing the identity of those to blame for the disasters and miscarriages of history and current affairs, but it was in collective rather than in individual identity that they conceived the essence of the matter to lie. (To say that 'the Jesuit Ravaillac' had killed Henri IV was to find a more detailed way of saying that the Jesuits had killed him, but not, in their view, to say something more exactly true.) In fact, as has been seen, they believed that Jesuits simply could not be considered as individual personalities. The notion that Jesuits were barely human might in theory have stimulated a determination to hunt them down like vermin (as happened later with the Jews); it seems, however, seldom to have done so. Instead, it was on Jesuitism as a collective spirit that anti-jesuits concentrated, and this they considered to be best revealed by its traditionally characteristic fruits.

The prevailing rhetorical strategies of anti-jesuitism thus reflect the crucial role of myth in shaping anti-jesuit perceptions. This brings our exploration of the anti-jesuit conspiracy theory on to the third—the structural—level. For what the myth provided was not simply a catalogue of the major traditional forms of Jesuit iniquity, with supporting examples, but an overarching vision of Jesuit conspiracy. Though this vision allowed nineteenth-century anti-jesuits room for manœuvre in their selection of themes and employment of arguments, it supplied a basic framework for their interpretations, and one whose principal characteristics those interpretations on the whole merely accentuated. By comparing these characteristics with those of the equivalent visions of conspiracy generated in other historical circumstances or within other traditions of conspiracy theory, we can begin to give the anti-jesuits of nineteenth-century France their place in a broader typology and longer history of the paranoid style.

The characteristic secular conspiracy theories of the eighteenth century, as studied most notably by historians interested in the ideological background to the American Revolution, but also by historians of Britain and France, were (by nineteenth-century standards) relatively small in scale.[4] The conspiracies they described—

[4] See the works of Wood, Bailyn, Christie, and Kaplan, listed in the Bibliography.

be they ministerial intrigues, plots against the government, or *complots de famine*—were typically ones hatched by a small number of men of recognized public prominence or political importance— ministers, courtiers, or notable representatives of sectional interests. These men were imagined to be moved by personal ambition, greed, or lust for power, and to be conspiring for some relatively limited and specific purpose (such as to enslave the colonies, to control the government, or to starve the people), and the life-span of their conspiracies was accordingly to be measured in years, perhaps decades, but not centuries. The French Revolution both inherited and transformed this pattern of conspiracy theory; its evolving discourse on conspiracy began by transmitting a series of images of limited intrigue of the familiar eighteenth-century kind, and ended, in the Terrorist rhetoric of the Year II, by conflating an ever-expanding series of them into one vast, rambling, and seem- ingly open-ended vision of conspiratorial Counter-Revolution. This vision, however, retained two of the distinctive features of its eighteenth-century predecessors: the restricted time-span (in this case generally beginning with the Revolution itself) and the attri- bution of conspiracy to known political actors (foreign govern- ments, royal ministers, the Girondins, the Hébertistes, Danton and his associates).[5]

The major nineteenth-century traditions of conspiracy theory— and this is as true of the predominantly right-wing anti-masonic and anti-Semitic traditions as it is of the anti-jesuit one—projected a vision of conspiracy which differed from this eighteenth-century secular model in at least five notable ways. First, conspiracy was now located not among the ostensible holders of power and influ- ence, but in a group whose existence or whose membership or whose political character was a secret; the primary revelations of conspiracy theory now concerned the activities of hidden political actors, rather than the hidden motives of public figures. Second, the motives of the conspirators were taken to be collective rather than personal; it was devotion to the interest of the organization (or the race, in the Jewish case) that determined their behaviour. Third, the relatively limited aims attributed to conspiracy in the eighteenth century were now replaced by ones of effectively limit- less scope, like world domination, or the destruction of all order

---

[5] See Cubitt, 'Denouncing Conspiracy'.

and authority, or the undermining of Christian civilization. Fourth, and in keeping with this extreme breadth of purpose, the conspiracies now described embraced a much wider range of methods and activities than those previously envisaged. Finally, since these conspiracies were taken to be the work of organizations capable of pursuing constant aims despite the deaths or defeats of their individual members, and devoted to ends so ambitious they could scarcely ever be perfectly fulfilled, they seemed almost infinitely durable. The idea of Jesuit (or masonic or Jewish) conspiracy tended to serve as a sort of standing explanation, always ready to absorb new phenomena or fresh events. Conspiracy theories turned into ever more elaborate and extensive accounts both of history and of current affairs.

How were these highly developed visions of all-encompassing conspiracy able to take root and to exert an influence? It is no doubt possible, on some level, to trace a connection between evolutions in conspiracy theory and changes in concrete political conditions. The imagined conspiracies of the eighteenth century roughly fitted the limited and élitist world of pre-Revolutionary politics; those of the nineteenth perhaps accorded with the broader and more complex realities of a political world increasingly shaped by electoral considerations, by politically conscious public opinion, and by new forms of political association. The explanatory force of such an observation is, however, limited. In the first place, it rests on too sweeping a summary of political development: the political culture of late eighteenth-century Britain and America (which generated the best-known cases of the relatively limited style of conspiracy theory) already had much of the complexity and social depth which we associate with the nineteenth century, while the influence of the great nineteenth-century conspiracy myths was not confined to countries with highly developed arenas of public politics. Even were this not the case, however, it would seem implausible to treat conspiracy theories (with their claim to reveal what is hidden) simply as straightforward reflections of practical political conditions. Some fuller understanding of the basic functions which conspiracy theories perform, and hence of the possible bases of their appeal, is required if their variations and transformations on the structural level are to be comprehended.

It was suggested in passing at the beginning of this book that conspiracy theories do three things: explain what happens as the intended product of conscious human volition; establish the division of humanity into two opposed camps; and affirm a discrepancy between the surface appearance and the hidden reality of human affairs. For convenience, these may be called the 'intentionalist', the 'dualist', and the 'occultist' functions of conspiracy theory.[6] They are held together, within the structure of a conspiracy theory, by that structure's central organizing device, the notion of a unique and effective conspiracy. They need not, however, receive equal emphasis within that structure, or be equally important in securing assent for it, at any given historical moment. Conspiracy theories, in short, do not exist in a state of perfect and perpetual three-point balance; they are prone to list and spiral.

An effort to explore the eighteenth- and nineteenth-century transformations of the paranoid style in these terms may usefully begin with the interpretation of eighteenth-century conspiracy theories offered (with American examples primarily but not exclusively in mind) by Gordon S. Wood. Wood's purpose is to argue against the view (once dominant in studies of the paranoid style) that conspiracy theories are manifestations of 'irrationality', whose influence in history can only be attributable to psychological aberrance. On the contrary, he suggests, those of the eighteenth century were closely connected with a fundamental project of the rationalistic Enlightenment: the effort to found a science of human affairs on the same paradigm of mechanistic causality that the scientific revolution of the late seventeenth century had established as the basis of the physical sciences. Anxious to posit an indissoluble connection between cause and effect, and to exclude from their explanations the operations both of chance and of an interventionist divinity, yet reluctant (for the sake of morality) to abandon the principle of free will, the 'enlightened' men of the eighteenth century were led inexorably to assign the role of causes to human intentions. Cause and effect were assumed to be morally identical: good effects stemmed from good intentions, and bad from bad. Effects forming a discernible pattern were presumed to be the consequence of concerted intentions. Since evil effects were not always visibly accompanied by correspondingly evil intentions, those who thought in these terms tended also to become obsessed

---

[6] The analytical apparatus used here is set out more fully in Cubitt, 'Conspiracy Myths', 13–18.

with the prevalence of duplicity' and deception in human affairs. Where their Puritan predecessors had scanned the surface of events for evidence of God's will in operation, they learnt to scan it for evidence of hidden conspiratorial designs. In short, Wood argues, eighteenth-century 'enlightened' thought 'was structured in such a way that conspiratorial explanations of complex events became normal, necessary, and rational'.[7]

Wood's account is one which stresses what I have called the 'intentionalist' function of conspiracy theories, and which gives their 'occultist' function a significant but dependent role: conspiracy theories are held to have appealed because they made it possible to sustain a certain causal theory, and to have done so partly by dwelling on the deceptiveness of surface appearances in the study of human character and motives. This makes good sense of the particular characteristics of eighteenth-century secular conspiracy theories. If their role was essentially to provide causal explanations of events, while preserving intact the notion of individual moral responsibility, it is not surprising that such theories concentrated on interpreting the motives of public figures, that they sketched those motives largely in personal terms, and that the patterns they detected in events reflected a limited vision of conspiracy's scope and durability.

What happened to conspiracy theory at the end of the eighteenth century and in the course of the nineteenth, however, remains problematic. In Wood's own view, the French Revolution dealt it a slow death-wound: an event so vast and complex and tumultuous simply ruptured the frameworks of 'enlightened' causal theory. While pioneers like Hegel moved towards a quite different conception of the flow of history, those who clung to the old explanatory habits were forced to make their conspiracy theories ever more elaborate and speculative to keep abreast of the turbulent flood of modern events. Increasingly deserted by the intellectual mainstream of Western culture, conspiracy theory began a slow but inexorable drift to beach itself in the cranky margins of political debate.[8]

Such a view harbours an element of truth and an element of over-simplification. It seems plausible enough to interpret the extravagant growth of conspiracy theory in Revolutionary France

---

[7] G. S. Wood, 'Conspiracy and the Paranoid Style: Causality and Deceit in the Eighteenth Century', *William and Mary Quarterly*, 3rd ser. 39 (1982), 411–29 (quotation 421).   [8] Ibid. 431–2.

itself, based as it was on a constant scrutiny of the actions and suspicious probing of the motives of public political figures, as in part the product of a desperate effort to apply the assumptions of 'enlightened' causal theory in unprecedentedly unpromising historical circumstances. Whether such an interpretation tells us as much about the extravagances of the major nineteenth-century conspiracy visions is less clear. No doubt the 'intentionalist' assumptions about causality that were implicit in conspiracy theories did command less general assent in the century following the Revolution than in the century preceding it, and no doubt greater inventiveness was needed to sustain them. It need not follow, however, that the Revolution's long-term effect on the foundations of conspiracy theory was purely destructive, and the nineteenth-century histories both of anti-jesuitism and of anti-masonry (to say nothing of the late nineteenth- and early twentieth-century history of anti-Semitism) may lead us to question whether this was the case. Something more than the tortured straining of a superannuated explanatory mode may be reflected in the structural hyper-development of nineteenth-century conspiracy theories; it may also reflect a shift in the primary functions which conspiracy theories performed. If the French Revolution had eroded the philosophical foundations of the 'intentionalist' function, it had done nothing to undermine the 'occultist' interest in hidden meanings, and had positively encouraged the 'dualist' description of human affairs.

'Occultism', here, may be understood in either a stronger or a weaker sense. In the stronger, it refers to the sheer (and often apolitical) appetite for concealed truths and mysterious realms of meaning that was a common feature of nineteenth-century European culture, and one which any decay in the fabric of eighteenth-century rationalism was only likely to encourage. Considered in this light, conspiracy theories appear as part of a broader picture that includes the occult sciences, Spiritualism, Theosophy, magic, astrology, Symbolist art, and fascination with secret societies both artistic and political.[9] The point here is not that conspiracy theories and other forms of occultism had overlapping constituencies (though

[9] This dimension to conspiracy theories is highlighted by J. Webb, *The Occult Establishment* (Glasgow, 1981), 213–73. See also R. Thurlow, 'The Powers of Darkness: Conspiracy Belief and Political Strategy', *Patterns of Prejudice*, 12 (1978), 4–12, on the division between 'occultists' and 'materialists' among modern British conspiracy theorists.

some conspiracy theorists certainly had broader esoteric interests), but that they were capable of expressing a similar cult or dramatization of hidden reality. Post-Barruelian anti-masonry, obsessed with Freemasonry's subjection to the occult directorship of the 'arrière-loges' and the sinister messages encoded in masonic ritual, perhaps provides the most striking examples, but references to secret texts, secret identities, occult language, and occult leader-ship were almost equally commonplace in the mythology of anti-jesuitism. Like other fashionable bodies of occultist lore, repeated allusions to the secret structures of conspiracy perhaps reflected a need to reconstruct a sense of the order and connectedness of things, which the confusing experience of modern life had jeopardized.

'Occultism' in this strong sense (the development of a formalized mythology of the secret) fed upon 'occultism' in the weaker sense —a preoccupation with the illusory quality of outward appearances or conventional descriptions of reality. Both in the political and in the social arena, the changes associated with the Revolution did much to transform the grounds for such a preoccupation, but can scarcely be said to have removed them. The implications of this refocusing of 'occultist' anxieties for our understanding of the poss-ible functions of conspiracy theory are most obvious in the realm of political analysis. The occult reality of politics, for the secular conspiracy theorists of the pre-Revolutionary age (and indeed of the Revolution itself), had essentially consisted of the hidden motives of political actors; the surface appearance with which it had been contrasted had consisted of these actors' publicly advertised characters. The occult reality had been detected by noting the moral discrepancy between this appearance and the effects to which the actors' conduct was perceived to contribute. The positing of an occult reality was thus part and parcel of the affirmation of relations of mechanistic causality in human affairs. It was also, however, frequently part of an analysis of power relations within the political system: the sinister influence of a ministerial cabal might, for example, be the occult reality which undercut the surface appear-ance of royal authority. Conspiracy theory, in other words, took root in the tension between the practical complexity (and hence opacity) of political power and the clarity of its official descriptions. This tension, however, was by no means peculiar to the small-scale court politics of the *ancien régime*, which the Revolution swept away;

in many ways, it was more pronounced and more endemic in the new forms of politics that the Revolution helped to launch.[10] For post-Revolutionary politics—whether its forms were those of Jacobin democracy, of liberal parliamentarism, or of populistic nationalism—was ideologically founded on the attribution of sovereign authority to an abstract entity (the people or the nation); its discourse and practice reflected the constant necessity and difficulty of defining and enacting that entity's elusive will. Politics were more public than hitherto, but political systems for that reason more complicated, and the actual location and operation of political power therefore more deeply mysterious. Occasions to imagine the circumvention of visible structures by clandestine ones, of the general interest by the partial, of legitimate authority by surreptitious influence, thus abounded, and were accepted both by those who admired the ideological claims of the new politics and had to account for its less glorious reality, and by those who rejected those claims and were concerned to expose its hypocrisy. Both on the Right and on the Left, conspiracy theories grew out of and systematized such suspicions.

In another way, too, the 'occultist' function of conspiracy theories remained important in the nineteenth century. In ceasing to make exposure of the secret motives and character of prominent public figures the central effect of their political analyses, nineteenth-century conspiracy theorists by no means lost interest in discrepancies between the surface appearance and the inner reality of individual character; this interest simply revealed itself in new analytical contexts, suggested by different social or ideological conditions. In a study of the use made of the paranoid style during the conflicts over slavery which preceded the American Civil War, David Brion Davis suggests a connection between the widespread belief in conspiracy and 'a sharp increase in confusion over social roles', produced by the unprecedented geographical and social mobility of the antebellum decades. In circumstances where self-conscious role-playing was the key to social success, there developed on the one hand 'a virtual obsession with hoaxes, imposters, frauds, confidence men, and double identities', on the other 'a yearning for authenticity, spontaneity, and naturalness'; conspiracy

---

[10] For a somewhat similar argument, see P. Nora, '1898: Le Thème du complot et la définition de l'identité juive', in M. Olender (ed.), *Le Racisme: Mythes et sciences* (Brussels, 1981), 158–9.

theories reflected these dispositions in the terms of political analysis.[11] Though Davis's argument can only be transposed with
caution to the less fluid social conditions of nineteenth-century
European states, the themes of fraudulent identity and deceitful
simulation (and the corresponding cult of honesty and spontaneity)
ran with equal persistence through the literatures of conspiracy
theory in countries like France; ample illustrations from the anti-
jesuit tradition have already been given. Social uneasiness of the
type referred to by Davis may have had something to do with this,
but the peculiar emphasis placed, in both the anti-jesuit and the
anti-masonic literatures, on the corporate nature of the false identity
and the depersonalized character of the conspirators suggests, as
I have argued earlier, that the insecurities (for the Left) and
perceived hypocrisies (for the Right) of post-Revolutionary liberal
individualism were also deeply involved. Once again, the gap between neat official description (of a society of independent, rational,
and responsible individuals bound together in equal and unmedi-
ated loyalty to the State) and confusing practical reality (of a society
teeming with partial, divided, and conflicting loyalties, and prone
to internecine strife) provided a promising terrain for the development of conspiracy theories, with their themes of deception and
hidden reality.

The continued relevance of their 'occultist' dimension, in the
altered circumstances of the post-Revolutionary world, thus helps
to explain the sheer tenacity of 'conspiratorial' explanations in
the secular thinking of the nineteenth century. It does less, on
its own, to explain their new-found scale and complexity. Here
the resurgence of dualism promoted by the French Revolution is
more important. Viewed from this angle, the relevant affinities of
nineteenth-century conspiracy theories are neither with Enlightened
science nor with occultist lore, but with religious ideologies. Indeed, it is to the religious conspiracy theories of the sixteenth and
seventeenth centuries (whether Protestant or Catholic), rather than
to the secular ones of the eighteenth, that the major nineteenth-
century specimens can most readily be compared; here one finds the
same sense of unmitigated and undying conflict between Good and
Evil, the same reductionism (the Protestant sectary or the Anglican

---

[11] D. B. Davis, *The Slave Power Conspiracy and the Paranoid Style* (Baton Rouge,
La., 1969), 26–9.

bishop as Papist in disguise), the same repetitive recourse to a constantly reusable stock mythology. These religious conspiracy theories left their mark on the secular ideologies they had helped to shape, even when the religious hatreds of the early modern period receded, and traces of their cosmic dualism coexisted with the rationalistic elements discussed by Wood even in the 'paranoid' rhetoric of the later eighteenth century.[12] Nor should their contribution to the conspiracy theory traditions of the nineteenth century be underestimated. If Barruel's counter-revolutionary denunciation of the *philosophe* conspiracy had its most immediate roots in the polemics which he and others had carried on before the Revolution in the periodical *Année littéraire*, these themselves have been seen as involving 'a secularization of anti-Protestant arguments about heresy', previously developed by seventeenth-century writers like Bossuet and Varillas.[13] Strongly Catholic in emphasis, nineteenth-century anti-masonry continued to assimilate present enemies to the age-old heretic tradition. In the case of anti-jesuitism, the continuity is both more and less obvious: more so, because the villains of an old religious conspiracy theory retained their original identity; less so, because primarily religious interests no longer inspired the majority of their denouncers.

Both in the anti-masonic and in the anti-jesuit case, this revival or reworking of styles of conspiracy theory familiar from an earlier age of religious strife reflected and sustained the influence of a deeply dichotomized vision of contemporary reality, whose immediate origins must be sought in the dramatic impact of the French Revolution on European imaginations. By its suddenness, by its violence, by the force of the pretension, embedded in its rhetoric and reflected in its practice, to rupture the course of history and bring forth a new order of existence, the Revolution left those who lived through it with the sensation of being placed (as the comte d'Allonville told his sons) 'on the frontiers of two worlds almost unknown one to the other'.[14] The new world, however, remained

[12] This is recognized by Wood, 'Conspiracy and the Paranoid Style', 420. The connection is explored more fully in T. M. Brown, 'The Image of the Beast: Anti-Papal Rhetoric in Colonial America', in R. O. Curry and T. M. Brown (eds.), *Conspiracy: The Fear of Subversion in American History* (New York, 1972), 1–20.

[13] Hofman, 'The Origins of the Theory of the *Philosophe* Conspiracy', 163–70.

[14] Comte d'Allonville, *Mémoires secrets, de 1770 à 1830*, 6 vols. (Paris, 1838–45), i. 4.

unstable, under threat; the Revolution thus became, for the nineteenth century, the dividing line of present politics as well as of history. Everything, wrote abbé de Pradt in 1825, was now reducible 'to these two words: for or against the Revolution, before or after the Revolution'.[15] Had the projector of history jammed for good, with the frames of old and new neatly frozen, reductionism of this kind might have found a stable footing. Instead, the navigational instruments of a dualism fashioned in the brutal but deceptive clarity of the Revolutionary dawn were called on, by both Left and Right, to fix the imagined hard outlines of old and new, Revolution and Counter-Revolution, good and evil, in the nineteenth century's swirling and unremitting blizzard of historical change. Terms like 'the Revolution' or 'the *ancien régime*' acquired a sense that went well beyond their reference to fixed historical periods or events; they stood for the opposing forces or movements whose war to the death was taken to be the essential drama of contemporary history. While the Right encompassed in its notion of 'the Revolution' each perceived threat to the Christian and monarchical order, men like Jules Ferry cut through the treacherous flux of modern politics to an equally simple core:

Today, there is a veiled but persistent struggle, between the society of former times, the *ancien régime* with its edifice of regrets, of beliefs and institutions, which does not accept modern democracy, and the society which emerges from the French Revolution; there is in our midst an *ancien régime* that is still persistent, still active, and when this struggle, which is the very root of the modern anarchy, when this intimate struggle is over, the political struggle will be over at the same stroke.[16]

Both on the Left and on the Right, conspiracy theories played an important practical part in this binary patterning of contemporary history. They helped not only to explain events, but to arrange them. An event or circumstance attributed to Jesuit (or masonic) action was marked out, and brought into significant connection with a host of others, on a map of history whose dualistic design was thus continually reinforced, or on a map of politics whose essential integration with that of history was constantly reaffirmed. In accounting for the lavish dimensions of nineteenth-century conspiracy theories, the imperatives of dualism are probably more

[15] Pradt, *Du jésuitisme ancien et moderne*, 237.
[16] Ferry, *Discours et opinions*, i. 304–5 (speech at the Salle Molière, 10 Apr. 1870).

important than any deep commitment of conspiracy theorists to a particular causal theory.

Placed in a comparative context, then, the anti-jesuit conspiracy theory studied in this book emerges as a specimen of a particular type, whose characteristics were shaped by and served the mental needs of an age subject simultaneously to the inherited shock of sudden revolution and to the sustained uncertainties of accelerating social and political and economic change. Elements in the detailed mythology of such conspiracy theories helped to express the anxieties of such an age; their overall structures helped to reduce those anxieties to order.

Remarks of this general nature, however, do not exhaust the question of why (and with what significance) the anti-jesuit conspiracy theory in particular exerted such an influence. Nor is the gap completely filled by returning to the more specific remarks made in Chapter 1, concerning the Jesuits' suggestive roles (as counter-revolutionaries, as Ultramontanes, as unauthorized possessors of a collective identity) in nineteenth-century political and religious affairs, though these help to explain how anti-jesuit inspirations could find a contemporary footing. When the general and the particular remarks are brought together, there remains something striking and apparently paradoxical about the readiness of so many self-styled champions of modernity to invest so heavily in a myth so graven with the preoccupations of former centuries.

To ask what lay behind this appropriation of the Jesuit and anti-jesuit past is to probe some complex tensions involved in the efforts of nineteenth-century French liberals and republicans to formulate a political understanding of the contemporary world and of their place within it. Though Right and Left alike had reason to crave the dualistic coherence that conspiracy theories could give to their accounts of modern experience, its achievement posed problems for the Left that the Right (at least in its dominant Catholic and monarchist form) largely avoided. For the Right seldom tied its determined rejection of the Revolution and 'the modern world' to a deep insistence on their novelty; it was ready enough to add them to the long and repetitive line of Satanically inspired wars on the divine order, which stretched back, through countless heresies, to the Crucifixion or to Eden.[17] Only in the more recent passages of

---

[17] See Cubitt, 'Catholics versus Freemasons', 129–30.

this epic conflict of Good and Evil had the Satanic onslaught taken the name of Revolution and a masonic organizational form; these changes marked a moment of great danger in the struggle (as the Reformation had done before), without, however, affecting its basic nature. It was the opposition of God and Satan, not that of old and new, that was fundamental. The Right, in short, experienced no real difficulty in blending its chosen conspiracy theory into the broader pattern of its dualism. Difficulties arose for the Left in so far as it committed itself to the notion that history was broken at the Revolution. If this rupture was taken to be fundamental, the basic conflicts of the modern age could not, in any straightforward sense, simply continue the hostilities of the old world. Nor, on the other hand, could they entirely be separated from them, if the old world remained present (in some sense) as the antagonist of the new. In short, the relationship between a bisected history and a binary present was problematic: liberals and republicans needed old enemies to establish their own modernity; to reveal the chasm of the Revolution, they needed to span it.

No iron law, of course, compelled admirers of the Revolution to treat it as a new departure in history. One powerful strand in left-wing thinking, whose most influential exponent was the historian Augustin Thierry, adopted a position quite close in formal terms to that just attributed to the Catholic Right. In a moral inversion of the aristocratic ideology of writers like Boulainvilliers, it traced a single unbroken thread of racial antagonism through fifteen centuries of French history, treating both the Revolution and the present as episodes in the long struggle between the subject Gauls and their Frankish conquerors.[18] This was a forceful and generally intransigent vision, with an obvious appeal to those whose radicalism was rooted in an enduring sense of social exclusion or oppression (not for nothing did Marx call Thierry the 'father of the class war in French historiography'[19]), and it was perfectly compatible with an ardent passion for the Revolution, but for a Revolution running with, rather than erupting across, the older current of history.

---

[18] See E. Weber, ' "Nos ancêtres les gaulois" ', in his *My France: Politics, Culture, Myth* (Cambridge, Mass., 1991), 21–39; L. Poliakov, *The Aryan Myth: A History of Racist and Nationalist Ideas in Europe* (London, 1971), 17–36.

[19] Quoted in Weber, ' "Nos ancêtres" ', 27.

When the anti-jesuit description of past and present is set along-side this alternative thesis of racial struggle, its significance as an ingredient in the mentalities of liberals and republicans begins to emerge more clearly. Several differences between the two visions are apparent. The Jesuits were an enemy drawn from the past but not, as the Franks were, from a past that was virtually immemorial: they belonged to the *ancien régime*. Their passage from past to present, on the other hand, was not continuous (as that of the Frankish element was taken to be), but was broken by a period of suppression coinciding with the Revolution itself. The importance of these facts is suggested by the rareness of attempts to undermine them; so imaginative in other ways, the anti-jesuits of the nineteenth century never seriously tried to give Jesuit conspiracy a pre-Jesuit ancestry, and seldom claimed that it had played a role during the Revolutionary years. The moral identity between old and new Jesuit orders which was implied in the nineteenth-century appropriation of previous anti-jesuit myth had its basis not in alleged physical continuity, but in a quasi-magical resurrection, made possible by the sinister potency of the Jesuit *Constitutions*. It was as if the shock troops of reaction were parachuted into the modern world, bearing the insignia of the old, but leaving the frontier intact. In short, a revived and revitalized anti-jesuitism helped (in a way that the racial thesis did not) to reconcile the absolute status of the Revolution as the moment of foundation of a new world with the practical requirements of post-Revolutionary dualism.

It also helped give to French struggles a more than French significance. The racial thesis turned French history in on itself (though it allowed analogous conflicts elsewhere); anti-jesuitism traditionally linked it to a broader international drama of Jesuit villainy. It fitted well, as a result, with the liberal Left's usual conviction of the basic universality of the conflict between Revolution and Counter-Revolution (while remaining capable, if necessary, of expressing the more xenophobic vision of a France victimized by foreign or cosmopolitan powers).

Finally, the usefulness of anti-jesuitism in the present was enhanced by its diversity in the past. The passage of time and the breakages of history ensured that what had once been narrow or partisan hostilities to the Jesuits reached the majority of modern Frenchmen only as ingredients in an eclectic anti-jesuit tradition. The comparison with the racial thesis is again revealing. The latter (once again resembling the thinking of the Catholic Right, which had the one eternal Church wrestling with disparate waves of *suppôts de Satan*) focused its dualistic vision at the positive (Gaulish) pole. Thierry narrated French history as the *Histoire véritable de Jacques Bonhomme* (not the story of bad Frank the Frank): while the faces of the 'Frankish' tyrants changed with the centuries, the same personification of the Gaulish people endured each fresh oppression. Gaulish suffering, not Frankish aggression, set the agenda and limits of the tale.[20] The anti-jesuit presentation of history, in its usual nineteenth-century form, embodied the opposite focus: the Jesuit order, fixed and durable in its vicious identity, held the attention; its victims and opponents—kings, bishops, Parlements, Protestants, Jansenists, *philosophes*—came and went. Each cohort of antagonists made its contribution to the accumulating fund of anti-jesuit wisdom; each, however, lost its discordant peculiarities in the nebulous harmony of the anti-jesuit chorus. As a result, application of the myth of Jesuit conspiracy to nineteenth-century circumstances implied no automatic commitment to any particular antecedent tradition in politics or religion. Instead it made possible a limited (and sometimes one-sided) *rapprochement* between traditions, allowing liberals or republicans, for example, to cultivate an affinity (part real, part fictitious) with the Gallican Church, with the watchful traditions of the old Parlements, with the conservative anticlericalism of a Montlosier (with whom, as an unreconstructed self-proclaimed Frank,[21] no reconciliation on the terrain of the racial thesis was conceivable).

Two different conceptions of anti-jesuitism, in fact, were kept in play by the anti-jesuit myth. The first, rooted in the myth's dualism, posited anti-jesuitism as the opposite of Jesuitism, hence something absolute and sharply defined—which the Left identified with the Revolution, with its connotations of liberty, progress, and enlightenment. The second, rooted in the myth's cumulative story of past resistance, construed anti-jesuitism as a capacious (and ideologically indeterminate) tradition of public vigilance. The myth's special service to the mentalities of the Left was to permit the installation of the first of these conceptions in the central vacancy of the

[20] A. Thierry, 'Histoire véritable de Jacques Bonhomme d'après les documents authentiques', in his *Dix ans d'études historiques* (Paris, 1835).

[21] Thierry's reaction to Montlosier's arrogantly 'Frankish' pronouncements is in his article 'Sur l'antipathie de race qui divise la nation française', ibid. 295–6.

second. Placed within the magic circle of the longer, vaguer tradition, loyalty to the Revolution had its purity confirmed, and its partisan connotations suspended. The structures of the anti-jesuit myth helped to make thinkable and presentable the politics of a moderate Left.

More was at stake here than an abstract kind of intellectual coherence. French politics from the Restoration to the early Third Republic were conducted in a fluctuating but almost perpetually ambiguous ideological climate, each successive regime embodying a different compromise or amalgam of old and new elements, each proclaiming its difference from its predecessor, while affirming its ties with a longer tradition. The ways in which Frenchmen perceived and conceptualized continuity and change, and forged their own political identities in relation to them, were not, in these circumstances, insignificant matters. Under the Restoration, when anti-jesuitism made its first and arguably deepest impact on nineteenth-century France, the viability of Liberal politics depended to a large extent on its ability to place the pragmatic defence of Revolutionary achievements under the protection of acceptable pre-Revolutionary traditions. The legitimacy of its conservative continuations under the July Monarchy depended, conversely, on a successful appropriation of the Revolutionary heritage. The essence of the politics of Republican defence at the end of the 1870s lay in a combination of the two manœuvres: the Republic was to be presented simultaneously as the definitive advent of Revolutionary principles long denied, and as the continuation of the true traditions of French government. In all these cases, the practical dilemmas of legitimization were structured in ways which left scope for the operations of the anti-jesuit myth.

The old myth of Jesuit conspiracy took new root in the paradoxes of a Revolution defined both as rupture and as heritage, of a modern world experienced both as realm of novelty and as field of contestation, of an *ancien régime* consigned to its grave yet feared as a perpetually resurgent presence. It spoke to the needs of a Left which oscillated (under the influence of these paradoxes) between the rhetoric of conflict and the invocation of unity, between the proclamation of modernity and the appeal to established values. It did not, in any neat sense, 'resolve' the paradoxes or abolish the oscillation, but it imposed an imaginative structure on the former that helped to keep the latter within bounds which permitted liberals and republicans to feel themselves the possessors of a coherent and continuous political identity.

It did so, of course, at a cost. The Left's appetite for the myth of Jesuit conspiracy, like the Right's fascination with masonic plotting, infused into French politics a subtle blend of alarmism and complacency, which dramatized insecurities and systematized mistrust, and which did much to encourage the habits of rhetorical intransigence and moral ostracism that bedevilled French public debate on numerous occasions in the century and a half after the Revolution. There was a tendency to self-fulfilment in the conspiracy theorists' warnings of national division, and a discouragement to political imagination in the political picture they themselves imagined. Sustained, both on the Right and on the Left, by a nervous reaction to the endemic uncertainty of the modern age, conspiracy theories denied the improvisational element in human affairs and the inherent openness of historical outcomes—denied, in other words, the conditions whose acceptance would have made strategies of flexibility or compromise seem normal. The myths which supplied a footing in the flood of events stimulated the politics of confrontation and exclusion. Too much sense, arguably, was being made of the mysteries of modern life.

Bibliography

Archives

Archives Nationales:

F[7] (Police) 6706, 6751, 6769–72, 6779, 12324.
F[17] (Education) 6830, 8828.
F[18] (Press) 20.
F[19] (Religion) 6252, 6287, 6288.

Bibliothèque Nationale: département des manuscrits:

Nouvelles acquisitions françaises 15520.

Bibliothèque Nationale: département des estampes:

Tf 57, 58, 130, 530.
Collection de Vinck 89, 90.
Collection Hennin 164, 165.

Parliamentary Debates

The text of these has been taken from the following sources:

Archives parlementaires de 1787 à 1860 (for the years up to 1837).
Le Moniteur universel (for the years 1843–50).
Annales du Sénat et du Corps Législatif (for the years 1865 and 1869).
Annales du Sénat et de la Chambre des Députés (for the years 1876–80).

Newspapers and Periodicals

The place of publication is Paris except where stated. Complete references are given for periodical collections; the dates given for newspapers denote the years referred to for this book. Periodicals with only one author (e.g. Raspail) and isolated titled articles from other periodicals (e.g. those of Libri) are listed under their authors among the other printed sources below.

L'Album, 7 vols. (1821–3).
L'Almanach du mois, 5 vols. (1843–6).
L'Ancien Album, 4 vols. (numbered 8–11) (1828–9).

Le Bien social, 2 vols. (1844–5).
La Caricature morale, politique et littéraire, 9 vols. (1830–5).
Chronique religieuse, 6 vols. (1819–21).
Le Citateur politique, moral et littéraire, 1 vol. (1820).
Le Constitutionnel (1823–30, 1843–5).
Le Courrier français (1826–8).
Le Drapeau blanc (1825).
Les Droits de l'homme (1876).
L'Événement (1879).
La Gazette des tribunaux (1826, 1828, 1876–7).
L'Intermédiaire des chercheurs et curieux, 76 vols. (1864–1940).
Journal de la liberté religieuse, 1 vol. (1843–4).
Le Journal des débats (1826–8, 1843–5).
La Lanterne (1879–80).
Le Mercure du XIXe siècle, 18 vols. (1823–7).
La Minerve française, 9 vols. (1818–20).
New Monthly Magazine, 2nd ser. 149 vols. (London, 1821–71).
L'Observateur catholique, 19 vols. (1855–67).
L'Opinion nationale (1868).
Petite République française (1876, 1879).
Le Rappel (1879–80).
La République française (1876).
Revue ecclésiastique, 9 vols. (1838–48).
La Semaine anti-cléricale (1879–80).
Le Siècle (1843–5).
La Silhouette, 4 vols. (1829–31).
L'Union chrétienne, 11 vols. (1859–70).

Other Printed Sources

Square brackets are used to show the authors of anonymous works (where known), and the identities of authors usually known by their pseudonyms.

[AGIER, P.-J.], *Commentaire sur l'Apocalyse*, 2 vols. (Paris, 1823).
ALBERT, E., introd. to G. Dairnvaell, *Code des jésuites*, 18th edn. (Paris, 1879).
ALLONVILLE, A. F., comte d', *Mémoires secrets, de 1770 à 1830*, 6 vols. (Paris, 1838–45).
Almanach des jésuites, contenant un crime ou une sottise pour chaque jour de l'année (Paris, 1846).
AMIABLE, L., *L'Internationale noire et la francmaçonnerie* (Paris, 1884).
ANDRÉÏ, A., *Les Jésuites* (Paris, 1872).

ANDRIEUX, L., *Souvenirs d'un préfet de police*, 2 vols. (Paris, 1885).

APPONYI, R., *Vingt-cinq ans à Paris (1826–1850)*, ed. E. Daudet, 4 vols. (Paris, 1913–26).

ARNOULD, A., *Les Jésuites depuis leur origine jusqu'à nos jours: Histoire, types, mœurs, mystères*, 2 vols. (Paris, 1846).

AUFFRAY, J., and CROUSAZ-CRÉTET, L. DE (eds.), *Les Expulsés devant les tribunaux: Recueil des décisions judiciaires relatives à l'exécution des décrets du 29 mars 1880* (Paris, 1881).

AUGIER, E., *Lions et renards: Comédie en 5 actes, en prose* (Paris, 1870).

AULARD, A., *Polémique et histoire* (Paris, 1904).

BAILLOT, D., introd. to P. Landerset, *Opinions prononcées dans le Grand Conseil de Fribourg, les 16 janvier 1817 et 15 septembre 1818, au sujet de l'admission des ligoriens et des jésuites* (Paris, 1819).

BALZAC, H. DE, *Œuvres complètes*, ed. M. Bouteron and M. Longnon, 40 vols. (Paris, 1926–63).

BARANTE, A.-G.-P. BRUGIÈRE, baron de, *Souvenirs, 1782–1866*, 8 vols. (Paris, 1890–1901).

BARTHÉLEMY, A.-M., and MÉRY, J., *Les Jésuites: Épître à M. le président Séguier* (Paris, 1826).

BÉRANGER, P. J. DE, *Œuvres complètes* (Brussels, 1844).

BERT, P., *La Morale des jésuites* (Paris, 1880).

—— *Le Cléricalisme: Questions d'éducation nationale* (Paris, 1900).

BESCHERELLE, L.-N., *Nouveau Dictionnaire national; ou Dictionnaire universel de la langue française*, 4 vols. (Paris, 1887).

BLANC, L., *Discours politiques (1847 à 1881)* (Paris, 1882).

BONNEVILLE, N. DE, *Les Jésuites chassés de la maçonnerie, et leur poignard brisé par les maçons* (London, 1788).

BORDAS-DEMOULIN, J.-B., *Mélanges philosophiques et religieux* (Paris, 1846).

BOUCHÉ, J.-B., 'Préface appréciative sur l'état actuel de la Compagnie de Jésus', in J.-B. Salgues, *L'Antidote de Mont-Rouge*, new edn. (Paris, 1845).

BOUCHER, A., *Histoire dramatique et pittoresque des jésuites, depuis la fondation de l'ordre jusqu'à nos jours*, 2 vols. (Paris, 1845–6).

BOUIS, C., *Calottes et soutanes: Jésuites et jésuitesses* (Paris, 1870).

[BOURGUIGNON D'HERBIGNY, P.-F.-X.], *Revue politique de la France en 1826* (Paris, 1827).

BROT, A., and LURINE, L., *Les Couvents* (Paris, 1846).

[BUSCH, F.], *Découvertes d'un bibliophile; ou Lettres sur différents points de morale enseignés dans quelques séminaires de France*, 2nd edn. (Strasbourg, 1843).

CANAYE, P., *Lettres et ambassade de messire P. Canaye, sieur de Fresne*, 3 vols. (Paris, 1635–6).

CARADEUC DE LA CHALOTAIS, L. R. DE, *Résumé de la doctrine des jésuites*, ed. J.-A.-S. Collin de Plancy (Paris, 1826).

CARADEUC DE LA CHALOTAIS, L. R. DE, *Résumé des Constitutions des jésuites*, ed. J.-A.-S. Collin de Plancy (Paris, 1826).

CASTAGNARY, J.-A., *Les Jésuites devant la loi française* (Paris, 1877).

CAUCHOIS-LEMAIRE, L.-A.-F., *Lettres historiques adressées à Sa Grandeur Monseigneur le Cte de Peyronnet, Garde des Sceaux, Ministre de la Justice* (Paris, 1827).

CAYLA, J.-M., *La Conspiration cléricale* (Paris, 1862).

—— *Ces bons messieurs de Saint Vincent-de-Paul* (Paris, 1863).

—— *Les Jésuites hors la loi* (Paris, 1869).

—— *L'Expulsion des jésuites* (Paris, 1876).

CHARBONNEL, V., *L'Origine musulmane des jésuites* (Paris, 1900).

CLEMENCEAU, G., *Contre la justice* (Paris, 1900).

COLAU, P., *Derniers Efforts du jésuitisme expirant, ses infamies, ses crimes et ses complots, définition de ce qu'on appelle la Congrégation, du danger qu'il y aurait si une liberté mal entendue empêchait qu'on réprimât ses nouvelles tentatives* (Paris, 1830).

COLLIN DE PLANCY, J.-A.-S., *Histoire des jésuites, en 82 couplets, sur de beaux airs de complaintes, avec des notes instructives, depuis la naissance de saint Ignace, en 1492, jusqu'à cet an de grâce 1826* (Paris, 1826).

La Commission extraparlementaire de 1849: Texte intégral des procès-verbaux, ed. G. Chenesseau (Paris, 1937).

COMPAYRÉ, G., *Curiosités pédagogiques: L'Orbilianisme; ou L'Usage du fouet dans les collèges des jésuites au dix-huitième siècle* (Toulouse, 1878).

CONSIDÉRANT, V., 'Avertissement', in J. Leone, *Conjuration des jésuites* (Paris, 1848).

Les Constitutions des jésuites, avec les déclarations, texte latin, d'après l'édition de Prague (Paris, 1843).

CORBIÈRE, E., *Trois jours d'une mission à Brest* (Paris, 1819).

COTTU, C., *De la situation du clergé, de la magistrature, et du ministère, à l'ouverture de la session de 1827, et du moyen de consolider en France le gouvernement constitutionnel* (Paris, 1826).

—— *Considérations sur la mise en accusation des ministres* (Paris, 1827).

COURIER, P.-L., *Œuvres complètes*, Pléiade edn. (Paris, 1851).

CUCHEVAL-CLARIGNY, A., 'Le Révérend Père Loriquet: Sa vie et ses écrits', *La Liberté de penser*, 1 (1847), 165–99.

DAIRNVAELL, G., *Code des jésuites, d'après plus de trois cents ouvrages des casuistes jésuites, complément indispensable aux œuvres de MM. Michelet et Quinet* (Paris, 1845).

[DESCHAMPS, N.], *Le Monopole universitaire destructeur de la religion et des lois; ou La Charte et la liberté de l'enseignement* (Lyons, 1843).

DESMALIS, J., *Le Cri d'alarme; ou La France aux prises avec l'hydre jésuitique* (Paris, 1828).

DEVAUX, H., et al., *Consultation sur la dénonciation adressée à la Cour Royale par M. le comte de Montlosier* (Paris, 1826).

DINOCOURT, T., *L'Ombre d'Escobar* (Paris, 1826).

—— *Le Camisard*, 2nd edn., 4 vols. (Paris, 1833).

Doctrines morales et politiques, cas de conscience et aphorismes des jésuites, textuellement extraits et traduits des écrivains de la Compagnie de Jésus (Paris, 1844).

DOUARCHE, A., *Les Jésuites confesseurs des rois de France* (Carcassonne, 1880).

DUCANGE, V., *Les Trois Filles de la veuve*, 6 vols. (Paris, 1826).

—— and GUILBERT DE PIXÉRÉCOURT, R.-C., *Le Jésuite: Drame en 3 actes et en 6 tableaux* (Paris, 1830).

DUCHATEAU, S., *Dénonciation contre la Société des Bonnes Études, comme affiliation jésuitique, pour servir d'appendice à la dénonciation de M. le Cte de Montlosier* (Paris, 1826).

DUCROIX, F., *Les Frères, les jésuites, l'Université* (Thiers, 1843).

Du jésuitisme: Troisième annexe sur la justice et les juges, par trois procureurs généraux, deux de l'ancienne monarchie, le troisième de la monarchie constitutionnelle (Paris, 1874).

DUMAS, A., *Le Vicomte de Bragelonne*, 6 vols. (Paris, 1851).

DUMESNIL, A., *Considérations sur les causes et les progrès de la corruption en France* (Paris, 1824).

—— *Les Jésuites tricolores: Un chapitre de mœurs politiques* (Paris, 1830).

DUPARC, H., and COCHIN, H. (eds.), *Expulsions des congrégations religieuses: Récits et témoignages* (Paris, 1881).

DUPIN, A.-M.-J.-J., *Éloge d'Étienne Pasquier: Discours prononcé à l'audience de rentrée de la Cour de Cassation, le 6 novembre 1843* (Paris, 1843).

—— *Mémoires*, 4 vols. (Paris, 1855–61).

—— *Libertés de l'Église gallicane: Manuel du droit public ecclésiastique français*, 5th edn. (Paris, 1860).

—— *et al.*, *Consultation sur la dénonciation adressée à la Cour Royale par M. le comte de Montlosier* (Paris, 1826).

DUPORT, P., and [MONNAIS, E.], *La Contre-lettre; ou Le Jésuite: Drame en deux actes, mêlé de chant* (Paris, 1830).

DURANTIN, A., *Un jésuite de robe courte* (Paris, 1870).

—— *Un élève des jésuites* (Paris, 1880).

Du rétablissement des jésuites en France sous le nom de Pères de la Foi: Par M.G., avocat (Paris, 1819).

DURUY, V., *Notes et souvenirs (1811–1894)*, 2 vols. (Paris, 1901).

DUVERGIER DE HAURANNE, J.-M., *De l'ordre légal en France, et des abus d'autorité*, 2 vols. (Paris, 1826–8).

ERCKMANN, J., *Les Disciples d'Escobar* (Paris, 1846).

ERCKMANN-CHATRIAN [E. Erckmann and A. Chatrian], *Histoire du plébiscite, racontée par un des 7,500,000 oui*, ed. 'Aux bureaux . . . du *Soir*' (Paris, 1872).

ESTAUNIÉ, E., *L'Empreinte* (Paris, 1896).

FAGE, E., *Souvenirs d'enfance et de la jeunesse* (Tulle, 1901).

FERRY, J., *Discours et opinions*, ed. J. Robiquet, 7 vols. (Paris, 1893–8).

—— *Lettres, 1846–1893* (Paris, 1914).

FÉVAL, P., *Jésuites!* (Paris, 1877).

FLOCON, F., and BECKHAUS, A., *Dictionnaire de morale jésuitique* (Paris, 1824).

FRÉNILLY, A.-F., baron de, *Souvenirs*, ed. A. Chuquet (Paris, 1909).

FREYCINET, C. DE, *Souvenirs 1878–1893*, 4th edn. (Paris, 1913).

GAMBETTA, L., *Discours et plaidoyers politiques*, ed. J. Reinach, 11 vols. (Paris, 1881–5).

—— *Dépêches, circulaires, décrets, proclamations et discours*, ed. J. Reinach, 2 vols. (Paris, 1886–91).

—— *Lettres, 1868–82*, 3rd edn. (Paris, 1938).

GÉNIN, F., *Les Jésuites et l'Université* (Paris, 1844).

—— *Ou l'Église ou l'État* (Paris, 1847).

GILBERT DE VOISINS, P.-P.-A. (ed.), *Procédure contre l'Institut et les Constitutions des jésuites, suivie au Parlement de Paris, sur l'appel comme d'abus, interjeté par le procureur-général du roi* (Paris, 1823).

—— (ed.), *Nouvelles Pièces pour servir de complément à la Procédure contre les jésuites* (Paris, 1824).

[GOHIER, L.-J.], *Un mot sur le procès intenté par la famille La Chalotais, contre le journal l'Étoile* (Paris, 1826).

GOHIER, U., *L'Armée contre la nation* (Paris, 1899).

[GOUBEAU DE LA BILENNERIE, J.-F.], *Histoire abrégée des jésuites et des missionnaires pères de la foi, où il est prouvé que ces religieux et toutes corporations ecclésiastiques régies par l'institut de la Société de Jésus ne sont tolérables chez aucunes nations policées*, 2 vols. (Paris, 1820).

GRASSI, A., *La Sainte-Alliance, les Anglais et les jésuites: Leur système politique à l'égard de la Grèce, des gouvernements constitutionnels et des événemens actuels* (Paris, 1827).

GRAUX, G., *Les Amours d'un jésuite: Histoire vraie*, 9th edn. (Bordeaux, 1872).

GRÉGOIRE, H.-B., *Histoire des confesseurs des empereurs, des rois et d'autres princes* (Paris, 1824).

GUETTÉE, R.-F.-W., *Histoire des jésuites, composée sur documents authentiques en partie inédits*, 3 vols. (Paris, 1858–9).

—— *Souvenirs d'un prêtre romain devenu prêtre orthodoxe* (Paris, 1889).

GUILLAUME, C., *1er pamphlet: Il ne faut point de sociétés dans la société* (Dôle, 1844).

—— *2e pamphlet: Les Ultramontains ou jésuites* (Dôle, 1844).

GUIZOT, F., *Mémoires pour servir à l'histoire de mon temps*, 8 vols. (Paris, 1858–67).

HAURÉAU, B., 'Jésuitisme', in *Dictionnaire politique: Encyclopédie du langage et de la science politiques, rédigés par une réunion de députés, de publicistes et de journalistes* (Paris, 1842).

Bibliography

HÉNIN DE CUVILLERS, E.-F. D' (ed.), *La Monarchie des solipses, par Jules Clément Scotti, sous le nom emprunté de Melchior Inchofer, traduite de l'original latin, par P. Restaut, avocat au conseil du roi, accompagnée de notes, de remarques et de pièces, précédée d'un discours préliminaire* (Paris, 1824).

HUGO, V., *Les Châtiments*, Gallimard edn. (Paris, 1977).

HYACINTHE, N., *Coup d'œil dans l'intérieur de Saint-Acheul; ou De l'éducation que donnent les jésuites modernes à la jeunesse française* (Paris, 1826).

Institut royal de France: Discours prononcés à l'Académie Française pour la réception de M. le baron Pasquier, le 8 décembre 1842 (Paris, 1842).

Instructions secrètes des jésuites: ou Monita secreta Societatis Jesu (Paris, 1824).

Instructions secrètes des jésuites: ou Monita secreta Societatis Jesu, précédées de l'histoire et de la morale des jésuites depuis la fondation de leur société jusqu'à nos jours (Blois, 1845).

ISAMBERT, F.-A., *Consultation sur la dénonciation adressée à la Cour Royale par M. de Montlosier* (Paris, 1826).

JACQUEMONT, F., *Examen impartial du jésuitisme ancien et moderne, par un ami sincère de la religion et du roi* (Lyons, 1828).

JACQUES, A., 'Bulletin: Supplément à l'histoire de France depuis la mort de Louis XVI jusqu'à l'an 1816, par A.M.D.G.***', *La Liberté de penser*, 1 (1848), 398–400.

Les Jésuites et l'affaire Debuck, 6th edn. (Brussels, 1864).

Les Jésuites et l'Inquisition: Histoire populaire et anecdotique des Compagnies de Jésus et de Saint Dominique (Paris, 1869).

Les Jésuites et la propriété: Lettre grenobloise aux conservateurs (Grenoble, 1880).

Les Jésuites marchands, usuriers et usurpateurs: Par G***** de N****, volontaire royal en 1815 (Paris, 1824).

KÉRATRY, A. H. DE, *Documents pour servir à l'histoire de France en 1820*, 4th edn. (Paris, 1820).

—— *La France telle qu'on l'a faite; ou Suite aux Documents pour servir à l'intelligence de l'histoire de France en 1820 et 1821*, 2nd edn. (Paris, 1821).

LACRETELLE, C. DE, *Histoire de France depuis la Restauration*, 4 vols. (Paris, 1829–35).

—— *Testament philosophique et littéraire*, 2 vols. (Paris, 1840).

—— *Discours prononcé à la Faculté des Lettres, le 29 novembre 1843, suivi d'une lettre à M. de Lamartine sur les rapports de l'Église et de l'État* (Paris, 1843).

LAMENNAIS, F. DE, *Œuvres complètes*, 10 vols. (Paris, 1843–4).

LARCHEY, L., *Dictionnaire historique, étymologique et anecdotique de l'argot parisien*, 6th edn. (Paris, 1872).

LAROUSSE, P. (ed.), *Grand Dictionnaire universel français*, 17 vols. (Paris, 1865–90).

LAUMIER, C., *L'Enfant du jésuite*, 2 vols. (Paris, 1822).

LAUMIER, C., *Résumé de l'histoire des jésuites, depuis l'origine jusqu'à la destruction de leur société, suivi de considérations sur les causes de leur élévation et de leur chute, et d'un examen critique de leurs Constitutions* (Paris, 1826).

LAURENS, J., *Le Cas d'un curé gallican* (Paris, 1879).

—— *Le Cas d'un curé gallican; ou Explication de l'infaillibilité du pape et de l'Église ultramontaine: Deuxième lettre* (Paris, 1879).

LEBRUN, I., *Du sacrilège et des jésuites* (Paris, 1825).

—— *La Bonne Ville; ou Le Maire et le jésuite*, 2 vols. (Paris, 1826).

LEMER, J., *Dossier des jésuites et des libertés de l'Église gallicane* (Paris, 1877).

LEONE, J., *Conjuration des jésuites: Publication authentique du plan secret de l'ordre*, ed. V. Considérant (Paris, 1848).

LIBRI, G., 'Lettres sur le clergé français', *Revue des deux mondes*, 2nd ser. 2 (1843), 329–56 and 968–81.

LITTRÉ, E., *Dictionnaire de la langue française*, 5 vols. (Paris, 1863–72).

[LOMBARD DE LANGRES, V.], *Des sociétés secrètes en Allemagne et en d'autres contrées, de la secte des illuminés, du tribunal secret, de l'assassinat de Kotzebue, etc.* (Paris, 1819).

LONGHAYE, G., 'Types cléricaux dans le drame et le roman modernes: Étude morale et littéraire: Troisième article', *Études religieuses, historiques et littéraires*, 4th ser. 5 (1870), 345–72.

[LORIQUET, J.-N.], *Histoire de France à l'usage de la jeunesse: Par A.M.D.G. ****, 2nd edn., 2 vols. (Lyons, 1816).

MAGALON, J.-D., *Ma translation; ou La Force, Sainte-Pélagie et Poissy* (Paris, 1824).

MAGNIER, L., *Considérations sur les jésuites* (Paris, 1819).

MAISTRE, J. DE, *Correspondance diplomatique, 1811–1817*, ed. A. Blanc (Paris, 1860).

—— *Lettres et opuscules inédits*, ed. R. de Maistre, 2 vols. (Paris, 1861).

—— *Œuvres inédites (Mélanges)*, ed. C. de Maistre (Paris, 1870).

MARCET, M., *Les Jésuites modernes, pour faire suite au Mémoire de M. le comte de Montlosier* (Paris, 1826).

—— *Mémoires d'un jeune jésuite; ou Conjuration de Mont-Rouge, développée par des faits* (Paris, 1828).

—— *Nouveau Mémoire à consulter du jeune jésuite sur l'état actuel des jésuites en France, des évêques et des prêtres, suivi de la pétition à la Chambre des Députés* (Paris, 1829).

—— *Les Sept Bêtes de Montrouge: Prophétie et apocalypse: Manuscrit trouvé dans le noviciat des jésuites de Paris* (Paris, 1829).

—— *Mémoire à consulter sur le rétablissement légal des jésuites en France* (Paris, 1845).

MICHAUD, E., *Le Mouvement contemporain des églises: Études religieuses et politiques* (Paris, 1874).

MICHEL, A., *Les Jésuites* (Paris, 1879).

MICHELET, J., *Des jésuites*, forming the first part of J. Michelet and E. Quinet, *Des jésuites*, 7th edn. (Paris, 1845).

—— *Du prêtre, de la femme, de la famille*, 3rd edn. (Paris, 1845).

—— 'Le Collège de France', in *Paris-guide, par les principaux écrivains et artistes de la France*, 2 vols. (Paris, 1867), i. 136–45.

—— *Journal*, ed. P. Viallaneix, 4 vols. (Paris, 1959–76).

[MICHON, J.-H.], *Le Maudit*, 3 vols. (Paris, 1864).

[——] *Le Jésuite*, 2 vols. (Paris, 1865).

MIRBEAU, O., *Sébastien Roch: Roman de mœurs* (Paris, 1890).

MONGLAVE, E. DE, and CHALAS, P., *Histoire des conspirations des jésuites contre la maison de Bourbon en France* (Paris, 1825).

MONNAIS, E., and [ARAGO, E.], *La Demande en mariage; ou Le Jésuite retourne: Comédie-vaudeville en 1 acte* (Paris, 1830).

MONTALEMBERT, C. F., comte de, *Œuvres*, 9 vols. (Paris, 1860–8).

MONTLOSIER, F. D. DE REYNAUD, comte de, *Mémoire à consulter sur un système religieux et politique tendant à renverser la religion, la société et le trône*, 4th edn. (Paris, 1826).

—— *Dénonciation aux Cours Royales, relativement au système religieux et politique signalé dans le Mémoire à consulter; précédée de nouvelles observations sur ce système, et sur les apologies qu'on en a récemment publiées* (Paris, 1826).

—— *Pétition à la Chambre des Pairs, précédée de quelques observations sur les calamités, objet de la pétition* (Paris, 1827).

—— *Les Jésuites, les congrégations et le parti prêtre en 1827: Mémoire à M. le comte de Villèle, Président du Conseil des Ministres* (Paris, 1827).

MORTONVAL [A.-F. Guesdon], *Le Tartufe moderne*, 3 vols. (Paris, 1825).

MOULS, X., *Les Mystères d'un évêché: Scènes du jésuitisme et de la rénovation chrétienne*, 2 vols. (Brussels, 1872).

MUN, comte A. DE, *Nouvelle Réponse à une vieille accusation renouvelée contre l'École Sainte-Geneviève* (Paris, 1899).

Les Nihilistes de robe noire: Les Jésuites, leur enseignement: Par un professeur de l'Université (Paris, 1879).

Observation sur le vœu spécial d'obéissance que font au pape les jésuites profès des quatre vœux (Paris, n.d.).

ORDINAIRE, D., *Seize lettres aux jésuites* (Paris, 1879).

—— *Lettres aux jésuites* (Tours, 1883).

PARADIS, E., *Les Jésuites* (Paris, 1873).

PASCAL, B., *Les Provinciales; ou Les Lettres écrites par Louis de Montalte à un provincial de ses amis et aux RR.PP. jésuites*, Classiques Garnier edn. (Paris, 1965).

PEYRAT, A., *Histoire et religion* (Paris, 1858).

Physiologie du jésuite (Paris, 1844).

Pièces historiques, rares ou inédites, pour servir à l'instruction du temps présent (Paris, 1830).

POMPÉRY, E. DE, *Les Jésuites et le jésuitisme* (Paris, 1879).

PRADT, D.-G.-F. DE, *Du jésuitisme ancien et moderne* (Paris, 1825).

PRESSENSÉ, E. DE, *La Liberté religieuse en Europe depuis 1870* (Paris, 1874).

Procès Affnaer, Cour d'Assises de la Seine, audience des 8 et 9 avril 1845 (Paris, 1845).

Procès d'Affenaer: Vol de 333,000 francs, au préjudice des jésuites (Paris, 1845).

Procès du Constitutionnel et du Courrier, accusés de tendance à porter atteinte au respect dû à la religion de l'État (Paris, 1826).

QUINET, E., *Des jésuites*, forming the second part of J. Michelet and E. Quinet, *Des jésuites*, 7th edn. (Paris, 1845).

—— *Œuvres complètes*, 10 vols. (Paris, 1857–8).

QUINET, H., *Edgar Quinet avant l'éxil*, 2nd edn. (Paris, 1888).

RABAN, L.-F., *La Femme jésuite: Histoire véritable, écrite par une victime du jésuitisme* (Paris, 1826).

RASPAIL, F.-V., *Revue élémentaire de médecine et pharmacie domestiques, ainsi que des sciences accessoires et usuelles mises à la portée de tout le monde*, 2 vols. (Paris, 1847–9).

—— *La Lunette du donjon de Vincennes: Almanach démocratique et social de l'Ami du peuple, pour 1849* (Paris, 1848).

—— *La Lunette de Doullens: Almanach démocratique et progressif de l'Ami du peuple, pour 1850* (Paris, 1849).

—— *Revue complémentaire des sciences appliquées à la médecine et pharmacie, à l'agriculture, aux arts et à l'industrie*, 6 vols. (Paris, 1854–60).

—— *Nouvelles Études scientifiques et philologiques* (Paris, 1864).

—— *Prévision du temps: Almanach et calendrier météorologique pour l'année [——]*, (Paris, annually 1865–77, except 1871).

RAVELET, A., *Traité des congrégations religieuses: Commentaire des lois et de la jurisprudence, précédé d'une introduction historique et économique* (Paris, 1869).

RAVIGNAN, X. DE, *De l'existence et de l'institut des jésuites* (Paris, 1844).

Recueil complet du procès intenté par les héritiers de M. de La Chalotais, ancien procureur-général au Parlement de Bretagne, contre les éditeurs du journal dit l'Étoile (Paris, 1826).

REINACH, J., *Histoire de l'Affaire Dreyfus*, 6 vols. (Paris, 1901–8).

RÉMUSAT, C. DE, *Mémoires de ma vie*, ed. C. Pouthas, 5 vols. (Paris, 1958–67).

Réquisitoire de M. le procureur général près la Cour Royale de Paris, contre le Constitutionnel, suivi des articles incriminés dans le Constitutionnel, à la suite du réquisitoire, ainsi que de l'ordonnance de M. le premier président, et de l'exploit de signification (n.p., 1825).

Résumé de la doctrine des jésuites; ou Extraits des assertions dangereuses et pernicieuses soutenues par les jésuites dans leurs ouvrages dogmatiques, recueillies et imprimées par ordre du Parlement en 1762 (Paris, 1826).

[REYBAUD, F.], *La Protestante; ou Les Cevennes au commencement du XVIIIe siècle*, 3 vols. (Paris, 1828).

ROUSSE, E., *Consultations sur les décrets du 29 mars 1880 et sur les mesures annoncées contre les associations religieuses* (Paris, 1880).

ROUSSEL, N., *Jésus et jésuite* (Paris, 1845).

SAINTE-BEUVE, C.-A., *Les Cahiers* (Paris, 1876).

SAINT-SIMON, L., duc de, *Mémoires*, ed. A. de Boislisle, 41 vols. (Paris, 1879–1928).

[SALGUES, J.-B.], *Courtes Observations sur la Congrégation, les jésuites, et les trois discours de M. le Ministre des Affaires Ecclésiastiques, prononcés à la Chambre des Députés, les 25, 26, et 27 mai 1826* (Paris, 1826).

[——] *Étrennes aux jésuites, pour l'édification des personnes pieuses affectionnées à la société* (Paris, 1826).

—— *L'Antidote de Mont-Rouge; ou Six questions adressées à Mgr. l'évêque d'Hermopolis sur le projet de rétablir ou de tolérer les jésuites, et suivies de l'examen de leurs modernes apologistes, MM. Tharin, de Bonald, etc., etc.* (Paris, 1827).

—— *Pétition sur l'exécution des lois ecclésiastiques relatives à la Compagnie de Jésus, présentée à la Chambre des Députés* (Paris, 1828).

SAND, G. [A.-L.-A. Dupin], *Mademoiselle La Quintinie*, 2nd edn. (Paris, 1863).

SANTO-DOMINGO, J.-H. DE, *Plaidoirie . . . devant la Cour Royale* (Paris, 1824).

—— *Les Jésuites en action sous le ministère Villèle* (Paris, 1828).

SAUVESTRE, C. (ed.), *Monita secreta Societatis Jesu: Instructions secrètes des jésuites, suivies de pièces justificatives* (Paris, 1861; 2nd edn. 1862; 3rd edn. 1863).

—— *Lettres de province* (Paris, 1862).

—— *Mes lundis* (Paris, 1864).

—— *Les Congrégations religieuses: Enquête* (Paris, 1867).

—— *Sur les genoux de l'Église* (Paris, 1868).

—— *La Sonnette du sacristain* (Paris, 1869).

—— *Les Jésuites peints par eux-mêmes, suivi du Syllabus romain* (Paris, 1878).

SCHEFFER, A., *Précis de l'histoire générale de la Compagnie de Jésus, suivi des Monita secreta* (Paris, 1824).

[SILVY, L.], *Les Jésuites tels qu'ils ont été dans l'ordre politique, religieux et moral, contre le système d'un livre intitulé 'Mémoires pour servir à l'histoire ecclésiastique pendant le dix-huitième siècle'* (Paris, 1816).

[——] *Du rétablissement des jésuites en France*, 2nd edn. (Paris, 1816).

[——] *Henri IV et les jésuites* (Paris, 1818).

[——] 'Dissertation sur la foi qui est due au témoignage de Pascal dans ses Lettres provinciales', appended to [L. Silvy], *Henri IV et les jésuites* (Paris, 1818).

[——] *Les Jésuites ennemis de l'ordre social, de la morale et de la religion, par leur probabilisme, leur doctrine régicide et leur conduite dans les missions et leur système de calomnie: Le Tout prouvé par des pièces authentiques et par des lettres originales déposées aux Archives du Vatican* (Paris, 1828).

SIRVEN, A., and LE VERDIER, H., *Le Jésuite rouge: Roman contemporain* (Paris, 1879).

SMITH, G., *The Use and Abuse of Free-Masonry: A Work of the Greatest Utility to the Brethren of the Society* (London, 1783).

STENDHAL [H. Beyle], *Le Rouge et le noir* (Paris, 1830).

STRAUSS, H., *Drumont-jésuite et ses complices démasqués A.M.D.G.* (Paris, 1892).

SUE, E., *Le Juif errant*, 5 vols. (Brussels, 1844–5); 4 vols. (Paris, 1845).

—— *Les Mystères du peuple: ou Histoire d'une famille de prolétaires à travers les âges*, Librairie du progrès edn., 10 vols. (Paris, 1881).

[TABARAUD, M.-M.], *Du pape et des jésuites* (Paris, 1814).

—— *Lettre à M. Bellart, procureur-général à la Cour Royale de Paris, sur son réquisitoire du 30 juillet contre les journaux de l'opposition* (Paris, 1825).

—— *Essai historique et critique sur l'état des jésuites en France depuis leur arrivée dans le royaume jusqu'au temps présent* (Paris, 1828).

TAINE, H., *Voyage en Italie*, 9th edn., 2 vols. (Paris, 1898).

TAPON FOUGAS, F., *Le Jésuite . . . pour rire en loterie: Comédie en 1 acte et en vers* (Brussels, 1857).

—— *Sur la mort d'Eugène Sue: Humble Avis d'un démocrate* (Brussels, n.d.).

TAXIL, L. [G.-A. Jogand-Pagès], *C'est nous qui fouettons ces vieux polissons!* (Paris, 1879).

—— *Calotte et calotins: Histoire illustrée du clergé et des congrégations*, 3 vols. (Paris, 1880).

—— *Les Amours secrètes de Pie IX, par un ancien camérier secret du pape* (Paris, 1881).

[THARIN, C.-M.-P.], *Nouvelles Considérations philosophiques et critiques sur la Société des Jésuites, sur les causes et les suites de sa destruction* (Versailles, 1817).

THIERRY, A., *Dix ans d'études historiques* (Paris, 1835).

VATIMESNIL, A. F. DE, *Lettre au R.P. de Ravignan, suivie d'un extrait d'un mémoire sur l'état légal en France des associations religieuses non autorisées* (Paris, 1844).

VÉRON, L.-D., *Mémoires d'un bourgeois de Paris*, 6 vols. (Paris, 1853–5).

VILLÈLE, J., comte de, *Mémoires et correspondance*, 5 vols. (Paris, 1888–90).

VILLENEUVE, T. DE, and BOURGEOIS, A., *Le Congréganiste; ou Les Trois Éducations: Comédie-vaudeville en 3 actes* (Paris, 1830).

La Voix du peuple est la voix de Dieu: Plus d'abus dans la religion catholique, plus de jésuites, plus de couvents, et la France et l'Italie délivrées: Par un catholique (Carouge, 1862).

WALLON, J., *La Vérité sur le Concile* (Paris, 1872).

—— *Jésus et les jésuites: Moïse—Jésus—Loyola, les jésuites dans l'histoire* (Paris, 1879).

—— *Un collège de jésuites, auquel on a joint le Jésus-ouvrier, le Jésus-roi, le Jésus-industriel, le Jésus-homme de lettres* (Paris, 1880).

ZOLA, E., *L'Affaire Dreyfus: La Vérité en marche* (Paris, 1901).
—— *Vérité* (Paris, 1903).

Secondary Literature

ACOMB, E., *The French Laic Laws, 1879–89: The First Anticlerical Campaign of the Third French Republic* (New York, 1941).

APPOLIS, E., 'Une tentative de schisme vieux-catholique dans le Tarn en 1879', *Bulletin de la Société des Sciences, Arts et Belles-Lettres du Tarn*, NS 12 (1951), 197–209.

—— 'Un évêque ennemi des jésuites sous la Monarchie de Juillet', *Actes du 81e congrès national des sociétés savantes: Section d'histoire moderne et contemporaine* (1956), 715–20.

ASHE, K., *The Jesuit Academy (Pensionnat) of Saint Michel in Fribourg, 1827–1847* (Fribourg, 1971).

AUBERT, R., *Vatican I* (Paris, 1964).

BAILYN, B., *The Ideological Origins of the American Revolution* (Cambridge, Mass., 1967).

BARBER, M., 'Lepers, Jews and Moslems: The Plot to Overthrow Christendom in 1321', *History*, 66 (1981), 1–17.

BARDOUX, A., *Le Comte de Montlosier et le gallicanisme* (Paris, 1881).

BERTIER DE SAUVIGNY, G. DE, *Le Comte Ferdinand de Bertier, 1782–1864, et l'énigme de la Congrégation* (Paris, 1948).

BERTRAND, L., *Histoire des séminaires de Bordeaux et de Bazas*, 3 vols. (Bordeaux, 1894).

BILLIG, M., *Fascists: A Social Psychological View of the National Front* (London, 1978).

BIRNBAUM, P., *Le Peuple et les gros: Histoire d'un mythe* (Paris, 1979).

—— *Un mythe politique: 'La République juive' de Léon Blum à Pierre Mendès France* (Paris, 1988).

BLIARD, P., *Le Père Loriquet: La Légende et l'histoire*, 2nd edn. (Paris, 1922).

BORY, J.-L., *Eugène Sue: Le Roi du roman populaire* (Paris, 1962).

BRISSON, E., 'Le Tribun du Collège de France devant la presse', in P. Viallaneix (ed.), *Michelet cent ans après* (Grenoble, 1975), 166–95.

—— 'L'Enseignement de Quinet au Collège de France d'après la presse parisienne, 1842–1845', in S. Bernard-Griffiths and P. Viallaneix (eds.), *Edgar Quinet, ce juif errant* (Clermont-Ferrand, 1978), 89–108.

BROU, A., *Les Jésuites de la légende*, 2 vols. (Paris, 1906–7).

BROWN, T. M., 'The Image of the Beast: Anti-Papal Rhetoric in Colonial America', in R. O. Curry and T. M. Brown (eds.), *Conspiracy: The Fear of Subversion in American History* (New York, 1972), 1–20.

BRUGERETTE, J., *Le Comte de Montlosier et son temps (1755–1838)* (Aurillac, 1931).

BURNICHON, J., *La Compagnie de Jésus en France: Histoire d'un siècle, 1814–1914*, 4 vols. (Paris, 1914–22).

BURY, J. P. T., *Gambetta and the National Defence: A Republican Dictatorship in France* (London, 1936).

—— and TOMBS, R. P., *Thiers, 1797–1877: A Political Life* (London, 1986).

BUSH, J., 'Education and Social Status: The Jesuit *Collège* in the Early Third Republic', *French Historical Studies*, 10 (1975), 125–40.

CANRON, A., *Les Jésuites à Avignon: Esquisse historique* (Avignon, 1875).

CAPÉRAN, L., *Histoire contemporaine de la laïcité française*, 3 vols. (Paris, 1957–61).

CARAYON, A., *Bibliographie historique de la Compagnie de Jésus; ou Catalogue des ouvrages relatifs à l'histoire des jésuites depuis leur origine jusqu'à nos jours* (Paris, 1864).

CASANOVA, R., *Montlosier et le parti prêtre: Étude, suivie d'un choix de textes* (Paris, 1970).

CHADWICK, O., *The Popes and European Revolution* (Oxford, 1981).

CHEVALLIER, P., *La Séparation de l'Église et de l'école: Jules Ferry et Léon XIII* (Paris, 1981).

CHOLVY, G., and HILAIRE, Y.-M., *Histoire religieuse de la France contemporaine*, 2 vols. (Toulouse, 1985–6).

CHRISTIE, I. R., 'Myth and Reality in Late-Eighteenth-Century British Politics', in I. R. Christie, *Myth and Reality in Late-Eighteenth-Century British Politics and Other Papers* (London, 1970), 27–54.

CLIFTON, R., 'The Popular Fear of Catholics during the English Revolution', *Past and Present*, 52 (1971), 23–55.

COHN, N., *Warrant for Genocide: The Myth of the Jewish World Conspiracy and the 'Protocols' of the Elders of Zion* (London, 1967).

CRÉTINEAU-JOLY, J., *Histoire religieuse, politique et littéraire de la Compagnie de Jésus*, 6 vols. (Paris, 1844–6).

CUBITT, G. T., 'The Myth of a Jesuit Conspiracy in France, 1814–1880', Ph.D. thesis (Cambridge, 1984).

—— 'Conspiracy Myths and Conspiracy Theories', *JASO* (*Journal of the Anthropological Society of Oxford*), 20 (1989), 12–26.

—— 'Denouncing Conspiracy in the French Revolution', *Renaissance and Modern Studies*, 33 (1989), 144–58.

—— 'Catholics versus Freemasons in Late Nineteenth-Century France', in F. Tallett and N. Atkin (eds.), *Religion, Society and Politics in France since 1789* (London, 1991), 121–36.

CUNO, J., 'The Business and Politics of Caricature: Charles Philipon and La Maison Aubert', *Gazette des beaux-arts*, 106 (1985), 95–112.

DAMAS D'ANLEZY, comte de, 'L'Éducation du duc de Bordeaux', *Revue des deux mondes*, 5th ser. 11 (1902), 602–40.

DAVIS, D. B., *The Slave Power Conspiracy and the Paranoid Style* (Baton Rouge, La., 1969).

—— (ed.), *The Fear of Conspiracy: Images of Un-American Subversion from the Revolution to the Present* (Ithaca, NY, 1971).

—— 'Some Themes of Counter-Subversion: An Analysis of Anti-Masonic, Anti-Catholic, and Anti-Mormon Literature', in D. B. Davis, *From Homicide to Slavery: Studies in American Culture* (Oxford, 1986), 137–54.

DEBIDOUR, A., *Histoire des rapports de l'Église et de l'État en France de 1789 à 1870* (Paris, 1898).

DEDEREN, R., *Un réformateur catholique au XIXe siècle: E. Michaud, 1839–1917: Vieux-Catholicisme, œcuménisme* (Geneva, 1963).

DELATTRE, P. (ed.), *Les Établissements des jésuites en France depuis quatre siècles: Répertoire topo-bibliographique*, 5 vols. (Enghien, 1949–57).

DUDON, P., 'La Résurrection de la Compagnie de Jésus (1773–1814)', *Revue des questions historiques*, 133 (1939), 21–59.

DUROSELLE, J.-B., 'L'Abbé Clavel et les revendications du bas-clergé sous Louis-Philippe', *Études d'histoire moderne et contemporaine*, 1 (1947), 99–126.

—— 'Les "Filiales" de la Congrégation', *Revue d'histoire ecclésiastique*, 50 (1955), 867–91.

EPSTEIN, K., *The Genesis of German Conservatism* (Princeton, NJ, 1966).

FURET, F., *Interpreting the French Revolution* (Cambridge, 1981).

GADILLE, J., 'La Politique de la défense républicaine à l'égard de l'Église de France, 1876–1883', *Bulletin de la Société d'Histoire Moderne*, 4th ser. 1 (1967), 1–6.

—— 'Le Jansénisme populaire: Ses prolongements au XIXe siècle: Le Cas du Forez', *Études foréziennes*, 7 (1975), 157–67.

GARNIER, A., *Les Ordonnances du 16 juin 1828, d'après des documents inédits tirés des Archives du Vatican et des Archives Nationales* (Paris, 1929).

GAZIER, A., *Histoire générale du mouvement janséniste depuis ses origines jusqu'à nos jours*, 2 vols. (Paris, 1922).

GIBSON, R., *A Social History of French Catholicism, 1789–1914* (London, 1989).

GIRARDET, R., *Mythes et mythologies politiques* (Paris, 1986).

GOUGH, A., *Paris and Rome: The Gallican Church and the Ultramontane Campaign, 1848–1853* (Oxford, 1986).

GRANDMAISON, G. DE, *La Congrégation (1801–1830)* (Paris, 1889).

GRAUMANN, C. F., and MOSCOVICI, S. (eds.), *Changing Conceptions of Conspiracy* (New York, 1987).

GRIFFITHS, R., *The Use of Abuse: The Polemics of the Dreyfus Affair and its Aftermath* (New York, 1991).

GRIMAUD, L., *Histoire de la liberté d'enseignement en France*, new edn., 6 vols. (Grenoble, 1944–54).

GUERBER, J., *Le Ralliement du clergé français à la morale liguorienne: L'Abbé Gousset et ses précurseurs (1785–1832)* (Rome, 1973).

GUIBERT, J. DE, *The Jesuits, their Spiritual Doctrine and Practice: A Historical Study*, 2nd edn. (St Louis, 1972).

HARPAZ, A., *L'École libérale sous la Restauration: Le Mercure et La Minerve, 1817–20* (Geneva, 1968).

HENRION, A., *Vie du Révérend Père Loriquet, de la Compagnie de Jésus, d'après sa correspondance et ses ouvrages inédits* (Paris, 1845).

HIBBARD, C., *Charles I and the Popish Plot* (Chapel Hill, NC, 1983).

HOFMAN, A., 'Anatomy of Conspiracy: The Origins of the Theory of *Philosophe* Conspiracy, 1750–1789', Ph.D. thesis (Chicago, 1986).

—— 'The Origins of the Theory of the *Philosophe* Conspiracy', *French History*, 2 (1988), 152–72.

HOFSTADTER, R., *The Paranoid Style in American Politics, and Other Essays* (New York, 1965).

HOUTIN, A., *Le Père Hyacinthe*, 3 vols. (Paris, 1920–4).

HUNT, L., *Politics, Culture, and Class in the French Revolution* (London, 1986).

IMLAH, A. G., *Britain and Switzerland, 1845–60: A Study of Anglo-Swiss Relations during some Critical Years for Swiss Neutrality* (London, 1966).

JACQUEMONT, E., *Une âme de janséniste: François Jacquemont, curé de Saint-Médard-en-Forez, 1757–1835: Sa vie et sa correspondance d'après des documents inédits* (Lyons, 1914).

JOHNSON, D., *Guizot: Aspects of French History, 1787–1874* (London, 1963).

KAPLAN, S., *The Famine Plot Persuasion in Eighteenth-Century France* (Philadelphia, 1982).

KATZ, J., *Jews and Freemasons in Europe, 1723–1939* (Cambridge, Mass., 1970).

—— 'A State within the State: The History of an Anti-Semitic Slogan', in J. Katz, *Emancipation and Assimilation: Studies in Modern Jewish History* (Farnborough, 1972), 47–76.

KREISER, R. B., *Miracles, Convulsions, and Ecclesiastical Politics in Early Eighteenth-Century Paris* (Princeton, NJ, 1978).

KUISEL, R., 'The Legend of the Vichy Synarchy', *French Historical Studies*, 6 (1970), 365–98.

LANGDON, J., 'The Jesuits and French Education: A Comparative Study of Two Schools, 1852–1913', *History of Education Quarterly*, 18 (1978), 49–60.

LAVALLEY, G., 'Les Duellistes de Caen de l'an IV à 1848: Le Bretteur Alexis Dumesnil', *Mémoires de l'Académie Nationale des Sciences, Arts et Belles-Lettres de Caen* (1913), 325–96.

LEFEBVRE, G., *The Great Fear of 1789: Rural Panic in Revolutionary France* (London, 1973).

LE FORESTIER, R., *La Franc-maçonnerie templière et occultiste aux XVIIIe et XIXe siècles* (Louvain, 1970).

LEMAIRE, J., *Les Origines françaises de l'antimaçonnisme (1744–1797)* (Brussels, 1985).

LIDSKY, P., *Les Écrivains contre la Commune* (Paris, 1970).

LIGOU, D. (ed.), *François-Vincent Raspail; ou Le Bon Usage de la prison, précédé de l'Étude impartiale sur Jean Paul Marat* (Paris, 1968).

LIMOUZIN-LAMOTHE, R., and LEFLON, J., Mgr. *Denys-Auguste Affre, archévêque de Paris (1793–1848)* (Paris, 1971).

LINEHAN, D. M., 'The Society of Jesus in France, 1870–1880', Ph.D. thesis (London, 1984).

LIPSET, S. M., and RAAB, E., *The Politics of Unreason: Right-Wing Extremism in America, 1790–1970* (London, 1971).

LIRAC, A. [C. Clair], *Les Jésuites et la liberté religieuse sous la Restauration* (Paris, 1879).

MARCHASSON, Y., *La Diplomatie romaine et la République française à la recherche d'une conciliation, 1879–1880* (Paris, 1974).

MARQUANT, R., *Thiers et le baron Cotta: Étude sur la collaboration de Thiers à la Gazette d'Augsbourg* (Paris, 1959).

MAURAIN, J., *La Politique ecclésiastique du Second Empire de 1852 à 1869* (Paris, 1930).

MAYERS, M. J., *The Jesuit and Sonderbund Contest in Switzerland* (London, 1847).

MELLON, S., *The Political Uses of History: A Study of Historians in the French Restoration* (Stanford, Calif., 1958).

MELLOR, A., *Histoire de l'anticléricalisme français* (Paris, 1978).

MICHAUD, L.-G. (ed.), *Biographie universelle ancienne et moderne*, 2nd edn., 45 vols. (Paris, 1843–65).

MITCHELL, D., *The Jesuits: A History* (London, 1980).

MONOD, G., 'Les Troubles du Collège de France en 1843', *Séances et travaux de l'Académie des Sciences Morales et Politiques (Institut de France)*, 172 (1909), 407–23.

—— 'La Politique secrète des jésuites et les Monita secreta', *Séances et travaux de l'Académie des Sciences Morales et Politiques (Institut de France)*, 173 (1910), 210–29.

—— *La Vie et la pensée de Jules Michelet, 1798–1852*, 2 vols. (Paris, 1923).

NORA, P., '1898: Le Thème du complot et la définition de l'identité juive', in M. Olender (ed.), *Le Racisme: Mythes et sciences* (Brussels, 1981), 157–65.

NOURRISSON, P., *Histoire légale des congrégations religieuses en France depuis 1789*, 3 vols. (Paris, 1928–30).

ORHAND, *Le Révérend Père Pillon de la Compagnie de Jésus et les collèges de Brugelette, Vannes, Sainte-Geneviève, Amiens, Lille* (Lille, 1888).

PADBERG, J., *Colleges in Controversy: The Jesuit Schools in France from Revival to Suppression, 1815–1880* (Cambridge, Mass., 1969).

332 Bibliography

PALANQUE, J.-R., Catholiques libéraux et gallicans en France face au Concile du Vatican, 1867–1870 (Gap, 1962).

POCHON, J., 'Edgar Quinet et les luttes du Collège de France, 1843–1847', Revue d'histoire littéraire de la France, 120 (1970), 619–27.

POLIAKOV, L., La Causalité diabolique, 2 vols. (Paris, 1980–5).

—— The Aryan Myth: A History of Racist and Nationalist Ideas in Europe (London, 1971).

PONLEVOY, A. DE, Vie du R.P. Xavier de Ravignan, de la Compagnie de Jésus, 6th edn., 2 vols. (Paris, 1862).

—— Actes de la captivité et de la mort des RR.PP. P. Olivaint, L. Ducoudray, J. Caubert, A. Clerc, A. de Bengy, de la Compagnie de Jésus (Paris, 1871).

PONTEIL, F., L'Opposition politique à Strasbourg sous la Monarchie de Juillet (1830–1848) (Paris, 1932).

POWERS, R. H., Edgar Quinet: A Study in French Patriotism (Dallas, 1957).

RACHMAN, O. A., Un périodique libéral sous la Restauration: Le Mercure du XIXe siècle, avril 1823–mars 1826, suivi du répertoire daté et annoté (Geneva, 1984).

RÉMOND, R., L'Anticléricalisme en France de 1815 à nos jours (Paris, 1976).

—— 'Anticlericalism: Some Reflections by Way of Introduction', European Studies Review, 13 (1983), 121–6.

RIMBAULT, M., Histoire politique des congrégations religieuses françaises, 1790–1914 (Paris, 1926).

ROBERTS, J. M., The Paris Commune from the Right, English Historical Review Supplement 6 (London, 1973).

—— The Mythology of the Secret Societies, 2nd edn. (St Albans, 1974).

ROCHEMONTEIX, C. DE, Les Congrégations religieuses non reconnues en France, 1789–1881, 2 vols. (Cairo, 1901).

ROGALLA VON BIEBERSTEIN, J., Die These von der Verschwörung 1776–1945: Philosophen, Freimaurer, Juden, Liberalen und Sozialisten als Verschwörer gegen die Sozialordnung (Berne, 1976).

—— 'The Story of the Jewish–Masonic Conspiracy, 1776–1945', Patterns of Prejudice, 11/6 (1977), 1–8 and 21.

ROLLIN, H., L'Apocalypse de notre temps: Les Dessous de la propagande allemande d'après des documents inédits, 7th edn. (Paris, 1939).

ROSETTE, A., La Compagnie de Jésus à Dôle après sa rétablissement: Un siècle de labeur, 1823–1920 (Paris, 1945).

ROSSIGNOL, D., Vichy et les francs-maçons: La Liquidation des sociétés secrètes 1940–1944 (Paris, 1981).

SALVAN, P., 'Le Tartuffe de Molière et l'agitation anticléricale en 1825', Revue de la Société d'Histoire du Théâtre, 12 (1960), 7–19.

SAVART, C., L'Abbé Jean-Hippolyte Michon, 1806–81: Contribution à l'étude du libéralisme catholique au XIXe siècle (Paris, 1971).

SÉCHÉ, L., Les Derniers Jansénistes, depuis la ruine de Port-Royal jusqu'à nos jours (1710–1870), 3 vols. (Paris, 1891).

SEVRIN, E., *Les Missions religieuses en France sous la Restauration, 1815–1830*, 2 vols. (Paris, 1948–59).

SOMMERVOGEL, C. (ed.), *Bibliothèque de la Compagnie de Jésus*, 12 vols. (Paris, 1890–1960).

SPENCER, P. H., *Politics of Belief in Nineteenth-Century France: Lacordaire, Michon, Veuillot* (London, 1954).

SUTTO, C., introd. to E. Pasquier, *Le Catéchisme des jésuites* (Sherbrooke, 1982), 11–121.

TAVENEAUX, R., 'Permanences jansénistes au XIXe siècle', *XVIIe siècle*, 32 (1980), 397–414.

THACKRAY, I., 'Zion Undermined: The Protestant Belief in a Popish Plot during the English Interregnum', *History Workshop*, 18 (1984), 28–52.

THUREAU-DANGIN, P., *Histoire de la Monarchie de Juillet*, 7 vols. (Paris, 1884–92).

THURLOW, R., 'The Powers of Darkness: Conspiracy Belief and Political Strategy', *Patterns of Prejudice*, 12/6 (1978), 1–12 and 23.

TUDESQ, A. J., *Les Grands Notables en France, 1840–1849: Étude historique d'une psychologie sociale* (Paris, 1964).

VALLIN, P., 'La Nouvelle Compagnie en France', in *Les Jésuites, spiritualité et activités: Jalons d'une histoire* (Paris, 1974), 155–96.

VAN AKEN, *La Fable des Monita secreta ou instructions secrètes des jesuites: Histoire et bibliographie* (Brussels, n.d.).

VAN KLEY, D., *The Jansenists and the Expulsion of the Jesuits from France* (New Haven, Conn., 1975).

VIALLANEIX, P., introd. to J. Michelet and M. Quinet, *Des jésuites*, Libertés 35 (Paris, 1966).

WEBB, J., *The Occult Establishment* (Glasgow, 1981).

WEBER, E., ' "Nos ancêtres les gaulois" ', in E. Weber, *My France: Politics, Culture, Myth* (Cambridge, Mass., 1991), 21–39.

WEINER, D. B., *Raspail: Scientist and Reformer* (New York, 1968).

WIENER, C. Z., 'The Beleaguered Isle: A Study of Elizabethan and Early Jacobean Anti-Catholicism', *Past and Present*, 51 (1971), 27–62.

WOOD, G. S., 'Conspiracy and the Paranoid Style: Causality and Deceit in the Eighteenth Century', *William and Mary Quarterly*, 3rd ser. 39 (1982), 401–41.

ZELDIN, T., 'The Conflict of Moralities: Confession, Sin and Pleasure in the Nineteenth Century', in T. Zeldin (ed.), *Conflicts in French Society: Anticlericalism, Education and Morals in the Nineteenth Century* (London, 1970), 13–50.

—— *France 1848–1945*, 2 vols. (Oxford, 1973–7).

Index